T0386102

DRAGONSLAYER

DRAGONSLAYER

*The Legend of Erich Ludendorff
in the Weimar Republic
and Third Reich*

JAY LOCKENOUR

CORNELL UNIVERSITY PRESS
ITHACA AND LONDON

First published 2021 by Cornell University Press

Printed in the United States of America

Library of Congress Cataloging-in-Publication Data

Names: Lockenour, Jay, 1966– author.
Title: Dragonslayer : the legend of Erich Ludendorff in the Weimar
    Republic and Third Reich / Jay Lockenour.
Description: Ithaca [New York] : Cornell University Press, 2021. |
    Series: Battlegrounds : Cornell studies in military history |
    Includes bibliographical references and index.
Identifiers: LCCN 2020025192 (print) | LCCN 2020025193 (ebook) |
    ISBN 9781501754593 (hardcover) | ISBN 9781501754609 (ebook) |
    ISBN 9781501754616 (pdf)
Subjects: LCSH: Ludendorff, Erich, 1865-1937. | Generals—Germany—
    Biography. | Germany—Politics and government—1918–1933. |
    Germany—History—1918–1933.
Classification: LCC DD231.L8 L59 2021 (print) |
    LCC DD231.L8 (ebook) | DDC 355.0092 [B]—dc23
LC record available at https://lccn.loc.gov/2020025192
LC ebook record available at https://lccn.loc.gov/2020025193

For Andrea

CONTENTS

Illustrations

Figures

Maps

ACKNOWLEDGMENTS

My interest in Erich Ludendorff began in the late 1980s when as an undergraduate at the University of California, I wrote my senior thesis on Hindenburg and Ludendorff's Third Supreme Command with guidance from the late Gerald Feldman. I am enormously indebted to Feldman and two other giants of our profession who are no longer with us, Russell Weigley and Dennis Showalter. All three provided not only models of professional behavior and scholarship, but also guidance at critical moments in my career.

I am grateful to Richard S. Levy, who years later, at Feldman's prompting, asked me to contribute articles on Erich, Mathilde, and their publishing company for his *Antisemitism: A Historical Encyclopedia of Prejudice and Persecution* (ABC-CLIO, 2005). Research for those essays opened my eyes to the fascinating postwar careers of the couple, their associates, and followers. To Paul Steege, David Imhoof, Julia Sneeringer, Heikki Lempa, Rita Krueger, Belinda Davis, Paul Hanebrink, Melissa Feinberg, Jeffrey Johnson, Greg Eghigian, Andy Lees, and other occasional attendees of our Philadelphia Area Modern Germany Workshop a big thank you for all the insightful comments. Thanks to current and former colleagues Beth Bailey, David Farber, Richard Immerman, and Gregory Urwin for reading chapters and book proposals. Temple graduate students Lynnette Deem and Erik Klinek served as research assistants for the project. Special thanks to Jonathan Zatlin who generously took time from his own research to provide materials from the Zentralarchiv zur Erforschung der Geschichte der Juden in Deutschland. Archivists and staff at the various archives I visited were uniformly helpful. Klaus A. Lankheit of the Institut für Zeitgeschichte proved an enormously helpful guide to their collections. Thanks to Mike Bechtold for the beautiful maps.

Finally, I could not have written this book without the patient support of my wife, Andrea, who not only tolerated my frequent absence on research trips but also softened the emotional and physical toll wrought by such a difficult and time-consuming task.

Abbreviations

AC	Apologetische Centrale der Deutschen Evangelische Kirche, Evangelical Church Defense Organization
BA	Bundesarchiv, Koblenz, German Federal Archive, Koblenz
BAMA	Bundesarchiv-Militärarchiv, Freiburg, German Federal Military Archive, Freiburg
DDP	Deutsche Demokratische Partei, German Democratic Party
DNVP	Deutschnationale Volkspartei, German Nationalist People's Party
DVFB	Deutschvölkische Freiheitsbewegung, German Völkisch Freedom Movement
DVP	Deutsche Volkspartei, German People's Party
DVSTB	Deutschvölkischen Schutz- und Trutzbund, German national protection and defiance federation
GGS	*Großer Generalstab*, Great General Staff
HKA	Hauptkadettenanstalt, Cadet Academy

IfZ	Institut für Zeitgeschichte, München, Institute for Contemporary History, Munich
IG Farben	Interessengemeinschaft Farbenindustrie Aktien Gesellschaft, German chemical firm
NSDAP	Nationalsozialistische Deutsche Arbeiterpartei, National Socialist German Workers' Party
NSFB	Nationalsozialistische Freiheitsbewegung, National Socialist Freedom Movement
NV	Nationale Vereinigung, Nationalist Association
OHL	Oberste Heeresleitung, Army Supreme Command
OKH	Oberste Kommando des Heeres, Army Supreme Command
SA	Sturmabteilung, NSDAP Stormtroopers
SPD	Sozialdemokratische Partei Deutschland, Social Democratic Party
SS	Schutzstaffel, NSDAP bodyguard and paramilitary organization
UFA	Universum Film-Aktien Gesellschaft, Universum film company
USPD	Unabhängige Sozialistische Partei Deutschlands, Independent Socialist Party of Germany, forerunner of the German Communist Party

Dragonslayer

1

MYTHIC LIFE

Erich Ludendorff lived a life of legend. Partly through action, partly through self-conscious construction, often with the assistance of others, he fashioned a life story that secured his place as one of the most prominent (and despicable) Germans of the twentieth century. Between 1914 and his death in 1937, Erich Ludendorff was a war hero, a dictator, a right-wing activist, a failed putschist, a presidential candidate, a publisher, and a would-be prophet. He guided Germany's effort in the Great War between 1916 and 1918 and then set the tone for a politics of victimhood and revenge in the postwar era. Other major characters appear in Ludendorff's story. He witnessed firsthand the downfall of Kaiser Wilhelm II, the last king of Prussia and German emperor. Ludendorff served under legendary military figures such as Count Alfred von Schlieffen, Helmut von Moltke the Younger, and Field Marshal (and later Reich president) Paul von Hindenburg. Ludendorff jousted with the famous military historian Hans Delbrück and Crown Prince Rupprecht of Bavaria. Adolf

Hitler appears in the tale as both protégé and bitter rival. Ludendorff's second wife, Mathilde von Kemnitz, née Spiess, exerted a powerful editorial influence.

Through 1925, Ludendorff told his story primarily through action. He earned the prestigious military award Pour le Mérite for his role in the capture of the Belgian fortress at Liège in August 1914. He led German armies to victory at the Battle of Tannenberg later that fall. He pushed Russian armies out of East Prussia and Poland in 1915. After 1916, he directed the entire war effort from his position as first quartermaster general of the German Army. He called for unrestricted submarine warfare against the United States. Ludendorff brought German industry and media into the service of the war. He masterminded Germany's last desperate effort to win the war, Operation Michael, in 1918. On September 28, 1918, he recommended that the German Empire seek an armistice with its enemies, bringing about the end of the war a little over six weeks later.[1]

Ludendorff has been compared by contemporaries as well as historians to the greatest warriors of history. The variety is bewildering: from the sovereign-strategist Frederick the Great to the slave-rebel Spartacus. From the genius Napoleon Bonaparte to the organizers Gerhard von Scharnhorst and August Neidhardt von Gneisenau. From the German nationalist icon Ludwig Yorck von Wartenburg to the protocapitalist mercenary Albrecht von Wallenstein.[2] To some, he was the German Oliver Cromwell.[3] His name carried nonmilitary associations as well. Ludendorff was the "Atlas" who bore the burdens of Germany on his shoulders during the war. Sympathizers of his worldview classed him alongside Friedrich Nietzsche as an intellectual.

In June 1917, H. L. Mencken wrote for the *Atlantic Monthly* a column reporting on his recent experiences in Berlin, before the United States had entered the war. He described a gathering of reporters in January of that year at which his colleagues discussed the recent declaration of unrestricted submarine warfare. "I chiefly listened," wrote Mencken, "and the more I listened the more I heard a certain Awful Name." Ludendorff. His fellow reporters yammered on about the mysterious figure behind the scenes. "Ludendorff is the neglected factor in this war—the forgotten man," they said. "The world hears nothing about him, and yet he has the world by the ear."[4]

Ludendorff maintained that grip for many years. He championed the cause of the radical right wing in Germany throughout the early 1920s and lent his name and considerable prestige to various efforts to overthrow the Weimar Republic. From behind the scenes, he masterminded the abortive Kapp Putsch of 1920. From the head of a marching column, he led Adolf Hitler's motley band of National Socialists through the streets of Munich in 1923. In photographs of Ludendorff and Hitler's subsequent trial for treason, Ludendorff, in full military regalia, appears center frame.[5]

After 1918, however, he also began a campaign of self-conscious construction aimed at retelling the story of his life according to his own fantasies. Ludendorff experienced Germany's defeat in the Great War as a profound personal crisis. Many of his military colleagues agree that he suffered a mental collapse in September 1918, caused by the strain and impending failure of his wartime efforts. That collapse and his subsequent flight to Sweden to escape the revolutionary violence that swept Germany in November 1918 were indelible stains on his honor, so dearly prized in the circles in which he moved, as well as on his manhood.

In a fit of authorial energy, he penned the first volume (and first of many versions) of his memoirs in a mere three months.[6] The book sold hundreds of thousands of copies and was quickly translated into many languages. But *Meine Kriegserinnerungen* (*My War Memories*) was only the first salvo fired by Ludendorff in a long campaign to tell the "real" story of the war, Germany's subsequent history, and (more importantly for him) Ludendorff's place in that history. Subsequent works elaborated the themes laid down in his memoirs: the valiant German army, the brilliant German leadership (at least after 1916 when he was in charge), and the failure of the home front. To make this latter point, Ludendorff pointed increasingly to Jews, Freemasons, and Catholics as participants in a vast conspiracy to undermine German power. With his second wife, Mathilde, he draped the trappings of a pagan religion around this conspiracy theory and appointed himself prophet of a movement to harden the German "soul" against the attacks of these "supranational powers."[7] His enormous and diverse portfolio makes Ludendorff a frustrating and enigmatic subject for historical study. He published dozens of confrontational, self-justifying, and often inscrutable books and pamphlets. His highly developed sense of personal honor led him into countless battles, in print, in the courtroom, and elsewhere, over perceived slights. His pagan religious philosophy, his messianic fantasies, and his paranoid conspiracy theories practically defy rational analysis.[8]

In the face of these facts, most biographers and historians of Ludendorff have relied on the alleged mental collapse in 1918, brought on by the strain of managing Germany's war effort from his perch on the Army Supreme Command (OHL), to explain Ludendorff's subsequent behavior. Using the device of mental illness, his descent into political radicalism, pagan religion, and crackpot conspiracy theories is relatively easily explained. Most historians treat his life after 1918, including his flirtation with Adolf Hitler, as a mere epilogue—the descent of a once-powerful man into a sad and lonely isolation. D. J. Goodspeed suggests he may have had a stroke.[9] Roger Chickering diagnoses "paranoia or 'delusional disorder.' "[10] Richard Watt dismisses him as "half insane."[11] His most recent biographer wisely avoids a diagnosis but quotes Heinrich Mann calling the postwar Ludendorff a "lunatic" and includes Heinrich's younger brother Thomas's judgment that Ludendorff was "not to be taken seriously" after the war.[12]

Clearly, Ludendorff experienced a crisis in September 1918 that led him to seek the help of a psychiatrist.[13] He had difficulty sleeping. He suffered fits of crying. His colleagues worked in fear of his raging temper. It surprised no one that he should be suffering from nervous exhaustion, given his workload over the previous four years. It should be noted that even if he did show signs of exhaustion and suffered a crisis at some point, many observers testified to quite normal behavior in the days and weeks after the alleged breakdown.[14]

That Ludendorff's "nerves" became the focus of such attention both during and after war doubtless wounded him deeply. As Paul Lerner points out, in the German Empire, nerves were a "metaphor for vitality and fitness" and "a well-balanced nervous system were the keys to successful military service." Lerner quotes Kaiser Wilhelm II himself from a speech in 1910: "It is through nerves that [the next war's] outcome will be decided."[15] Nervous ailments were diagnosed as hysteria and attributed to a lack of willpower.[16] But it is not necessary to posit mental illness (in fact it is in some ways counterproductive or even exculpatory) to explain Ludendorff's pronounced antisemitism and flirtation with Adolf Hitler. Long before his alleged 1918 crisis, Ludendorff and those around him saw themselves at war not merely with the Entente but also with shadowy forces aimed at destroying Germany.

In order to achieve a more complete understanding of Ludendorff's place in German history after 1918 (including the post-1945 history of the Federal Republic of Germany), this work will take a biographical approach that differs from traditional biography in two ways. First, it will reduce to a bare minimum the story of the First World War, arguably the most eventful and important years of our subject's life. Ludendorff's roles and activities from 1914 to 1918 are very well known, and a recent German biography by Manfred Nebelin should be considered definitive on the subject.[17] Rather than rehearse that well-known story in detail, I chose instead to focus on two battles from 1914, Liège and Tannenberg, which appear out of all proportion in Ludendorff's postwar writings. These battles establish characteristics—bold, courageous action and operational genius in defense of Germany—that Ludendorff wanted to associate with his mythos. I also survey his role in the Third Supreme Command after 1916, which earned him (in the minds of many, including himself) the sobriquet "Feldherr," or "master of battle," which became the preferred form of address among his followers. The title testified to Ludendorff's presumed strategic genius that allowed him to comment with authority on world affairs and the changing nature of war.

Second, this work gives significant attention to Ludendorff's importance as a prolific writer—of autobiography, political commentary, pseudo-philosophy and -history, and prophecy. A glance at the bibliography will show the dozens and dozens of books and pamphlets he authored between 1918 and 1937, many coauthored with his second wife Mathilde and appearing in their publishing house, Ludendorffs Verlag, established in 1929. Ludendorff was also the principal contributor to the many periodicals that issued from his various organizations, including *Deutsche Wochenschau* and *Ludendorffs Volkswarte*. Two subjects dominated his oeuvre: autobiography/commentary intended to defend and burnish his own reputation; and second, the machinations past and present of the "supranational powers"—the Catholic Church, Freemasonry, and Jews.

One does not find in the historical record prior to 1918 anything to rival Ludendorff's later rants against Jews, Freemasons, and Jesuit agents. But there is no doubt that those with whom Ludendorff worked and lived before 1918 held antisemitic beliefs that must be described as more than "typical" for elite German and European society. The most notable offender in this regard is certainly Colonel Max Bauer, who served Ludendorff as an artillery specialist as well as political adviser. Bauer was especially vitriolic in his wartime denunciations of Socialists, "Jewish liberals," and "Jewish demagogues" who were undermining the war effort.[18] Generals Max Hoffmann and Wilhelm Groener as well as other colleagues of Ludendorff shared these suspicions, even if they voiced them less vehemently. By the end of the war, Kaiser Wilhelm himself decried President Woodrow Wilson's support for Freemasonry and "international Jewry" in their efforts to put the Bolsheviks in power in Russia and dethrone the Hohenzollerns in Germany.[19] From Ludendorff's own pen we read in 1917 thinly veiled references to "state-destroying elements" who attempt to spread unrest while egotistically pursuing their own profits.[20] Such terminology comes straight from the lexicon of antisemites who saw Jews as the premier practitioners of both capitalist profiteering and Socialist rabble-rousing.

Nor was Ludendorff alone in clinging to fantasies of victory very late in the war. Alfred von Tirpitz, prewar chief of the German Navy and influential right-wing figure long after the war, maintained his faith in German victory (and of naval contribution thereto) long after the "Black Day" in August 1918 when Allied troops broke through at Amiens.[21] Tirpitz, like Ludendorff, lived after the war in an "illusionary" world of conspiratorial politics and scapegoats. According to a biographer, Tirpitz, like Ludendorff, "saw himself and fellow rightists as the high priests of national self-realization."[22] Ludendorff took his priestly vows a bit more literally than did others.

Rather than attempt to diagnose Ludendorff's particular malady, I will argue that Ludendorff's mental state is largely irrelevant for understanding his historical significance. Something was going on, but rather than disabling Ludendorff, it endowed him with even greater energy to trace the alleged roots of Germany's defeat. Though Ludendorff's beliefs and actions appear to historians as misguided, illogical, or bizarre (not to mention morally repugnant), they are not dependent on a psychosis in any individual or a clinical sense. Nor were his core beliefs the primary reason for his political failure and eventual (relative) isolation. In fact, some of Ludendorff's attributes that today strike us as strange were those that guaranteed him a high public profile and a secure place in the German pantheon, at least until 1945.

In his psychological and political milieu, occupied by a huge proportion of the German citizenry, his beliefs and behaviors made a certain kind of sense, no matter how farfetched they seem to us or how baseless in historical fact they were. Shortly after his dismissal as the commander in chief of the German Army, Werner von Fritsch, usually seen as somewhat of a resistance figure of the period for his opposition to Hitler's plans for war, spoke of Germany's need to combat the working class, the Catholic Church, and Jews.[23] Ludendorff took his beliefs further than most Germans were willing to go, particularly in attacking Christianity, but his style of politics based on struggle and heroic action; his refusal to accept Germany's defeat as the result of anything but treachery; and his scapegoating of Jews, Catholics, and Freemasons were not, by any meaningful definition, "insane."[24]

In his writings, Ludendorff placed himself at the center of a mythic universe while simultaneously explaining his personal failures through the heroic tropes of treason and betrayal. By his actions, he placed himself at the center of a movement to renew Germany, spiritually and militarily, which encompassed millions of nationalist Germans. Even before 1918, Ludendorff imagined a world of "mythic politics" in which good battled evil for the soul of the nation.[25] In such a world, honor, decisiveness, and courage were paramount. Opposition, discussion, and compromise could not be tolerated. Obedience was prized; disagreement was treason.

This book began as an effort to write the "Ludendorff Myth"—to do for Erich Ludendorff what Ian Kershaw has done for Adolf Hitler.[26] In his 1987 work *The Hitler Myth*, Kershaw argues that Hitler's actual biography is less important for understanding his power than the propaganda image that Joseph Goebbels and others built up around him. For Kershaw, this image "was indispensable in its integrative function, firstly as a counter to the strong centrifugal forces within the Nazi Movement itself, and secondly in establishing a massive basis of consensus among the German people for those aims and policies identifiable with the Führer."[27] This "myth" played an indispensable part both in keeping the fractious Nationalsozialistiche Deutsche Arbeiterpartei (National Socialist German Workers' Party—NSDAP) together and in mobilizing support for Hitler's goals.[28] Though he would later write a definitive and more traditional biography of Hitler, Kershaw described the "Hitler Myth" as "not, in fact, primarily concerned with Hitler himself," but about the construction and reception of the myth that surrounded him. I wanted to write a biography of Erich Ludendorff (even if only a partial one) that focused not just on his life, but also on the stories about that life that seemed to have broader political and cultural significance. Ludendorff exerted real influence both before and after 1918, and those stories make that influence clear. Ludendorff was a principal author of those stories, but by no means the only one.

Wolfram Pyta has also published a biography of Paul von Hindenburg that attempts something similar, while also serving as a definitive, traditional biography.[29] Pyta argues that Hindenburg's power, which formed a bridge between the Hohenzollern dynasty and the Hitler dictatorship, was not bureaucratic (i.e., based on the power of his office, either as head of the Supreme Command in wartime or as president of the Weimar Republic) or even strictly charismatic, in the Weberian sense, but rather "mythic."[30] According to Herfried Münkler, political myths "define a dualistic-dichotomic worldview in which good and evil, the beautiful and the ugly, true and untrue, are clear and unambiguously separated from each other and are therefore distinguishable."[31] Political myths are comprised of three elements: narrative structure, iconography, and ritual performance.[32] Political myths "give orientation to political action," foreclose some options while providing alternative models of political behavior.[33]

Jan Assman suggests that such political myths operate most actively in times of forced integration into larger political units such as empires.[34] But they can also operate powerfully during times of reform or revolution, stress and disintegration.[35] The lost war, the imposition of the Treaty of Versailles, the shattered economy created powerful urges to unify and renew Germany. The person or group who created the most satisfying narrative, who embodied those aspirations most transparently, could wield enormous influence. Pyta argues that was the source of Hindenburg's strength, his "symbolic competence," his ability to wield symbolism in the service of his political aims.[36] Kershaw makes a similar argument about Hitler.[37]

In the same year that Pyta published his biography, Jesko von Hoegen published a work specifically on the Hindenburg mythos, and two years letter Anna von der Goltz examined the impact of Hindenburg's myth both during and after the Great War. According to Hoegen, myths can give meaning to a difficult past by emphasizing certain events, repeating and ritualizing certain versions of a story.[38] For Goltz, such myths, including Hindenburg's, embody values and "generate meaning by acting as a filter of reality."[39]

It is in the same sense that I seek to examine Erich Ludendorff—not simply because he wielded real, unquestioned authority from 1916 to 1918 and exerted powerful influence on the events of the immediate postwar period, but because he was engaged in a similar struggle to create a "mythos." That mythos allowed Ludendorff, as it did Hindenburg and eventually Hitler, to tap into deep wellsprings of cultural power and symbolism, even if his mythos can be rightly be judged to have had less direct political influence than theirs.[40]

Ludendorff's case is worth of study even though he never achieved high office after 1918 and despite his failure to build a truly mass organization like the NSDAP. His failure was not for lack of trying. He was the power behind the Kapp Putsch. He tried (and failed) to wrest control of the NSDAP from Hitler while the latter was in prison following the Beer Hall Putsch. He ran for president of the republic as a Nazi in 1925 and garnered a miserable 1 percent of the vote. His Tannenberg League (Tannenbergbund), founded in 1926 may have attracted as many as one hundred thousand members at its peak, but its vocal anti-Christian and esoteric ideology, based on the writings of Ludendorff's second wife, Mathilde, limited it to the relative fringes of German society and politics.

As he told his and Germany's story in countless books, pamphlets, and newspaper articles from 1919 until 1937, he fashioned a character for himself. A hero. While Ludendorff's heroic conception of himself was particularly pronounced, it was part of a larger phenomenon of mythic politics that powerfully shaped the history of the Weimar Republic. Prominent political figures of the Weimar era (and of many other eras, to be sure) imagined themselves on an epic stage. Ludendorff's peers on the political right shared with him a mythic self-image, but theirs were subtly different. Ludendorff's partner-cum-rival Paul von Hindenburg, the wartime supreme commander and later Reich president, frequently cast himself as Cincinnatus, the Roman general called out of retirement to defend Rome who then returned to his estate for a peaceful civilian life.[41] Adolf Hitler's fantasies went in many ways even further than Ludendorff's so that he could imagine himself not merely as a hero but as Germany personified.[42] Ludendorff styled his own mythos, sometimes consciously and sometimes subconsciously on the hero of Germanic mythology, Siegfried.[43]

Siegfried, Dragonslayer

> Hjördis bore a son, whom she named Sigurd. So say the Nordic poets. Further to the south they say he was called Siegfried. . . . Of no man have the poets of yore sung or said more, no man have they loved more. He was the model of all heroes, and the fate of many a man and even the fate of peoples are mirrored in his fate.
>
> —Die Nibelungen-Sage

Siegfried, son of the Rhenish King Siegmund, was the most handsome, brave, and honorable knight of his day.[44] He vanquished kings and seized untold treasures. He slew a dragon and acquired virtual invulnerability by bathing in its blood. He won the hand of the fairest and most virtuous princess in Europe, Kriemhild of Burgundy.

But Siegfried's was a tragic fate. Hagen of Troneck, a warrior at the Burgundian court, despised the noble Siegfried. For years he nurtured his hatred of the hero. He duped Kriemhild into revealing Siegfried's one vulnerable spot, a small space between his shoulder blades where a fallen linden leaf had prevented the dragon's blood from working its protective magic. Hagen enlisted the help of Kriemhild's brother, King Gunther of Burgundy, who proclaimed a hunt, during which Hagen and Gunther could lure Siegfried to his death. Exhausted from chasing game, Siegfried knelt at a cool spring to quench his thirst. The deceitful Hagen used this one moment of distraction to thrust a spear into Siegfried's back. Siegfried died among the blood-soaked flowers of the meadow, but not before begging Gunther to remain loyal to his sister, Siegfried's wife Kriemhild.

Kriemhild harbored a grudge. She mourned Siegfried for years but eventually remarried, this time to the Hunnish king Attila (Etzel). Plotting vengeance she feigned forgiveness and invited her brother and the entire Burgundian court to Attila's capital. She provoked a bloody battle between the Huns and Burgundians that climaxed in the great hall, which was set ablaze at Kriemhild's order. There, the last of the Burgundians,

Gunther and Hagen, splashed through pools of their comrades' blood to fend off waves of attackers. They were captured at last, to be taunted and eventually beheaded by Kriemhild. Kriemhild was slain in turn by a Hunnish knight, outraged that two noble men, enemies though they were, would be cut down by a woman. Thus was the Burgundian dynasty annihilated and Siegfried finally avenged.[45]

"Ludendorff is our Siegfried" asserted one right-wing German newspaper in November 1923.[46] In so referring to Ludendorff, that journalist was merely making explicit a linkage that Ludendorff himself had encouraged since at least 1917 and which he would promote with increasing vigor for the rest of his life. Doing so salved his conscience, stroked his ego, and helped him maintain his position as the preeminent nationalist and military expert in the 1920s. As Siegfried, Ludendorff could argue that the fate of many men and even the fate of Germany were mirrored in his fate.

The Siegfried Legend in Imperial Germany

The legend of the hero Siegfried occupies an important place in German culture. The *Nibelungenlied* (Song of the Nibelungs), which tells the story of Siegfried's murder and Kriemhild's revenge, was written by an anonymous poet around the year 1200, though it likely had older oral and written antecedents. The *Nibelungenlied* has been called "the German *Iliad*" in that it is an epic poem comparable in some respects to Homer's masterpiece. The German romantics and nationalists of the early nineteenth century discovered the tale as a useful, native alternative to counter the then-dominant admiration for the culture of classical antiquity.[47]

Herfried Münkler has argued that the Siegfried legend poisoned German political culture after 1800.[48] The adoption of the mythic hero as a model, first by liberal, romantic nationalists in the Napoleonic era and later by authoritarian conservatives subtly shaped and limited the policy choices available to Germany's ruling elite, creating a Manichean universe in which unwavering loyalty, heroic aggression, and decisive action became the dominant political virtues.[49] The story of Siegfried provided a historical and ethnic foundational myth for Germany. It also served to "reduce political complexity through the rejection of discursive decision-making processes." It allowed elites to cast their own interests in universal

moral and aesthetic terms and then to escape responsibility for the consequences of their actions by "stylizing history as predestined fate."[50] Myths
operate not just as instruments of power. As Münkler shows, they also
seep into the heads of those using them and become a perverted filter
for reality. The Siegfried myth played itself out in Germany over many
decades, culminating, for Münkler, in the *Götterdämmerung* (Twilight of
the Gods) of the Third Reich in 1945.

Early Reliance on the Siegfried Motif

Richard Wagner's operas powerfully shaped the popular imagination of
the Siegfried legend in the nineteenth century. Though at least one scholar
of the epic warns that "it is fatal to approach the *Nibelungenlied* from
Wagner," many of Ludendorff's contemporaries probably did.[51] Wagner
based his operatic masterpiece, the *Ring of the Nibelungen*, which premiered between 1869 and 1876, not only on the *Nibelungenlied*, but on
several other medieval and contemporary sources as well.[52] In addition
to the thirteenth-century epic poem itself, Wagner augmented his studies
with two important Nordic tales, the *Völsungasaga* and the *Poetic Edda*.
He studied the works of the Brothers Grimm, *Deutsche Mythologie* and
Deutsche Heldensage. Wagner took significant artistic license with all of
these materials. The result was that in 1848, when he wrote the famous
"sketch" for the opera, his "mind was a tangled mass of German myth,
legend, history, and tradition."[53]

Out of this mass grew a story that retained the basic elements of the
original *Nibelungenlied*, such as Siegfried's heroic feats, his betrayal and
murder, while introducing a few significant changes. In Wagner's work,
the gods play a much more prominent role, for example, and it is they
who suffer destruction in the finale (Götterdämmerung or Twilight of the
Gods), not (merely) the Burgundian dynasty. Along with other works on
similar themes (Friedrich Hebel's *Die Nibelungen* trilogy, for example),
Wagner's *Ring* conspired to keep the story of Siegfried (even with Wagner's variations) firmly entrenched in the public imagination.[54] Wagner
also wrote a poem in 1871, "To the German Army before Paris," calling
them "Siege-Fried" (Victory-Peace).[55]

Ludendorff claimed to enjoy the theater and may very well have attended performances of Wagner's *Ring* in Berlin, Bayreuth, and elsewhere.[56] Nevertheless, the original epic story, retained its relevance for Ludendorff and others. Wagner's opera ends with the "twilight of the gods," yet the destruction of the Burgundian dynasty in the hall of King Attila resonated with the German public and politicians alike. Wagner's *Ring* altered the motives for and details of Siegfried's murder in significant ways, yet the *Nibelungenlied*'s plot remained familiar.

With increasing frequency after the turn of the century, the original Siegfried story colored political discourse. It provided the metaphors to which political actors could refer in confidence that their audience would understand. In his notorious speech to German troops departing for China to quell the Boxer Rebellion in 1900, Kaiser Wilhelm invoked the *Nibelungenlied* when he called on his soldiers to behave as Huns: "Just as a thousand years ago the Huns under their King Attila made a name for themselves, one that even today makes them seem mighty in history and legend, may the name German be affirmed by you in such a way in China that no Chinese will ever again dare to look cross-eyed at a German."[57]

Chancellor von Bülow coined the phrase *Nibelungentreue* (Nibelung loyalty) in a 1909 speech discussing the alliance of Germany and Austria-Hungary.[58] Like Hagen and Völker, who stood watch against Hunnish treachery during the Burgundians' stay at Attila's court, Germany and Austria-Hungary would stand by each other. Of course, the loyalty of the Burgundians in the story brings them only utter destruction. The climax of the poem sees the dynasty slaughtered to the last man in the halls of Attila. In 1914, Franz von Liszt, a member of the Reichstag and professor at the University of Berlin, dismissed this troubling detail with the observation that in the context of World War I, it was the Serbs and their supporters who had committed the "sinful" murder of Franz Ferdinand and therefore they would suffer the fate that the Burgundians had brought on themselves by murdering Siegfried.[59] The fact that the analogy made by Bülow and Liszt required mental gymnastics to overcome such contradictions speaks to the fervor with which many Germans clung to the epic storyline.

Ludendorff, like most Germans of his generation, would have been steeped in the story of Siegfried. The *Nibelungenlied* was a staple of German school curricula in the nineteenth and into the twentieth century.

Beginning in 1815 and then increasingly after 1848, the *Nibelungenlied*, appeared in new editions and was excerpted for use in school textbooks. Renowned scholars emphasized the work's utility in inculcating national, moral values of loyalty, glory, and strength. It was touted as the German national epic, Germany's founding myth.[60] One pedagogue in the *Zeitschrift für deutschen Unterricht* recommended in 1917 that graduating students could be filled with patriotic enthusiasm by the great deeds depicted in the *Nibelungenlied*.[61] More editions and variations appeared during the years of the Weimar Republic and the National Socialist regime featured it prominently in its curricula.[62] Between 1918 and 1945, Germany maintained an "unrelenting fascination" with the story.[63] Ludendorff certainly shared that fascination.

Once he rose to a position of responsibility, Ludendorff himself adopted the Siegfried motif for propaganda purposes.[64] In the spring of 1917, anticipating a French offensive, German troops retreated to a more defensible line of fortifications named by Ludendorff the "Siegfried Line." The program of scorched earth carried out in the area vacated by the German Army proceeded under the codename "Alberich," the dwarf in the *Nibelungenlied* who originally guarded the hoard of gold claimed by Siegfried.[65] It was from these defenses that the German Army in July 1918 launched attacks preparatory to the planned "Hagen" offensive and to which they retreated after that offensive failed.[66] Some German troops still held positions in the Siegfried Line when Ludendorff called for an armistice in September 1918.

But it was in linking his personal story to the Siegfried legend that Ludendorff differed. Ludendorff's adoption of the Siegfried persona served political/propagandistic as well as psychological functions. He perceived Germany's defeat in November 1918 as a personal one, and spent the rest of his life attempting to wash away the stain of that failure. Rather than subject Germany's wartime conduct to rational analysis, Ludendorff (and many other Germans as well) fabricated conspiracies to explain the defeat and relied on mythology to bolster their case. Ludendorff in fact authored the most widespread and influential explanation for the lost war: the "stab in the back," or *Dolchstoß*.[67] According to this theory, the German Army, like Siegfried, could not be defeated in battle. Rather, it had been betrayed by internal enemies (Socialists, Communists, and/or Jews in most accounts) intent on dishonoring and destroying Germany.

There are subtle variations in the story, ranging from extreme versions that blame Jews, Marxists, and other "outsider" groups for calling for an armistice in the fall of 1918 (Hitler and Ludendorff favored this version, of course) to more moderate stances suggesting only that domestic unrest and economic weakness had undermined the army's fighting ability at the front. The powerful resonance of the "stab in the back" myth both for Ludendorff personally and for so many German nationalists is related to the deep semiconscious attachment to the legend of Siegfried.[68]

The notion of a "stab in the back" relies on a seriously distorted view of the actual military situation in 1918 and had its roots in the frustrations of the German General Staff with the Reichstag's desire for peace in 1917.[69] "Why are we still fighting?" asked General Wilhelm Groener in July 1917. "The home front has attacked us from the rear and so the war is lost."[70] In a letter to his sister-in-law Gertrud, Ludwig Beck, then a major in the General Staff, described how "in the most difficult moment of the war the revolution,—of this I now have no more doubt—prepared

Figure 1. *Dolchstoß*: Siegfried (Paul Richter) in Fritz Lang's 1924 film *Die Nibelungen: Siegfried*. Courtesy of Friedrich Wilhelm Murnau Stiftung.

long beforehand, fell on our rear." In a most cowardly manner, the revolution (always personified) took advantage of Germany's defenselessness behind the front, Beck insisted.[71] Clearly the idea of a "stab in the back" was in the air. Stories abound as to the exact origin of the phrase *Dolchstoß*. A December 1918 article in the *Neue Zurcher Zeitung* attributed to the British general Sir Frederick Maurice the opinion that "the German army was stabbed in the back by the civilian population."[72] Walter Görlitz, in his *History of the German General Staff*, claims that a different English general, Sir Neill Malcolm, visited Ludendorff in Berlin before his departure for Sweden and heard him complaining of being betrayed by the entire German people. "Are you endeavouring to tell me, General, that you were stabbed in the back?" According to Görlitz (who cites no source for the encounter), Ludendorff shouted "That's it! They gave me a stab in the back—a stab in the back!"[73] Perhaps it was at that moment that Ludendorff cast himself as the noble hero.

Siegfried's betrayal at the hands of Hagen surfaced repeatedly as a compelling trope for explaining Germany's defeat. Addressing the German National Assembly at the end of October 1919, the German nationalist Albrecht von Graefe made the link with the *Nibelungenlied* explicit when he said, "[The German Army] lay on the ground, in a repeat of the image that the old heroic epic of Siegfried and Hagen prophesied for us as an ever-repeating symbol of German history; the spear that was thrust by Hagen from behind into the body of Siegfried, was forged long ago."[74]

But the image became fixed in the German psyche by the statement read by Field Marshal Paul von Hindenburg on November 18, 1919, before the special commission investigating the reasons for the defeat. He quoted General Maurice: " 'The German army was stabbed in the back'— where the blame lies is clear. If one needs proof, it can be found in the above quote of an English general and in the boundless disbelief of our enemies about their victory."[75] The statement Hindenburg read had been drafted at the insistence of and in consultation with Erich Ludendorff.[76] Hindenburg drove the point home (and made explicit the connection to Siegfried) in his memoirs: "It was the end. Like Siegfried, stricken down by the treacherous spear of savage Hagen, our weary front collapsed."[77]

Since, as H. L. Mencken observed in 1917, "the army is Ludendorff,"[78] it was possible for Ludendorff to see the stab in the back as both a personal and a national tragedy. He could readily adopt the role of Siegfried.

Ludendorff would say that he too had been betrayed. His orders at the end of the war had been countermanded or misunderstood, he claimed. According to Ludendorff, it had been his dismissal in 1918 that had opened the floodgates of revolution. He was fond of quoting himself at the audience with the Kaiser on October 26 as saying, "In fourteen days there will be no more monarchy." The Kaiser fled Berlin on November 9, fourteen days later.[79] His dismissal from the position of first quartermaster general of the army was, according to Ludendorff, the key blow that undermined the stability of the front and led to the military collapse and revolution that followed.

Both the appearance of Ludendorff and Hindenburg before the committee and the stab in the back legend were politicized by rightist forces in Germany throughout the 1920s and 1930s. The Deutsche Schutz- und Trutz Bund decried the "Jewish Inquisition" to which the pair were subjected.[80] The "stab in the back," for example, was used for propagandistic purposes within the Reichswehr in order to bolster the morale of the rank and file. In his daily orders to the First Armeekorps immediately following the signing of the Treaty of Versailles in 1919, General Ludwig von Estorff reminded his troops of the countries great need. Not only did Poland threaten in the East but domestic enemies "in Berlin, Hamburg, Frankfurt" and elsewhere threatened domestic order. These revolutionary forces, "who were to blame for our great misfortune" were readying an attack on the state.[81]

The "stab in the back" is only one of the most striking ways in which Ludendorff's life intersected that of the heroic Siegfried. Ludendorff's personal life also merged with the Siegfried legend in ways both significant and trivial. For example, Siegfried was famously handsome. "When he was young," wrote the poet of the *Nibelungenlied*, "marvels could be told of the honours that accrued to him and of his handsome looks, so that women of great beauty came to love him. . . . Indeed many ladies both married and maidens, hoped he would always wish to come [to his father's court]; for (as lord Siegfried was aware) no few were well-disposed towards him."[82] Woodcuts and drawings that accompanied the countless editions of the Siegfried story depict him as a paragon of manhood: tall, muscular, clear-eyed, and with an attractive shock of waving blond hair.

Though photos of the barrel-chested and jowly Ludendorff belie the direct comparison of their looks, some contemporaries found him

Figure 2. Paul Richter as Siegfried. Courtesy of Friedrich Wilhelm Murnau Stiftung.

handsome. A colonel on Ludendorff's staff in 1918 described the general as a "truly handsome Germanic hero-figure." When Ludendorff entered headquarters, burdened by the untenable situation at the front on October 1, the officer wrote: "I had to think of Siegfried with the mortal wound in his back from Hagen's spear."[83]

While Ludendorff may have lacked Siegfried's Adonislike appearance, he did possess the hero's piercing blue eyes. When in his youth, Siegfried approached the smith, Mimir, to offer himself as an apprentice, Mimir and his companions thought "that the sun had arisen. So much radiance sprang from the glowing blue eyes."[84] Ludendorff's associates frequently spoke of his commanding presence, singling out his piercing gaze as his most notable feature. "Whosoever just once saw those blue eyes blazing has seen the living manifestation of the eternal Germanic god of war. From that moment on, he knows what filled the Romans with horror when they spoke of the terrible gaze of the Germans."[85] Like the slightly vain Siegfried, Ludendorff knew the effect that his gaze had. It conveyed to his supporters conviction, resolution, and insight. His eyes bored through the paper of nearly every photograph taken.

The two images, the handsome stalwart Siegfried and the clear-eyed visionary Ludendorff, came together most obviously in the banner of

Figure 3. Erich Ludendorff in 1915. Bundesarchiv, Bild 183-2005-0828-525, photographer unknown.

Figure 4. Erich Ludendorff in 1935. Photo by KEYSTONE-FRANCE / Gamma-Rapho via Getty Images.

Ludendorff's paper, *Volkswarte*, the mouthpiece of his Tannenberg League formed in 1925.

Like so many politicians today, Ludendorff struggled to balance his later wealth and fame with a narrative of his humble beginnings. Though there is no indication that his early life was anything but comfortable, Ludendorff continually highlighted the many obstacles to his achievement. He took particular pride in being a commoner in the company of so many aristocrats in the German officer corps. The autobiography of his early life, *Mein militärischer Werdegang*, drips with resentment

Figure 5. Masthead of *Ludendorffs Volkswarte*. Bundesarchiv, Nachlaß Holtzmann N1079/26/242.

toward those who owed their positions in the army to family connections. In the German Supreme Command (OHL) after 1916, it was a man with not one but two "vons"—Paul Ludwig Hans Anton von Hindenburg und von Beneckendorff—whom the Kaiser appointed commander in chief, but it was Erich Ludendorff who was the brains of the operation. Of course, Ludendorff had many patrons during his career—most notably Helmut von Moltke (the Younger), but he cast himself as a self-made man.[86]

Perhaps surprisingly, this motif of self-reliance is also present in the story of Siegfried. Siegfried was the eldest son of a king, so humble origins play no role, but Siegfried's father King Siegmund refused to treat his son differently than any of the other warriors in his household. "He should earn his heroism through his own merit," insisted Siegmund. "Siegfried agreed."[87] Although he would inherit his father's throne, Siegfried made his own way in the world, apprenticing himself (in many versions of the story) to a smith, single-handedly slaying a dragon, and seizing the Nibelungen hoard from the dwarf Alberich. So while his title was hereditary, Siegfried's fame and fortune, like Ludendorff's were his own.

Ludendorff: Dragonslayer

According to the widely held consensus in Germany concerning the First World War, Ludendorff was the *Feldherr*, the battle lord, who had shown his prowess at Liège and Tannenberg and then held off Germany's enemies through more than two years of war. The Kaiser called Ludendorff "the Siegfried of our time."[88] According to his narrative, Ludendorff's titanic efforts were only undone when, like Siegfried, he was betrayed, "stabbed in the back," and driven from power. Ludendorff became both spokesman for and symbol of many Germans' thirst for retribution, thereby embodying *both* elements of the Nibelungen story: heroism and revenge.[89]

These associations and this story gave Ludendorff a prominence practically unparalleled in the early years of the Weimar Republic. After his brief exile in Sweden, he returned to wealth and fame in Germany. He testified before the special committee examining the causes of the lost war. Foreign governments monitored his movements, still convinced that he could play kingmaker, and they were not entirely misguided. Ludendorff conspired with Wolfgang Kapp in the abortive putsch in 1920 that bears Kapp's name. He was at the head of the young National Socialist movement when Adolf Hitler and his followers marched through Munich on their way (so they thought) to Berlin in 1923. He sold hundreds of thousands of copies of books in the 1920s and 1930s about the war and his life. Upon his death in 1937, the paeans surpassed even those offered to the former field marshal and Reich president Paul von Hindenburg, Ludendorff's wartime partner.

Ludendorff became such a prominent public figure because he was at least partly successful in attaching the symbolism of Siegfried to his person and embodying (in his own telling at least) the qualities of Siegfried. He was able to tap into a powerful cultural current—one that cast politics in heroic terms, one that believed in Manichean struggles, one given to fears of conspiracy and fantasies of revenge—in order to maintain a prominent profile on the extreme nationalist right. From that position of prominence he helped to set the tone for military and political debate in the Weimar Republic even as he became increasingly isolated due to his personal dogmatism and growing anti-Christian convictions.[90]

In this context Ludendorff's postwar political machinations, his publications, his conspiracy theories, his spiritual quest look not insane or quixotic (as other historians have described them) but rather heroic. It was to this hero that hundreds of thousands of Germans looked at that crucial moment in their history when they sought to build a new Germany out of the ruins of the Empire and the Great War.

2

VICTOR OF LIÈGE AND TANNENBERG

Of the mighty barons the tale doth tell that they desired the youth
unto their lord, but of this the stately knight, Sir Siegfried, listed
naught. Forasmuch as both Siegmund and Siegelind were still alive,
the dear child of them twain wished not to wear a crown, but fain
would he become a lord against all the deeds of force within his
lands, whereof the bold and daring knight was sore adread.

—THE NIBELUNGENLIED

His father desired that he should not have it better than any other
knight. He should earn his heroism through his own merit.
Siegfried agreed.

—DIE NIBELUNGEN

Erich Friedrich Wilhelm Ludendorff was born on a small estate in Krusze-
wnia (Posen), now part of Poland.[1] Despite the many references one finds
to Erich *von* Ludendorff, he was not an aristocrat—a fact in which he
would take no small pride.[2] After Ludendorff achieved fame, however,
some followers grasped for such connections. His mother had an aristocratic heritage that genealogists would trace back to Gustav I, king of
Sweden.[3] Admirers of Ludendorff saw the connection to Gustav I as particularly important, most likely because Gustav, known as "Vasa," led
the Swedish War of Liberation (1521–23) against Denmark, winning
Sweden's independence. Gustav's dynasty also included Gustavus Adol-
phus, the great Swedish soldier-king of the Thirty Years' War, so one could
argue that military genius ran in the family.[4] On Ludendorff's father's side
one researcher found a tenuous link to Frederick the Great.[5] His father's

family had been merchants and shipowners near Stettin as far back as the seventeenth century. The father's family had no military heritage to speak of, though one uncle did serve as an officer in a regiment of Hussars. Ludendorff's father was a reserve officer in the Twelfth Hussar Regiment and was recalled to service for the wars in 1866 and 1870 against Austria and France, respectively.

Ludendorff credited his father's example and his pride in service to the crown for his own decision to enroll in the cadet school at Plön, where he was accepted in 1877 at the tender age of twelve.[6] The aloofness and lack of humor that less friendly observers noted in Ludendorff in later life seems to have been evident at an early age. Even Ludendorff himself described his difficulty in establishing friendships at school. Unable to relate to boys his own age, he channeled his loneliness and his energy into making a successful career. After only a year at the school, he was promoted to "squad room elder," giving him responsibility for order and regulations in his unit. One can only imagine how this affected his chances of endearing himself to his classmates.[7]

In 1879 he moved to the main cadet school at Groß-Lichterfelde, near Berlin, to continue his training. Two years later, at age sixteen, he passed an exam formally to become a *Fähnrich*. As at Plön, his keen intellect earned him a position of authority. He had done well enough on his Fähnrich exam to earn a prized spot among the Selekta, the group of officers in training who would command their fellow cadets. Selekta status also meant that Ludendorff would have a shorter period of study (one year instead of two) and would emerge from Groß-Lichterfelde as a second lieutenant, as opposed to an ensign (*Portepée-fähnrich*) or brevet ensign (*characterisierte Portepée-fähnrich*).[8] Ludendorff relished the responsibility of maintaining order in the barracks and leading his classmates, including many older than he, to meals and to their duties. He also enjoyed the opportunity to be in Berlin, where he could visit relatives of his mother as well as attend the theater and opera on occasion.

One detects the obvious pride that young Erich felt at rising so quickly within the German officer corps still dominated by aristocrats. In 1860, 65 percent of Prussian officers were of noble birth.[9] The percentage of noble officers declined in the course of the nineteenth century as the German military expanded and faced the challenges of increasingly modern, industrialized warfare. But as late as 1895, 44 percent of all officers still

Figure 6. Ludendorff as cadet circa 1880. Photo by Hulton Archive / Getty Images.

featured a "von" in their names, and the highest echelons of the military were still staffed almost exclusively with the scions of old, aristocratic military families.[10] Two-thirds of the officers in the Great General Staff in 1872 were of aristocratic origin.[11] The most prestigious positions, even in the officer training schools, were largely reserved for those with the right family connections, and Erich confessed to some jealousy when he saw his noble classmates selected to serve as pages at the court or in other capacities where the opportunity to cultivate important career connections existed.[12] Despite such obstacles, Ludendorff was promoted to lieutenant on April 15, 1882, just days after his seventeenth birthday.[13] He hoped to make a career for himself in the artillery, where his proficiency in mathematics would serve him well and where chances for bourgeois officers were greater. But his first posting was to the Fifty-Seventh Infantry Regiment in Wesel on the Lower Rhine.[14]

In 1933, when Ludendorff recounted his early life in *Mein militärischer Werdegang*, he was deeply committed to *Deutsche Gotterkenntnis* and its anti-Catholic, antisemitic, and anti-Freemason credo. When he looked back at his time in the Catholic Rhenish region, he could easily descry the symptoms of corruption that he attributed to Catholics and Freemasons later in life. He credited himself with no great insight at the time and described only his sense of unease at the power wielded by priests in the region. He called the Catholics "poor people without a homeland who only lived in German houses."[15] The air in their homes seemed foreign to him, he recalled.

Ludendorff, like so many Germans of his days, could not resist the temptation to wax eloquent about the mighty "German river" that flowed "majestically" past Wesel and along which he would march for the next five years.[16] He spoke of the region's pagan past with fondness, and he specifically mentioned visiting the "saga-entwined" city of Xanten, just across the river from Wesel.[17] Having only read the *Nibelungenlied* in school, this visit to Siegfried's birthplace must have been Ludendorff's first tangible encounter with the legend.

Like many young officers of middle-class background, Ludendorff struggled to avoid debt while serving in the army. An officer's pay never sufficed, with the cost of several different and expensive uniforms, costs for any entertainments indulged in, and many other incidental expenses besides. His parents supplemented his income as best they could, but Ludendorff did not lead a lavish lifestyle.

Ludendorff returned to Berlin in February 1887 to take command of the *Militärturnanstalt* there, where cadets learned gymnastics, swimming, and enjoyed other sports.[18] He welcomed the return to Berlin with its theaters and nightlife. A small supplement to his pay, granted to commanding officers, allowed him to visit the theater more frequently. Ludendorff confessed a love for Shakespeare.[19] And for the first time, apparently, he sought the attention of the young ladies of Berlin. Yet life in the city was also bittersweet. His father's agricultural holdings had failed while Erich was away in Wesel, and the father had been forced to move to Berlin to find work as an insurance official for the Norddeutschen Hagelversicherungsgesellschaft. Ludendorff was able to see his family more often but their circumstances were not what they had been.

The posting to Berlin did not last long, in any case. In April of that same year, he received orders to report to Wilhelmshaven to serve in a marine infantry unit as a liaison to the German Navy. Service in the "Seebattalion" was both a blessing and a curse for Ludendorff. In one sense, it represented a significant honor. The transfer came with a back-dated promotion. Not for the last time would Ludendorff be singled out for advancement ahead of his peers. It was also a position that was always filled very carefully by the leadership of the army because that unit served as a model battalion intended to, as Ludendorff expressed it, "display for the sailors and other naval detachments . . . the discipline of the army."[20] For an officer without family connections, it represented real advancement. Soon, Ludendorff was dining with General Leo von Caprivi, then chief of the Admiralty, and Crown Prince Wilhelm himself. During his tour, Ludendorff visited many of the nations bordering the North Sea and the Baltic (Sweden, Denmark, Great Britain, Norway) and made his first impressions of foreign peoples and foreign armies. Ludendorff's unit accompanied the Kaiser to the Isle of Wight in August 1889 when the newly crowned Wilhelm II made a state visit to his grandmother, Queen Victoria of Great Britain. As the commander of the unit inspected by Victoria's son Edward, Ludendorff received a minor decoration from the Kaiser himself.

But life among the naval officer corps did not sit well with Ludendorff. He found them ill-disciplined and petty, jealous of the resources lavished on the army. They resented his position and treated him with hostility. With only small units to command and little to do onboard ship, Ludendorff felt himself "flapping in the breeze."[21] He used the time to read works of military history and military science and to study for the entrance exams for the Kriegsakademie. After a brief visit to newly acquired Heligoland in the North Sea, Ludendorff was admitted to the Kriegsakademie in the summer of 1890. After a short stay in Frankfurt an der Oder, Ludendorff moved to Berlin for his three-year stint that October. The Kriegsakademie admitted only the one hundred best applicants each year, and so Ludendorff had once again distinguished himself.

The Kriegsakademie as it existed in 1890 had been created in 1858, though it traced its roots to the reform era following Prussia's disastrous defeat at the hands of Napoleon.[22] The curriculum was built around military topics such as tactics, fortifications, and military law as well as academic subjects such as French, Russian, and physics. Ludendorff judged the curriculum at the academy to be insufficient in virtually all areas except tactics and military history. In other fields, such as fortifications, general history, and geography, Ludendorff felt that the lessons were outdated and of little utility. Ludendorff learned Russian while at the academy. Each year was punctuated by a summer posting to a different branch, where officers could learn the capabilities of the artillery and cavalry, for example. A maneuver presided over by Helmuth von Moltke (the Younger) in the summer of 1893 culminated Ludendorff's career at the Kriegsakademie.[23] His commander judged that Ludendorff "had a good head, which combined good knowledge and good ability with good form."[24] Indeed, he was marked for higher responsibilities within the army. After an army-funded trip through Russia to solidify his language skills, Ludendorff was promoted to captain and reported for duty with the Great General Staff (GGS) in April 1894.[25]

It bears repeating what an exclusive club Ludendorff joined. At the turn of the twentieth century, only about two hundred of German's finest officers served on the GGS at any point.[26] The majority, though an increasingly slim one, could rely on an aristocratic name and a long family tradition of military service to ensure that their talents were not unnoticed.[27]

The GGS was "a body of General Staff officers not attached to Army Corps" and was "entrusted, under the immediate supervision of the chief of the General Staff, with drawing up and preparing possible plans of operation."[28] In 1894, the GGS consisted of a number "sections" each presided over by a section chief. The most important was the second, or "German," section, which devised deployment plans and supervised railways, in addition to other duties. The first section dealt with Russia and the states of Eastern Europe. The third covered France as well as England, Belgium, and the United States. Officers in these two sections were responsible for keeping abreast of military developments in those regions. Other sections related to fortresses, training, cartography, maneuvers, and other tasks.[29]

To his chagrin, Ludendorff was placed in a division of the Russian section, which according to one of his colleagues offered few opportunities for advancement.[30] He was responsible for covering military affairs in Northern Europe, the Balkans, and Asia, including China and Japan. The inclusion of the latter states under his purview proved propitious for Ludendorff, as war broke out between those two states that summer. A short piece he had written on the growing tensions between Japan and China caught the attention of Count von Schlieffen, the chief of the General Staff.[31] His superiors had initially been shocked that Ludendorff predicted a swift Japanese victory but were convinced by Ludendorff's arguments. Ludendorff's star rose when the course of the war largely conformed to his predictions, and Ludendorff was promoted to the rank of captain in the General Staff in March 1895.

One gets the sense that Ludendorff, for all of his success, was not very well liked within the officer corps. In his account of his early military career Ludendorff frequently cites the satisfaction of his superiors and the gratitude of his subordinates but rarely mentions personal relationships or private connections at all. He evaluated all those around him by a strictly military yardstick. Those who commanded competently he praised; those who succeeded through family connections were mocked; those who appeared to be self-serving he condemned. The few who do appear by name serve primarily as models against which to compare prominent rivals whom Ludendorff wished to discredit.

Whatever Ludendorff may have lacked in charisma, he clearly compensated for with his work ethic. His professional fortunes continued to rise, and in March 1896 he was named a general staff officer (Ib) in the staff of the Fourth Army Corps, stationed in Magdeburg and commanded by General Carl Eduard von Hänisch. There Ludendorff learned the basics of staff work, both by observing his Ia counterpart, who was responsible for maneuvers and mobilization plans, and by performing his own more limited duties. In the German Army of the time, the Ib staff officer managed training and maneuvers, kept tabs on foreign armies, and supervised the production of maps.[32] The highlight of Ludendorff's service in Magdeburg was the annual maneuvers. There he accompanied the commander on horseback and learned the basics of large-unit command.

After two years on the Fourth Army Corps staff, Ludendorff transferred as a company commander to the Sixty-First Infantry Regiment located in Thorn.[33] Spending time with troops in the field was a component of staff training that was considered indispensable to high rank in the Great German General Staff. Army commanders and members of the General Staff were expected to be leaders and not just theoreticians. Experience in troop commands would keep staff officers grounded in reality and connected to the real capabilities of their soldiers.

Ludendorff found his company in a state of disarray. His predecessor had neglected the basics of discipline, and Ludendorff made it his goal to repair the damage. He relied heavily, he later recalled, on physical fitness, target practice, bayonet drills, and history lessons. With these devices, Ludendorff claimed to have salvaged his unit by the fall so that incoming recruits imbibed only the pure military spirit that Ludendorff thought necessary.

Thorn, where Ludendorff's unit was based, was a major fortress complex on the Weichsel River in East Prussia, near the Russian border. It was a fairly dismal posting, made worse in the summer of 1898 by torrential rains that flooded the company out of its barracks. From his vantage point in 1933, the service in Thorn seemed especially significant because the area was largely Polish and had been swapped back and forth between Prussia/Germany and the various independent Polish states of the previous few centuries. In 1933, Thorn lay in the "Polish corridor" and therefore served for Ludendorff and his readers as a reminder of Germany's present "defenseless" state.

Ludendorff's General Staff colleagues consistently described him as "energetic." General Max Hoffmann, whose path would cross Ludendorff's several times over the years, mentions his high profile in military circles.[34] Others perceived Ludendorff's influence deriving from his work ethic. The historian Karl Hampe noted Ludendorff's "brutal energy" more than once in his wartime diary.[35] Ludendorff's superior through much of the war, Paul von Hindenburg, saw his own job as giving "free scope to the intellectual powers, the almost superhuman capacity for work and untiring resolution of [his] Chief of Staff."[36] Ludendorff hoped for a place among the German expedition to quell the Boxer Rebellion in China in 1900. He traveled to Berlin personally to beseech Alfred von Schlieffen for a spot on General Alfred von Waldersee's staff, but his request was denied. His term of service in the field had ended, and Ludendorff transferred to the staff of the Ninth Division of the Fifth Army Corps in Posen and Lower Silesia. His success in the maneuvers and exercises carried out by the division won him the promotion to Major in September 1901.[37] He assumed the important position of staff officer Ia in the Fifth Army Corps the following year. Ludendorff felt the tremendous responsibility of the position, which required him to prepare mobilization plans down to the very last detail. He applied to the work his usual fervor and exactitude. The time spent preparing these enormously complicated plans would stand Ludendorff in good stead in the coming years, the high point of his prewar career. In March 1904, Ludendorff was made chief of the division dealing with the army in the "German" section of the Great General Staff. Here Ludendorff renewed his acquaintance with Counts Schlieffen and Moltke. Schlieffen served as chief of the General Staff until December 1905 when he was replaced by Moltke, who had served as Oberquartiermeister I (supervisor of the "German" and the railway sections) in preparation for the job.[38] Ludendorff admired both men for their strategic insights.[39] Ludendorff now dealt with the organization, training, equipment, and mobilization of the German Army.[40]

In January 1906, Ludendorff's father passed away, so he foreswore the stint as battalion commander that would normally have followed his tenure as section chief and requested a position at the Kriegsakademie in order to remain with his mother in Berlin. Ludendorff taught tactics and military history and reveled in the opportunity to share his knowledge and shape young military minds. He drew his lessons largely from the Prussian wars against Austria and France in 1866 and 1870–71, respectively. That the numerically inferior Prussian Army could so handily defeat the Habsburgs and their allies was proof, for Ludendorff, of the superiority of the Prussian Army's training, equipment, and tactical leadership. Ludendorff's lectures on the Franco-Prussian War in the spring of 1908 were interrupted, however, by his recall that March to the Great General Staff. When the section leader of the "German" section moved up to the position of Oberquartiermeister I in 1908, Ludendorff succeeded him.[41]

Shortly thereafter, in May, Ludendorff received the promotion to lieutenant colonel.

A word concerning sources is in order here. Much of Ludendorff's early memoir, the only document containing information about his prewar life, is fairly reliable. He marches his reader through his early career with only occasional references to the conspiracy theories that would occupy him in later life. When he recounts his time in Poland, he embarks on one brief tangent concerning the pernicious influence of the Catholic Church there, and he makes occasional reference to a Masonic plot. But these are only asides and unrelated to the basic narrative of his activities.

The passages dealing with his time as chief of the "German" section are different. Chief of the "German" section was an important position because that officer would serve as chief of operations in the event of war. He would serve at the side of the chief of the General Staff directing the entire war effort. In this position, Ludendorff worked closely with the chief of the General Staff, Count Helmuth von Moltke (the Younger). By 1933, when he wrote *Mein militärischer Werdegang*, Ludendorff was convinced that Moltke had been under occult, Masonic influence for years prior to 1914. According to Ludendorff, Moltke's wife and another woman, Lizbeth Seidler, exerted spiritual control over Moltke as part of a Masonic plot hatched in 1889 to entangle Germany in a war in 1914. Ludendorff's conviction that Moltke was an "internally broken man" compromises his narrative in this section in a fairly direct way, and so the work must be read with greater than usual caution from this point on.[42]

Ludendorff remained section chief, a position of enormous responsibility, from 1908 until 1913. In this role, he not only prepared mobilization plans but also oversaw the technical section of the General Staff. In this capacity, Ludendorff was responsible for modernizing Germany's artillery, managing the army's communications, and evaluating and incorporating new technologies such as automobiles and aircraft.[43] Correspondence within the GGS indicated Moltke and Ludendorff's curiosity concerning the capabilities of aircraft, including bomb loads and night operations.[44]

From this post, Ludendorff would champion the cause of army enlargement. Whereas Moltke the Elder had lamented the changing character of modern war while he conducted the brutal siege of Paris, Ludendorff was already convinced that "real" war would be total. To win the next war, Ludendorff believed that the entire manpower strength of Germany should be mobilized for the engagement with the enemy. As he became acquainted with the details of the Schlieffen Plan and saw the results of exercises based on that plan, Ludendorff became disturbed by the disparity between the forces called for in the Schlieffen Plan and the real numbers and capabilities of the German Army. For one thing, Schlieffen based his attack on a number of divisions larger than the German Army commanded. According to Ludendorff, Schlieffen also equated the capabilities of standing and reserve units, an assumption Ludendorff knew to be faulty from his time at Thorn, Magdeburg, and elsewhere.[45]

Ludendorff mobilized his now considerable circle of allies to lobby on behalf of his scheme. The official memorandum, composed in 1912, proposing the enlargement bore Moltke's signature but it was (now Colonel) Ludendorff's plan. He noted that France mobilized 82 percent of its eligible recruits each year, whereas Germany only drew in 52–54 percent. If Germany matched France's effort, 150,000 more men each year could enter the ranks. Germany's peacetime strength would be increased by 300,000. Such growth would enable the creation of at least three new army corps for use in battle. Given the Entente's numerical superiority, the current shortfall could be disastrous, Ludendorff predicted.[46]

The stumbling block was money. To pay for the increase, both the War Ministry and the Reichstag would have to approve the necessary funds, and neither body was eager. The character of the Reichstag had fundamentally changed in 1912 when elections had for the first time produced a plurality for the Social Democratic Party (SPD). Though by any measure a gradualist, as opposed to a revolutionary, Marxist party, the SPD knew that one of the principle tasks of the German Army was to quell domestic unrest and their constituency could be in the crosshairs of those new recruits with a single command.[47]

To overcome such resistance, Ludendorff took the step radical for a military man and sought to enlist public opinion. Retired general August Keim introduced Ludendorff to Heinrich Class, leader of the Pan-German League. Together, they created the Wehrverein to lobby for the interests of the army in general and of Ludendorff's proposed increase in particular. They succeeded in squeezing 106,000 men as well as new equipment (especially artillery and aircraft) out of the reluctant Reichstag.[48]

I have already warned of Ludendorff's bias in reporting his years on the General Staff. Regarding the issue of army enlargement, Ludendorff could add a less idiosyncratic reason for playing up his role. Foregrounding his involvement allowed him after the war to claim not only to have been the Feldherr but a prophet as well. Page after page of *Mein militärischer Werdegang* is devoted to substantiating, often with long citations from documentary evidence, Ludendorff's perception of the problems faced by Germany in any future war with the Entente powers. He detailed his proposals for larger forces, for the disposition of reserve divisions, and for the defense of Schleswig-Holstein against an anticipated British landing.

Not that Schlieffen had been blind to the problem. Before his departure, Schlieffen lobbied the War Ministry ceaselessly to approve various increases. He hoped, for example, to outfit "irregular" divisions to perform occupation, guard, and transport duties, thereby freeing the field army for combat alone. Ludendorff would make a similar argument, based on his reading of the problems encountered by the Prussian Army in France in 1870 and 1871.[49] Ludendorff also proposed activating certain reserve divisions or mobilizing larger numbers of reserve troops (the plan carried out in 1914 left 600,000 trained men unmobilized, according to Ludendorff).[50]

The proposal to field additional divisions ran into opposition from a variety of sources both military and civilian. The Reichstag resisted the budgetary implications that the increase would entail (and the growing Socialist plurality probably just enjoyed flexing its muscle a bit). More serious for Ludendorff was resistance within the War Ministry. The War Ministry feared that it would be unable to find sufficiently reliable officers to staff the new army corps, with the usual circles among which the army recruited its officer corps stretched thin already.[51]

In hindsight, of course, these decisions appear fateful. Whether any additional troops could effectively have been brought into action in August and September of 1914 is, however, debatable. What impact the loss of those manpower reserves would have had on the economic situation in Germany is unclear. For Ludendorff, none of these considerations mattered. If the war could have been won in 1914, no greater economic mobilization would have been required. The army had been neglected, Ludendorff was convinced, so that Wilhelm II could squander his war chest on a navy that would contribute little to the German war effort. "If my proposals had been accepted," Ludendorff argued, "the Volk would have been saved."[52]

Ludendorff was probably not mistaken in seeing his transfer in January 1913 to a minor field command in Düsseldorf (Niederrheinsischen Füsilierregiment Nr. 39) as retribution for championing the cause of army enlargement. As an "inconvenient prophet" (a phrase frequently repeated in eulogies to Ludendorff in 1937), he was sent packing.[53] His receipt of a decoration that summer was (in Moltke's words) "recognition for his work on the army increase" and would not have lessened the sting.[54] Ludendorff languished in Düsseldorf until just before the outbreak of war in August 1914, though he attacked his duties as regimental commander with the energy and precision for which his staff work was known.

In hindsight, Ludendorff credited his time in Düsseldorf with increasing his awareness of the significance of industry and labor to Germany's war effort. His previous position on the General Staff had placed him in charge of technical questions concerning military technology. With his new barracks situated near the Rheinische Metallwarenfabrik that would supply munitions during the war (and with Krupp nearby), Ludendorff had a palpable sense of Germany's industrial might. But he claimed also to notice the growing dissent among Germany's working class. It was in Düsseldorf that Ludendorff suffered the death of his mother in March 1914.[55]

Liège

Shortly before the fateful summer of 1914, Ludendorff received a brigade command (Eighty-Fifth Infantry Brigade) in Strasbourg and a promotion to major general.[56] They say that fortune favors the bold, and Ludendorff found fortune within the first days of the war. While his Rhenish commands had been a form of exile from Berlin, his superiors at the GGS had clearly not forgotten him. Immediately upon the outbreak of war, orders arrived sending Ludendorff to join the Second Army commanded by General Karl von Bülow at Aachen, where he would be attached to General Otto von Emmich of the Tenth Corps. The Second Army (along with the First) had an extremely crucial role to play in the early stages of the Schlieffen Plan. They were responsible for spearheading the German advance through Belgium and around the left flank of the main French forces arrayed along the German border. Emmich commanded six brigades (drawn from a variety of divisions) tasked with capturing the all-important Belgian fortress at

Liège. All German forces would have to be funneled through the relatively narrow strip of territory between the Ardennes and Holland. Liège and its twelve subsidiary fortresses sat astride that meager gap. It had been one of Erich Ludendorff's tasks while on the General Staff to solve the problem of Liège by any means necessary.

Ludendorff developed a bold plan. Rather than trying to disassemble the mutually supporting network of fortifications, German forces would exploit their detailed knowledge of Belgian terrain (some gained during secret vacation trips by staff officers to the area) to bypass the surrounding forts and strike directly at the main citadel itself.[57] With the command and support center of the fortification complex in their hands, German troops could race ahead across Belgium while follow-on forces surrounded the remaining defenders and used extremely heavy new howitzers (developed at least in part at Ludendorff's insistence for precisely this purpose) to reduce the forts.[58] While the operation can hardly be deemed a "surprise" attack (the usual literal translation of *Handstreich*) given the general knowledge of German intentions combined with the ultimatum of August 2, it would serve the Germans well if the Belgian defense could be unhinged before it had a chance to establish itself more firmly through the call up of reserves and the advance of the field army to support the garrison. In order to accomplish the *Handstreich*, German units were sent across the Belgian border only partially mobilized.[59]

Moltke and Ludendorff recognized the weakness of the Belgian system: that the forts were poorly sited to cover the approaches, and that the city lacked a wall. If German units could enter the city, the forts would not shell it and would likely surrender, he believed. Moltke recognized that the plan was risky but felt secure because "in any case the heaviest artillery will be ready, so that in case the *coup de main* fails the fortress can be taken with an abbreviated siege."[60]

So it was no coincidence that from his exile in Strasbourg, Ludendorff would be summoned to the critical point to advise and support the commander of Second Army, Tenth Corps, General Otto von Emmich, as his deputy chief of staff (quartermaster general).[61] His position was a complicated but not unusual one. He was to serve as a liaison between the Second Army command and Emmich's staff. As such, he had no power to issue formal orders but had significant independence and authority by virtue of his connection to the General Staff.

The German plan called for an attack by General Otto von Emmich's Tenth Corps, part of the Second Army commanded by Generaloberst Karl von Bülow.[62] The Tenth Corps included six infantry brigades (Thirty-Fourth, Twenty-Seventh, Fourteenth, Eleventh, Thirty-Eighth, and Forty-Third) as well as the Second, Fourth, and Ninth Cavalry divisions. By the third day of mobilization (August 4 in this case) the Second Cavalry Division and Thirty-Fourth Infantry Brigade would advance from Aachen to seize the Meuse crossings at Visé in the north and protect the northern flanks of the units attacking Liège.[63] The Twenty-Seventh Brigade would pass the gap between the forts at Barchon and Évegnée, while the Fourteenth Brigade would take the most direct route, aiming for the village of Retinne that sat between Évegnée and Fléron. The German Eleventh Brigade would advance from Eupen via Verviers to enter Liège south of Fléron. The units mobilized at Malmedy (Thirty-Eighth and Forty-Third Brigades and the Ninth Cavalry Division) would cross the tributary Ourthe River south of Liège and attempt to flank the city from that direction. In all, roughly thirty-three thousand German troops were committed to the initial operation.[64]

The fortress complex at Liège had been designed in 1888 by renowned Dutch-born engineer Lieutenant General Henri Alexis Brialmont along with the other important fortresses of Belgium (such as the much larger complex at Antwerp built in 1868).[65] Brialmont recognized that Belgium would be the likely battleground for the inevitable future conflict between France and Germany, and he designed the fortress system of Belgium for that eventuality.[66] It was built for a total cost of 100 million francs, finished in 1892, and was supposed to hold out for one year against a force of 300,000.[67] After the war, the Belgian commander confessed that he only had provisions for one month.[68] It was modern by the standards of the 1890s, built to withstand the fire of the largest guns then available, around 21cm, but no improvements had been made since.[69] Brialmont's forts were made of modern concrete, using Portland cement, but were not reinforced with steel, a technique invented in the 1890s.[70]

There were twelve subsidiary forts surrounding the citadel in Liège itself.[71] The forts formed a circle roughly six or seven kilometers from the center of the city. Each fort was approximately four kilometers from its neighbor. Though they were intended to be mutually supporting, several of the forts were just outside the range of their neighbors' guns. Fort

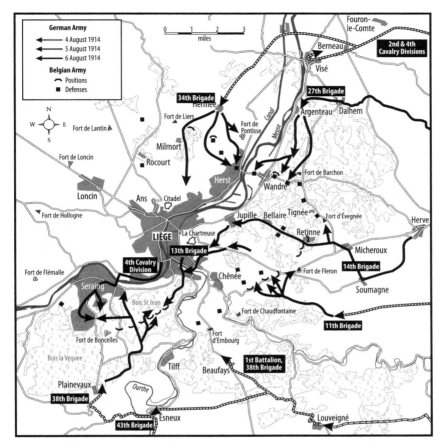

Map 1. Battle of Liège, August 4–6, 1914. Map by Mike Bechtold.

Boncelles, for example, was particularly exposed: sixty-four hundred meters from Embourg to the east and fifty-six hundred meters from Flémalle
on the left bank of the Meuse.[72]

Some observers faulted the layout of the forts for not adequately covering certain low-lying stretches of terrain that the Germans were sure to
use for their approach.[73] Their commander in 1914 complained that these
"deep valleys led right up to our ramparts as if the enemy had excavated
them to create a sheltered path."[74] Upon the outbreak of the war, the Belgians did their best to place obstacles and troops in these "blind spots" to
impede the German advance, but with limited success. Two further works

in the city itself, the citadel and La Chartreuse were deemed of very little military value. In fact, the citadel proved of use only to the Germans, who occupied it in order to menace the town of Liège and encourage the quiescence of its population.[75]

The forts were usually empty in peacetime. Engineers toured the facilities occasionally to make repairs and test equipment.[76] Once activated, each fort contained a garrison of between one hundred sixty-nine and two hundred men, supported by elements of the field army. One advantage that the Belgians did possess was that they mobilized in response to the German ultimatum and fully expected an attack from the direction of Aachen. The Germans would face far more troops than they expected. Estimates of the size of Belgian forces near Liège range from twenty-two thousand to thirty-two thousand men—a formidable number.[77] By comparison, the Germans had expected to face only six thousand Belgian soldiers, bolstered by a smaller number of members of Belgium's Garde Civique.[78]

In the event, German forces moved quickly, crossing the border on schedule on August 4. Germans forces arrived at Visé, north of Liège to find the Meuse Bridge had been destroyed.[79] Stymied at Visé, cavalry units managed to cross the Meuse closer to the Dutch border at the fords of Lixhe.[80] To the south, units of the Ninth Cavalry captured the undamaged bridge across the Ourthe at Poulseur.

On August 5, the Belgians repulsed the initial German attacks on the fortress complex, inflicting heavy losses.[81] German units continued to make contact with Belgian forces during the course of the day on Wednesday, August 5, and prepared for a massive attack all along the eastern edge of the fortress ring that evening. The main attack on the fortress complex began in the evening of Wednesday, August 5. At 2:30 that afternoon, units of the Thirty-Fourth Brigade crossed the Meuse at Lixhe, spurred on by Ludendorff himself, then proceeded down the left bank of the Meuse to occupy the small village of Hermée and invest Fort Pontisse, which overlooked the river and therefore most directly threatened the main German advance, which was to take place between Liège and the Dutch border.[82] German guns opened fire on the fort, trying to disable its guns with artillery fire.[83] German units attempted to storm Pontisse in the dark but suffered heavy losses in fighting with the Belgian Eleventh Line Regiment.[84] Heavy fighting also occurred at several other forts. The Germans seized a portion of the high ground south of the city and could bring guns to within range of Liège. They shelled the city for the first time at 4:00 a.m. on August 6.[85]

Ludendorff roamed the battlefield. On the night of August 5, Ludendorff was in the center with of the German line. After becoming separated from his fellow officers in the dark of the village of Retinne, Ludendorff and a small detachment encountered the heap of dead and wounded soldiers belonging to the Fourteenth Brigade, including its commander, Generalmajor Friedrich von Wussow.[86] On his own initiative, Ludendorff assumed command and led the remainder of the brigade on toward the city.[87] In Retinne, he outflanked the defenders who had cut down Wussow, taking one hundred Belgians prisoner and capturing several guns. When his men stalled on the road, he urged them on saying: "Don't let me go on alone!"[88] The village of Queue du Bois fell next, and the remaining Belgian defenders fled.[89] A few more German units straggled in, as did General von Emmich.[90]

As the Germans advanced Belgian commander Gérard Leman decided to withdraw his headquarters to Fort Loncin, as the strongest fort that commanded the best view of the Germans' most likely route. There Leman received one grim report after another. His Fourteenth Brigade had been forced back and the Germans were threatening to break through in numerous locations. His troops, including many aged militiamen, were exhausted after two days of fighting a vastly superior enemy. After a brief consultation with his staff, Leman decided to order a general retreat rather than expose his Third Division to wholesale destruction or capture in their positions around Liège. The retreat in the direction of Waremme began at 2:00 p.m.[91] As the Belgian troops passed through Liège, townspeople admired their continued good spirit but also saw many toss aside their knapsacks to save weight.[92]

Just before noon on August 6, Emmich and Ludendorff ascended to the heights near the disused La Chartreuse fortress east of the city. Seeing a white flag flying over the citadel, Emmich sent Captain von Harbou to investigate. Toward evening, Harbou returned with the news that the flag had been raised in error.[93] Ludendorff and his fifteen hundred men, low on ammunition and guarding Belgian prisoners (whose numbers had swollen to one thousand), bivouacked at La Chartreuse for the night of August 6–7.[94] They were the only German soldiers inside the ring of fortresses.[95]

Having secured a few of the undamaged Meuse bridges during the night, Ludendorff took his men across the river early on August 7.[96] Ludendorff ordered Colonel Burghardt von Oven's 165th Infantry Regiment to take the citadel. Ludendorff then commandeered a vehicle and followed with his aide.[97] For some reason, Oven had gone to Fort Loncin instead of the citadel, so when Ludendorff arrived, no German soldiers were apparent. Ludendorff rapped on the gate of the citadel with his sword. When Belgian officers answered his call, Ludendorff, thinking quickly, convinced them that he was at the head of a large body of troops and called on the hundred or so Belgians present to surrender.[98] Miraculously, they complied.

With the Germans now shelling Liège itself more heavily, the mayor surrendered the town rather than face further destruction. But without control of the outlying forts, the German foothold in Liège itself was tenuous. Troops and supplies passing through the town could still be attacked by artillery fire from the forts, which also harassed Germans trying to cross the Meuse.[99]

Each fort was equipped with a large howitzer, so it should have been possible to fire on the Germans even in the defiles out of sight of the fortresses, but Liège had not been equipped sufficiently with observation posts or the communication network necessary to enable such attacks. General Leman lamented the inadequate observation facilities at his disposal, which prevented accurate fire on the Germans beyond one or two thousand meters from each fort.[100] Once the Germans occupied Liège itself, they could move much more openly, as the Belgians were reluctant to bombard their own city.

A few of the forts fell in the following days, but most held out until the arrival of the heavy German siege guns on August 12. Ludendorff himself had demanded the creation of batteries of large mortars in order to reduce border fortifications quickly in time of war. In a report dated February 8, 1911, Ludendorff called for mobile batteries of 30.5 and 42cm mortars.[101]

The combination of gases from high explosives and horrible stench from malfunctioning or inadequate latrines actually caused or contributed to the surrender of eight of the twelve forts, including the large forts Pontisse, Fléron, Flémalle, and Boncelles.[102] Leman noted that while Brialmont might have been a scientific genius, he had neglected to consider that his works were constructed for men, whose "natural functions" where not suspended under bombardment—"quite the contrary[!]"[103] The garrison of Fort Pontisse earned Leman's praise for resisting to the maximum despite the pestilential conditions. The fort took more than a dozen hits from the massive 42cm siege mortars. Its concrete defenses were in ruins and its artillery was utterly incapacitated. Despite piling mattresses against any openings, the infiltration of noxious gases (combined with the stench of their own latrines), forced the defenders out. Remarkably, the garrison suffered only three dead and thirty wounded in the barrage.[104]

One by one, the surrounding forts fell, but the explosion of Fort Loncin, which housed General Leman, got the lion's share of attention in subsequent accounts. Loncin was shelled by 10.5cm and 21cm guns on the twelfth and thirteenth but suffered very little damage.[105] It was not until August 14, after the city itself had been in German hands for one week, that the great Krupp siege mortars were ready to do their terrible work on this critical installation, which guarded the important rail line heading west from Liège. The final phase of the bombardment began at 5:30 a.m. on August 15. The Germans fired from the center of town, and the concussion from the massive guns broke windows and knocked tiles from the roofs of nearby houses.[106] The fort endured for twelve hours until, at 5:20 p.m. on August 15, an enormous explosion shattered the main gallery and entombed most of the garrison.[107]

It seems clear from the magnitude of the damage that the fort's magazine, containing twenty-four thousand pounds of black powder, had exploded but whether from a direct hit by the Germans (the German theory) or due to a smoldering fire caused by the lengthy shelling (as claimed by the Allies) remained in dispute.[108] A Belgian officer, surveying the damage, called the devastation "indescribable" but then proceeded to describe it. "A broken cataract of blocks of stone, of concrete, of fragments of cupolas, which crushed beneath it almost the whole garrison, which had already been decimated by the violence of the explosion. The explosion was succeeded by a silence as of death."[109]

Of the fort's garrison, swollen to 500 after other forts had been evacuated, 350 were dead and only a handful remained uninjured.[110] The minatory explosion of Loncin led to the collapse of moral in the neighboring fortress of Hollagne, which surrendered after a much shorter bombardment on August 16.[111] The large Fort Flémalle surrendered at about the same time.

The battle had been a costly one. The German Army ended up pouring nearly 100,000 troops into the siege and suffered notable casualties. Conservative estimates indicate that the six original brigades committed to the Handstreich lost over five thousand men just in the first few days.[112] The official German history details the losses of the Thirty-Fourth Brigade as 1,150 soldiers and thirty officers in just the fighting on August 5.[113] Ludendorff's Fourteenth Brigade that entered Liège on August 7 was below 50 percent strength. Figures for the battle as a whole, including the investment of the ring fortresses, range much higher. One should of course be skeptical of Allied sources on the subject, but Holger Herwig writes that the Belgian Army lost an estimated 20,000 in Liège's defense—so perhaps the high estimates of German losses are not so farfetched.[114]

The Battle of Liège minted the first heroes of the war. Kaiser Wilhelm II decorated both Emmich and Ludendorff with the Pour le Mérite—the first recipients of the Great War. The victory at Liège made Ludendorff a national hero and remained firmly associated with his name.[115]

Tannenberg

Germany's military leadership had other plans for the now-famous general. The situation on the Eastern Front was dire. Russian armies threatened East Prussia and the commander of the Eighth Army, General Maximilian von Prittwitz seemed to be losing his nerve. The Eighth Army had been mauled in battles along the frontier with Russia's First Army, commanded by General Pavel Rennenkampf. Though Rennenkampf's forces had also taken a beating and were plagued by supply problems, Prittwitz felt threatened by the approach from the south of General Sergei Samsonov's Second Army. Prittwitz urged a retreat behind the Vistula, effectively abandoning East Prussia to the Russians.

Moltke turned to his former partner Ludendorff, whom he rapidly shipped off to salvage the ominous situation.[116] He (and the new nominal commander of the Eighth Army, Paul von Hindenburg) won a seemingly miraculous victory at Tannenberg on August 30, 1914, which secured his reputation as the greatest general of the war both in German and in foreign eyes.[117]

Ludendorff expressed concerns over the state of the Eighth Army but he was determined to exploit the opportunity provided by the terrain in East Prussia to move on interior lines and defeat the advancing Russian armies piecemeal. The area around Tannenberg, where Teutonic Knights had suffered a disastrous defeat at the hands of Polish and Lithuanian forces in 1410 (also known as the Battle of Grünewald), was rugged and effectively broken by myriad small bodies of water known as the Masurian Lakes. Staff studies had for decades recommended using the shelter of the lakes to launch an offensive against the necessarily divided Russian forces that would approach from the east in the next war.

The speed with which the Russians mobilized and advanced had unsettled German commanders both locally and at Supreme Headquarters in Koblenz. Sensing that his small forces, not yet reinforced by troops returning from the expected victory against France, could not carry out the necessary spoiling offensive, Prittwitz looked to the Vistula as the next major line of defense. But members of his staff, especially Max Hoffmann, continued to develop plans along prewar lines: retreat slowly, but attack decisively if the Russian armies appeared unable to support each other because of terrain and distance.[118] Ludendorff issued very similar orders from Koblenz on his way to assume his post in East Prussia. The benefits of German staff training manifested in more ways than just a common approach to operational problems; Hoffmann and Ludendorff knew each other well and respected each other's judgment, having worked and lived together while stationed in Posen and Berlin. After the battle, Hoffmann was certain that Ludendorff was "the right man for this business—ruthless and hard."[119]

The Russian First Army had inflicted serious losses on the Germans at the town of Gumbinnen on August 20 but followed up with no more than a desultory pursuit despite a heavy superiority in cavalry forces. In the meantime, Samsonov's Second Army had pressed on westward, no doubt hoping to outflank the German forces defending East Prussia. He had no way of knowing that the German forces retreating in the face of Rennenkampf's advance were being directed toward his line of march.

On August 26, Samsonov's army marched blindly into the trap laid by Ludendorff and Hoffmann. Two German corps (Seventeenth and First Reserve) achieved complete surprise in their attack on the Russian Sixth Corps and inflicted over five thousand casualties. Though his units occupied the critical position on the Second Army's right flank, the commanding Russian general neglected to inform his superiors of his defeat for several hours.[120] On the morning of August 27, General Hermann von François's First Corps unleashed a furious attack on the Russians' left wing to the south, forcing it into headlong flight.[121] The Russian center lay exposed, and the German commanders recognized their opportunity to turn a spoiling attack into a battle of annihilation.

On August 28, Ludendorff ordered a general attack that resulted in the encirclement of virtually the entire Russian Second Army. The Germans captured ninety-two thousand prisoners and hundreds of Russian guns. Fifty thousand Russians lay dead under the August sun. Only two thousand Russians escaped the battle to reach friendly lines.[122] Dennis Showalter, while refusing to call Tannenberg a "battle of annihilation," highlights the effect of the defeat on Russian morale at the highest levels. What had seemed like an opportunity for a crushing victory by Russian forces developed into a humiliating, if not fatal, defeat.[123]

East Prussia was not yet secure, however. One of the reasons Rennenkampf had been unable to support Samsonov effectively was that his army was headed for the fortress complex at Königsberg to secure the Russian right flank for the advance into Germany. Rennenkampf's large forces were a formidable opponent for Eighth Army's soldiers. While some German units had gained crucial battlefield experience and a measure of confidence in their victories over Russia's Second Army, the German Eighth Army still relied on relatively large numbers of substandard garrison troops or units cobbled together from a variety of other sources.

Despite suffering ten thousand to fifteen thousand casualties of their own, the Germans now prepared to face the remaining Russian force commanded by Rennenkampf. New forces arrived from the Western Front and between September 10 and 12 a furious battle raged around the East Prussian villages of Rastenberg and Bartenstein. Only by ordering a general retreat in a timely fashion did Rennenkampf escape the destruction meted out to Samsonov. The Russian First Army left East Prussia with 100,000 men fewer than it had when it entered.[124] The victorious Germans chased the Russian armies across Poland throughout the fall and restored order to what in August had looked like a catastrophe in the making.

For the remainder of 1914 and into 1915, Hindenburg and Ludendorff stayed on the offensive, driving the Russian Army out of East Prussia and then out of Poland in what are generally acknowledged to have been a model series of well-planned offensives against a large but admittedly inferior and dispirited enemy. Friedrich von Rabenau dates Ludendorff's ascension to fame from the Battle of Masurian Lakes.[125]

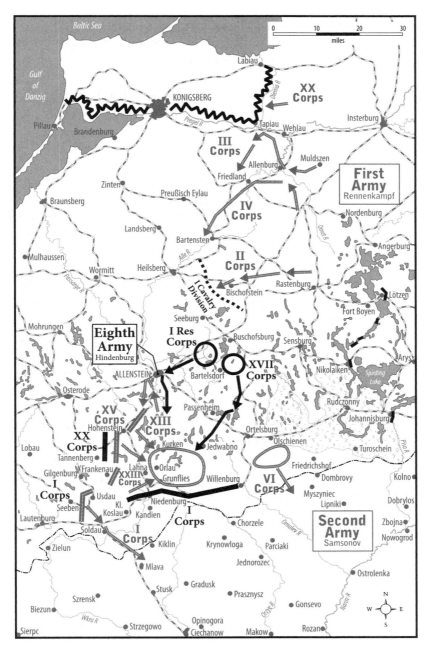

Map 2. Battle of Tannenberg, August 26–27, 1914. Map by Mike Bechtold.

It may have been at Tannenberg that Ludendorff's fantasy life took off. Groener describes Ludendorff earlier as not overly ambitious or self-confident. But according to Groener, "the victory at Tannenberg was his victory, his deed. After such a victory, his immortality seemed secure."[126] "Glory took possession of [Ludendorff's] mind" after Tannenberg, according to Karl Novak in his introduction to Max Hoffmann's 1929 published diaries.[127]

The decision to name the battle that concluded on August 30, 1914, "Tannenberg" is powerful testimony to the sway that the quasi-mythic past had on Germany's military leadership. The battle would be more aptly named "Frögenau," for the village that formed the command center of the Eighth Army. A small monument to Hindenburg and Ludendorff was in fact constructed there.[128] The battle instead became linked, at the explicit command of Ludendorff and Hoffmann, with the imperium of the Teutonic Knights who ruled the area in the Middle Ages.[129] It was at Tannenberg that the Polish king Vladislav II Jagiello defeated the German Order (Teutonic Knights) in 1410. Many historians accept Max Hoffmann's claim to have suggested the change to Ludendorff, because of Tannenberg's historical resonance.[130] It is clear that the Eighth Army command petitioned the Kaiser for permission to use the name.[131] Frithjof Benjamin Schenk in his article on the subject concludes that the existing documentation does not allow the decision to be attributed to any one individual.[132] Ludendorff naturally claimed credit for the decision, hoping to enhance his own prestige by casting the 1914 victory as revenge for the German defeat five hundred years earlier.[133]

The twin victories at Liège and Tannenberg established Ludendorff's reputation as a courageous officer and gifted operational commander. Relying on nothing but his own brains and his iron will, with no aristocratic background to gain him favor, Ludendorff had risen to the top of his profession. Like Siegfried, Ludendorff now "aspired to dominion that he might ward off all the violence which he feared for his country."[134]

3

THE FELDHERR

Siegfried of the Netherlands was bent on wresting victory from the
brave Saxons, of whom many were now wounded, and the weight of
his blows sent the bolts and braces flying from their shields.

—DIE NIBELUNGEN

Victories at Liège and Tannenberg firmly established Ludendorff's reputation as a courageous tactician and inspired operational planner, and Ludendorff rested on those laurels for the remaining decades of his life.[1] He
linked both battles explicitly to his later political activities, claiming, for
example, that the same spirit that drove him forward at Retinne led him to
call for the march through Munich on the night of November 8–9, 1923.[2]

Even more important for Ludendorff's postwar image making was his
claim to strategic talent, to the title Feldherr. It was the epithet "battle
lord" (or battle master) that justified both his claim to influence after 1918
and the "stab in the back" myth that he fostered. His many great strategic
triumphs as first quartermaster general of the Third Supreme Command
(OHL), from swiftly knocking Romania out of the war in 1916 to managing the occupied territories known as Ober Ost, to defeating the Russian
colossus at the end 1917 were proof, he and his followers believed, of
his genius.[3] That, like Siegfried, this unconquerable hero had nevertheless
been defeated had to be the result of treachery, of a betrayal in this case by

cowardly Socialist and Jewish politicians on the home front, who encouraged defeatism among soldiers returning to the battle front and ultimately drove Germany into the throes of revolution.

This chapter can hardly be a comprehensive survey of Ludendorff's activities as first quartermaster general. That story is well known and convincingly told by the many biographers and historians who have written about Ludendorff and the German effort in the Great War.[4] Rather, its purpose is to highlight those aspects of the German war effort that Ludendorff used to cement his legend as Feldherr and as the embodiment of German revenge fantasies in the interwar period.

The rise of Ludendorff the Feldherr began after the spectacular victory of the Eighth Army over the Russian Second and First armies at the battles of Tannenberg and Masurian Lakes, respectively. With news of those victories still in the air, the Kaiser dismissed Helmuth von Moltke, the war's first chief of the General Staff, and replaced him with war minister Erich von Falkenhayn. Bitter over the fall from power, Moltke sought to have himself reinstated, and when that proved impossible, to maneuver his protégé, Ludendorff, into the position. In several letters written from his internal exile, Moltke lobbied to have Ludendorff placed somehow in charge. Moltke recognized that Ludendorff was too young to serve as chief of the General Staff, but as chief of operations, or Oberquartiermeister, he would be excellent.[5]

A two-year-long conspiracy ensued, aiming to undermine the strong support that Falkenhayn enjoyed with the Kaiser and his military cabinet. The struggle was partly over personality but also about strategic focus. Ludendorff confessed a powerful hatred of Falkenhayn.[6] Hindenburg and Ludendorff believed that 1914 had proven that the decisive front in the war was the eastern one. Well-equipped armies operating in the relatively confined quarters of Belgium and northern France had succeeded only in grinding themselves to pieces. A weaker foe and greater maneuverability in the east, however, seemed to offer continued prospects not only for battlefield victories but the defeat of Russia itself. Falkenhayn disagreed. He pursued instead a strategy of attrition, eventually settling on Verdun as the target of an attack in early 1916 meant to bleed the French white.[7] Falkenhayn believed that despite gains made in Poland and the Baltic region, Russia would always be able to trade space for time and elude any crushing blow that Germany might wish to inflict.[8]

While Moltke conspired Hindenburg and Ludendorff were not idle. After the victory at Tannenberg and Masurian Lakes, the pair planned a series of offensives using the three armies available to them to first push the Russians out of East Prussia and drive them out of Poland. With East Prussia free of Russian troops after January and February, Hindenburg and Ludendorff combined forces with the (much-depleted) Habsburg army for a campaign designed to annihilate Russian forces in the theater. It began with a strike into Galicia in the south in May and became a more general advance across the entire front by the summer of 1915.[9]

As German victories in the East mounted, Ludendorff also oversaw the occupied territories of Lithuania, and Courland (modern western Latvia), called Ober Ost. As Vejas Liulevicius argues in one of the first studies of the administration, Ludendorff strove (in vain) to create a "military utopia" in Ober Ost, a perfectly ordered region from which resources and manpower could be extracted in the service of the war effort.[10] According to Liulevicius, the German experience in Ober Ost transformed their conception of "the East" from a land inhabited by people who could be "cultivated" to a state of civilization and productivity to a "space" occupied by an inferior race suited only for removal or extermination.[11]

Plans for exploitation of Ober Ost clearly reflected one of Ludendorff's fundamental insights about the current and future wars. Resources would be critical. As the press agency of the Ober Ost administration wrote (with a sense of growing frustration one surmises) in 1917: "If one could breed the people to order . . . this area could become a bread basket of wheat and cattle, wood and wool."[12] The experience in the east may have prepared Ludendorff to think more deeply (if no more successfully) about the link between economic, cultural, and military affairs that would define his later stint in the Supreme Command.

Third Supreme Command (OHL)

By 1916, Falkenhayn had failed to gain any momentum on the Western Front despite his exertions at Verdun, and the military and public alike clamored for change.[13] The surprising entry of Romania into the war in August 1916 finally prompted Falkenhayn's dismissal. On August 29, 1916, the Kaiser offered Hindenburg the supreme command of Germany's armies.[14] Ludendorff, not content with being second-in-command, crafted for himself the rank of first quartermaster general of the army, sharing responsibility for decision making with Hindenburg but in fact operating largely autonomously. "Deputy chief of staff" did not sound like the appropriate title to describe Ludendorff's role. He preferred a newly invented title probably because it elided the hierarchy that "deputy chief" would imply.

After the war, Hindenburg and Ludendorff engaged in a running battle (with Ludendorff most often on the offensive) over who deserved credit for their success or blame for their failures as a pair. A personality cult built up around Hindenburg, whose massive, grandfatherly figure stood in for Bismarck, for the old regime, for a fictional undefeated Germany.[15] It is probably fairest to say that they made a powerful combination and should share both the plaudits and the blame. Otto Geßler's description of the pair is apt: "One thing was certain, that Ludendorff was the active element, the motorized willpower of the military leadership circle; but one cannot dismiss Hindenburg, who in his lucid calmness made the final decision and provided the balancing force, acting to promote or deter simply through his authoritative presence."[16] Certainly Geßler's viewpoint was prevalent among those with little or no stake in the struggle between the two men.

Martin Kitchen, in his 1976 work on Hindenburg and Ludendorff, labels the team "a militarized form of bonapartism" because they secured the economic and political interests of the existing elite (the revived alliance of "rye and iron") against the growing demands of the German labor force and much-suffering citizenry. The popularity of the pair, highlighted at the end of the previous chapter, guaranteed, at least temporarily, public support for a maximum war effort aimed at total victory. Only a complete military triumph would enable the kind of German economic domination and territorial ambitions of men like Hugo Stinnes, Heinrich Class, and others.[17]

Whether bonapartist or not, Ludendorff's power was dictatorial. Roger Chickering helpfully reminds us that no dictator's power is absolute. Ludendorff had to contend with myriad social, political, and bureaucratic forces that sought to block or amend his policies. Nevertheless, he concludes that for the final two years of the war, "Ludendorff was the most powerful man in Germany."[18] Ludendorff's power developed over time as part of a political process that had antecedents that predated the war and that would be felt for decades after. Nor can it be said that any particular measure was the fruit of Ludendorff's sole creativity. Hoffman, Bauer, Rathenau, and others deserve a great deal of the credit for these innovations. But Ludendorff had the sense to listen to their advice and support their initiatives with the power of the General Staff, the Eighth Army command, and eventually the OHL.

From this perch, Ludendorff directed the German war effort, and his increasing control over not only the armed forces but the economy and media has led historians to label his tenure "the silent dictatorship."[19] This appointment was the pinnacle of Ludendorff's already illustrious military career. While a cult built up around the father-figure Hindenburg, Ludendorff remained the power behind the scenes, prompting the American H. L. Mencken to remark (as quoted in my introduction) "The world hears nothing about him, and yet he has the world by the ear."[20] It was Ludendorff's tenure as first quartermaster general from 1916 to 1918 that laid the foundation for his claim to have been the Feldherr—the Battle Lord of Germany.

The Hindenburg Program

As first quartermaster general, Ludendorff was one of the principal architects of the Hindenburg Program to retool the German economy for war. Ludendorff's reputation as "genius of war," as the Prometheus of modern warfare, is based in large part on his conscious and sometimes skillful harnessing of German economic might to the war effort after his appointment in 1916. What became known as the "Hindenburg Program," was a complex set of laws, administrative reforms, proposals, and edicts that began flowing out of the OHL in the fall of that year, aimed at exploiting all available manpower and dramatically increasing the output of war material, especially artillery tubes, machine guns, and the ammunition to supply those weapons.[21] Chickering calls the Hindenburg Program "an attempt to realize Ludendorff's vision of war," in which, in the words of Hindenburg, "men would be more and more replaced by machines."[22]

Even before his appointment to the Supreme Command in 1916, Ludendorff had been approached by prominent German industrialists eager to impress on him the need for more rigorous control of the economy.[23] In particular, men like Hugo Stinnes were concerned to secure reliable supplies of raw materials and to wield more powerful weapons against the demands of labor unions on wages and working conditions. Ludendorff was primed to sympathize with such arguments by his prewar association with men like the Pan-German League's Heinrich Class, within whose orbit Stinnes and many other prominent industrialists moved.[24] As mentioned in chapter 2, Ludendorff had found Class and his allies useful in pressing for army expansion in 1912.[25] Now Ludendorff was the insider, sitting at the peak of the German military establishment, and again he found alliance with the industrial magnates, with both economic and media resources at their disposal, to be indispensable.

Just two days after assuming command, Hindenburg signed a memorandum directed at the minister of war, Adolf Wild von Hohenborn, demanding greater efforts to enlist all able-bodied men for the war effort. The enemies "inexhaustible" supply of manpower was beginning to tell at the front. The German workforce would need to be combed for suitable recruits and their places taken by older or militarily unsuitable men or even, Hindenburg suggested, by the thousands of "women and girls who are running around doing nothing." "Those that do not work, should not eat."[26]

In the OHL's original conception, universities would be closed. Young men would receive military training beginning at age sixteen. A memo of September 13 made the same point to the chancellor, Theobald von Bethmann-Hollweg. Bethmann's response (dated September 30) was polite but initially negative, to the effect that wartime reality had already accomplished most of what the OHL was proposing to dictate. The vast majority of healthy men already served in the military or worked in war-related industries. Higher wages in heavy industry had either pulled, or the collapse of most non-war-related industries had pushed, workers in this direction. Teenage Germans already worked in industry and agriculture, so additional military training at that age would negatively impact the economy.

On the issue of women, Ludendorff advocated for their inclusion but General Wilhelm Groener, the soon-to-be appointed head of the new War Office (Kriegsamt), and Bethmann-Hollweg remained opposed.[27] Bethmann recognized the value of female labor (in appropriate industries, of course) and lamented that if women were idle, it was because of the lack of work for them, not their lack of willingness. General Groener like-wise tried to rationalize in a postwar essay that German factories were at near full capacity in any case, so there was less need to intensify co-ercion.[28] Germany's economic problems would not be solved, Bethmann concluded, through "authoritarian decrees."[29]

The OHL sent a copy of the September 13 memorandum to the minister of war, Adolf Wild von Hohenborn. In a cover letter, the OHL proposed the creation of the War Office to govern the distribution of labor and food in order more effectively to marshal Germany's economic resources.[30] Pre-viously, such controls as had existed were under the purview of the War Ministry, the only power center in the German military structure that could rival the General Staff and the Supreme Command. The War Ministry, however, had constructed a decentralized and inefficient system for manag-ing the economy that, in the view of Ludendorff and others, lacked mean-ingful provisions for enforcement.

Given his initially hesitant response to Hindenburg's September memo-randum, Chancellor Bethmann-Hollweg had to be cajoled to support the OHL's move. He insisted that the new office exist under the command of the Prussian War Ministry. But when Ludendorff arranged for the dis-missal of Wild von Hohenborn and his replacement by the more compli-ant General Hermann von Stein that October, the OHL took effective control of the agency.[31] The Kriegsamt therefore represented a meaningful accretion to the OHL's political power.

The authority of the Kriegsamt was to be given teeth by the passage of an Auxiliary Service Law (Hilfsdienstgesetz) that Ludendorff hoped would amount to the labor "draft" suggested in the series of original notes to the chancellor and war minister. Under the terms eventually negoti-ated by the Supreme Command, the chancellor, and other agencies, every healthy male aged seventeen to sixty not already in the military could be forced into service in a war-related industry. The ability of workers to change jobs in search of higher wages would be curtailed. With the labor force under military control, unruly workers could be threatened with service in frontline trenches. Ludendorff was confident that such a law would be passed by the Reichstag and would serve as an expression of Germany's will both to foreign and domestic audiences.[32] He later justi-fied the Auxiliary Service Law as more in keeping with ancient Germanic notions of duty and service.[33]

The debate in the Reichstag surrounding the new law revealed the extent to which the course of the war and privations on the home front had fractured the *Burgfrieden* (the sense of political solidarity and social peace) of 1914.[34] The Reichstag's Socialist and progressive liberal factions amended the law significantly in favor of organized labor. While the politicians agreed to the basic provisions of the law regarding national service, they granted labor representation on the committees and councils that oversaw its implementation. Most significantly, German unions for the first time received the right to represent workers in war industries. So important were these gains that after the war and revolution, the Socialist unions compromised their stated position on the abolition of private property in return for their continuation in the Weimar Republic.[35]

Even before the Reichstag debate, the OHL's suspicion of politicians and the home front in general was palpable. The home front was rife with shirkers. Men who "sit safely at home" and concern themselves with their profits, the women who "run around doing nothing," students who refused the call to the colors in order to skip ahead of their classmates to gain advantage after the war.[36] Without much tangible evidence, the Supreme Command was laying the groundwork for the "stab in the back." The failure of Germany to win by 1916 was unthinkable unless some native source was holding back. Strikes that ensued after the "turnip winter" of 1916–17 must have been, in the eyes of the new war minister Stein, the work of "provocateurs and foreign money."[37]

Concern for manpower also prompted the German War Ministry to undertake the notorious "Jew count" (*Judenzahlung*) in late 1916. On October 11, 1916, shortly before his dismissal, War Minister Adolf Wild von Hohenborn asked all commanders to determine how many Jews were serving in the German Army and in what capacity.[38] The ministry had been for months receiving complaints, usually anonymous and probably coordinated by antisemitic groups like the Pan-German League, that Jews were shirking their duties, finding easy exemptions from service from sympathetic Jewish doctors or using connections to land relatively safe assignments behind the front lines.

As he stated in the order, Wild von Hohenborn ostensibly wished to counter these rumors with definitive evidence, if it could be provided, so the motivation for the order may not have been entirely antisemitic. But news of the census struck German Jews hard, particularly those in uniform but also the vast majority of Jewish civilians who patriotically supported the war. If such questions about shirking needed to be asked, why were they not asked of all religious denominations? Singling out Jews only fed existing stereotypes and increased Germans' hostility, they argued. In the end, the results of the census where never fully published, and whatever results did exist were destroyed in the Second World War. Fragmentary and questionable information leaked out, usually in the memoirs of anti-semites like Ernst von Wrisberg, who had access to the documents in his capacity as director of the ministry's General War Department.[39]

As the *Judenzahlung* was initiated just weeks after Ludendorff's ap-pointment in August, it is tempting perhaps to link it to Ludendorff's later and pronounced antisemitism. Such a linkage seems unfounded, however. It may well have been Ludendorff's insistent demands for manpower fol-lowing the intense operations at the Somme and elsewhere that prompted Wild to act on the many complaints he was receiving. Ludendorff seems to have taken no special interest in the census at the time. Indeed, Albrecht von Thaer, longtime member of Ludendorff's staff, remembers Ludendorff dismissing antisemitism as inherently irrational.[40] After the war, of course, he could point to the census as evidence of his early concern about Jewish influence. But very little about the "Jew Count" suggests that it was of particular interest to Ludendorff at the time.[41]

In November 1916, Ludendorff appointed General Wilhelm Groener, a general staff officer with a reputation as an organizational mastermind, to lead the new War Office. Groener turned out not to be the pliant tool that Ludendorff had perhaps expected him to be, however. Despite ap-parently sharing the class prejudices of most of his colleagues (he once infamously referred to striking workers as "scoundrels" and threatened to prosecute them for treason), Groener seems to have approached the task of maximizing the efficiency of the economy with at least a modicum of attention to the political complexities involved.[42] Groener seemed genuinely interested in pursuing a conciliatory policy toward labor unions and in avoiding confrontation and coercion whenever pos-sible. He resisted the industrialists and the OHL when they called for more controls and more compulsion under the terms of the Auxiliary Service Law. However, many commanders exhibited more sympathy for the demands of industry than labor. Groener's dismissal in August 1917 exacerbated that problem.[43]

Ludendorff eventually soured on Groener, deeming him insufficiently dedicated to extracting maximum effort from the German economy in the service of victory.[44] On August 16, 1917, Ludendorff removed Groener from the War Office and placed him in command of the Thirty-Third Division.[45] His successor, Scheüch, barely warrants mention in the historical record, in part because he was forced by political circumstances, despite the demands of the OHL and the industrialists, to continue Groener's quasi-conciliatory policies. By 1917, the ominous situation of the home front simply would not allow any dramatic revisions of economic policy that might impact morale.

The Hindenburg Program for the German economy should be judged an overall failure. Hindenburg called for an immediate doubling of munitions production and a tripling of the stock of machine guns and artillery. But efforts to satisfy that demand threw much previous careful planning into chaos. Many small businesses, deprived of labor or resources, closed. The production of explosive powder actually declined.[46] The Auxiliary Service Law did transfer some manpower from the front to the factory, but tellingly, steel production in February 1917 was lower than it had been six months earlier.[47] The truce that had governed labor and industry relations was broken.[48]

Ludendorff's military efforts enjoyed somewhat more success. A combined attack by German and Austro-Hungarian forces, alongside new ally Bulgaria, quickly dispatched Romania, whose entry on the side of the Entente was the final straw that led to Falkenhayn's dismissal. On the Western Front, the Third OHL called off the campaign around Verdun and moved to the strategic defensive.[49] Rather than defending frontline trenches strongly, the Germans after 1917 left fairly weak screens in the forward trenches and massed troops further back (out of artillery range when possible) to conduct blistering counterattacks on attacking Allied soldiers. Between March 16 and 20, 1917, Ludendorff ordered the German Army to conduct a massive withdrawal to well-prepared positions in the so-called Siegfried Line. Under the codename "Alberich," retreating troops conducted a scorched earth campaign and planted booby traps in order to deny the enemy resources and an easy advance. These moves removed some of the strain on German manpower and dramatically raised the price the Allies would pay in blood for future offensives.[50]

Groener believed 1917 was when Ludendorff was at the peak of his powers. "The strategic defensive in the west with the clever withdrawal into the Siegfried line was masterfully organized," Groener wrote. "It was the highlight of his achievements overall and contributed positively to the overall strategic and political situation."[51] It is worth tracing the development (and eventual decline) of Ludendorff's dictatorship through a series of political, economic, and military events critical to the outcome of the war.

Unrestricted Submarine Warfare

The most fateful decision Ludendorff made during the war was to resume unrestricted submarine warfare on February 1, 1917.[52] Unrestricted attacks on merchant shipping had ceased in April 1916 in order to ease the strain on relations with neutrals, especially the United States. Ludendorff and others, however, believed that striking a decisive blow at Britain was more important than the prospect of American entry into the war. The decision seems to reflect truly sloppy management on the part of the entire German establishment. Bethmann-Hollweg essentially handed the decision over to Ludendorff, arguing in his memoirs that having convinced the Kaiser to replace Falkenhayn, he had to give Hindenburg and Ludendorff their chance to win the war.[53] Oddly, Ludendorff seems to have accepted the German Navy's argument, based largely on guesswork, that submarines could quickly starve Great Britain out of the war. In a fit of bravado, German naval commanders promised that not a single American soldier would reach France.

Initial results of the campaign were excellent. In April 1917, German submarines sunk a remarkable 841,118 tons of Allied shipping, beyond what the Germans calculated Great Britain could replace, but by the summer, the crisis for Britain had passed.[54] Several factors turned the tide. For one, the Allies (now fighting alongside the United States), instituted convoys, which the Germans had dismissed as being too slow. The British were able to increase cereal production, which replaced some of the losses, and issued ominous warnings to neutral nations whose ships refused to sail in the face of the submarine threat.[55] In the final year of the war,

"British and American shipyards were producing twice the tonnage that the Germans were sinking."[56]

Germany's submarine force was simply insufficient (numerically, technologically) to accomplish the goals the Supreme Command set for it. Anthony Watson argues that the initial successes had less to do with the new rules of engagement than with a larger submarine force and ferocious (and unsustainable) operational tempo.[57] The convoy system made hunting merchant shipping a dangerous business. Roughly 50 percent of German submarine crews did not survive the war.[58]

Ludendorff may also have considered the United States' increasingly evident hostility to Germany as being tantamount to war in any case, so that an actual declaration would matter less.[59] Whatever the rationale, submarine attacks did very quickly bring the United States in to the war against Germany. After repeated protests, Woodrow Wilson asked the United States Congress for a declaration of war and received it on April 6, 1917. By the summer of 1918, 100,000 American troops were arriving in France each month.

Because of Bethmann's foot-dragging on the submarine issue as well as his willingness to flirt with a negotiated peace, the military establishment as a whole, and Hindenburg and Ludendorff in particular, had become disenchanted with his leadership.[60] To Ludendorff's mind, Bethmann was unwilling to go far enough in matters of economic policy, censorship, or war aims. His pursuit of the "politics of the diagonal"—an effort to seek a consensus among the parties of the Reichstag enthused no one.[61]

So Bethmann had to go. But who should replace him? Few suitable candidates surfaced. The finance minister Dr. Karl Helfferich's name was tossed around in various quarters. Later putschist Wolfgang Kapp and many others preferred Admiral Alfred von Tirpitz, who seemed eager for the job.[62] Not long after Ludendorff's appointment as first quartermaster general, his name also began to surface as a candidate for the chancellorship itself. Ludendorff's prestige was very high, but many doubted his political abilities. "It would be desirable," thought General Max Hoffmann, "that Tirpitz should merely keep the place warm, and that Ludendorff should succeed him later."[63] Tirpitz, however, had quarreled with the Kaiser over naval policy and could not be considered.[64]

It appears that Ludendorff himself did not want the job.[65] It would be too generous to suggest that Ludendorff recognized his own limitations in the realm of politics. Rather, Ludendorff's reluctance was more likely based on the seemingly paradoxical belief that his power was more secure the more it operated behind the scenes. The "silent dictatorship" depended on having a (preferably weak) chancellor to act as a "lightning conductor" for controversial, unpopular, or failed policies.[66] In his postwar memoir, Ludendorff took exactly this approach when he lamented the general impression that he was responsible for the defeat. "Unfortunately, in public, the Government did not state sufficiently clearly and emphatically that it, and not General Ludendorff, was in supreme command."[67]

Bethmann limped along, attacked from many sides, through the winter of 1916 and the spring of 1917. By the summer, he was politically paralyzed and almost universally despised. Ludendorff abhorred Bethmann's flirtation with peace and suffrage reform.[68] Even those parties in the Reichstag whom he had tried to appease by his "politics of the diagonal" had abandoned him, convinced that he was under the control of the OHL, which was not far from true, despite Ludendorff's enmity. Bethmann had supported the Auxiliary Service Law and the other elements of the Hindenburg Program. He supported Ludendorff's demand for unrestricted submarine warfare. Menaced by Hindenburg and Ludendorff, who threatened their own resignations, the Kaiser dismissed Bethmann on July 13.[69] Georg von Müller, the chief of the Kaiser's Naval Cabinet wrote in his diaries just a few days before Bethmann's departure, "What an irony of Fate! . . . [The chancellor] is falling victim to the High Command, to the Hindenburg-Ludendorff team whom he once firmly placed in the saddle."[70]

That was not the only irony in Bethmann's fall, which cemented Hindenburg and Ludendorff's political as well as military control. Bethmann's replacement was Georg Michaelis, a little-known figure understood to be doing the army's bidding. In the words of Prince Max von Baden, who would later become chancellor himself, with Michaelis's appointment Ludendorff's political desires "acquired the character of 'inevitable natural law.' "[71]

Ludendorff's increasing political role was not unopposed. No less a personage than Max Weber repeatedly decried the "irresponsible cogovernment" of the OHL.[72] Weber's attacks naturally earned him the enmity of Ludendorff, though Weber felt that he had the best interests of the military at heart. He did not wish it said later of the army that "what they achieved with the sword was later spoiled by their pen."[73] Max Hoffmann alludes to a movement in military as well as political circles to remove Ludendorff, but Hindenburg's prestige and loyalty protected him. Even his enemies recognized that toppling Ludendorff would mean that Hindenburg would resign as well.[74]

Especially beginning in 1917, Ludendorff took a major interest in propaganda as a means of bolstering support for the war and the annexationist aims he favored. As a young lieutenant, he had been responsible for the "patriotic instruction" of new recruits in the Fifty-Seventh Infantry Regiment. Looking back on those years from the vantage of 1933, Ludendorff lamented the poor state of their knowledge of history.[75] Soldiers and citizens could not possibly understand the war's aims, he believed, if they did not have the proper historical perspective. "Words are battles," Ludendorff's longtime colleague Hans von Haeften wrote, and the right words could so damage the enemy's morale that he would give up the war.[76] To bolster morale and support a patriotic political message, Ludendorff supported the creation of the first film studio in Germany, Universum Film-Aktien Gesellschaft (UFA).

On war aims, Ludendorff was consistently and aggressively expansionist. He never countenanced the sacrifice of Belgian gains or Alsace-Lorraine, for example, for a free hand in the east.[77] Especially after the October Revolution in Russia, with Entente fears about Bolshevism, such a deal might have been a possibility. The Kaiser, despite becoming increasingly irrelevant during the war, may have become a stumbling block had such moves been considered. Other forces, such as the Fatherland Party, also worked to sabotage any peace efforts that envisioned concessions in either east or west, let alone any thoughts of renouncing wartime gains.

Even more striking is the nearly unquestioned assumption that any result short of a complete German victory would only mean a pause in hostilities. To a very great extent, Ludendorff and his entourage were fighting as much for victory as to secure territory and resources for a future conflict—most likely against England.[78] For this reason, Belgium could not remain free, as Major Georg Wetzell, head of the Operations Section in the General Staff, wrote in a 1917 memorandum.[79] Many critics of the OHL blamed Ludendorff's intransigence over Belgium for the failure of any negotiated peace.[80] In this belief, Ludendorff was consistently bolstered by Admiral Alfred von Tirpitz, for whom Belgium was the foundation of Germany's future security.[81] Tirpitz, as head of the Fatherland

Party after 1917 (see below) lobbied aggressively to maintain at least a foothold on the Belgian coast as well as important iron and coal resources in the regions bordering Germany.[82]

But it was in the East where Ludendorff's dreams of expansion flourished. As mentioned above, while he and Hindenburg had commanded armies on the Eastern Front, Ludendorff also supervised the military occupation of the Baltics and other regions seized from the Russians.[83] The military command, known by the shorthand "Ober Ost," amounted to a personal kingdom for Ludendorff. The region as well as the rest of Eastern Europe, remained important for Ludendorff as first quartermaster general, since it could be a source of supply for the German Army. German control of Lithuania would be assured by a combination of formal and informal measures. There was much wrangling over the issue with Austria, but Ludendorff favored seizing Polish territory as a military buffer zone (whether or not an independent Poland continued to exist). Romania with its rich oil reserves Ludendorff imagined as a German protectorate. Even in July 1917, as the situation on the Western Front was threatening to unravel, Ludendorff insisted at a conference at Spa that huge chunks of Livonia and Estonia should be seized for German settlements.

Ludendorff's vision is revealed most clearly in the negotiation of the Treaty of Brest-Litovsk at the end of 1917. Once Lenin triumphed in Russia, and after long negotiations, Ludendorff forced that punitive treaty on the beleaguered Bolsheviks. The stunning territorial arrangements imposed on the Russians by that document made clear to the remaining Allied combatants what a German victory in the west might look like. The Russians lost huge swaths of territory along their western border, all the way from the Crimea to Finland. Ninety percent of their coal mines, half their industrial capacity, and nearly one-third of their territory went to the Germans or their allies.[84] With this example of rapacity in mind, peace through negotiation with the Western Allies became much less likely as a result.

Fatherland Party and "Patriotic Instruction"

To generate popular enthusiasm for both the tighter controls and the expansive war aims that the OHL envisioned, Ludendorff provided crucial support for the foundation of the Fatherland Party in 1917. The Fatherland Party was the brainchild of Wolfgang Kapp and Alfred von Tirpitz, who hoped to unite the disparate forces of the German right under a prowar banner. It was not a parliamentary party, per se, but more akin to the many military and defense leagues that had cropped up in the two decades prior to the war (Kolonialverein, Wehrverein). Indeed, one of its most influential corporate members was the Pan-German League, whose leader, Heinrich Class, perhaps had a prewar association with Ludendorff as already mentioned.

Ludendorff's involvement with the Fatherland Party is one of the reasons Martin Kitchen and Raffael Scheck describe the dictatorship of the OHL as "bonapartist." The aims of the group were "to divert attention from domestic reform and to foster a bonapartist synthesis of military victory and popular military dictatorship."[85] Ostensibly politically neutral and with a broad class base (the founders placed a working man on the executive committee), the Fatherland Party in fact represented the same industrial and agrarian interests included in the old "alliance of rye and iron" of the prewar period.[86]

Nevertheless, the Fatherland Party appealed to a large constituency. Near its peak in July 1918, it could boast 1.25 million members.[87] Its leadership controlled major media outlets, and thanks in large part to the special allowances granted by the OHL for the party's press appeals, its programs reached a wide audience. Ludendorff was also a strong supporter of the Pan-German League during the war. Just before his dismissal in October 1918, Ludendorff wrote a letter thanking Class for the important work of the Pan-German League.[88]

For Ludendorff, the Fatherland Party represented a domestic corollary to the system of "patriotic instruction" already instituted in the ranks of the armed forces. The emphasis that Ludendorff placed on propaganda and the "spiritual armament" of the German people is clear in the curriculum that he and his allies devised for the army. Ludendorff saw the "necessity that conviction, duty, and whole-hearted resolve should become the Army's weapons."[89] The "enthusiasm and the discipline" exhibited by the German Army in 1914 had been the result of "prolonged peace[-time] training."[90] He recognized the long war had created hardships that potentially weakened those foundations, so special effort was needed to strengthen that resolve.

His scheme for patriotic instruction consisted of a set of specially trained field commanders who would be responsible for the education of the troops in matters regarding the conduct of the war, peace proposals, and other patriotic matters. The outline of the program consisted of structural diagrams showing the flow of information from the chief of the General Staff (Hindenburg), through the various levels of the military hierarchy, to both the field troops *and* the civilian population. A prodigious list enumerated the means of communication, ranging from military journals, newspapers, leaflets from aircraft, and posters "such as the troops are likely to understand," to chaplains and field cinemas.[91] "The enemy's determination to destroy us," as Ludendorff put it in his memoir, was obvious to frontline troops enduring the storm of battle.[92] But troops behind the front lines, in garrisons, or along the supply lines, seemed vulnerable to a loss of will and so would receive special attention. The themes of the instruction were the causes of the war and the economic necessity of victory despite the mounting costs. The common German soldier, especially the one with a working-class background, should understand that without victory, his livelihood and that of his family would be threatened. Strikes undermined the battle front. Peace proposals only prolonged the war.[93]

In his memoir, Ludendorff lamented that the Reichstag could only criticize the proposal and seemed unwilling to shoulder the burden of similarly educating the civilian population. Indeed, Reichstag delegates from the Social Democratic Party attacked the program as pure propaganda for the Pan-Germans and the Fatherland Party.[94] In response War Minister Stein contended that the program was aimed purely at the "spiritual nourishment" of the men in the trenches, and that the lectures, plays, music and theater presented by the army commands were purely apolitical. Measures were necessary, he argued, because of the effective propaganda of the enemy. Catcalls from the Social Democrats elicited the admission that in rare instances, some patriotic speaker may have overstepped his bounds, but Stein insisted that these rare occurrences were dealt with appropriately.[95]

Domestic programs alone would not win the war. By the end of 1917, Ludendorff had concluded that he had to gamble all in an attack on the Western Front in 1918. The balance of forces had shifted in Germany's favor for the first time in many years thanks to the withdrawal of Russia from the war. Germany's allies would only grow weaker. American forces would not be a major factor until later in the following year. No other front, not Italy, not Macedonia, promised the results that a victory in the West would deliver.[96]

An oft-cited quote from Ludendorff in regard to the March offensives reveals his strategic concept—or lack thereof: "We shall punch a hole, as for the rest, we shall see."[97] Later critics ridiculed this statement for its apparent blindness to the importance of strategy, of linking together victories at the tactical and operational level in the service of a war-winning or political aim. In *Mein militärischer Werdegang*, Ludendorff tried to justify his seeming reversal of normal military practice. In that work, Ludendorff writes that in a war of movement, the tactical attack brings strategy to its culmination; in a war of position, it is reversed. Tactical success restores movement and enables strategy.[98] He also made a judgment based on morale and leadership, areas in which he judged the British to be the weaker foe.[99] For all that the comment above seems to display a willful negligence of his duties as commander, Ludendorff did manage to punch quite a hole.[100]

To prepare for the attacks, Ludendorff ordered the German Army to develop infiltration tactics to break the stalemate of trench warfare. German soldiers left the line for special training in these new tactics—a move made possible by the construction of more elastic (and shorter) defensive lines in 1917. Instead of lengthy artillery barrages in preparation for an attack, which told the enemy exactly where the attack would be and facilitated the timely arrival of reserves, the Germans would attempt to attack with surprise. Troops would approach the enemy lines as stealthily as possible; brief but targeted artillery fire would unhinge the enemy defense; attacking troops would bypass strongholds when possible to disrupt rear areas. Especially in the March offensives of 1918, these tactics met with some success.

The German Army launched five offensives between March and July 1918.[101] The first two, Operations Michael and Blücher, were very successful at the tactical level but only worsened Germany's strategic problems.[102] The British Army reeled under the initial blows: ninety thousand British soldiers surrendered, and the Germans captured thirteen hundred guns.[103] The German gains were shocking yet fell short of expectations. The offensives created a dangerous salient that would be untenable in the long run. Logistical problems and years of relative privations led German troops to forage for food and raid Allied supply depots. As a result, the offensives moved more slowly than necessary.[104] The German Army suffered terrible losses in the March offensives, nearly 40,000 casualties on the first day and 239,800 in the month of March alone, making it the bloodiest month of the entire war. The combined offensives through June 5 cost the Germans 249,530 casualties and the Allies 382,076.[105] Rarely in World War I were casualties so lopsidedly in favor of the attacker, but these were losses the Germans could not replace, while fresh American troops arrived in France at a quickening pace over the same period.

The "we shall see" in Ludendorff's statement was the final operation named for Siegried's murderer, Hagen. All of the "punching" along the Marne convinced Ludendorff that a final powerful blow against the British in Flanders would be decisive.[106] To pull off Operation Hagen, though, the Germans would have to capture the important rail junction at Rheims. Without it, Ludendorff would not be able logistically to support the operations to the north. Hagen quickly petered out, having accomplished only the further exhaustion of the German Army. Ludendorff's nerves and constant meddling in the planning process had exhausted its leadership as well.[107] Writing his memoirs in Sweden in 1918, Ludendorff lamented the delays imposed by the Soviets at the Brest-Litovsk negotiations, which prevented an earlier withdrawal of greater numbers of German troops from the Balkans and the Eastern Front. As with the failure of submarines to achieve decisive results, he shifted blame for the problems onto others, in this case, an insufficiently urgent attitude on the part of the diplomatic corps and the gullibility of Reichstag delegates who saw in Bolshevik obfuscation only their own pacifist tendencies confirmed.[108]

The Allied counteroffensive that greeted the end of Ludendorff's attacks was the first in a series of blows that would bring Germany to its knees by the end of October. At the Second Battle of the Marne, begun on July 18, 1918, the Allies captured twenty thousand German soldiers on the first day, and the effect on German morale, and Ludendorff's in particular, was pronounced.[109] More bad news followed. On August 8, 1918, the German Army suffered what Ludendorff called its "black day" at the Battle of Amiens.[110] There, seventeen thousand German soldiers surrendered in the face of waves of British tanks. With the 1918 offensive, Groener wrote, Ludendorff lost his genius. "Hubris had taken hold of him."[111]

It was in the late summer of 1918 that Ludendorff's longtime confidante, Colonel Max Bauer, began expressing concerns about Ludendorff's mental state.[112] He seemed never to sleep; colleagues reported seeing fits of crying. Bauer recommended, and Ludendorff received, treatment by a Dr. Hochheimer, who prescribed breathing exercises, massage, and "looking at mountains."[113] But many disputed the conclusion, used so often by biographers to dismiss Ludendorff as irrelevant after the war, that Ludendorff suffered a "nervous breakdown." Most of Ludendorff's close associates insisted that if Ludendorff's focus did ever wane, the condition was only temporary.[114] Looking at mountains couldn't have hurt, in any case, and Ludendorff exhibited no troubling symptoms for the remainder of the war.

For Germany it was too late. The long war, the growing material and manpower superiority of the Allies, and the collapse of Germany's partners in the Balkans finally opened Ludendorff's eyes to the growing possibility of a complete collapse. Ludendorff seemed to take the "betrayal" of Bulgaria on September 28 particularly hard.[115] In the back of many Germans' minds was the specter of Bolshevism and civil war playing out in the new Soviet Union. The only bulwark against the spread of Bolshevism to Germany, Ludendorff believed, was the German Army. It had to be preserved at all costs to maintain domestic order.

As a consequence, at a meeting on September 29, 1918, with State Secretary Otto von Hintze, Ludendorff asked that the government seek an armistice with the Allies. Meaningful offensives were no longer possible, Ludendorff believed, and so some sort of negotiated peace would be necessary. An armistice would allow the army to find its footing again, consolidate its defensive positions, and perhaps present a sturdy enough obstacle to the Allies to gain leverage at the peace table. Hintze and Ludendorff secured the Kaiser's agreement, but all believed that the current chancellor, Count von Hertling, could not make the approach to President Wilson. A new liberal government would eventually be formed under Prince Max von Baden, whose relatively liberal beliefs and ties to Great Britain the Germans believed might allow him to secure better terms.

Of course Ludendorff tried to shift the blame for the whole situation to the politicians. "I had been writing to the Government for two years on end," he insisted in his memoirs, "with reference to the shortage of reinforcements, the Auxiliary-Service Law, my efforts to have it amended and to bring women more and more into service, my suggestions for rounding up shirkers and deserters at home." His appeals had fallen on deaf ears. To his colleagues in the OHL, Ludendorff explained that he had insisted that the Kaiser now choose a chancellor from among "those circles within the government whom we mainly have to thank that we have gotten to this point." "They should conclude the peace that now must be made. They should now eat the soup that they have cooked for us!"[116]

Prince Max's government negotiated with the Allies over terms through the early weeks of October, while the military situation deteriorated further for Germany. A breakthrough at Cambrai in late September still threatened the entire front. German soldiers showed little interest in dying in what now seemed to be the waning moments of a lost war. Ludendorff, who had gotten the ball rolling, now thought the government had adopted too weak a position, unwilling to mobilize the last of Germany's resources to confront Allied requirements for an armistice.[117] Ludendorff later claimed that he had always been ready to take up the sword again in one last effort to save German honor or to die trying. The fire and blood of Kriemhild's revenge in Etzel's hall might result, but honor would be restored.[118]

On the evening of October 25, Ludendorff indeed signed an order to the army, explaining the need to resist the Allied demands, which amounted to an unconditional surrender in his view.[119] When the government and the Reichstag objected to the call to arms, Ludendorff decided to resign. On the morning of October 26, Ludendorff sat in his office, drafting his letter of resignation, when he and Hindenburg were summoned to an audience with the Kaiser. In his memoirs, Ludendorff claims to have spoken to the Kaiser alone and to have offered to resign. The Kaiser accepted, and Ludendorff returned to his office to put affairs in order for his successor.[120] Ludendorff makes no mention of Hindenburg remaining at his post, a decision that clearly enraged Ludendorff and led eventually to a bitter feud between the two men.[121]

Ludendorff told his colleague and confidant Albrecht von Thaer a much different story in the aftermath of the meeting. To Thaer, Ludendorff described a tense meeting, in which Ludendorff defended the OHL and the telegram of the twenty-fourth, adding brusquely, that if the Kaiser had lost faith in him or if he were a hindrance to the peace process, he would go. The Kaiser at first refused, but when Ludendorff offered a second time to resign, the Kaiser accepted. Ludendorff refused the Kaiser's offer of a field command (Falkenhayn had been given command of the Ninth Army after his dismissal), and stormed from the room.[122]

Hindenburg, who had remained largely silent during the entire meeting, found Ludendorff in the waiting room outside the audience chamber a few minutes later. The Kaiser had asked him to remain for the sake of the army, he told his old comrade. Ludendorff became angry and accused Hindenburg of having left him in the lurch. Ludendorff would not even ride in the same car as Hindenburg back to headquarters. When asked why not, Ludendorff snapped back: "I refuse to have anything to do with you, after you have treated me so disgracefully."[123]

Unrest among workers and desertion among soldiers had been on the rise since early 1918, and the decision to seek an armistice in October of that year provoked revolution. On November 3, sailors at the German naval base in Kiel mutinied and formed self-governing "councils" to replace the military chain of command. Workers in factories and soldiers elsewhere followed suit. On November 9, Philip Scheidemann, the leader of the Social Democratic Party (SPD), in an effort to prevent further radicalization of the widespread uprising, declared Germany a republic and set about, with Friedrich Ebert, creating a provisional government. Seeing the handwriting on the wall, the Kaiser fled to Holland and later formally abdicated.

Hans von Seeckt compiled a sympathetic, if not uncritical, assessment of Ludendorff's impact shortly after his dismissal in October 1918. "I am sure Ludendorff made the sacrifice willingly for the sake of the entire cause," Seeckt wrote to his wife. "I acknowledge his outstanding energy, his capacity for work and his organizational talent. Militarily we would not have been able to fight the war so long without him."[124] Seeckt's wife, Dorothea, implicitly granted Ludendorff a much more significant role, claiming during the 1925 presidential election campaign that Hindenburg owed his fame entirely to Ludendorff's technical abilities.[125]

Strategically, however, Ludendorff proved inept. Quite often, military and political calculations would conflict, as when Ludendorff ordered the resumption of unrestricted submarine warfare in 1917. Ludendorff, like his protégé, Adolf Hitler (whom admirers also referred to as Feldherr), had very little sense for the relationship between politics and strategy.[126] David Stone, in his recent work on Russia in the Great War, portrays

Ludendorff as increasingly overconfident and generally "blind to strategic considerations."[127]

While many have credited Ludendorff with important tactical and operational achievements and even with innovating a new form of "total war," most historians have judged Ludendorff's political escapades to have been disastrous. Through him, parties favoring the most extreme annexationist policies maintained their voice long after Germany's armies could enforce them. Historians rate Ludendorff's handling of the collapse of Russia as exceptionally bad. He helped to foment the Russian Revolution by transporting Lenin from Switzerland to Finland (in a sealed train) so that Lenin could direct Bolshevik agitation against the Kerensky government. Rapacious demands for Russian concessions prolonged the negotiations for an end to the war on the Eastern Front.[128]

Nor were contemporaries very flattering. No less an authority than Hans Delbrück blamed Ludendorff and his allies for the collapse of morale both at home and on the battlefront. He countered Ludendorff's stab in the back claim by insisting that it was not domestic politics per se, but the extreme annexationist desires of the political right and the Supreme Command that embittered the soldiers. They were willing to fight to defend Germany but not for the interests of industrialists and others.[129]

Ludendorff's military peers offered both criticism and praise. Hans von Seeckt did not judge Ludendorff's political ability as very high. But even here, Seeckt was in a forgiving mood, acknowledging that Ludendorff's impact in the political arena would not have been so harmful had he not faced "zeroes or worse" in his domestic and diplomatic counterparts.[130] Ludwig Beck saw Ludendorff as the principal obstacle to peace in 1918. Ludendorff was so secure in the trust of the army and the people that he ignored any advice that did not correspond to his own increasingly unrealistic views of the war. Still, Beck remained an admirer of the "outstandingly competent, clever, and energetic man" to whom Beck would turn after 1934 as the symbol of the imperial army.[131]

Ludendorff's sudden departure in October 1918 and the subsequent rapid collapse of Germany into revolution brought down on Ludendorff's head the wrath of millions of Germans who felt betrayed and disoriented in defeat. In no small part due to the Supreme Command's control of the media, most Germans were unaware of the dire condition of the front, even if they could sense in their stomachs the troublesome supply situation.

Germany's defeat in 1918 hit Ludendorff hard. It had been *his* war, at least since 1916, and his many accomplishments—the battles of Liège and Tannenberg but also the victories over Romania and Russia and the massive effort to mobilize the German economy—had come to naught. He was the Feldherr, who demanded (and received) recognition for his deeds, but such recognition did not explain his failure to achieve ultimate victory over Germany's foes. That failure required explanation, and Ludendorff eventually found it in the machinations of the "supranational powers": Judaism, Catholicism, and Freemasonry.

4

PUTSCHIST

Kriemhild's mind was heavy with fresh sorrow over her husband's
end, and because they had taken from her all her wealth. Her plaints
ceased not in all her life, down to her latest day.

—THE NIBELUNGENLIED

It is difficult to surmise how Ludendorff envisioned his postwar life in the
years prior to 1918.[1] He had had his personal effects shipped from his
prewar station in Düsseldorf to Berlin in the expectation that he would
make his home there after the war. Whether he imagined himself returning to Berlin after the war as chief of the General Staff, as a cabinet member, or as a simple pensioner is not evident in the documents. Germany's
defeat precluded those outcomes in any case. Instead, Ludendorff found
himself without occupation, embittered by the perceived betrayal of his
colleagues, defamed by much of the increasingly vocal revolutionary and
antiwar forces in Germany, and driven almost to distraction by the unac-
customed inactivity.[2] There is a certain irony (not lost on Ludendorff himself) that he was attacked *both* for being an impediment to peace *and* for
seeking an armistice at an inopportune moment at the end of the war.[3]

After his dismissal, Ludendorff traveled to Berlin and stayed in a pension in the Keithstrasse.[4] Ludendorff viewed the revolutionary occurrences
in Berlin firsthand with horror and no doubt some measure of fear. Berlin

was not a safe place for Ludendorff to be in November 1918. Ludendorff tells of strangers inquiring about his whereabouts and army intelligence officers warning him to leave the pension for security reasons. Paranoid Ludendorff might have been, but that does not mean someone was not out to get him. He fled briefly to Potsdam, to stay with his brother (a physicist), then returned to the Berlin residence of an officer acquaintance, Captain Wilhelm Breucker.[5]

Flight to Sweden and Memoirs

A more permanent solution was needed. An acquaintance in the German embassy in Copenhagen suggested that Ludendorff might find asylum there. Ludendorff and Breucker used their connections to arrange for forged travel documents. Sporting blue glasses, a false beard, and a Finnish passport, "Ernst Lindström" fled Berlin under cover of darkness on November 15.[6] Ludendorff knew from reading detective novels that the initials of his pseudonym should correspond to those of his real name.[7]

The circumstances of his departure did not accord with Ludendorff's heroic nature, so he and his allies took pains in later years to make his flight seem more honorable. His friend, Breucker, later wrote a very sympathetic account of his time with Ludendorff, which Ludendorff quotes extensively in his own memoir. According to Breucker, Ludendorff's trip was meticulously prepared with the permission of the War Ministry and even Friedrich Ebert, the head of the Provisional Government. Ludendorff first sought assurances of his safety from the government and only when those were not forthcoming did he take the drastic step of fleeing his homeland not so much for his own safety as for the safety of those who would offer him refuge. Ludendorff promised his government contacts that he would return to account for his wartime deeds should they wish.[8] Though Ludendorff's (and Breucker's) account perhaps overstated the orderliness and honorability of his flight, his first wife Margarethe, who remained behind in Berlin for some time, does confirm in her memoir (written after their divorce) that Ludendorff's life was in danger and that he took the trouble to inform the Reich government of his intentions.

The trip to Copenhagen did not pass without incident, however. On board the ferry to Copenhagen, the crew recognized Ludendorff and so his arrival in Denmark could not remain a secret. The constant attention prevented him from writing in peace and so he carried on to Sweden where he eventually found refuge on the country estate of a well-known equestrian named Ohlsen in Heßleholm (Hässleholm), in Sweden's southern interior, northeast of Malmö.[9] While in Heßleholm, Ludendorff penned his memoirs in just ten weeks. He would remain nearly as prolific for the rest of his life, writing dozens of pamphlets, several books, and innumerable contributions to various journals and newspapers.

In one of the first reviews of his memoirs, his old colleague Colonel Max Bauer extracted from the lengthy tome the key elements of Ludendorff's legend. Readers of Berlin's *Der Tag* in August 1919 were reminded that it was Ludendorff who in 1912 had called for a larger army; it was Ludendorff who took special pains to improve Germany's heavy artillery, so crucial for the opening battles of the war; it was Ludendorff alone who carried the incredible workload and the enormous responsibility of Supreme Command after 1916.[10] Bauer took for granted Ludendorff's claim that it was the Social Democrats that brought about his downfall, not a nervous breakdown. It was the failure of the Reich's political leadership, not of Ludendorff's military genius, that lost the war for Germany.[11]

Ludendorff interrupted his work only for meals and for his daily walk, during which he kept abreast of developments in Germany by reading Swedish and German newspapers. He responded with predictable horror to the terms of the Treaty of Versailles when they were publicized. Germany would lose large swaths of territory—in the East, in Alsace-Lorraine and would suffer the humiliation of occupation in its western industrial provinces. Its army would be limited to a token force of 100,000 men and denied most modern weapon systems. The Allies would force Germany to pay an as-yet-unspecified sum as reparation for the cost of the war and the nation would be tarnished with the responsibility for starting the war by the terms of the notorious "war guilt clause." On a personal level, to which we will return momentarily, Ludendorff also faced the danger of extradition and prosecution for war crimes.

Ludendorff saw all of his most dire predictions fulfilled in the territorial and military restrictions placed on Germany by that treaty. It was no doubt a hard blow to see the army for which he had worked his whole life reduced to insignificance by the limitations on its size and armaments. In his memoirs, he stressed his willingness to resume hostilities in

October 1918 as a way of maintaining German honor. Cowardly politicians would deny him the opportunity, according to his version of the story. Michael Geyer has shown us that in fact it was Ludendorff who balked at a face saving levée en masse proposed by Walther Rathenau and seriously discussed in the cabinet of the recently appointed Chancellor Max von Baden. Ludendorff's desire for an epic final battle may have been mere rhetoric.[12]

From the perspective of his embittered idleness, Ludendorff saw the events of late 1918 and 1919 in very personal terms. Hindenburg, the Spartacists, the army—were intent on blaming Ludendorff for the lost war and Germany's problems.[13] Hindenburg's alleged "betrayal" Ludendorff felt particularly strongly. That his wartime partner did not rise to Ludendorff's defense after the war seemed shameful. Hindenburg owed his fame, Ludendorff believed, to Ludendorff's prowess at Tannenberg. The burdens of the OHL had been on Ludendorff's shoulders had they not? Ludendorff discerned a pattern tracing all the way back to Hindenburg's remaining in the Supreme Command after Ludendorff's dismissal in October. Ludendorff now saw Hindenburg's offer to resign at the time as half-hearted and his willingness to accede to the Kaiser's request to stay as too great. Forces seemed to be moving against Ludendorff from all sides. Having finished his manuscript, Ludendorff departed for Germany on February 21, 1919.[14]

When Ludendorff returned to Germany from Sweden on February 26, he bristled with rage and manly indignation.[15] His wife records his attempt at prophecy: "It was the greatest stupidity for the revolutionaries to allow us all to remain alive. Why, if ever I come to power again, there will be no pardon. Then, with an easy conscience, I would have Ebert, Scheidemann and company hanged and watch them dangle."[16] It is difficult to know whether such hyperbole was the mere bravado of a defensive conscience. Certainly Ludendorff behaved ruthlessly toward his rivals during the war, but not murderously. Ludendorff spent the next several years attempting to reestablish both his reputation and his authority.

In his war memoir, Ludendorff was content to blame the revolution primarily on Bolshevism. The revolution had been prepared by the Independent Socialists (USPD, synonymous with Bolshevik in his usage), he declared.[17] "Long, systematic underground work," presumably by these same Bolshevik elements, had laid the foundations for the soldier's and worker's councils that appeared in 1918 with what Ludendorff deemed to be suspicious suddenness.[18] It was impossible for a man of Ludendorff's temperament to believe that such widespread and similar actions could have been spontaneous and uncoordinated. The irony that he was responsible for sending Lenin to Russia and thereby contributed to the Bolshevik triumph he obfuscated by calling the decision "our government's."[19]

Nor is antisemitism much in evidence in his first work on the war. It may have been that his time in Ober Ost had instilled in him a suspicion of Jews, whom he encountered in large numbers in Eastern Europe and the Baltic. Certainly, other Germans in the völkisch milieu of postwar Germany credit their time on the Eastern Front or on the Ober Ost administration with fostering their own antisemitism.[20] Ludendorff took for granted the assertion of General Max Hoffmann that Jewish traders in the East, presumably black marketers, had had a "corrupting" influence on the German troops stationed there. Those soldiers, exposed also to Bolshevik propaganda in Russia and elsewhere, often reached the Western Front, if they did not desert, in a very poor state of morale.[21] While these do not represent neutral sentiments, they hardly rise above the prejudices of most Germans of the time, particularly toward eastern Jews. Nor do such statements suggest that Ludendorff thought Jews bore any particular responsibility for the lost war.

On the other hand, for Ludendorff, Bolshevism (not yet linked to Jews, apparently, in Ludendorff's thought) seemed the greater danger. Bolshevism had eaten like a cancer at Russia, had destroyed the Russian Army, and threatened Germany itself with corruption. Bolsheviks undermined German control in Ukraine and the Baltic states.[22] Bolsheviks inspired the strikes that broke out in Germany in the spring of 1918, according to Ludendorff.[23]

The first notable appearance of antisemitism in Ludendorff's writings occurs in 1922's *Kriegsführung und Politik*, in which he more fully develops his notion of the "stab in the back."[24] In that work Ludendorff claimed that the "supreme leadership of the Jewish people were working hand in hand with France and England. Perhaps even leading them" during the Great War. Notwithstanding the fact that Jews fought for Germany in the war, which Ludendorff acknowledged, all Jews strove for Germany's defeat, according to him. German Jews profited disproportionately from the war, Ludendorff claimed, and "sold out and betrayed" the German people.[25]

Return to Berlin

After 1918, Ludendorff remained nearly constantly in the public consciousness, not only in Germany, but abroad as well. His hastily completed memoir, *Meine Kriegserinnerungen*, went through multiple printings and was quickly translated into English, French, Russian, and Turkish. The thirst for his insights in Germany was nearly insatiable. By 1921, the German language version was in its seventh edition.[26] No sooner had he returned to Berlin in 1919 than he began to assemble the documents necessary for his second postwar work, *Urkunden der Obersten Heeresleitung über ihre Tätigkeit, 1916–18*, which first appeared in 1920.[27]

Foreign newspapers tracked his movements and speculated about Ludendorff's involvement in government, as when Romain Rolland spoke of a "Scheidemann-Erzberger-Noske-Ludendorff Bloc" in a January 1919 article. A less probable association is difficult for this scholar to imagine, but Rolland's usually keen political sense must have perceived something in the works.[28] Foreign observers assumed Ludendorff to be the lodestone for monarchist officers and to be the sponsor of General Rüdiger von der Goltz's campaign in the Baltic in 1919.[29] Ludendorff's name appeared over two hundred times in London's *The Times* in 1919 and 1920 alone. Bold, full-column ads touted his publications in both book and serial form.[30]

Ludendorff felt that he had to tread carefully in the tumultuous environment of Berlin but began quickly to gain his bearings. He was cheered by a large crowd when he unexpectedly appeared on the streets in the spring.[31] According to a statement by the Nationalverband Deutscher Offiziere, Ludendorff appeared both surprised and embarrassed when the public recognized him at a large gathering to protest the terms of the Treaty of Versailles on March 23, 1919.[32]

Ludendorff certainly lived in style in Berlin, staying for at least the first several weeks at the fashionable Hotel Adlon. According to Margarethe, the proprietor was kind enough to arrange for them to occupy a room with its own exit onto the street, so that Ludendorff would not have to encounter the scores of Entente officers also in the hotel, which served as Entente headquarters in Berlin.[33] Ludendorff stayed under an assumed name, "Karl Neumann," but it beggars the imagination to believe that British and French officers would not have recognized their arch-enemy at such close proximity. Apparently, at least some British officers sought

Ludendorff's company during this time, since, as mentioned in chapter 1, the origin of the phrase "stab in the back" is often attributed to a dinner conversation between Ludendorff and General Sir Neill Malcolm at this time.[34]

During this time, Ludendorff also renewed several political contacts, in particular with the Freikorps leader Reinhardt and his entourage.[35] He spoke to youth organizations.[36] He mingled with former officers and later claimed responsibility for establishing Oskar von Hutier as head of the Deutsche Offizierbund, a veterans' organization focusing primarily on the economic interests of career soldiers.[37] He was present at the ceremony planned by Nazis to commemorate the death of Leo Schlageter in Munich.[38]

In April 1919, Karl von Treuenfeld kindly arranged for the Ludendorffs to move to his mother-in-law's luxurious apartment in the Viktoriastrasse. Margarethe compared the lodgings to a "private museum," tastefully decorated with paintings by Cézanne, Manet, Degas, and others.[39] Here Ludendorff, living under the name Charles Newman, entertained representatives of the Hohenzollern family, the crown prince of Saxony, delegates of right-wing political parties, former colleagues, and other dignitaries.[40]

It was during this period that Ludendorff began to formulate ideas for military action against a government that would sign and ratify the Treaty of Versailles. Visitors planted the seed in Ludendorff's mind of using forces stationed in the east, particularly Freikorps, to force a rejection of the hateful treaty and liberate Germany, a la Yorck von Wartenburg, from the yoke of foreign occupation.[41] He moved in circles that one contemporary observer derided as "pompous" and "garrulous," made up mainly of "old officers, members of the landholding aristocracy and antisemites."[42]

Through at least January 1923, Ludendorff seems to have been working primarily for a Hohenzollern restoration of some sort, though he usually envisioned at least a period of personal military dictatorship.[43] Prior to the Kapp Putsch, he negotiated with Wilhelm II and his son about placing the crown prince on the throne. During his flirtation with a Central European alliance of Germany, Austria, and Hungary (see below), he saw himself acting in the interests of the Hohenzollerns (and against the Habsburgs), though his personal role became more pronounced. When the effort collapsed, his associate Max Bauer wrote that he had honorably and successfully advanced the Hohenzollern cause in the affair, but that his "actions perhaps better served a Ludendorff-Politik."[44] To foreign journalists visiting him around 1922, he claimed that he could not envision a restoration of the monarchy in Germany's current condition. The restrictions placed on Germany by the Entente would be unbearable for a monarch.[45] Instead, in his posthumously published memoir of the period, he said he favored a populist dictatorship. Of course, all of this was written (most likely) after 1933, so it could also be seen as a retrospective justification for Nazism.[46]

In 1919, Ludendorff was called to testify before the parliamentary committee investigating the causes of the German defeat. At first, he balked, fearing the negative press coverage his appearance was likely to generate. He stipulated that Field Marshal von Hindenburg must also appear. Hindenburg agreed.[47] The appearance of the two men at the Reichstag on Tuesday, November 18, caused a sensation.[48] Huge crowds gathered to cheer the former heroes, which surprised Ludendorff, who had expected a more hostile reception. On the contrary, even the chairman of the committee, Georg Gothein, was polite, and a bouquet of flowers, decorated with black, white, and red ribbons, awaited the men at their seats.[49]

Hindenburg read from testimony prepared with input from Ludendorff and Karl Helfferich and made the famous remark concerning the "stab in the back."[50] He claimed that all of the good work of the OHL and bravery of the troops had been undone by party interests and by politicians sowing disunity. For his part, Ludendorff staunchly defended the decision to wage unrestricted submarine warfare in an effort to deny Britain foodstuffs and the Entente armies war materiel.

The effect of the men's appearance was to firmly establish the "stab in the back" myth with the full weight of Hindenburg's significant authority behind it. Because of the deference shown by the committee chairman, almost none of the committee's prepared questions received the attention they deserved, while Hindenburg was given free rein to weave his tale of betrayal. In hindsight, at least, Ludendorff recalled noting the prevalence of Jews on the committee, a fact that even Max Weber had lamented, if for different reasons.[51] It is quite possible that the furor surrounding the committee's Jewish members, encouraged by the Schutz- und Trutzbund and other radical groups, pushed Ludendorff himself into a more uncompromising antisemitic stance.[52]

War Crimes

One other danger confronting Ludendorff in the period following the war was the ever-present threat of prosecution or extradition for war crimes. In Germany, the Spartacus League and other leftist groups had been calling for Ludendorff's head (and also Hindenburg's, Tirpitz's, and the Kaiser's) since as early as October 1918.[53] Even more significantly, articles 228–230 of the Versailles Treaty obligated the German government to "recognize the right of the Allied and Associated Powers to bring before military tribunals persons accused of having committed acts in violation of the laws and customs of war." Germany would be required not only to extradite those accused but also to support the prosecution through the provision of documents.[54] At least one German official grumbled that that had Serbia agreed to such conditions in 1914, there might not have been a World War.[55] Though the official list containing Ludendorff's name (along with those of close to nine hundred other officers, soldiers, and officials) did not appear until February 1920, it was widely assumed that the Allies would target their nemesis from 1916 on.[56]

Realistically, of course, Ludendorff could not be charged with involvement in the outbreak of the war, given his position as a troop commander at the time. But once he ascended to the position of first quartermaster general and became, especially in his own estimation, the Feldherr of the German Army, it is reasonable to lay responsibility for the conduct of the war and the misconduct of the troops under his command at his feet. Ludendorff directly ordered the resumption of unrestricted submarine warfare and thereby violated international norms of conduct, if not international law. The British and Americans, in particular, were anxious to punish Ludendorff for the predations of the German U-boat fleet.

Ludendorff, feeling his honor besmirched by the public charges of criminality, himself called for a trial so that he might defend himself properly.[57] Nationalist groups such as the Pan-German League rallied to the defense of Ludendorff and others threatened with prosecution.[58] Whether his offer to defend himself before a German court was genuine or not, Ludendorff was *not* willing to present himself to an Allied court for trial. No less a personage than Max Weber suggested in 1919 that Ludendorff voluntarily surrender to the Allies. Weber was excited by the example of the scuttling of the German High Seas fleet at Scapa Flow.[59] Perhaps Ludendorff could put on a similarly glorious show in defeat. At a public trial, Weber hoped that Ludendorff could defend not only himself but the army and by extension Germany as a whole against charges of criminal behavior. "The officer corps can be gloriously resurrected some day only if they [Ludendorff, Tirpitz, Bethmann, etc.] 'offer their heads' to the enemy," Weber told his sister.[60] Ludendorff could prove, Weber believed, that Germany's more extreme measures had been mere reactive, retaliatory, or necessitated by wartime emergency. Ludendorff would simultaneously restore the luster of the nationalist cause at home, as well.[61] The German people would never consider exoneration by a German court legitimate. They would see nationalist influence behind the scenes and assume the verdict was politically motivated. Seeing German officers and other leaders on trial in foreign courts would rally Germans of all political stripes against a common enemy.

Ludendorff would have none of it. Returning from Versailles, Weber visited Ludendorff in Berlin, where the two men spoke for several hours. Ludendorff was dismissive of Weber's suggestion: "The nation can go jump in a lake! Such ingratitude!" "Why don't you go see Hindenburg?" Ludendorff helpfully suggested. Weber cleverly stroked Ludendorff's ego, saying that Hindenburg's age was a factor "and besides, every child knows that at the time *you* were Number One in Germany."[62] Ludendorff, in his memoirs, remembered the exchange differently, arguing that it would stain Germany's honor to have former leaders like himself dragged through the mud by Allied judges.[63] The conversation dragged on and eventually the two parted amicably. But Weber lost faith in Ludendorff. "Perhaps it is better for Germany that he does not give himself up," Weber concluded. "The enemy would find *once again* that the sacrifices of a war which put this type out of commission have been worthwhile. Now I understand why the world resists the attempts of men like him to place their heels upon the necks of others. If he should again meddle in politics, he must be fought remorselessly."[64]

Not only was Ludendorff unwilling to turn himself over for prosecution, he played a key role in organizing the resistance to the extradition of other officers who appeared on Allied lists of war criminals. He introduced Albert Schiebe, a former naval captain, to Captain Heinz von Pflugk-Harttung, a staff officer in Colonel Wilhelm Reinhard's Fifteenth

Reichswehr Brigade. Beginning in the summer of 1919, Reinhard, Pflugk-Harttung, and Schiebe coordinated efforts to hide accused officers or help them flee to neutral countries overseas to escape prosecution.[65] In their efforts, Schiebe and the others had the full, though necessarily unspoken, support of the Reichswehr establishment.

Of course, hiding mid-ranking officers would be a much simpler matter than hiding prominent leaders such as Hindenburg, Ludendorff, or Tirpitz. They were too well known for them to assimilate silently into even the most well-meaning community. Their case had to be handled differently. At a "Feldherr conference" in October 1919, Ludendorff and other high-ranking officers debated the merits of going underground versus passive resistance (i.e., simply refusing to comply with extradition orders unless arrested by force). Ludendorff favored the former course of action, and the chief of the Admiralty, Vice Admiral Adolf von Trotha put Operation Ferienkinder into action.[66] Operation Ferienkinder, funded largely by the prominent industrialist Walter Simons, secreted hundreds of accused officers in safehouses throughout Germany or helped to smuggle them abroad under assumed names. Scandalously, the navy continued paying pensions to its officers who had fled without betraying their location to judicial officials.[67]

Meanwhile, the government set up a system to process Allied requests for extradition that contained so many obstacles and guarantees as to make it extremely difficult to bring alleged war criminals before foreign courts. Public opinion was overwhelmingly against the surrender of anyone to the Allies, and every political party of the center and right decried the Allied demands. Opponents of extradition staged rallies and flooded government offices with letters of protest. The right-wing newspaper *Der Tag* called the extradition list an "honor roll," since to be on it meant to be associated with the greatest Germans of the day.[68] To counter the demands for the extradition of prominent Germans, the Reich Foreign Office created a special commission under the leadership of Major Otto von Stülpnagel to gather information on offenses committed by Allied armies while at the same time collecting material likely to absolve those accused of war crimes.[69]

In the end, after much negotiation, the German government convinced the Allies to forego extradition in favor of prosecuting a much smaller (and less prominent) list of war criminals in a German court in Leipzig.

Gone were the complaints against Bethmann-Hollweg, Ludendorff, or Tirpitz for breaking international law. There remained instead only more easily provable cases against low-ranking officers and men for such universally execrated offenses as looting, mistreating prisoners, or attacking hospital ships at sea. Even in these cases, German foot-dragging meant that only a handful of cases were ever prosecuted, and those convicted received extremely light sentences.[70]

It is interesting to note that according to Paul Lerner's study of German psychiatry in World War I, national unity was seen as the appropriate corrective to wartime hysteria. Weakness of the individual will "could be counteracted and strengthened by the collective will of the national community."[71] Ludendorff, in his own agitated state, seemingly arrived at a similar cure on his own. Throwing himself into the "spiritual" project of redeeming Germany helped to mute any concern over his "nerves." Cultivating a *Volksgemeinschaft* (people's community) based on racial identity would strengthen the nation and allow it to overturn the verdict of the war. In his memoir, he chastised men who "lost their nerve and abandoned the army and the country, thinking of nothing but themselves."[72] Such language could easily be seen as a case of psychological projection, ascribing to others one's own shameful emotions or thoughts.

Kapp Putsch

Despite the terms of his departure and the different character of the Weimar regime, Ludendorff still occupied a prominent place in the minds of Germany's conservative and military elite. Hans von Seeckt, then head of the Truppenamt, missed "Ludendorff's strong hand" in dealing with the chaotic military situation along the eastern border in 1919. Ludendorff could have maintained order there, Seeckt insisted.[73] Kurt Lüdecke claimed Ludendorff was "behind [Cossack leader Pavel] Bermondt and General von der Goltz in the Baltic."[74] Lüdecke knew that Ludendorff supported the Kapp Putsch. "After that," "Lüdecke wrote, "wherever true German interests brought a group together, his name was spoken, his spirit felt—but only vaguely, for his hand was seldom seen."[75] Waiting for Ludendorff in 1922, Lüdecke knew that "here in this villa, many of the threads ran together that were being spun, wisely or unwisely, to strangle the Marxist Republic. Here it was that the Frei-Korps leaders and many others, active agents of all interested groups, came for advice and encouragement."[76]

The groundwork for the Kapp Putsch had been laid by Ludendorff himself as the OHL—and the army as a whole—became increasingly politicized after 1916.[77] Ludendorff had known Kapp during the war and found him a useful ally in his struggle against Chancellor Bethmann-Hollweg in 1917.[78] After the war, Ludendorff clearly saw Kapp (and later General Walther von Lüttwitz) as important leaders of a diffuse but growing nationalist movement. Ludendorff believed that his own actions, and especially his public appearances such as the testimony before the special committee investigating the causes of defeat, were instrumental in fostering that growth.[79]

Wolfgang Kapp, who kept a portrait of Yorck von Wartenburg in his Königsberg apartment, began planning immediately after the war.[80] Well before the National Assembly signed the Treaty of Versailles, Kapp was canvassing leading figures on the right to gain support for an uprising. "I remain convinced," he wrote in a letter to Colonel Wilhelm Heye, "that it is still not too late to revive the good spirit, the courage and the discipline in our troops" in order to resist.[81] In a later letter to Heye, Kapp promised that Ludendorff and other nationalists hoped soon to join with current and former soldiers in the east to overthrow the nascent republican government.[82] Difficulties transporting troops on rail lines subject to disruption by hostile workers gave the conspirators pause. Ludendorff suggested instead that the coup be launched in Berlin itself, closer to the centers of power.[83]

Beginning in the summer of 1919, Ludendorff became actively engaged in an effort to overthrow the still-provisional government.[84] In the chaos of postwar Berlin, sometime in the summer of 1919, several right-wing figures, mainly former officers, gathered to form the Nationale Vereinigung with Ludendorff's blessing. The key players were Waldemar Pabst, a former officer linked to the murders of Karl Liebknecht and Rosa Luxembourg, and Ludendorff's confidante, former colonel Max Bauer.[85] The Nationale Vereinigung (NV) established its offices in Berlin's Schellingstrasse, in the same building that had housed the Vaterlandspartei during the war.[86] While Ludendorff, as ranking officer, remained the nominal leader of the group, Bauer took over most of the day-to-day operations.[87]

The NV's official aims were innocent enough: to promote efforts politically and economically to rebuild Germany and to coordinate efforts to strengthen German national sentiment. The group hoped to maintain the traditions of the old army and to marshal forces in the event of a Communist uprising. The Berlin police were satisfied that the group was harmless. Those rosy phrases about a German renaissance masked the group's real intention, to stage the violent overthrow of the Weimar government, to establish a military dictatorship, and to break free of the shackles of Versailles.[88]

Adolf Vogt, whose biography of Max Bauer details the plans for the coup, speculates that their true aims were reflected in a pamphlet penned by Major F. E. Solf in 1919 titled "Deutschlands Auferstehung 1934." In this pamphlet, Solf imagines a cabal based in Berlin and headed by a man referred to only as "The General," who develops a detailed plan for overthrowing the Republic. In a moment that bears remarkable resemblance to later plans for and actions in Munich in 1923, The General gives the signal for armed units to storm the Reichstag and force the resignation of the cabinet and the president. The Reichstag grants The General dictatorial power in order to restore order, and the latter launches a war of revenge against France.[89] The General could only be Ludendorff. The main actors of the Kapp Putsch, and especially Max Bauer, consulted constantly with Ludendorff. It was the connections fostered by Ludendorff both during and after the war that had enabled the putsch in the first place.[90] Prior to the Kapp Putsch, the British government warned its German counterpart of an upcoming coup attempt by Ludendorff.[91]

In practical terms, the conspirators in the Nationale Vereinigung knew that they needed the support of the Reichswehr.[92] From the very beginning, Kapp himself saw the army as hanging in the balance. The success of any right-wing coup would depend on military might. Knowing this, the Weimar government, he assumed, would do everything in its power to weaken the army, not merely by fulfilling the terms of the Treaty of Versailles that called for Germany's virtual disarmament but also by weakening the army in battles in the east against primarily Polish forces. As a result, Kapp believed the clock was ticking. The conspirators needed to strike before the power of the Reichswehr waned any further. In a letter of July 5, 1919, he invoked Ludendorff's name and implored Colonel Wilhelm Heye, at the time chief of the General Staff of the Grenzschutz in

East Prussia to use his influence to sway his fellow officers and to preserve his forces for the domestic fight.[93] General Rüdiger von der Goltz, commander of the "Iron Division" of fighters in the Baltic, pledged his support if Ludendorff made the call.[94] The involvement of General Walther von Lüttwitz in the coup provided the formal link into the Reichswehr chain of command, but no doubt the prestige of Ludendorff could be influential in moving the troops to obey Lüttwitz's commands. Lüttwitz's involvement ultimately proved problematic, as we shall see.

The group held frequent meetings beginning in the summer of 1919, sometimes at the office in the Schellingstrasse and sometimes at the Treuenfeld's apartment where the Ludendorffs lived.[95] In early 1920, Kapp assembled a small subcommittee including himself, Ludendorff, Kuno Count von Westarp, and others, to lay the political foundation.[96] The putschists were also in contact with Hindenburg, then contemplating a run for the presidency of the Weimar Republic.[97]

Ludendorff, even in much later writings, remained somewhat cagey about his participation. He admitted to having contacts with Kapp in 1919 and even to having visited Kapp in Königsberg to discuss the undertaking. But Kapp seemed only to be offering Ludendorff a subordinate position, which Ludendorff declined. Ludendorff was willing to lead a nationalist dictatorship, but not to serve in second place. Kapp should inform his friends of Ludendorff's favorable attitude but not rely on his direct support, Ludendorff explained.[98] In their later correspondence, he and Bauer maintained the fiction that he had only lent his aid to the conspirators when they asked.[99] At a subsequent trial, Ludendorff categorically denied any involvement in the planning.[100]

Ludendorff's role was central, however. Partly to insulate himself from government prosecution and partly to avoid alienating individuals or groups hostile to his personage for some reason or another (there were many), Ludendorff remained in the background. Yet one government official called Ludendorff the "theater director" of the coup, and as Johannes Erger reminds us, "no important decision was made without his assent."[101]

Ludendorff was also an important fund-raiser for the putsch, using his popularity in the eastern provinces as well as his connections to heavy industry to secure generous financial support. Karl Fehrmann, an associate of Hugo Stinnes and representative of western industrial concerns, provided Ludendorff with 1.5 million marks in monthly installments.[102] I. G. Farben's Carl Duisberg and Othmar Strauß, part owner of a Cologne ironworks, also provided funds through their support of the Nationale Vereinigung.[103]

Ludendorff, wishing to remain behind the scenes as much as possible, frequently relied on Bauer to represent him. It was Bauer, for example, who canvassed the opinion of the British Military Government in Cologne on July 5, 1919. In a conversation with a Colonel Ryan, Bauer outlined the conspirators' plans to intervene in case the Weimar government proved unable to quell leftist unrest. Ludendorff would lead a brief military dictatorship with the aim of eventually establishing a constitutional monarchy under non-Hohenzollern leadership.[104] Bauer claimed the support of the Reichswehr and the conservative press for the endeavor. He asked in return only that the Freikorps be maintained and for the extradition issue to be settled. Both concessions would help secure order in the new state.[105]

It seems that Ryan himself was sympathetic, but other British officials doubted the sincerity of Bauer's promise that these groups merely wished to restore order so as to be in a position to fulfill German obligations under the Treaty of Versailles. The British secretary of state, Arthur Balfour, suspected that with Ludendorff involved, the endpoint was likely to be a military dictatorship.[106] There was some debate within the British government how to respond, and Balfour decided in the end to leave Bauer's inquiry unanswered.[107] Bauer persisted in his efforts to secure British backing by meeting later the same month with General Sir Neill Malcolm in Berlin. The plan as presented to Malcolm was more limited than the one described to Ryan, but Bauer led Malcolm to believe that action was imminent. Malcolm refused to take an official position but did suggest that his country would likely "support any stable Government in Germany."[108]

Despite the lack of formal approval, Bauer and Ludendorff proceeded as though the British were on board. No doubt Ryan's and Malcolm's sympathetic hearings played a role but so did Ludendorff's typical lack of political sensibility. Throughout the fall and winter, traffic in and out of Ludendorff's residence became more and more dense. Bauer, Pabst, and Kapp himself were frequent visitors. Margarethe Ludendorff helped to entertain generals Lüttwitz and Oven and the shadowy character Ignatius Trebitsch-Lincoln.[109]

If the conspirators had deluded themselves into believing that foreign support would be forthcoming, they held even greater illusions about their sources of domestic support. Ludendorff even believed that Kapp's new regime would be welcomed by the Social Democratic Party.[110] Bauer in particular was concerned to reconcile left and right in opposition to the Versailles Treaty. He had contact with an Independent Socialist (USPD) leader, William Wauer, for whom he arranged a series of meetings with Kapp on March 13 and 14. Wauer rather fantastically dubbed Ludendorff the "General of the Workers" and suggested that Ludendorff take the reins of the putsch more firmly in hand. Both Wauer and Bauer were tilting at windmills, however. Wauer's colleagues immediately excluded him from future party meetings, and Kapp never placed much stock in Bauer's suggestions for a more worker-friendly constitution.[111]

The plotters sense of urgency sprang from the impending deadline of April 1, 1920, spelled out at Versailles, by which the Freikorps must be disbanded and the Wehrmacht reduced to its 100,000-man limit. More immediately, Lüttwitz pushed the issue with provisional government head Friedrich Ebert on the morning of March 10. According to Gustav Noske, who was present for the meeting, Lüttwitz presented demands long associated with the German Nationalist People's Party (DNVP) and was relieved of his position. Rather than risk this important connection to the Reichswehr, Kapp decided to act.[112]

In later life, Ludendorff was keen to display omniscience or at least prophetic talent, and so in his memoirs he claims that he understood that the nationalist movement was weakening in early 1920 and the moment for the coup was inauspicious.[113] But with Kapp insisting that the appropriate political alliances had been made and Lüttwitz assuring Ludendorff that the Reichswehr was on board, the conspirators in 1920 were optimistic. In Ludendorff's account, on March 10, Lüttwitz met Ebert and Noske to request that they call elections as required by the constitution and delay the implementation of the military provisions of the Treaty of Versailles in order to stave off Bolshevik insurrection. Faced with Ebert's refusal, Lüttwitz moved into open opposition.[114] Even Kapp viewed the action as precipitous but decided to initiate the coup in any case.

Kapp and Lüttwitz issued a proclamation on March 13, declaring the current government deposed and naming Kapp the Reichskanzler and Prussian minister president, while Lüttwitz would take over the military as Reichswehr minister.[115] Their government platform, issued at the same time, enumerated the severe dangers facing Germany and promised to address them forcefully, through land reform and economic measures designed to tackle unemployment and labor unrest. Strikes and separatist movements would be dealt with harshly, the proclamation promised.[116] Despite the claims of some historians, the proclamation was not overtly antisemitic. It spoke the coded antisemitic language of the right, however, in promising to protect Germans from the "hard fate of enslavement to international capital."[117]

The network around Ludendorff began to hum. When Ebert ordered the arrest of the conspirators on the eleventh, Ludendorff suggested that they might find safe haven with Captain Hermann Ehrhardt, the leader of a nearby Freikorps brigade, one unit of which was camped, perhaps not coincidentally, at the end of Ludendorff's street by March 13.[118] Ludendorff claimed that his appearance at the Brandenburg Gate at the very moment that Lüttwitz and his troops passed through it in parade formation was a mere coincidence. He was out for his morning walk.[119] The Reich government immediately fled to Dresden but while they found temporary refuge there, doubts about the loyalty of the local Reichswehr commander, General Georg Maercker, uprooted them again for a trip to Stuttgart where both the state government and the Reichswehr commander, General Walter von Bergmann agreed to protect the cabinet and parliamentarians.[120]

By the fourteenth, the prospects for the coup looked somewhat favorable. A "cabinet meeting" on that day assessed the situation, and most present, including Ludendorff, were in favor of carrying on despite various problems, including the increasingly dangerous general strike.[121] Military commanders in Berlin, in the east and north, and several naval detachments had declared themselves for Kapp and Lüttwitz. Generals Maercker and Oskar von Watter gave ambivalent responses to requests for a declaration. Bavarian officials took a clear negative stance to the coup but rather more from their own desire to steer events than from their support of Ebert and his government. Gustav von Kahr and General Arnold von Möhl used the crisis as an excuse to topple the Social Democratic regime in Bavaria and establish their own special authority.[122]

But on the same day (fourteenth), an emissary from the German People's Party (DVP), Garnich, summed up what would become Kapp's biggest problem. No matter what declarations the government made or what policies it instituted, the vast majority would view the new government only as a reactionary clique because of its leadership.[123] Despite the steps taken by Ludendorff to remain behind the scenes, friend and foe alike knew who was pulling the strings. In their declaration of the general strike the SPD leadership called for factories to shut down "so long as the military dictatorship of Ludendorff reigned."[124]

In addition, the conspirators were unclear themselves as to what they sought. Lüttwitz envisioned a milder "reordering" of the national government in support of new elections and a stronger army, whereas Kapp strove for a more permanent dictatorship aimed at building an authoritarian state and constitution.[125] With the successful flight of the legitimate government to Stuttgart and their refusal to enter into meaningful negotiations with the conspirators, Lüttwitz saw his hopes for a "reordering" dashed. The inability of Kapp to muster support from other groups for his more radical transformation doomed the coup. The bureaucracy balked, the army wavered, and the more mainstream conservative political parties preferred to wait for the elections scheduled for later that spring, which they expected to dominate.

Ludendorff took an active, if nebulous, part in the proceedings. His name cropped up on both sides as a candidate for leadership positions following the coup. The legitimate finance minister, Eugen Schiffer, seemed to think that Ludendorff would play a role in the Reichswehr Ministry.[126] Ludendorff sought to win allies in the Truppenamt—a move which Seeckt quickly sought to hinder.[127] He acted as a sort of cheerleader for the coup, appearing here and there to bolster the conspirators or to browbeat wavering bureaucrats.[128] During the coup, Ludendorff received deputations from both the putschists and the legitimate government. He appeared frequently at the Reich Chancellery to advise Kapp and was in constant contact with officers throughout Germany trying to muster support for the coup.[129] The legitimate government understood that Ludendorff was the key to the situation. On the morning of March 16, at a meeting of the Reichsrat, the emissary from Württemberg, Hildenbrand, suggested that since Ludendorff had lent his name to the coup, he should be the one to urge the rebellious troops to withdraw.[130]

On March 16, Unterstaatssekretär Dr. Ramm visited Ludendorff at the apartment in the Viktoriastrasse on behalf of the officials who had met that morning. Ramm believed that Ludendorff alone could exert the necessary pressure on Lüttwitz to convince him to back down. Only with Lüttwitz's removal could the Reichswehr be reunified. Ludendorff flatly refused, arguing, no doubt disingenuously, that such a step would undermine military discipline and insert the ministry into command affairs where it had no business.[131]

Ludendorff had consistently exuded optimism and preached persistence during the coup but finally recognized the hopelessness of the situation. Indicative of the conspirators' political ineptitude was the suggestion, made on March 16 by Waldemar Pabst, that a People's Dictatorship, led by Ludendorff and none other than the USPD leader Ernst Däumig, was a viable alternative to a Kapp government. How the völkisch forces around Ludendorff would work with their archrivals on the far left Pabst never made clear.[132] Kapp's reputation even with the far right among the mainstream parties (in particular the DNVP and DVP) did not help the cause. Otto Geßler, one of the leaders of the centrist German Democratic Party (DDP), described him as a "blindly rabid pan-German fanatic."[133] On March 17, Ludendorff, who had been summoned to the Reich Chancellery where the leaders of the putsch had gathered finally consented to Kapp's resignation.[134] He departed the Reich Chancellery in the company of Lüttwitz, who dropped Ludendorff off at home before heading to his own office in Third Army Corps headquarters.[135]

Lüttwitz held out, with Ludendorff's support, for a bit longer in his effort to preserve a military dictatorship. A group of officers assembled in the Reich Chancellery on the morning of the seventeenth, where General von Hülsen pleaded with Lüttwitz to resign. The situation among the troops was becoming critical as some commanders supported the coup while others did not. Soldiers had not been trained for these situations and were losing faith in Lüttwitz. Ludendorff and Bauer tried in vain to convince the assembly otherwise but could not.[136] Lüttwitz finally relented in the face of collapsing support within the Reichswehr.[137] When the Reichswehr refused to support the coup, Bauer contemplated the desperate step of arresting the army's top leadership and placing Ludendorff in command. Nothing came of the plan, however.[138]

Many on the right, including Alfred von Tirpitz, considered the move ill-timed and poorly planned.[139] Max Weber feared that the repercussions of the Kapp Putsch would lead to the dissolution of the Reich. In a letter to his sister in May 1920 he worried about Bavarian separatism and leftist uprisings, writing that "if the Reich breaks up, then it will have been the work of these people (Kapp, Lüttwitz, and I fear I must add Ludendorff)."[140] When the putsch seemed likely to call forth the very leftist revolution it was supposed to prevent, most of its potential allies and friends deserted it.[141]

Ludendorff found little sympathy in Berlin. Captain Ehrhardt posted a twenty-four-man bodyguard around Ludendorff's house. He blamed the failure of the putsch on inadequate preparation and on the disloyal and selfish behavior of so many officers unwilling to follow Lüttwitz's lead.[142] Ludendorff fled at the end of March for the safety of Bavaria, where wealthy nationalists sheltered him, first in a castle overlooking the Inn Valley, then, near Rosenheim at the home of Baron von Halkett.[143] In August of the same year, he rented a house overlooking the Isar River near Munich in Ludwigshöhe.[144] The Munich Schutzpolizei provided Ludendorff with a car and an "adjutant" to accompany him as he traveled around the city.[145]

Few of the main conspirators received any kind of punishment. Several were indicted but not tried. Lüttwitz found shelter in Silesia with friends. Kapp fled to Sweden, Bauer and Ehrhardt to Munich. Only Traugott von Jagow served any time.[146] Ludendorff managed to avoid even the indictment for high treason that fell on Kapp, Bauer, and the others. The cabinet initially deemed it too dangerous to arrest Ludendorff. Seeckt agreed that for the sake of the troops—and because Ludendorff had not "actively participated"—his arrest was not necessary.[147] Ludendorff's reliance on Bauer as a go-between and his refusal to participate directly in the putschists' activities allowed him to keep his freedom.[148] Maintaining the fiction of noninvolvement, Ludendorff himself insisted publicly that had he taken a more active role, the coup might have succeeded. He would not repeat the mistake of remaining in the background the next time.

Many observers recall Ludendorff retreating to his villa at Ludwigshöhe in disgust after the ignominious collapse of the Kapp Putsch. Yet Ludendorff was not entirely out of the public eye nor isolated from conspiratorial friends. It is possible that he sent letters to Kapp in Sweden, using Hermann Göring as an intermediary.[149] As early as the summer of 1920, Reich Chancellery officials feared that Ludendorff was plotting an anti-Bolshevist crusade that might upset their plans to reduce political tensions with France.[150]

Ludendorff quickly reestablished contact with Bauer, hiding out for the time being in Garmisch-Partenkirchen. Having lost Prussia to "Jews and revolutionaries" after the failure of the Kapp Putsch, Bauer hoped to use Bavaria as a new base of operations to establish an anti-Versailles coalition around the Munich-Budapest axis.[151] Bauer was never one to think small. He envisioned an alliance of rightist forces in Berlin and Budapest that would overthrow the Social Democratic government in Vienna, unite with Freikorps units in northern Germany to invade Czechoslovakia, establish a military dictatorship in Berlin under Ludendorff, then assist the Russian Whites in the overthrow of the Bolshevik regime. The alliance would then partition Poland and the Baltic States. Ludendorff lent his support to Bauer without becoming too directly involved in the planning. He provided Bauer with a letter of introduction to Admiral Horthy in Budapest so that the two could discuss the future.[152] Somewhat surprisingly, Horthy assented to the fantastic scheme and established contact with Gustav von Kahr, minister president of Bavaria.[153]

Hungary under the Horthy regime was viewed as a kind of model by völkisch groups in Germany. Horthy was a nationalist, an antisemite whose regime catered to agricultural interests as well as the middle class. Horthy even seemed, to those with monarchist sympathies, to hold out the prospect for a restoration of Habsburg power that might help the Hohenzollern cause as well.[154] On April 19, 1920, Ludendorff wrote a long letter to Horthy, again expressing his support of the plan and his faith in Bauer. He called on the Hungarians for both military and financial support of the undertaking, but seemed unwilling to take further steps personally. Adolf Vogt speculates that Ludendorff was hoping to have the Hungarians apply pressure on the right-wing groups in Bavaria in support of his leadership.[155]

The project percolated for over two years but eventually foundered on personal conflicts and the issue of a Habsburg restoration. The Hungarians, Ludendorff, and those around him would not countenance it, while the return of the Habsburgs was sine qua non to many on the Austrian right. Many Austrians wanted to see their nation's power restored—not absorbed into a Greater Germany. As we have seen elsewhere, especially when Ludendorff was concerned, personalities also clashed. Ludendorff and Bauer could not get along with many in the Austrian camp. The experience also seemed to have further soured Ludendorff's relationship with

Crown Prince Rupprecht of Bavaria, with whom he had quarreled during and after the war.

Though he remained constantly on the lookout during this period for separatist forces at work among the Bavarians, he quickly established contact through Bauer with the Bavarian minister president Gustav von Kahr and with the Munich police chief Ernst Pöhner.[156] The latter Ludendorff clearly admired for his energetic actions against Communists in Munich and indeed in all of Bavaria. In return, Pöhner and his colleague Wilhelm Frick (later minister of the interior under Hitler) protected Ludendorff (along with Ehrhardt and others) from prosecution by the Reich government.[157] Ludendorff also reestablished his contacts with Captain Ehrhardt and numerous other former officers.[158]

In addition to his various Bavarian escapades, Ludendorff appeared frequently on the national stage as well. He was a prominent guest at many nationalist events, including the burial of Kaiserin Auguste Viktoria on November 19, 1920.[159] At the funeral service, Ludendorff received a loud ovation, which struck many observers as unseemly.[160] He was called to testify in December 1921 at the treason trials of Jagow, Wangenheim, and Schiele stemming from the Kapp Putsch.[161] Ludendorff was an honored guest of the nationalist factions assembled at Oberammergau in 1922 for the Passion Play.[162] He attended the gathering of the Reichsflagge group in Munich at the beginning of July 1923.[163] He attended the "German Day" celebration at Nuremburg in September 1923 to show his support for the right-wing groups gathered there.[164] He met with Heinrich Class of the Pan-German League and others.[165] Many have suggested that Ludendorff shares at least some responsibility for the murder of Foreign Minister Walther Rathenau, with whom he had worked closely during the war.[166] Ludendorff also became heavily involved in veterans' politics, appearing at ceremonies honoring the war dead and speaking before youth groups, such as the Kyffhäuser-Verband Deutscher Studenten until conflicts between that group and Ludendorff's own Tannenberg League caused him to resign his membership in 1927.[167]

Throughout 1921, government officials kept a close watch on Ludendorff, who remained constantly under suspicion for plotting some sort of coup in league with Ehrhardt, Bauer, Escherich, or others.[168] He frequently traveled throughout Germany, attending ceremonies in Frankfurt an der Oder, speaking to audiences in Berlin, and nurturing connections

Figure 7. "German Day," September 2, 1923. Bundesarchiv, Bild 102-00162, photographer Georg Pahl.

among nationalist groups.[169] At the invitation of the organizers and East Prussian officials (many of whom had worked for Ludendorff in Ober Ost), Ludendorff traveled to Königsberg to attend a special commemoration of the Battle of Tannenberg in 1921. In order to reach Königsberg, Ludendorff had to travel by ship so as not to cross Polish territory and risk arrest.[170] Ludendorff spoke briefly and the assembled veterans, students, and other citizens greeted him with thunderous applause.

Beer Hall Putsch

It was at the end of 1920 that Ludendorff first met Rudolf Hess, who shortly thereafter introduced the former general to the new leader of the National Socialist German Worker's Party, Adolf Hitler. Hitler impressed Ludendorff, who never joined the party formally but began helping the young Führer establish contacts in right wing circles.[171] Winfried Martini in 1949 wrote that Ludendorff "attached himself to Hitler."[172] From the perspective of 1920 or 1921, it was in fact the other way around. More frequent contact between Ludendorff and Hitler began as early as September 1922. Kurt Lüdecke and Ernst Count zu Reventlow visited the Feldherr on behalf of Hitler, to secure Ludendorff's endorsement of a mission to visit Benito Mussolini, the up and coming Fascist leader in Italy. Lüdecke thought the Nazis might learn from Mussolini's anti-parliamentary tactics and hoped to build a bridge to the staunchly anti-Bolshevik Italian party. He was convinced that Ludendorff's name would open doors.

Though one must read Lüdecke's memoir with caution, particularly when he describes his own pivotal role and powerful contacts, his account of the visit to Ludendorff at the villa in Ludwigshöhe is instructive.[173] It reflects the hopes that many placed in Ludendorff as a potential leader of Germany's revival. Ludendorff's public prestige was still enormously high, and his backing would instantly propel any party to the forefront of right-wing politics. Like so many others of the day, Lüdecke saw the pairing of Ludendorff and Hitler as magical: "What a combination," Lüdecke wrote. "Ludendorff, the General, with all that name implied of caste and authority, and Hitler, the dynamic corporal, coming from the people!"[174] The extraordinary reverence with which German nationalists approached an audience with Ludendorff became almost cliché. Joseph Goebbels, in his diaries, gushed for pages after Ludendorff appeared at a gathering in 1924.[175] While Lüdecke and Reventlow awaited Ludendorff in his study, Lüdecke professed his admiration for the "fine old General . . . possessed of the high qualities bred of the best German tradition."

Ludendorff's participation in the Beer Hall Putsch is often portrayed as merely tangential, but his role was crucial. He not only led the march through the streets of Munich that November morning, he helped to plan the coup, and his prestige was vital for the coup's prospects for success.[176] Ludendorff dates his own participation in the putsch to October 21, when he learned of the Bavarian state's move to control its own troops.[177] According to his testimony at the treason trial, Ludendorff viewed this as a mutiny and feared that Germany was about to be dismembered.[178] He met with General Otto von Lossow shortly thereafter to discuss the situation.[179] Of course, his links to Hitler go back further, but it served him well at the trial to claim that the specific situation in Bavaria encouraged their cooperation.

However, documents indicate that Ludendorff's flirtation with a coup alongside Hitler date from at least a few months earlier. At the "German Day" on September 2, 1923, Ludendorff promised publicly to lend his support to Hitler and the Kampfbund, a short-lived association of right-wing paramilitary groups including the Nazi Sturmabteilung (SA).[180] Hitler and Ludendorff together reviewed the parade of sixty thousand supporters who attended.[181] Even earlier meetings betray Ludendorff's engagement with Bavarian conspirators. Ludendorff was in frequent contact with Tirpitz who was forever trying to coordinate nationwide movements on the right. In June 1923, Ludendorff met with Tirpitz and Kahr to try to settle some disputes among the various right-wing groups in Bavaria. Hitler had been invited but could not attend.[182]

On August 27, 1923, a meeting took place in Hagen, near Dortmund, attended by Ludendorff, Göring, Hoffman, and Hitler, at which the general conditions for a coup were discussed. Ludendorff agreed completely to subordinate himself to Hitler in political affairs. He also expressed confidence, probably based on the experience of the Kapp Putsch in 1920, that Hans von Seeckt would eventually support the coup after some initial vacillation. An attendee named Gelberg assured the group that they would have the backing of the Reichswehr when the time came.[183] It was during this period that Gottfried Feder introduced Ludendorff to Frau Doktor Mathilde von Kemnitz.[184]

Nor had Ludendorff been negotiating only with Hitler at this time. At the invitation of Hugo Stinnes, Ludendorff traveled to the Berlin suburb of Wannsee on February 21, 1923, to meet with Chancellor Cuno and Hans von Seeckt, the head of the Reichswehr. Ludendorff believed it crucial that the program of passive resistance to the French occupation be strengthened by more active forms of opposition supported if not carried out by the Reichswehr. In general, Seeckt sought to insulate his Truppenamt from the influence of political soldiers like Ludendorff, but he agreed to the meeting.[185] Ludendorff suggested that he could enlist the support of armed völkisch groups to expel the French from the Rhineland, provided those forces remained under the control of their current leadership.[186] After a two hour meeting, Seeckt welcomed the promised support of the paramilitary bands but insisted that all military forces must remain under his command.[187]

Though generally confident of Reichswehr support, the conspirators around Ludendorff nevertheless sought to weaken Seeckt's position within the Reichswehr prior to any coup. The NSDAP, and likely Ludendorff as well, took action to discredit the head of the Truppenamt. Otto Geßler reported a mysterious visit to his Berlin apartment in September 1923 by a Bavarian officer, whom Geßler assumed to be an emissary of the right-wing officers represented by Ludendorff. The emissary departed without communicating his message, however, when Geßler insisted that Seeckt be present for the conversation, since it promised to deal with military affairs. At about the same time, the NSDAP's *Völkischer Beobachter* published an attack on Seeckt and his wife that Geßler assumed was part of a coordinated effort to besmirch Seeckt's reputation. Given the animosity between Seeckt and Ludendorff, it seemed likely that the self-proclaimed Feldherr was behind the attacks.[188]

The events of the Beer Hall Putsch itself are well known, but Ludendorff's critical role is perhaps less so. His associate, Scheubner-Richter, telephoned Ludendorff immediately after Hitler's speech in the Burgerbräukeller and raced to Ludwigshöhe to collect the general. The small gray Benz raced through the foggy night at high speed, returning with the Feldherr in less than twenty minutes, according to one account.[189] Ludendorff entered the beer hall and immediately went to the back room where Hitler had sequestered Kahr, Lossow, and Seisser. Lossow and Seisser declared themselves in favor of Hitler's scheme, but Kahr wavered. Only when Ludendorff intervened did Kahr agree to support the putsch.[190] Hitler departed the hall and shortly thereafter, Kahr, Lossow, and Seisser left as well, presumably to man their respective offices and bring their subordinates into line with the coup. Kurt Lüdecke lamented that Ludendorff had arrived for the coup dressed only in civilian clothes. Ludendorff's decorations, Lüdecke assumed, would have prevented Kahr from betraying the plot later in the evening.[191] That is what Kahr (and Lossow as well) did. As soon as they were out of Hitler's grasp, the two men began assembling forces to halt the plot. They ordered the bridges into Munich city center to be occupied.

Ludendorff himself first went to the local headquarters of the Reichswehr, which had recently been occupied by Ernst Röhm and Nazi forces. One account also has him visiting the Bavarian War Ministry that evening.[192]

Ludendorff's name was especially important in mobilizing the young soldiers of the Munich Infanterieschule to the cause of the putsch. Schutzstaffel (SS) Hauptsturmführer Richard Kolb, in his account of the evening, insists that it was only his presence in uniform (which the young cadets mistook for an army uniform) and the prestige of Ludendorff's name that got the cadets out of bed.[193] Friedrich von Rabenau, the editor of Seeckt's posthumous memoir, spoke with many participants from the school, who "without exception assured him that the name of the famous general of the Great War played a critical role. They truly believed that the persons giving them orders had come as representatives of Ludendorff." Ludendorff's involvement was sufficient to disrupt the normal chain of command, a fact that sent Hans von Seeckt into a rage when he discovered it.[194]

When Ludendorff began to suspect that Kahr had switched sides, he returned to the nerve center of the conspiracy, the Burgerbräukeller, to see what could be done. Some present wanted to retreat from Munich into the countryside to take up armed struggle. Ludendorff saw no hope for success in such a strategy. The völkisch forces were simply too weak. Rather, he preferred a grand gesture designed either to win the sympathy of Münchners or, as he later remembered it, to create for the movement a sanguinary, and therefore honorable, end.

Hitler testified in 1924 that his followers insisted he warn Ludendorff of the possibility they might be fired on. "We march!" Ludendorff shouted, and the Nazis and other sympathizers fell in behind Ludendorff and Hitler as they marched toward the center of Munich.[195] They crossed the Isar Bridge without incident but were met by a resolute detachment of Landespolizei and Reichswehr soldiers in the narrow passage between the Residenz and the Feldherrnhalle. Some in the column tried to shout to the policemen not to shoot out of respect for Ludendorff and Hitler but as the marchers approached the police barricade, shots were fired. The passive voice is necessary, unfortunately, since it has never been firmly established who fired first. Many of the marching Nazis were armed, and both sides naturally claimed the other fired first.

Several marchers in the front of the column fell to the ground, wounded or already dead. Others sprang for cover in nearby doorways or stairwells. Only Ludendorff remained upright and continued marching, although a Major Streck, who had initially taken cover, claimed to have sprung to Ludendorff's side once he saw the Feldherr proceeding alone. As his companion Albrecht von Graefe recalled, "Without hearing or heeding the cry to take cover, Ludendorff marched, straight ahead and upright, the few steps into the midst of the Reichswehr and police."[196] Ludendorff passed through the line of police and entered the Odeonplatz.

Ernst Röhm also tells the now-famous story of Ludendorff's unflinching progress in the face of the fire of the Landespolizei in his *Geschichte eines Hochverräters*.[197] "The victor of Lüttich and Tannenberg walked upright, without batting an eyelash or increasing his pace, through the ranks toward the fire."[198] A party member who was present gave a longer account:

> Those of us at the front raised our arms once more, yelling to the troops that Adolf Hitler and General Ludendorff were there. Then suddenly behind us a shot rang out. I turned around to see what had happened as we were fired on from all sides. My comrades and I threw ourselves to the ground and returned fire. I was shocked to see that my best friend, Kurt Neubauer, orderly to General Ludendorff, lay dying on the street . . . the country's youngest volunteer in the World War. I then witnessed a heroic deed that will remain with me the rest of my life. The greatest general of the war climbed over my body, and standing tall with his left hand in his pocket, marched right into the line of fire.[199]

Only when he turned to enter the Briennerstrasse did a police officer dare to approach the war hero and ask him, politely, whether he would mind accompanying the officer into the police command center inside the Residenz. As he looked back down past the Feldherrnhalle he saw only the dead and wounded among the marchers. The rest of the formerly jubilant column had seemingly evaporated.[200]

Two men with close ties to Ludendorff perished in the gunfire and became martyrs for the Nazi cause. Max Erwin von Scheubner-Richter had served under Ludendorff in the General Staff and also worked in the Ober Ost administration during the war.[201] Another victim, Kurt Neubauer, had served as Ludendorff's orderly after the war. Ludendorff was clearly deeply affected by Neubauer's loss and had an inscription placed on his grave.[202] Many witnesses reported fearing that Ludendorff too had been killed in the hail of gunfire. Those quickly taking cover or further back in the ranks of the marchers likely missed the scene at the police cordon described by Röhm. For some, it was a moment of relief when they were

Figure 8. Sketch from the Beer Hall Putsch, November 9, 1923. Karl Neubauer tries to protect Ludendorff. Sketch by Thöny; photo by ullstein bild / ullstein bild via Getty Images.

brought to the Residenz to find Ludendorff sitting on a couch. "Luden-dorff is unbroken," recalled one witness. "The same figure that had be-come known to us in the images of the supreme headquarters. Icy calm. But inside the general a storm visibly raged."[203]

In the police station, Ludendorff was treated with great respect, and he asked to telephone Röhm, still occupying the military headquarters. Ludendorff convinced Röhm to surrender peacefully. A state prosecutor interviewed Ludendorff for several hours, but the general was allowed to return home that evening on only his word of honor. Only then did he learn that his servant, Kurt Neubauer, was among those killed that morn-ing.[204] Ludendorff was not convinced that he himself was out of danger. In the month after the coup, Ludendorff feared for his life, and there are reports that his compound was heavily guarded. He seemed convinced, as he had been in 1919, that his enemies would put him to death.[205]

Ludendorff's role in the putsch had indeed been decisive. Kurt Fügner gives Ludendorff credit both for the idea of the march (to gauge the mood of the city) and for the courage to brave fire. According to Fügner, Hitler had wanted to retreat to Rosenheim but Ludendorff dissuaded him. Fügner also claims that Ludendorff sent his surviving stepson Heinz Pernet home to be safe.[206] "Ludendorff alone is to be thanked that the march took place and what is more that the völkisch movement did not collapse."[207] Kurt Lüdecke claims that Ludendorff's pressure was instrumental in securing Kahr's support for the proposed march on Berlin.[208] His arrival in the beer hall on November 8 instantly brought Lossow into line.[209] His popularity brought the Infanterie- und Pionerschule over to the side of the putschists, according to Seeckt.[210]

Trial

Ludendorff and Hitler's trial for treason began on February 26, 1924, and lasted until the verdicts were read on April 1 of the same year. Most his-torians refer to the trial as the Hitler-Ludendorff trial if they mention Lu-dendorff's presence at all. The most common photograph of the accused has Hitler in an overcoat, holding his hat, confidently standing beside the old Feldherr.

But Ludendorff, winner of the Pour le Mérite, victor of Liège and Tannenberg, Feldherr of the Great War, was the much more prominent figure at the time. Both Generalleutnant von Lossow and General von Seeckt in their correspondence following the coup refer to the impending legal proceedings as the Ludendorff-Hitler trial, indicating the centrality of Ludendorff's role and his fame relative to the little-known Hitler.[211] Similarly, reports of the coup that arrived in the Reichswehr Ministry in Berlin foregrounded Ludendorff's role at the expense of Hitler's.[212] The actual photograph taken on the steps of the courthouse reveals who was the center of attention at the time, and it was not the gentleman in the frumpy overcoat.

Adolf Hitler used the trial to catapult himself onto the national stage. Ludendorff was already there, and so his lengthy speech on February 29 also attracted significant attention. His defense was not nearly as poignant as Hitler's (even Ludendorff admitted as much). Ludendorff claimed to have been involved with the coup only since October 21, the day Kahr brought the Reichswehr under Bavarian control. Shedding crocodile tears,

Figure 9. Ludendorff and other defendants at trial for treason, 1924. Bundesarchiv, Bild 102-00344A, photographer Hoffmann.

Ludendorff called this move both mutiny and a breach of the Weimar constitution. According to him, it required a response.[213]

In typical fashion, Ludendorff attacked his enemies with their own words, justifying his attack on the Republic with old quotations from its founder, Scheidemann, expressing his hostility to the old ruling class and the undesirability of a German victory in war. "You could hear a pin drop," Ludendorff claimed, when he had finished his oration, but whether that was because the audience was impressed by the war hero's sincerity or put to sleep by the rambling, pedantic, almost documentary tone is unclear.[214]

As is well known, the judge gave the defendants significant leeway to speak at length and showed them other courtesies as well. Ludendorff enjoyed the opportunity to meet with his codefendants during trial recesses.[215] Hitler, in particular, held forth at length, in attempt to put the Weimar "system" itself on trial for not serving Germany's interests. His only goal, he claimed, was to restore national pride, national honor, and overthrowing the present government was the precondition. For his treason, the court sentenced Hitler to a mere five years, of which he served only nine months. Ludendorff's stepson, Heinz Pernet, received a sentence of one year.[216] Ludendorff was exonerated. None could question his patriotic bona fides, the court believed, and therefore his actions were considered to stem from purely justifiable motives.

Raffael Scheck claims that Ludendorff's reputation was "ruined" by the failed putsch, but he remained the focus of many in the völkisch milieu.[217] Insiders still hoped that Ludendorff, perhaps together with Hitler, would lead the national revolution. Siegfried Kasche, later an emissary to Zagreb and responsible for the deportation of Jews from Croatia, looked to both Hitler and Ludendorff in the early years after the putsch. In March 1925, he wrote to Ludendorff of his dismay over the apparent splintering of the völkisch movement after Hitler's release from prison. "We see Your Excellence as the great leader and Adolf Hitler as the fiery spirit . . . for our movement." Kasche sought guidance from Ludendorff as to how to reconcile the various factions in his local group. Ludendorff offered little, beyond an exhortation to serve "truth" and the "Volksgemeinschaft."[218]

Many outsiders also believed Ludendorff to be the focus of nationalist aspirations. Ludendorff's involvement in the Kapp and Hitler putsches, combined with his wartime fame, appeared to make him *the* leader among the German Right. In the months surrounding the Beer Hall Putsch, Ludendorff had several meetings with emissaries of Benito Mussolini. They found Ludendorff still in a fighting mood, still favoring the violent overthrow of the Weimar Republic.[219] According to these reports, conspiracies already occupied Ludendorff's mind. He told one visitor of a plot involving Bavarian separatists and the Catholic Church for a Danubian federal state being hatched in the salon of an Austrian grand duchess.[220] He told General Capello, touring Germany on Mussolini's behalf in the spring of 1924, that only the warning contained in Ludendorff's testimony at his trial for treason had prevented France and the Vatican from putting the plan into action.[221]

That the Germans wanted revenge, for the lost war, for Versailles, seemed obvious, and who better than the modern Siegfried to lead the charge.[222] Ludendorff disingenuously claimed in his memoir of the period (published posthumously and during Hitler's reign) that he never aspired to lead the völkisch movement in the aftermath of the failed putsch. Ludendorff sought only to bring together the disparate elements of the party to help them learn from each other and from him. Questions of leadership could await Hitler's release.[223]

Nothing could be further from the truth. Ludendorff was in fact busy trying to secure his own position as leader of the radical right. With Albrecht von Graefe and others, Ludendorff led the effort to lure members of the now-banned NSDAP into a new coalition, the Nationalsozialist-ische Freiheitsbewegung (National Socialist Freedom Movement—NSFB), sometimes also known as the Deutschvölkische Freiheitsbewegung (German Völkisch Freedom Movement, DVFB). Ludendorff explained the choice of "Nationalsozialistische Freiheitsbewegung" for the common list for the elections of 1924. Many of the North German supporters of the völkisch cause objected to the use of "workers' party" in a name and yet wanted to retain the cachet that National Socialism had acquired thanks to the publicity surrounding the putsch.[224] Tirpitz and other national leaders visited Munich in March 1924 to discuss potential alliances.[225]

The völkisch groups enjoyed considerable success in the spring elections, so Ludendorff, along with Graefe, Frick, and Gregor Strasser entered the Reichstag along with twenty-nine other delegates of the combined NSDAP/DVFB list. Ludendorff also led the radical right in the Bavarian Landtag elections of April 1924. Ludendorff's Völkischer Block won a major victory in the Bavarian Landtag, 23 of 129 seats, up from 2 of 158 in the 1920 elections.[226] Notwithstanding his relative success, Ludendorff despised parliamentary politics, as he had made clear in his wartime memoir, and appeared to be a fish out of water in his new environment. He called his tenure in the Reichstag "a punishment."[227]

Even less could Ludendorff tolerate (nor could he master) the divisions that quickly appeared within the ranks of his movement. Graefe and Hitler advocated different directions and within the NSDAP itself fissures arose. Ludendorff therefore convened a meeting of the principal leaders (except Hitler, who remained in prison) in Weimar from August 15–17, 1924. As a provocation and a protest, the leaders chose the same theater in which the National Assembly had gathered in 1919 for their venue.[228] Problems and disagreements plagued the meeting from the beginning, especially since Hitler remained silent on the issues facing the movement in his absence, namely, who should lead and how should the various factions within the völkisch movement cooperate. Ludendorff clearly commanded a great deal of respect, especially from the groups from Prussia and northern Germany, but Hitler retained the loyalty of not only his former core of supporters but also the many who had admired Hitler's performance at the trial. Ludendorff appointed Mutschmann (Sachsen), Dinter (Thüringen), Wulle, and Reventlow (Prussia) as regional leaders.[229]

Ludendorff claimed in his memoir that a wide range of issues were to be addressed at the gathering, including his later pet projects involving education and women. One should not trust these claims, however, given Ludendorff's propensity to order events in hindsight to suit his current purpose. In addition, it is always possible that the memoir covering this period, which appeared posthumously in 1940, had been "edited" by Mathilde or others in the Deutsche Gotterkenntnis movement.[230] Mathilde (still von Kemnitz) was, in any case, invited to deliver a speech at the gathering on "The Power of the Pure Idea" at the insistence of Gottfried Feder, who was fond of her work.[231] According to Ludendorff's former adjutant, Wilhelm Breucker, Ludendorff intended Mathilde's speech to be the keynote of the conference, expressing his desire to make her anti-Christian viewpoint the central plank of the völkisch movement.[232]

As the NSFB prepared for the second elections of 1924, its leadership published a handbook to provide speakers and other officials with short summaries of the party's platform. Ludendorff himself wrote several items that reflected his growing concern for Germany's spiritual renaissance. Over the resistance of Graefe, Ludendorff wrote the section on the relationship of the völkisch movement to religion based in large part on his nascent understanding of Mathilde von Kemnitz's work. Ludendorff insisted that völkisch groups did God's work by preserving and fostering a consciousness of racial identity. Ludendorff's "conversion" was evidently not yet complete, since he insisted at the end that the NSFB "stood on the foundation of a Christian worldview."[233]

The NSFB would soon crumble, with the defection of prominent allies Artur Dinter, Julius Streicher, and Hermann Esser on November 24. After the professions of "loyalty unto death" that he been offered at Weimar that summer, Ludendorff wondered sardonically whether Dinter was living "life after death."[234] The election on December 7 was even more disappointing, with the combined völkisch movement losing twenty of its previous thirty-two seats in the Reichstag.

As Hitler's intent to reestablish the NSDAP under his firm and unilateral control became clear, Ludendorff left Berlin in disgust and abandoned his duties in the Reichstag. His only consolation was that by his efforts he had strengthened the völkisch movement as a whole by instilling in at least some members of all the various factions a concern for the spiritual foundation of the movement and the threat posed by Rome.

Hitler praised Ludendorff upon his return from prison. In an open letter published in the *Völkischer Beobachter* on February 26, 1925, Hitler honored Ludendorff as "the most loyal and selfless friend of the National Socialist movement."[235] The relationship would never be the same, however. In a surprisingly critical passage of his final memoir, published in 1940, Ludendorff described his dismay when Hitler began to curry favor with the old conservatives among whom Ludendorff had once held so much influence. According to Ludendorff, Hitler abandoned his völkisch principles in expectation of even the slightest recognition from the old guard. Ludendorff, in contrast, claimed to stay true to his ideals.[236] Other critical passages were inserted for the 1941 edition of the work, including several biting remarks concerning Hitler's refusal to attack the Catholic Church.[237]

Despite his nascent estrangement from Hitler and the NSDAP, Ludendorff allowed himself to be nominated as the National Socialist candidate for the presidency of the republic when Friedrich Ebert unexpectedly died on February 28, 1925. Ludendorff later claimed to know that he stood no chance of winning and that his candidacy was merely symbolic—to protest the policy of fulfillment of the Treaty of Versailles advocated by the other non-Communist candidates. He certainly gave no major speeches and did virtually no campaigning personally. The Nazis published campaign materials and sponsored a few events, but to little effect. Ludendorff garnered roughly 285,000 votes in the first ballot, just over 1 percent of votes cast.[238] Ludendorff threw his support behind his old comrade, Paul von Hindenburg, who entered the campaign on the second ballot and subsequently won the election. Ludendorff retired to his villa to celebrate his sixtieth birthday on April 9, 1925.

The Beer Hall Putsch, the subsequent struggle for control of the remnants of the Nazi party, and the failed presidential bid laid bare Ludendorff's lack of political adroitness.[239] According to Hitler, Ludendorff needed to learn that he could not "command as if he had divisions and brigades in front of him, whom we could simply order to 'right face.'" Hitler also assumed (incorrectly) that with experience, Ludendorff would learn his lesson.[240] His egotism and dogmatism combined with an increasing tendency to see cabals behind every curtain disqualified him from leadership. Yet Ludendorff would find his niche. In the aftermath of his failure to wrest control of the NSDAP from Hitler, Ludendorff founded a rival organization, the Tannenberg League (Tannenbergbund), that would serve as his mouthpiece and absorb his energies until his death.

PROPHET

Tannenberg League and Deutsche Gotterkenntnis

From thy shoulders shake what shocking seemeth; seek thou
thy way thyself.

—PASSAGE FROM THE EDDA, RECITED AT LUDENDORFF'S
BIRTHDAY CELEBRATION, 1924

To the elements of his mythos that corresponded roughly to his history as
military officer and man of action, Ludendorff sought to add the mantle
of a prophet.[1] Though he never ceased to justify his wartime actions, he
increasingly turned to works of commentary and prophecy. These works
highlighted his prewar prescience, in calling for a larger army in 1912, for
example, and predicted future events that threatened Germany.

The failure of the Kapp and Beer Hall putsches and his inability to seize
control of the splintering völkisch movement in the mid-1920s were further personal defeats for Ludendorff. Those defeats began the process of
slowly dissolving most of the connections he had forged to various political movements and even to the many officers' and veterans' organizations
in which he had moved since the end of the war. As those bonds dissolved,
usually in acrimony, new ones were forged to an ideological movement
that would attract tens of thousands to Ludendorff's ideals.

Also dissolving was Ludendorff's marriage to Margarethe. He initiated divorce proceedings in September 1924. He offered various grounds

for the divorce, including Margarethe's apparent morphine addiction, but the courts ultimately ruled that Margarethe was the injured party. Erich was forced to make alimony payments of 10,000 Reichsmarks per year, roughly half his income at the time.[2]

It was fairly clear that another woman played a role. Mathilde von Kemnitz, née Spiess, was born on October 4, 1877, in Wiesbaden.[3] She studied medicine at the Universities of Freiburg, Berlin, and Munich, eventually earning her medical degree in 1913. At a time when few women entered the academy, she found a position as an assistant in the lab of noted psychiatrist Emil Kräpelin. Mathilde also practiced psychiatry during the war, partly in a rehabilitation center for military officers, and she became well known for her publications in the areas of war-induced neuroses, sexual reform, and the occult.[4] She had three children with her first husband, Gustav Adolf von Kemnitz, a lecturer on zoology and comparative anatomy at the University of Munich.[5] Kemnitz perished in an avalanche in 1917. A brief marriage (1919–21) to a retired major named Edmund Georg Kleine followed, ending quickly in divorce. After the war, Kemnitz made a splash in rightist neopagan circles with the publication of *Triumph des Unsterblichkeitwillens* (Triumph of the will to immortality).[6]

In the fall of 1923, Ludendorff met Mathilde through the offices of Gottfried Feder, and she quickly ingratiated herself.[7] Rumor had it that Mathilde had offered herself to Hitler as "Führerin," and when he rebuffed her, she set her sights on Ludendorff. She gave a speech on völkisch spiritualism at the celebration of Ludendorff's birthday in 1924 and may have met with Hitler on Ludendorff's behalf at least once.[8] In 1924, she also treated Ludendorff's first wife, Margarethe, in the Ludendorffs' house for her addiction, albeit unsuccessfully.[9] Her rather obvious pursuit of the Feldherr culminated in their marriage in September 1926, just two months after his divorce from Margarethe became official.[10] Erich and Mathilde remained close partners, dedicated to two projects, the cultivation of Erich's legend in the Tannenberg League and evangelizing for Mathilde's neopagan philosophy, "Deutsche Gotterkenntnis" (Germanic understanding of God).

Many of Ludendorff's contemporaries blamed Mathilde for turning Ludendorff into a deranged conspiracy theorist, searching for Freemasons, Jews, and Catholics in every cupboard. However, Ludendorff's search for scapegoats had begun even during the war. It took him several years to develop the appropriate vocabulary to describe what he later consistently referred to as the "supranational powers." One can, however, read hints in some of his earliest works, such as *Urkunden der Oberste Heeresleitung* and *Kriegsführung und Politik*, that he is moving beyond the more mainstream version of the "stab in the back."

At first, the references to the Germany's enemies were ambiguous. Ludendorff's 1922 work *Kriegsführung und Politik* clearly illustrates his evolution from the "stab in the back" of 1918–19 toward the full-blown belief in the pernicious influence of the "supranational powers" that fills the pages of his works by the late 1920s. In that book, Ludendorff ponders the contemporary world political situation and finds most Germans lacking in the necessary national sensibility. Instead, he sees a Germany plagued by a vague internationalism and pacifism.[11] According to Ludendorff, Weimar Germany undermined its own power by aping English parliamentarism and succumbing to Jewish influence.

That his particular conspiratorial beliefs evolved slowly is best indicated by the passages on Christianity in *Kriegsführung*. The notion of "Jewish influence" was widespread within the völkisch circles in which Ludendorff moved, but Ludendorff handled Christianity much more carefully. Christianity, he writes, "has through its sublime teachings brought so much to the individual and continues to do so." But its organization and historical development has led Germans away from their true nature. Of the two established churches in Germany, the Evangelical and the Catholic, he is more critical of the latter. His attack on "Rome," however, comes nowhere close the fantastic charges he would later bring against the pope and the Catholic Church. Ludendorff claims, echoing Otto von Bismarck in the days of the Kulturkampf of the 1870s, that Catholics are too beholden to a foreign power and therefore insufficiently "German." Evangelical ministers alone remain "sons of the German people." Of course, Ludendorff adds, there are exceptions to both rules, namely pacifist/international members of the Evangelical Church and good German Catholics, such as the Catholic priests who served as chaplains in the war.[12]

Similar sentiments were rife on the German right wing. By 1922, Ludendorff had moved beyond merely seeing Germany's waning strength during the war and the revolution of 1918 as the result of shadowy domestic forces to seeing a broader conspiracy. To Kurt Lüdecke, the emissary from Hitler, Ludendorff allegedly confessed: "Today, of course, I clearly see that conditions as they prevailed at home were merely the result of a policy already inaugurated before the outbreak of the war by interests beyond the control of any government—interests whose influence veritably overshadowed the power of the nation."[13] Already in 1922 he saw many groups on the right wing as infiltrated by "Romelings"— agents of the Vatican.[14]

Tannenberg League

After his failed bid to unite the NSDAP and the other fragments of the völkisch movement in the NSFB after the Beer Hall Putsch, Ludendorff set out to found his own organization, the Tannenberg League.[15] Capitalizing on the battle that he claimed "made possible the four-year-long resistance of the German people during the war," Ludendorff hoped to build a nationalist movement of his own.[16] His own well-cultivated association with the battle on the Eastern Front was an added bonus.

The league was the brainchild of Konstantin Hierl, along with several other prominent figures in the völkisch movement, such as Georg Ahlemann and Hans Weberstedt.[17] They met with Ludendorff and others in Regensburg on September 5, 1925, to establish the ground rules for the organization. It was not to be a political party like the NSDAP, but would rather promote a "Greater German, völkisch state that served the social and the national needs of the German people."[18] It would do so by bringing together young men and former soldiers to develop their "physical, spiritual, and moral" faculties and place them in the service of a new, revitalized state.[19]

For role models, the group chose the usual icons of the national past: Frederick II, Gerhard von Scharnhorst, Carl von Clausewitz, Prince Frederick-Karl, Helmuth von Moltke (the Elder), Alfred von Schlieffen, and Ludendorff. Karl Freiherr vom Stein and Otto von Bismarck also received praise.[20] The Tannenberg League glorified the Romantics as the vanguard of the attack against the "supranational powers" and the alien spirit of the Enlightenment that those powers championed. The Brothers Grimm, Immanuel Kant, Johann Fichte, and Georg Hegel, were all seen as taking up the noble struggle.[21]

The constitution and activities of the Tannenberg League were modeled (whether consciously or not is unclear) on those of other völkisch groups

with which Ludendorff was acquainted. The Deutschvölkischen Schutz-
und Trutzbund (DVSTB) in particular was very similar with its calls for
"spiritual rebirth" and the promotion of a peculiarly German "personality."[22] Like the Trutzbund, the Tannenberg League distributed brochures
and leaflets, held public events, trained speakers for the lecture circuit,
and used prominent war heroes to increase its visibility.[23] Estimates of the
Tannenberg League's early membership are from thirty thousand to forty
thousand.[24]

As one might assume from the emphasis on the "social" and "national" project in its bylaws, the league drew much of its language and
many of its policies from the same well tapped by the National Socialists.[25] The Tannenberg League also used the language of a coming "Third
Reich."[26] Georg Ahlemann delivered a lecture titled "The Third Reich:
On the Völkisch Greater Germany of the Future" to a large gathering
in Hamburg on March 20, 1926.[27] At the same event, a band played the
march "Heil Ludendorff," composed by the Tannenberg League's *Ober-
musikmeister* Hauptmann. The Tannenberg League championed many of
the causes eventually associated with the National Socialists. They despised the Dawes and later Young plans. The League of Nations was,
they claimed, merely a tool of international Jewry to contain German
power. Events sponsored by the Tannenberg League called for "irredentist
Germany" to return "Heim ins Reich."[28] The Tannenberg League found
itself in direct competition in many places with the local National Socialist groups. They competed for audiences especially to hear lectures on
the evils of Jews and Freemasons, which were also favorite themes of the
Nazis.[29] Speakers at Tannenberg League events addressed topics such as
Jesuit and Masonic influence, the goals of Ludendorff and the Tannenberg
League, or current events relating to their enemies in National Socialism
or the Catholic Church.[30] Lectures on these topics seemed regularly to attract crowds as large as several hundred—on a few occasions as many as
one thousand—listeners.[31]

Beginning in July 1927, the Tannenberg League divided Germany into
six areas (*Länder*): South (Bavaria), East (Danzig and East Prussia), Central (Saxony, Hessen), Southeast (Brandenburg, Silesia), West (Westphalia,
Rhineland), and North (Hamburg, Schleswig-Holstein, Hannover, Meck-
lenburg, and more).[32] These *Landesverbände* which were then further par-
titioned into *Gaue* (regions) and "fighting groups." Thanks to Mathilde's

intervention, the group for the first time allowed women to join with full equality.³³ The league was organized hierarchically, with each group reporting monthly on its activities upward in the chain. The leader for each group was appointed by the organization above it, so that the Landesführer appointed the Gauführer, the Gauführer named each Kampfgruppenführer in his region, and so on. Each Kampfgruppe leader was supposed to name up to five assistants to aid him in conducting Tannenberg business. In practice, because of the small size of the individual groups, one or two people often filled all of the necessary positions (director, treasurer, press liaison, etc.).³⁴

The level of control exerted by Ludendorff and his inner circle was extraordinary. The leadership of the Tannenberg League issued guidelines to its affiliates concerning the conduct of operations in their respective areas. Every event needed to be carefully planned in advance, "with nothing left to chance." Each region should be carefully subdivided and authority delegated to reliable, well-trained subordinates. The subordinates received training in the form of weekly lectures and discussions that were organized for each fighting group. At these meetings, members would share successful strategies and, most important, discuss the recent issues of Ludendorff's newspaper.³⁵ Other training sessions, called *Kampfschulen* (fighting schools), were devoted to special topics such as "the essence of Roman fascism" or "What is the NSDAP fighting for?"³⁶ In Ludendorff's sense of politics, obedience was key. Disagreement was disloyalty and correspondents who argued even small points of policy or ideology often received stinging responses from the Feldherr.

Ludendorff used the Tannenberg League and its publications as a means to exonerate himself of the many charges leveled against him as a result of his wartime activities. He insisted that he had no annexationist desires, that he did everything possible to minimize casualties among his men, that he had *not* been responsible for transporting Lenin from Switzerland to Russia.³⁷ Ludendorff claimed to disdain politics, positioning himself as a "statesman in the deepest sense of the word, a free, unfettered, generous German man, beholden to no party or interest group."³⁸

Other connections to the war were also manifest, most notably the loyal membership of many former soldiers and officers, especially those who had worked with Ludendorff over the years. Guidelines for the group's events and speaker training were even reminiscent of Ludendorff's wartime program of "patriotic instruction" in the army. That program, like the Tannenberg League's, aimed at "enlightening" Germans concerning the national mission and exerting tight control over gatherings to prevent free-wheeling discussions from becoming derailed.[39]

Many völkisch groups fostered hopes of winning over the working class to the nationalist cause. Like the National Socialists, the Tannenbergers imagined a Germany free of class conflict, in which all classes of the Volk contributed to the national mission willingly. Not only the Nazis but also prominent groups like the Deutschvölkische Schutz- und Trutzbund lavished attention and propaganda on workers hoping to wean them from Marxism.[40] Ludendorff's Tannenberg League tried as well. Ludendorff claimed to have the trust of labor leaders such as Karl Legien as a result of satisfactory wartime cooperation. Whether Legien actually trusted Ludendorff or (much less) could have been won over to Ludendorff's schemes seems doubtful.[41] The group nevertheless tried to attract workers, not without success. Records are scanty, but mailing lists for one Landesverband name at least one or two recipients of Tannenberg publications from the working class.[42] Ludendorff's associate Robert Holtzmann deemed one working-class speaker, Allert, particularly effective in spreading the Tannenberg League's message, even though his presentations lacked the polish of a speaker with more formal education.[43]

The Tannenberg League claimed that Ludendorff's true feelings for the workers had manifested in the war. Ludendorff, they claimed, kept food prices low for the benefit of the working class. He fostered discussions between workers and employers about the issues important to them. If workers were unhappy, it was because their Socialist leadership and civilian government failed them.[44] In reality, of course, Ludendorff's star sat very low on the Socialist horizon. Wartime losses and Ludendorff's elbow-rubbing with industrialists during the war had not made him a popular figure among the class-conscious workers. Hitler himself in 1924 deemed Ludendorff a liability in trying to attract working-class support.[45] It wasn't for lack of trying. At various times, Ludendorff advocated a strengthened social safety net, with accident, old age, and unemployment benefits, and an eight-hour work day.[46]

In terms of an actual economic program, Tannenberger plans were often vague. Like the more conservative among his former National Socialist contacts, Ludendorff hoped to revive a healthy middle class of small shopkeepers and skilled craftsmen by rescuing them from the unfair competition of large concerns and trusts.[47] How the Tannenberg League would reconcile those goals with strengthening the working class remained largely unresolved, as they did with the Nazis.

Longtime associate of Ludendorff, Herbert Frank, wrote a manuscript titled "Aristocratic Leadership in Large Industry," in which he argues that great inventors and organizers create technology and lay the groundwork for economic progress but that later, lesser men focus too narrowly on profit and mechanization and cannot control the technology bequeathed to them. Man thereby becomes slave to the machine. What is needed, argued Frank, is a kind of "technical General Staff" to oversee the economy and direct it toward useful, productive, "völkisch" ends. New leaders would be born out of this staff system who could guide the economy and the nation toward a more fulfilling, "organic" future.[48]

However, Frank later admitted that the Tannenberg League had no economic program. "If the German people could have been helped by programs, then it certainly would have happened in the last years. . . . As a consequence, Ludendorff is an enemy of programs and recipes." The important thing was to keep the greater goal in mind, the freedom of the German Volk.[49] Everything else would work itself out. In a strange way, this approach sounds like the opposite of Ludendorff's plan for Operation Michael. In that endeavor, Ludendorff famously said that the important thing was to attack, to breakthrough. The overall strategy would work itself out later.

In keeping with typical völkisch belief, Ludendorff held that "the moral-spiritual and racial [*blutmäßige*] recovery of Germany demands an energetic peasantry, free of all bureaucratic and capitalist restraints, which at one time had provided the old armies with the most and the best recruits."[50] These peasants should be settled as thickly as possible near the Polish border in order to defend against Polish encroachment and to form a "basis for the recovery of German land." Sport and education would further the peasants' development and provide paramilitary training as well.[51] The same mailing lists cited above contained a significant plurality of farmers and independent landowners, so the group must have had some success in recruiting from the agricultural sector.[52]

With *Frau Doktor* Mathilde Ludendorff as the spiritual leader of the movement, the Tannenberg League could (and frequently did) make some

legitimate claims to representing the interests of women against the mi-
sogynist tendencies of other political groups. Especially after 1927, the
group supported women's suffrage and some measure of equal rights.
Erich Ludendorff claimed to have welcomed female suffrage in the new
constitution of 1919 because he had seen firsthand how men had failed to
govern.[53] In Mathilde's Gotterkenntnis, it was vital that women be directly
involved and have power, otherwise the "racial soul" would suffer.[54]

Numerous flyers and pamphlets issuing from the Ludendorff publishing house were dedicated to supposed women's issues: marriage, children,
or the persecution of women.[55] A Ms. L Oßwald from Heidelberg lent her
name to a booklet titled "Why Join Ludendorff's Tannenberg League?"
While not exclusively directed at women, the pamphlet emphasized how
dissatisfied Oßwald had been in the NSDAP, dominated as it was by men.
Whereas the NSDAP sought only women's votes and prevented them from
assuming responsible positions in the party, Oßwald believed that the
Tannenberg League valued women. She approvingly cites Erich Ludendorff: "Though their natures differ, woman and man are equal in the living
unity of the Volk. Women should regain the high position in the Volk and
in the family that they once held in the days of our ancestors, before the
infiltration of a foreign ideology."[56]

Increasingly after 1927, the same year Erich officially renounced his
Evangelical Church membership, the Tannenberg League promoted the
ideas of Mathilde Ludendorff and her "Germanic understanding of God,"
to the point that the distinction between the league ideals of promoting social and national goals, and the beliefs of the "Philosopheress" Mathilde
becomes meaningless.[57] The group developed an increasingly cultlike
character, with followers devoted to the "Feldherr couple" of Erich and
Mathilde.[58] When the Nazis banned the Tannenberg League in 1933 (see
below), this "religion" and the publishing house that peddled the Ludendorffs' wares became the home for Tannenbergers set adrift.

Deutsche Gotterkenntnis

In numerous works published between 1917 and her death in 1966,
Mathilde developed a spiritual program that she believed would ensure
the survival and prosperity of the German race.[59] Her first book was

1917's *Das Weib und seine Bestimmung* (Woman and her fate), which promised a new approach to female psychology, followed by *Erotische Wiedergeburt* (Erotic rebirth) in 1919.[60] As mentioned above, Mathilde made a splash in neopagan circles with her 1922 work, *Triumph des Unsterblichkeitswillen*.[61] In 1924, *Der Seele Ursprung und Wesen* (The soul: Its origin and nature) appeared, followed over the next decade by further volumes on that theme.[62] These works introduce certain key concepts that bound her philosophy together.[63] Even her first work shows the concern for "authenticity" and "truth" that would attract so many followers.

Like most religions, Deutsche Gotterkenntnis concerns itself with death and the nature of reality. According to Mathilde's view, man's current understanding of reality was clouded by the "mad teachings" of established religions, especially Christianity and Judaism.[64] Mathilde was educated as a scientist, a fact she never tired of reminding her followers. This scientific training, she claimed, enabled her to see through the façade of the world's religions to expose their superstitious and illogical cores. Belief in miracles and an afterlife, virgin birth and resurrection, for example, required a suspension of reason that was incompatible with reality.[65] Her belief was spiritual, she claimed, and yet nevertheless fully congruent with modern science.[66]

She touted her revelations as realistic, even if painful, because she recognized the inevitability of death, and yet promised no salvation or eternal life. Rather, one found immortality through one's racial belonging. By working on behalf of the racial community, maintaining its purity, and cultivating its inherent strengths, one did ensure an afterlife, of a kind, in the undying race to which one belonged. Just as important, one would achieve a self-awareness denied to subscribers of other beliefs as well as a heightened ability to experience pleasure in life's simplest occurrences.[67] Above all, the Ludendorffers valued "freedom." Believers described Erich Ludendorff as one of only a handful of truly "free Germans."[68] "Bound" (*gebunden*) was the codeword to describe adherents of Freemasonry and the other supranational powers. Ludendorff's followers were "free," and most signed their correspondence "Long live Freedom!" even when doing so could bring the unwelcome attention of the Gestapo after 1933.

Her philosophy is usually described as neopagan, and yet the "god" that Mathilde sought to understand is hardly a "god" in the usual pagan (let alone Judeo-Christian) sense. God is rather the ineffable essence that permeates the world and every individual in it. This "god" leads human beings to higher levels of self-awareness, provided they properly prepare themselves for the experience. Each individual's soul develops just as an organism does, through various stages of consciousness toward enlightenment, according to Mathilde.[69]

In the Gotterkenntnis system, each race possessed its own particular (*arteigene*) sense of the godly. The notion of individual races each possessing a unique path to the understanding of god's "will" is not inherently racist, Ludendorff would argue. In fact, many commentators have noted a certain understanding among some völkisch ideologues for the Zionist project.[70] Even in the 1930s, believers sometimes took great pains to emphasis that their philosophy was not inherently xenophobic. "Deutsche Gotterkenntnis shows respect to other peoples and races as manifestations of God," wrote one commentator in 1935, "but requires [one] to protect the maintenance, freedom, and spiritual life [*Gotterleben*] of one's own Volk."[71] A faithful Christian, for example, "deserves tolerance and respect for his conviction," provided he does not seek to force his beliefs on a true German.[72]

But the practical result of such a philosophy (and the firm conviction of most followers) was the forceful exclusion of non-Germans and especially Jews, from German political, social, and economic life, since their "alien" worldview made them unsuitable to wield any influence. Failure to live according to one's own sense of the divine would lead to "racial death." Racial mixing was viewed a mortal danger to the Volk, as were "foreign beliefs."[73]

Reality, or truth, could only be "revealed" by careful recognition of the forces inhibiting our perceptions. For Mathilde, and increasingly for Erich as well, these forces were the "supranational powers" of Judaism, Catholicism, and Freemasonry. In a 1960 article on Mathilde, one reporter described the pair's philosophy aptly as a "cabinet of horrors. Freemasons, Jesuits, Christian clergy in general and Socialist functionaries were at times exposed by [Ludendorff] as spineless tools of that worst of all the 'supranational powers,' namely Jewry, at other times however, he presented them as wildly antagonist fellow aspirants for world power."[74]

More sensational publications also generated attention for her fundamental ideas. *Erlösung von Jesu Christo* (Salvation from Jesus Christ), which appeared in 1931, argued that Christianity was merely a fiction invented by Jews in order to alienate Germans and other races from their true natures, weakening them by imposing a foreign belief system based on pacifism and the fantasy of an eternal afterlife.[75] *Christliche Grausamkeit an deutschen Frauen* (Christian atrocities committed against German women) (1934) detailed the rape and corruption of women that allegedly took place under the auspices of Catholicism.[76] Leering priests, dark-robed representations of Death, and other ominous images adorned the covers of many of the Ludendorff Verlag's books.

To describe Mathilde Ludendorff's entire philosophy is, as one postwar detractor described it in a fit of understatement, "extraordinarily difficult." Part of the difficulty stems from her prose style, which reflects "a vagueness of thought that is often mistaken for "depth" among a readership living in a musty state of half-education."[77]She presents her ideas as a series of revelations, uncovering truths hidden by the machinations of the supranational powers.[78] Readers should feel privileged to receive Mathilde's insights into the nature of reality. Even her first work, *Erotische Wiedergeburt*, written before her Gotterkenntnis philosophy matured, reflects this conspiratorial tone. "Some life questions touch the destiny of the individual and the collective so deeply," she wrote, "that one is not supposed to write books about them."[79] The danger was too real that both the author and the reader would lose their naïveté and be forced to confront the reality of existence. Her book promised to answer just such fundamental questions.

Once her work began to attract prominent criticism, she began to prophesize such attacks. Others, she warned, especially those beholden to the supranational powers, might mock or threaten believers who spread Gotterkenntnis. They might call one crazy for doubting the truth of Christianity, for example. Their scorn was only proof of one's correctness, she argued; their hostility was proof that one had become a threat to expose their lies. "The great goal of [Ludendorff's] struggle is to restore freedom to the German soul through the creation of a unity of blood and belief. Self-preservation in the service of preserving the Volk, Volk-preservation in the service of preserving God, and the creating of God [*Gottgestaltung*] in the Volk are the guiding principles for living in Deutsche Gotterkenntnis."[80]

In 1929, after falling out with the publisher of the Tannenberg League newspaper, *Deutsche Wochenschau*, the couple founded their own publishing company, Ludendorffs Verlag.[81] They started a new paper, now

Figure 10. Ad for Mathilde Ludendorff, *Erlösung von Jesu Christo*, 1931.
Institute für Zeitgeschichte, Munich, Library Holdings Ok180.

dubbed *Ludendorffs Volkswarte* and marketed the works of both Erich and Mathilde, as well those of fellow believers. Owning the company almost entirely themselves, the Ludendorffs were also able to profit handsomely from the continued national resonance of the Feldherr's name and the not-insignificant sales of Mathilde's works.

Both Ludendorffs were enormously prolific. I have already described the feverish pace at which Erich composed his wartime memoirs. In the early 1920s, he authored several more books and documents collections, and after 1925, the pace hardly slowed. Further editions of memoirs, including his pre- and postwar life, appeared. The publishing house produced countless pamphlets and booklets promoting his worldview. His newspaper, *Ludendorffs Volkswarte* and its successors, relied on regular contributions from the Feldherr to maintain readers' interest. In addition to the works described above, Mathilde authored numerous pamphlets and contributed frequently to the various journals their group published.[82]

Coworkers and family described some of the habits that sustained this enormous output. Wilhelm Freiherr von Gayl, who during the war headed the Ober Ost Political Department and later became interior minister, wrote that Ludendorff seemed to have a cabinet in his head, with countless drawers that he could open at a moment's notice, so that he would have "all the facts and a few well-considered thoughts" before him.[83] Erich's first wife, Margarethe recalled Erich receiving many visitors after the Beer Hall Putsch, and "every account and observation seemed to be of importance to him." He called this kind of work, "mosaic work," piecing together small details in order to acquire a truer picture of the whole.[84] Visitors to Ludendorff's house recall seeing his work area strewn with books, journals, newspapers and other documents.[85] Obviously, such an approach could also produce lunatic conspiracy theories, not just truth. It was Ludendorff's urge to connect disparate events and facts (the date of Luther's death, an utterance of Kaiser Wilhelm I, the words engraved on a soldier's belt buckle) that produced the globe-spanning conspiracy involving the "supranational powers."

Conspiracy sold and kept the Ludendorffs quite comfortable, at least. According to sources loyal to Ludendorff, he received as a retired commanding general a pension of 17,333 marks, which was reduced to 12,000 (1,000/month) by Reichstag legislation.[86] Ludendorff liked to claim that the publishing company generated little income and that most profits went back into advertising and spreading Gotterkenntnis. However, the fervor with which he pushed sales representatives, dismissed employees he thought were not pulling their weight, sued business partners, and the sheer volume of materials emanating from the publishing house would seem to belie the claim. "The Haus Ludendorff was able to turn [their] outrageous propaganda [against Jews, Freemasons, and Christians] into clinking coinage," writes Bettina Amm, a scholar of the Ludendorff movement.[87] In 1929, Ludendorff reported to his Landesführer a net profit for the publishing company of 3,300 Reichsmarks as well as a significant contribution to the advertising budget of 15,000 Reichsmarks. Ludendorffs Verlag carried a significant debt burden, but overall seemed healthy.[88] No records are available, but Ludendorff must also have earned significant income from his memoirs, which sold in the hundreds of thousands in Germany and abroad.

Supranational Powers

In the Ludendorffs' worldview, world history had been steered for hundreds of years by a global conspiracy of Jews, Catholics, and Freemasons. In a previous chapter, I described Erich Ludendorff's growing antisemitism after 1919. By 1922, he had begun to see other forces, Freemasons and the Catholic Church, at work, sometimes in league with Jews and at other times in competition.[89] These Ludendorff dubbed the "supranational powers" (*überstaatliche Mächte*).

Similar ideas were prevalent in the völkisch milieu. Ludendorff's convictions mirrored those of members of the Deutschvölkische Schutz- und Trutzbund, established by the leaders of the Pan-German League after the war to spread an antisemitic message to the masses. Antisemitism meshed quite easily with anti-Masonic beliefs and provided a reliable means to slander one's opponents. If an enemy could not be proven to be Jewish, then they must be Freemasons, whose alleged secrecy both precluded the need to provide evidence of membership and prevented those so-labeled from effectively defending themselves.[90]

What distinguished Ludendorff's group from most others was its profound anti-Catholicism and its willingness openly to attack Christianity as a whole.[91] "I am anti-Christian and a pagan and proud of it," proclaimed

Ludendorff to his followers, in order to clarify his religious affiliation.[92] Ludendorff's stance on Christianity was not unique, but like other elements of the Tannenberg program, was cobbled from ideas already common in the völkisch milieu in which he moved after 1919. Theodor Fritsch, whose Reichshammerbund, founded in 1912, was both antisemitic and anti-Christian, called for the maintenance and promotion of a "healthy German character [*Eigenart*]" in terms very much like those Ludendorff would later use.[93]

It was central to the Ludendorffs' belief system that Christianity was an alien, non-German import that was incompatible with the German spirit. In her most extreme expression, Mathilde insisted that Christianity was concocted by Jews out of a mishmash of Jewish tradition and Hindu spiritualism. Bizarre contradictions sometimes arose from their anti-Christian stance. When one Tannenberger tried to argue, à la Julius Langbehn or Ludwig Woltmann, that since the ancient Germans were the wellsprings of all culture, Jesus and Mary of Nazareth must have been *Germanen*, he received a sharp rebuke from the regional leader of the group.[94]

Ludendorff certainly avowed an anti-Christian belief but it was primarily anti-Catholic. As Steigmann-Gall argues, Ludendorff's attacks on Christianity nevertheless reflect a Protestant upbringing and hint that Protestantism could perhaps be salvaged if it opened its eyes to the Roman/Jesuit threat. To many nationalists, Protestantism was one of the symbols and products of a proud German culture.[95] Observers at the time and since have speculated that Ludendorff's origins in the borderlands of Posen, so near to Polish Catholic territory, heightened his sense of the correlation of German and Protestant.[96]

Like most of his conspiratorial fantasies, Ludendorff's hostility to Catholicism, though eventually far-reaching, had at least tenuous roots in his real wartime activities. Pope Benedict XV made several fruitless appeals to the warring powers to cease hostilities. One appeal, made in August 1917, though officially ignored by all but the United States, seems to have irked Ludendorff, who at the time was nearing the high point of his confidence in the prospects for German victory. The pope's messenger to the German government was none other than Eugenio Pacelli, papal nuncio for Bavaria and later the controversial Pope Pius XII. One can only imagine the fits Ludendorff would have thrown if he had lived to see his nemesis named pope in 1939.

Ludendorff's convictions concerning the supranational powers led him to stances that sharply differentiated him from the nationalist circles with which one might usually associate him. For example, the Teutonic Knights, staples of nationalist lore, are for Ludendorff representatives of a more ambiguous legacy. While they spread German culture, which pleased Ludendorff, they did so at the behest of the Catholic Church, which made them suspect. According to Ludendorff's "research," these crusaders extinguished in East Prussia a native German pagan culture whose heritage the Tannenberg League was struggling to recover.[97] Even the motto of the old imperial army was suspect in Ludendorff's eyes. "With God for King and Fatherland" significantly omitted the word *Volk* and substituted *Fatherland*, which represented for Ludendorff either a glorification of the state at the expense of the people or a sinister reference to Israel, referred to by Jews also as "Fatherland."[98]

Leaders of the Christian churches in Germany struggled with how to respond to the various attacks issuing from the Haus Ludendorff. As mostly reasonable and rational men and women, they were sorely tempted to ignore the flimsy pamphlets issuing from the Ludendorff press. As mostly patriotic Germans, they were understandably reluctant to attack the former general who had fought so hard for Germany in the Great War. But for this very reason, because of Ludendorff's prominence, they also feared that he and his wife might sway some Germans with their pseudo-scientific approach to spirituality.

During his 1924 trial for treason, for example, Ludendorff claimed to have exposed the ultramontanist, separatist aspirations of Bavaria's Catholic establishment, prompting the *Bayerischer Kurier* to collect the hostile responses of Germany's Catholic press to Ludendorff's suggestions. Ludendorff's attacks harked back to the violent days of the Reformation and Thirty Years' War, wrote the *Kölnische Zeitung*, while other papers saw him reviving the Kulturkampf of the nineteenth century.[99]

Each book and pamphlet authored by the Ludendorffs, especially those that carried Erich's name, tended to generate a flurry of rebuttals. For example, the coauthored Ludendorff publication, *Das große Entsetzen; die Bibel nicht Gottes Wort* (The great horror—the Bible is not the word of God), prompted Hans Freiherr von Soden, a professor of theology at the University of Marburg, to pose the rhetorical question, *Hat Ludendorff recht?* (Is Ludendorff right?) in a pamphlet of his own.[100] The Ludendorffs' book adopted the premise that since the Bible has historical origins, it cannot be the word of God. Soden attacked the very premise of the book as flawed, noting that Christian scholarship, which the Ludendorffs ignore, does not consider the historical origins of the work to impact its divine provenance. Of course it is an historical work, written by human hands, but it contains the spirit of God, Soden insisted. The fact that there is uncertainty and interpretation associated with the Bible was, for Soden, only proof of man's imperfection, not of the Bible's inauthenticity. Scholars are not, as the Ludendorffs claim, covering up their findings on the Bible's origins. They are published for all to see. It is just that the Ludendorffs have ignored that literature.[101]

Typical of these defenses, and revealing of Ludendorff's place in German political culture, is that even his vocal critics pay homage to his great achievements during the war. Hans Freiherr von Soden acknowledged Ludendorff's leadership at Liège and the great responsibility that the Feldherr bore as part of the Supreme Command. However, just as someone who is not a doctor should not treat the sick and someone who knows nothing of the sea should not captain a ship, Ludendorff should not comment on religious matters, Soden believed.[102] Others seemed to want to ignore the degree to which Ludendorff himself guided the actions of the Tannenberg League. A hostile newspaper article about a Tannenberg lecture in Rosenow (near Rostock) lamented that the "soldier Ludendorff, highly respected by millions of Germans, would be connected with the disgusting rabble-rousing of the so-called Tannenberg League."[103]

It is often surprising how seriously their Christian opponents took the Ludendorffs outlandish charges. Critics disputed on very technical grounds the Ludendorffs' use of specific Bible passages. They cited recent scholarship that belied specific claims, such as the charge in *Das große Entsetzen* that the apostles copied the Bible from various Hindu texts.[104] In 1936, the Apologetische Centrale (AC) of the Evangelical Church, a group founded in 1921 to combat anti-Christian movements, published as systematic an analysis as possible of Ludendorff's central claims and methodology.[105] The church acknowledged Ludendorff's powerful influence, not just within his own circle, but on the broader public through the circulation of *Am heiligen Quell* (which the AC estimated at seventy thousand biweekly issues) and through his early powerful influence on völkisch ideology of the type represented by Alfred Rosenberg and others. One had to recognize the fundamental principles on which Ludendorff based his arguments if one did not want to be drawn into a fruitless debate over the historical details—that "mosaic"—that Ludendorff mastered.

For Ludendorff, Christianity was merely a form of Jewish propaganda, designed to blind and weaken European peoples through the promulgation of Jewish law (the Old Testament) and the promulgation of a "depraved" fantasy of human equality and salvation. These teachings blinded Germans to the importance of race. Therefore, according to Ludendorff, "the rejection of Christianity's teachings was the most logical sort of antisemitism."[106] The Catholic Church in its form reflected Jewish teachings, Ludendorff claimed. The power of the priests and the supremacy of the pope atop his enormous hierarchy contradicted Christ's teachings of equality and reflected instead the practices and worldview of the (Jewish) Old Testament (as Ludendorff understood it).[107] Therefore, while Rome, as one of the supranational powers, fought its own battle for supremacy, it was crippled by its origins in its struggle with its supranational rival, "international Jewry."

Protestantism and Freemasonry, which similarly preached equality and the brotherhood of man, were merely creations of the Jewish power to counterbalance the strength of the pope. The Catholic Church responded by founding the Jesuits, so that the competition for world power could continue—a battle Ludendorff compared to the "battle between the sons of the dwarven king Alberich for the Nibelung hoard."[108] Ludendorff's worldview was merely a particularly radical form of the völkisch ideology. "Although the supranational powers fought amongst themselves, they present for Ludendorff in his secular mindset a significant internal unity, because their origins and their goals are the same."[109]

Attacks coming from the mainstream churches, and later from the Nazis themselves, Ludendorff would parry by wrapping himself, hypocritically one might judge, in the Weimar constitution. That document guaranteed religious freedom and the rights of Jews and other religious minorities but also, of course, created space for Ludendorff and other neopagans.[110] Likewise, point 24 of the NSDAP 25 Point Program promised freedom of religion. Ludendorff found that principle incompatible with the statement that followed, espousing "Positive Christianity," but nevertheless insisted after 1933 with some success that his group be afforded the same rights.

Ludendorff Publishing House

The predominance of Deutsche Gotterkenntnis and the fixation on the supranational powers within the Tannenberg League became complete with the creation of the publishing company, Ludendorffs Verlag. Individual members of the Tannenberg League were responsible for canvassing a given region, distributing flyers and pamphlets, contacting subscribers of *Volkswarte*, and enlisting new members. Judging from the amount of correspondence concerning the provision of speakers, lectures were the centerpiece of the Tannenberg League's activities. These ranged from small "discussion evenings," sometimes held in private homes, to large public lectures in beer halls or other auditoriums. The Tannenberg League held annual, or sometimes biannual conferences at the national and Gau levels. The larger gatherings required extensive preparations. Members sold tickets well in advance. The central leadership insisted that lectures be well advertised and no more than two hours long. They instructed organizers to choose catchy titles and print flyers, whenever possible, in German script (*Fraktur*). Larger gatherings presented the opportunity not only to induct new members but to turn a profit through the sale of books and other Ludendorff materials.[111]

Ludendorff placed great significance on winning as many new subscribers to his *Volkswarte* as possible. Individual Kampfgruppen received a kickback from the publishing house for each new subscriber.[112] The group hoped to persuade through the distribution of literature. The press distributed free copies of their newspapers and pamphlets liberally. Ludendorff placed special emphasis on the recruitment of members of the military and saw the permission to distribute his journal in military barracks as one of the key victories won during his gradual reconciliation with the Nazis.[113] Ludendorff always commented on military affairs in the journal, hoping thereby to pique the interest of officers in his larger ideological program.[114]

The publishing company targeted specific social and occupational groups by offering works that would presumably interest them. The press adopted a multipronged approach to marketing. Teachers might be interested in *Des Kindes Seele* (The soul of a child), while *Blut, Glaube, Recht* (Blood, belief, law) might appeal to lawyers. Ludendorff was a popular figure, and his books always sold more widely than Mathilde's or those produced by other authors in the group. Knowing that his works would reach many not already committed to Deutsche Gotterkenntnis, he would sprinkle his mainstream works with references to the more provocative materials published by the press. A military history buff or current and former officers might pick up Erich Ludendorff's *Mein militärischer Werdegang* (My military career) hoping to learn more about the war hero before he joined the Supreme Command in 1916.[115] The book does describe Ludendorff's life in the old army, as the subtitle promises. But it also details Erich's discomfort at being quartered in Catholic homes, which he described as having a "foreign air."[116] The reader would "learn," while reading the account of Kaiser Wilhelm's trip upon assuming the throne in 1888 to visit his grandmother, Queen Victoria (Ludendorff was serving as an army liaison with the German fleet that visited the Isle of Wight), that the future king of England, Edward, was a dedicated Freemason, intent on destroying Germany. Further details could be found, Ludendorff reminded the reader, in his 1931 book, *Kriegshetze und Völkermorden* (War fever and racial murder).[117] The company targeted schools, reading circles, army reading lounges, pubs, and any other location where their message might find sympathy.

The Ludendorff press tried to capitalize on current events in order to maximize their audience and their sales. In conjunction with the approaching twentieth anniversary of the Tannenberg battle in 1934, for example, the publishing company notified its representatives to expect greater interest in the Feldherr's "historical" works and to promote that interest through advertising. Works such as *Wie der Weltkrieg "gemacht" wurde* (How the World War was "made") and *Mein militärischer Werdegang* could be expected to sell especially well.[118] When the Nazi regime introduced conscription in 1935, coincidentally the year that Ludendorff would celebrate his seventieth birthday, the Feldherr predicted greater interest in his works. The press produced a special birthday edition of *Am heiligen Quell* to fill that need.[119] Periodic big pushes were made to peddle a certain specific title as with *Das Volks Schicksal in christlichen Bildwerken* (The fate of the people in Christian imagery, 1934) or, even more so, *Der totale Krieg* (The total war), when it appeared in 1935.[120]

Tannenbergers sold wherever they could. A casual meeting on a train could lead to further contacts, as it did when Georg Eitzen sent some of Ludendorff's publications to a Herr Heinrichs of Hamburg after such a chance encounter.[121] In order to attract new followers, the Ludendorffs created materials in a variety of formats, ranging from pamphlets costing only a few pennies to introduce people to the concepts of Deutsche Gotterkenntnis to full-fledged books that developed Erich and Mathilde's ideas more fully. One gets the sense, however, that their efforts, while not completely in vain, produced disappointing results. It is perhaps telling that the Reich leadership of the Tannenberg League warned its affiliates that some Germans might be unwilling to subscribe because they feared the scorn of their neighbors when *Volkswarte* arrived in the mail. In such cases, they advised, the local leader should subscribe for the person in question and personally deliver the paper to the house. I suppose they had not yet invented the brown paper wrapper.[122]

The regional representatives of the publishing company were constantly beseeching their local salespeople to work harder, to advertise more, to generate more subscribers. Occasional successes would be loudly trumpeted in monthly circulars to show less productive reps what was possible. In September 1935, the Ludendorff paper—now dubbed *Am heiligen Quell Deutscher Kraft* (At the holy source of German strength), in order to avoid a Nazi ban—had a circulation of 66,572, which seems sizable.[123] A monthly subscription in 1938 cost only sixty-four pfennige.[124] Often, however, new subscribers to *Am heiligen Quell* could be counted in single digits for a given month. Cards registering new converts to Deutsche Gotterkenntnis would trickle in to Ludendorff in ones and twos.[125] Judging from the amount of correspondence, representatives spent much of their time entreating booksellers to carry their works and businesses to take out ads in their journals.[126]

Most early gatherings of the Tannenberg League would likely have been barely distinguishable from NSDAP rallies or the meetings of other groups on the völkisch right wing. Fiery speakers would rail against "international capital," "Jewish banking," liberal democracy, and the Weimar Republic, calling for a repeat of November 9, 1923, that would finally overthrow the hated Weimar system.[127] The only notable difference in the early years might be the Tannenberg League's more pronounced anti-Catholicism.[128]

Gotterkenntnis gatherings had a more esoteric tone. Speakers were carefully trained in the tenets of Deutsche Gotterkenntnis and often in the techniques of public speaking. According to Erich Ludendorff, Gotterkenntnis speakers should not so much lecture as serve as "guides" into the works of his wife.[129] That meant the subject matter addressed could be fairly opaque to one not immersed in Mathilde's philosophy. A meeting in 1937 addressed topics from *Triumph des Unsterblichkeitswillen* such as "The origin of races [*Arten*] as the path to the meaning of life"; "Consciousness as the path to an eternal godly life"; "The gap between the struggle for existence and the meaning of life and how to overcome it"; "The meaning of life and the lesson of chivalric love [*Minne*]."[130]

By 1930, the leadership of the Tannenberg League was investigating how to have Deutsche Gotterkenntnis registered as a recognized religion, akin to Lutheranism and Catholicism. According the Weimar constitution, religious societies of a certain age and size were guaranteed the rights and protections of a public corporation.[131] The transformation from völkisch-nationalist association to spiritual community was nearly complete.

The Nazis banned the Tannenberg League on September 22, 1933, just nine months after Hitler's appointment as chancellor.[132] The Ludendorffs

Figure 11. Ludendorff Bookstore in Berlin. Photo by Keystone-France \ Gamma-Rapho via Getty Images.

had feared a Nazi takeover as early as 1931 or 1932 and had prepared for the eventuality.[133] Officially, Ludendorff dissolved the organization and released its members from related obligations. He tried to put as brave a face on the ban as possible, writing to his followers that he hoped the ban would allow believers to fight for the great "idea" that was Gotterkenntnis without the "difficulties" involved in managing an organization. But the dangers were clear. Without the organizational structure, the frequent meetings and discussions, the group threatened to disintegrate into its myriad factions.[134]

The league continued to exist in all but name only, however. The leadership of the league (the Gauführer and such) simply became "representatives" of the Ludendorff publishing house. Ludendorff bookstores became informal meeting places.[135] *Ludendorffs Volkswarte*, the organ of the Tannenberg League, ceased publication as ordered, but *Am heiligen Quell* moved from a monthly to a biweekly publication schedule and carried on very much in the vein of *Volkswarte*. Former Tannenbergers were urged to subscribe.[136]

Preparedness and *Der totale Krieg*

Ludendorff's voice was not entirely unwelcome in Hitler's Germany, despite the persecutions. In the areas of military affairs and preparedness, his historic stature gave his viewpoints weight, and they were sometimes even welcomed in National Socialist and military circles. For the Ludendorffs, freedom of the individual depended also on freedom of the state from domination by foreign powers. In their group's "battle aims," published in 1930, Ludendorff wrote: "Preparedness and freedom require a race that is strong and full of character, filled with a sense of its godly task, proud of its blood and the achievements of its forebears, aware of its power, its obligations, and its rights."[137] Such language lent welcome support to plans for rearmament and an end to the restrictions of the Versailles Treaty.

As with most of his activities, there was always element of self-promotion in his commentaries. He widely publicized his stance on disarmament, which he viewed as "immoral" and contrary to the Volk's will to self-preservation. A prominent article in *Das wehrhafte Volk* ("The people prepared"—a periodic supplement to *Volkswarte*), surrounded by thick black lines for emphasis, informed his readers that the League of Nations had even solicited Ludendorff's opinion. Never mind that Ludendorff despised the League of Nations. He informed the league's organ, *Journal des Nations*, that armaments were not a danger to peace per se. Rather, their misuse by "supranational secret powers" to pit the peoples of the earth against one another caused war. Therefore, he argued, only enlightening people to the dangers of these powers could preserve peace.[138]

Like Hitler and many others, Ludendorff saw in the Versailles Treaty's disarmament provisions an element of hypocrisy. The authors of the treaty couched those provisions that limited Germany's armed forces to a negligible minimum as part of a larger process of general disarmament. Of course most of the victorious powers, especially Britain and France, did not disarm in any meaningful way, needing military power to maintain their respective empires. Ludendorff therefore welcomed the disarmament talks taking place in Geneva in 1932 and 1933. Though he remained skeptical (he saw the influence of Jews and Freemasons in the British delegation, of course), he believed British prime minister Ramsay MacDonald's proposal to increase the size of Germany's armed forces (to 200,000) while placing limits on other powers in the context of mutual security guarantees was a positive step.[139]

Ludendorff and his followers were fond of pointing out, particularly after Hitler's abrogation of the limits imposed on the Wehrmacht in 1935, that Ludendorff had advocated a strong national defense long before any other contemporary politician or commentator and had risked his career to achieve it. Ludendorff claimed to have recognized the problem as early as 1895, when Chancellor Caprivi introduced a law to increase the effective size of the army by reducing the length of service to two years. Ludendorff lamented that nothing approaching a universal obligation to service was put into practice. Many able-bodied men escaped.[140] His championing the army increase in 1912–13 was a perennial theme.[141]

The announcement of conscription in 1935 reenergized Ludendorff in his efforts to proselytize Deutsche Gotterkenntnis. "An army is rooted in the Volk," he wrote in *Am heiligen Quell*. "Enemy air attacks and blockades strike [the Volk] and involve it." "In this great hour of new preparedness [*Wehrhaftseins*] perhaps my warning voice will now be heard more clearly than has been the case." "The Volk needs to be unified on the basis of its racial awareness, both biological and spiritual, as shown us by my wife."[142] It was presumably around this time that Ludendorffers began wearing black-white-red armbands that read "Be Prepared Again [*Werdet wieder wehrhaft*]—Ludendorff" written in the Feldherr's own hand.[143]

Ludendorff reached the culmination of his career as a military analyst with the publication of *Der totale Krieg* in 1935.[144] The publication of *Der totale Krieg* was meant to be a major event for the press. "Every reader of this book," the press promised, "will ascribe to it a powerful Volk-preserving importance. It is of great importance that above all in the Wehrmacht that every post, but also every officer and every non-com and soldier must take notice of this book." The press offered special discounts and incentives to bookshops and press representatives who sold large numbers of books.[145] Like many of Ludendorff's works, *Der totale Krieg* was translated into numerous languages and widely reviewed in the press both in Germany and internationally.

The book, while littered with the odd relics of Ludendorff's conspiratorial obsession, was one that many Germans grappled with, even if they ultimately rejected some of its conclusions.[146] It is by no means (or at least is not merely) an effort by Ludendorff to defend or apologize for his wartime failures, as some historians have suggested.[147] Rather, it represents the distilled thoughts of a man still respected for his military insights. Chief of the General Staff Ludwig Beck greeted the book with "enthusiasm" and studied the work carefully.[148] Beck found many of his own thoughts on national mobilization mirrored in its pages. In a draft lecture opposing Hitler's aggressive stance vis-à-vis Czechoslovakia intended for presentation to senior army commanders, Beck used Ludendorff's concept of "total war" to refute the idea that military action alone could decide a future war. The diplomatic and political context in which any attack on Czechoslovakia would take place would ensure a long, and in Beck's estimation, unwinnable campaign.[149]

In Beck's military-strategic works of the last decade of his life, he referred "repeatedly and prominently" to Ludendorff's theory. In 1942, Beck delivered a lecture to the famed "Mittwochgesellschaft" that critically engaged *Der totale Krieg*.[150] To Beck, at least initially, Ludendorff's theory addressed the need for "general mobilization of all national resources for a national struggle for existence." Beck refused, however, to countenance Ludendorff's call for the total submission to the will of the military leader in times of war. For Beck, in times of war as well as peace, the state's political and military branches had to share power and policy making.[151] It is perhaps not too much to see in Beck's grappling with (and partial rejection of) *Der totale Krieg* the origins of his later staunch resistance to Hitler and Nazism. Wolfgang Foerster nearly goes so far when he links Beck's insistence on a "morally grounded politics" to the general's grappling with the problem of civilian versus military control in wartime.[152]

Central to Ludendorff's argument about "total war" and the formation of policy was an explicit attack on the theories of Carl von Clausewitz. Something must have happened between 1931 and 1935 to change his view of Clausewitz, because in 1931, an article appeared in the "Wehrhafte Volk" section of *Ludendorffs Volkswarte* that declared Clausewitz's work an "imperishable legacy" and a "gift, whose worth one would treasure as long as a single spark of fighting spirit lived in mankind."[153] In 1935, however, "all of Clausewitz's theories should be dumped in the garbage," Ludendorff wrote. While his fundamental approach to the battlefield itself may still have had its merits, for Ludendorff, Clausewitz's political ideas were badly outdated. There would be no such thing as limited wars in the future, only total war. In total war, Clausewitz's notion that war is simply the continuation of politics with the admixture of other means, no longer applied. Instead, Ludendorff insisted that politics must be made exclusively to serve military purposes. At times, he could even marshal Clausewitz's support to rationalize this total commitment. Clausewitz once wrote: "That a people should respect nothing higher than its honor and its freedom to exist. That it should defend these with the last drop of blood."[154] To carry this notion to its logical conclusion, thought Ludendorff, led inevitably to the notion of subordinating politics to national defense.

Total war would therefore require a new, "total politics" that operated as part of an integrated system, with the military commander at the top and military requirements taking precedence over civilian ones. The task of the political leader, and here Ludendorff more often used the term *Führer*, would be to prepare and mobilize the civilian component of the war effort. There is some evidence that during Hitler and Ludendorff's early association circa 1922–23, they developed the notion of a dual dictatorship with Ludendorff and the military and Hitler as the political leader.

Ludendorff's notion of civil-military relations is not just Clausewitz turned on his head. It also reflected his obsession with conspiracy and what he referred to as the "supranational powers": Jews, Catholics, and Freemasons. According to Ludendorff the Great War had been "total" not merely for the reasons cited above involving the scope and intensity of the conflict. In addition, 1914 had been the moment when the machinations of the "Jewish people and the Catholic Church" aimed at bleeding dry and dominating the peoples of Europe were finally revealed to those observers with sufficient insight.[155] This element of the war, more than any other, convinced Ludendorff that the world had entered a new phase, in which the German Volk would struggle for its very existence against both other peoples and nations of Europe and these supranational forces aiming at global domination.

So Ludendorff's was a war total in both means *and* ends in a way that Clausewitz probably never imagined. Implacable enemies both external and internal would need to be fought with extraordinary energy. While it might be possible to infer genocidal intentions in Ludendorff's philosophy, it is too much simply to draw a straight line between Ludendorff's book and Hitler's policies in World War II.[156] Even Hitler, one of the few politicians whose rhetorical violence exceeded Ludendorff's, arrived at an actual policy of genocide through a process of evolution and circumstance. Ludendorff had over the years proven himself a consummate talker but successful execution had eluded him too consistently since 1918 to believe he could have carried out plans as brutal and far-reaching as Hitler eventually did.

Official and semi-official German publications extensively reviewed Ludendorff's *Der totale Krieg* in 1935. The *Nationalsozialistische Parteikorrespondenz* praised the book's insights on the nature of war "no matter what other topics preoccupy [Ludendorff]." Hitler, if he had read the work, would have found many of his own views on war confirmed.[157] The book was widely read in General Staff circles, though leaders like Beck, too firmly steeped in Clausewitzian philosophy, ultimately found it lacking.[158] Nevertheless, the work contributed to a public debate on the nature of war, not least by introducing the terminology of "total war" to a German readership.[159]

Here I disagree with Roger Chickering and Bettina Amm over the issue of *Der totale Krieg*'s influence. Chickering is in general too quick to dismiss Ludendorff and his work as insignificant. Walter Görlitz insists that the book was carefully studied by the General Staff even if they ultimately rejected Ludendorff's conclusions.[160] Groener may have dismissed the book as "propaganda," as Chickering points out, but it is not true that "nowhere, outside the Ludendorff's house organs, was the book even reviewed."[161] On the contrary, in addition to those mentioned above, the *Zeitschrift für Politik* devoted nineteen pages to a review in 1936. Dozens of German and non-German journals reviewed the work and numerous articles mentioned it as influential on "totalitarian war" in the years prior to 1945.[162] Chickering neglects to mention that the work was also translated into English, as *The Nation at War*, as well as many other languages. Given the miniscule appeal of Deutsche Gotterkenntnis outside of Germany, these editions must have sold to persons outside of the movement. Within a few years, it had appeared in French, Chinese, Portuguese, and even Bengali.

Further evidence for the influence of Ludendorff's work comes from a wide-ranging 1936 article titled "Politik und Wehrmacht als Mittel der Kriegsführung" that appeared in the *Militärwissenschaftliche Rundschau*, a prominent German military journal. The author, retired lieutenant colonel Wilhelm Müller-Loebnitz, engaged extensively with *Der totale Krieg*, as well as Ludendorff's 1920 compilation *Kriegsführung und Politik*. Müller-Loebnitz faulted Ludendorff for placing so much responsibility in the hands of the Feldherr that such an individual would have to be nearly superhuman—as Ludendorff's own experience at the end of the war should have shown.[163]

Nor was *Der totale Krieg* the only work of Ludendorff's to receive attention. Retired lieutenant general Konstantin von Altrock very favorably reviewed the memoir of Ludendorff's early life, *Mein militärischer Werdegang*, which appeared in 1933. Perhaps surprisingly, Altrock entirely ignores the references to the supranational powers littered throughout the book. His only criticism is that Ludendorff is too hard on the senior leadership of the army—especially those unable to defend themselves from the grave (presumably an allusion to Moltke). Nevertheless, like many other commentators of the time, Altrock lamented that Ludendorff had not had greater influence on the overall direction of the war in 1914. Instead, seniority determined military leadership for too long when greater merit should have been given to personal qualities, such as those Ludendorff possessed.[164]

Many biographers have described Ludendorff as increasingly isolated in his villa in Tutzing, south of Munich, during the final years of his life. There is a certain truth in that. Ludendorff and his followers simply could not match the activism of Hitler and the Nazis, either before or after January 1933.[165] Ludendorff's style of leadership was dogmatic, where Hitler (at least until the end of the 1930s) remained nimble enough to take advantage of political opportunity. Hitler could play both national savior and common man, while Ludendorff was by nature more aloof. He isolated himself intentionally, and it was grounds for expulsion from the Tannenberg League to write directly to Erich or Mathilde without permission.[166]

The preceding chapter has shown, however, that despite Nazi persecution and the unpopularity of his anti-Christian ideology, Ludendorff remained a figure of enormous public significance. It was because of Ludendorff's continued high profile and strong reputation for nationalism and military genius that both the National Socialist government and the German military sought to bring him back onto the public stage.

6

DUELIST

Ludendorff, Hindenburg, Hitler

> The dwarves brought so much gold and jewelry out of the mountain
> that more than a hundred wagons would not have been able to carry
> the treasure away. Siegfried divided the treasure honestly in two
> equal and equally valuable parts. But he received no thanks for his
> trouble. Schilbung as well as Nibelung called him an unfair judge
> and each of the men disparaged Siegfried for having cheated them.
> They even threatened Siegfried, called their warriors hither, and
> attacked him.
>
> —DIE NIBELUNGEN

Ludendorff's real political power had clearly peaked by 1925, and while
he continued to participate in political intrigues, he was never again the
man who "had the world by the ear" during the war (as mentioned by
Mencken earlier) or who pulled levers behind the scenes as he had been
during the Kapp and Beer Hall putsches.[1] He nevertheless remained an important part of a symbolic and political struggle for influence in German
political culture. Ludendorff was notoriously combative and fought publicly with many notable Germans of the era, from a lingering wartime feud
with Prince Rupprecht of Bavaria, to sparring matches with intellectuals
such as Hans von Delbrück and Max Weber. It was Paul von Hindenburg
and Adolf Hitler with whom Ludendorff most often and most significantly crossed swords. Ludendorff's separate but related battles with Hindenburg and Hitler to have his narrative of the war and revolution prevail

and to have his vision guide Germany's future most determined his significance for German political culture.

It became one of Ludendorff's many obsessions later in life to insist
that he alone was responsible for the great victories at Liège and Tannenberg. The story of Ludendorff's bravery at Liège was central to his
later efforts to combat the evidence of his "loss of nerve/breakdown" in
1918. As George Mosse points out, "willpower," so essential to the turn
of the century notions of mental health, "was usually equated with courage."[2] Ludendorff's "storming" of the citadel at Liège provided concrete
evidence of his courage and willpower.

Ludendorff played on the legend of Liège for the rest of his life, linking it
most prominently to his participation in the Beer Hall Putsch in 1923.[3] Liège
served to establish not only Ludendorff's personal bravery, but the battle also
became a metaphor for his promotion of German freedom through Deutsche
Gotterkenntnis. "In the attack on Liège German soldiers followed my instructions and my call, they did not leave me to force my way into the fortress
alone," Ludendorff wrote. The victory over "clerical reaction," he insisted,
would "make the way free for the German people's creation as once the taking of Liège opened the way for the German Army into enemy territory."[4]

Part of the significance of Tannenberg to postwar accounts of the war
was that it could be portrayed as defensive, as evidence that Germany had
been surrounded by aggressive enemies and forced into war. Ludendorff
guarded his reputation as victor of Tannenberg jealously, and it became
the subject of a direct struggle with Paul von Hindenburg over its symbolic power. During the war, it was the commander of the Eighth Army,
Hindenburg who received the lion's share of the credit for the victory in
the East. Appraisals of the battle written immediately after the war often
highlighted the roles of François and/or Hoffmann. Ludendorff could not
tolerate these perceived slights to his honor. At seemingly every opportunity, he lashed out at his former comrades in order to diminish either their
role in the battle or their character.

Hindenburg and Tannenberg

Ludendorff's animosity toward Paul von Hindenburg came into the open
only after 1927, but it had its roots in their wartime relationship. While

the published version of Ludendorff's memoir is kind to Hindenburg, the original draft apparently contained a scathing indictment of Hindenburg that friends of the field marshal convinced him to remove before publication.[5] He likewise provided positive commentary when Hindenburg's memoirs appeared in 1920—a decision he would later regret as Hindenburg came to occupy a central place in Ludendorff's cosmology of conspiracy.[6] By 1930, Ludendorff recanted the kind words used to describe Hindenburg in his memoirs. He claimed not to have realized until 1927 that Hindenburg had fallen under the influence of the "supranational" powers and was willing to enslave Germany for their benefit.[7]

The origin of the rift dates to October 1918, when, according to Ludendorff, Hindenburg had not sufficiently supported him during their final meeting with the Kaiser.[8] Ludendorff saw Hindenburg's offer to resign along with Ludendorff as half-hearted. That Hindenburg ultimately stayed at his post to oversee the armistice Ludendorff saw as a betrayal of their once-happy "marriage." Perhaps significantly, in Hindenburg's memoirs, the field marshal consistently refers to "we" when describing his work with Ludendorff. In Ludendorff's memoir, "I" dominates.[9]

According to Ludendorff, relations with Hindenburg remained cool until the spring of 1919 when mutual acquaintances approached Ludendorff concerning a reconciliation. Ludendorff insisted that his honor would only be satisfied by a direct approach from Hindenburg himself. The latter arrived in the form of birthday greetings in April 1919, and a "brisk correspondence" ensued.[10] In August 1921 Hindenburg urgently contacted Ludendorff, asking him to travel to his estate in Pomerania to discuss a confidential matter. Ludendorff complied and found Hindenburg extremely upset by the charges leveled at him by his former colleague Max Bauer, in a new book. Ludendorff privately concurred with some of Bauer's conclusions, but admitted that Bauer may have erred in some smaller points. He advised Hindenburg to contact General von Kuhl, who would best be able to refute Bauer's claims.[11]

New rifts appeared in 1925 when Hindenburg, recently elected Reich president, twice refused to meet with Ludendorff, once during a planned visit to Munich in early August and again on the anniversary of the Tannenberg battle. Ludendorff saw various Bavarian factions at work to drive a wedge between the two old friends. His suspicions were confirmed when he read an announcement of the planned meeting in the *Völkischer*

Beobachter. Ludendorff began to put together the pieces, as was his wont. Hidden hands had managed to place the announcement in the Nazi newspaper, giving the meeting of old comrades a "political character" and thereby precluding the possibility of Hindenburg visiting. The timing of Hindenburg's letter of regret, posted mere moments after the appearance of the newspaper in question, was for Ludendorff the final piece of the puzzle.[12] The jilted Feldherr wrote that he "looked forward to the day when Your Excellency [Hindenburg] would not feel compromised by a visit to a . . . former comrade and German man."[13]

Eventually, Hindenburg's memoirs became the focus of Ludendorff's anger. In numerous articles published in his postwar newspaper, *Ludendorffs Volkswarte*, such as "Hindenburg und ich," Ludendorff made it clear that the section of Hindenburg's memoir on Tannenberg, page eighty-seven to be exact, is the one that upset him most. On that page Hindenburg wrote of the critical phase of the Battle of Tannenberg when information about Rennenkampf's disposition threatened the operations against Samsanov. The German command, Hindenburg admitted, "vacillated" and weighed the possibility of adopting a more conservative approach in order to bolster defenses against the Russians to their north. Ludendorff's enemies seized on the passage in order to claim that the nervous and mercurial Ludendorff had lost his nerve at that point, only to be soothed by the steady hand of Hindenburg. Ludendorff demanded, incessantly and in vain, that Hindenburg issue a retraction.[14] It is indicative of Ludendorff's prickly nature that the passage in question only obliquely refers to a moment of doubt and never actually mentions Ludendorff by name. Hindenburg writes only of "our" doubts and of overcoming them collectively.[15] Ludendorff claimed (rightly) that Hindenburg did not write his own memoirs and that General von Merz, later president of the Reichsarchiv, had written the section on Tannenberg.[16] What Ludendorff might not have known was that Hindenburg himself had added the offending, if carefully worded, passage on his own, predicting its effect.[17]

It became important for Ludendorff to prove that he, and he alone, had developed not only the plans for the Eighth Army in the East but German strategy in the war from his position as first quartermaster general after 1916. Hindenburg he portrayed as at best a figurehead, at worst, a doddering old fool. His followers were fond, for example, of pointing to a tribute to Hindenburg's wife that contained the charming (or damning, depending on one's perspective) anecdote of Hindenburg bouncing his newest granddaughter on his knee while Ludendorff and the Kaiser argued in a nearby room about how to deal with the latest crisis.[18] Where Hindenburg's admirers saw an even-keeled and contemplative soul, Ludendorff portrayed a simpleton.

To counter claims that the victory at Tannenberg belonged to anyone other than himself, Ludendorff kept at his side a list of quotations from Hindenburg and others that corroborated Ludendorff's assertion that all of the important decisions had been his. Ludendorff and his allies especially liked to point to the judgment of Reichsoberarchivrat Dr. Theobald von Schäfer because it had the imprimatur of an official judgment. Schäfer wrote: "Hindenburg's leadership without Ludendorff is as difficult to imagine as King Wilhelm's without Moltke."[19] To be equated with Helmuth von Moltke the Elder, victor of Sedan in 1870, was just barely enough to satisfy Ludendorff's ego.

To commemorate the victory at Tannenberg, patriotic Germans erected a monument at Hohenstein, near the battlefield. A private foundation laid the cornerstone of the monument on August 31, 1924. Both Hindenburg and Ludendorff attended the ceremony.[20] The brothers Walter and Johannes Krüger won the design competition with a plan they likened to a "German Stonehenge."[21] Organizers solicited donations from veterans' organizations, public corporations, and private individuals, so that the project used no public funds. State representatives as such were not invited to the dedication ceremony on September 18, 1927, though then-Reichspräsident Hindenburg attended, for obvious reasons. The date was moved forward to coincide provocatively with the dedication of a French memorial at Verdun, though organizers claimed the move had been made to bring the ceremony closer to the field marshal's eightieth birthday.[22] Eighty thousand people reportedly attended the official opening.[23] Hindenburg spoke to the gathering and used the opportunity to reject the charge that Germany was responsible for the outbreak of war in 1914.[24]

The victory at Tannenberg was important both at the time (for repelling the Russians from German soil) and for the subsequent myth making about the war. Tannenberg, according to a blind, twisted sort of logic, refuted the postwar claim of German aggression. Tannenberg was a battle fought on the strategic defensive, with Russian hordes threatening the German homeland. The great victory also testified to the strength of the

Figure 12. Hindenburg and Ludendorff, fall 1916. Bundesarchiv, Bild 146-1970-073-47, photographer unknown.

German Army, and therefore bolstered the later claim to have been unde-feated in the field. Hindenburg, at the dedication of the Tannenberg mon-ument in 1927, made the point explicitly when he described the German Army taking the field "with pure hearts in defense of the Fatherland."[25] In gratitude for the valiant efforts of both Hindenburg and Ludendorff, the University of Königsberg granted both men honorary doctorates.[26]

The monument spoke volumes with its political symbolism. The archi-tects, Johannes and Walter Krüger, constructed a huge octagon one hun-dred meters across, with twenty meter towers at each corner. The layout was supposed to invoke Stonehenge as well as a medieval castle. Mod-ern observers (of photographic and other records since the monument is destroyed) note similarities with contemporary stage designs, including Fritz Lang's 1924 production of the Nibelungen story.[27] The monument became a regular stop on Hitler's itinerary after 1933 and was chosen (against the field marshal's wishes) as the burial site for Paul von Hinden-burg when he died in August 1934. Hindenburg's and his wife's bodies were moved to Marburg shortly before German engineers destroyed the monument in 1945.[28]

The monument and the various celebrations held at the site served as a focal point in Ludendorff's efforts to claim credit for the victory. Luden-dorff claimed to have gotten along well with Hindenburg at the 1924 gath-ering, though other generals treated him coldly.[29] Hans von Seeckt ignored Ludendorff completely and remarked that Ludendorff played no role at the ceremony.[30] At the 1927 ceremony, Ludendorff attended, but refused to associate with Hindenburg. He declined an invitation to an official ban-quet arranged for the evening before the ceremony. He refused to ride in Hindenburg's car, and he pointedly distanced himself from the Reich-spräsident on the podium as columns of Reichswehr soldiers marched by in review.[31] When Hindenburg approached him, with arms outstretched in greeting, some sources claim Ludendorff turned his back and moved five paces away.[32] To reinforce his displeasure with Hindenburg, he also forbade his followers from attending celebrations of the field marshal's eightieth birthday that year.[33] Despite his eventual reconciliation with Hit-ler, Ludendorff would not allow his bust to be placed in the Feldherrnturm of the Tannenberg memorial alongside Hindenburg's. Only after his death could it be placed there, just in time for the production of the official book on the memorial.[34]

Figure 13. Tannenberg memorial, September 18, 1927. On the tribune are Reich president Paul von Hindenburg, Field Marshal August von Mackensen, and Chancellor Dr. Wilhelm Marx. Standing in the lower left corner of the photograph is Erich Ludendorff. Bundesarchiv, Bild 102-04822, photographer unknown.

In 1928 Humboldt University professor Walter Elze wrote *Tannenberg; das deutsche Heer von 1914, seine Grundzüge und deren Auswirkung im Sieg an der Ostfront* (Tannenberg: The German army of 1914, its main features and its role in the victory on the Eastern Front).[35] The book had received the blessing of the Reichsarchiv but angered Ludendorff by its depiction of his alleged panic during the height of the battle on the August 26. Elze had relied on statements by Hindenburg to illuminate the crisis in Eighth Army headquarters, which Ludendorff always denied. Ludendorff fired off angry letters to Elze and quickly published *"Dirne Kriegsgeschichte" vor dem Gericht des Weltkrieges* in response.[36] Ludendorff sought to have Elze's book suppressed and eventually filed a lawsuit against the author.

The point about the loss of nerve at Tannenberg was important to Ludendorff because it lent support to the theory of a "nervous breakdown" in October 1918 that prompted Ludendorff to call for an immediate armistice. If Ludendorff could be shown to be susceptible to such episodes of panic, then the theory of the nervous breakdown in 1918 seems more plausible. Ludendorff energetically defended himself against such charges both because they linked him directly with Germany's rapid collapse in November 1918 and because they called into question his self-styled status as Feldherr, as the resolute and iron-willed leader of men.

Chancellor Heinrich Brüning added fuel to the fire when, in a speech calling for Hindenburg's reelection in 1932, he credited Hindenburg, rather than Ludendorff, with the victory at Tannenberg. Ludendorff had been on the verge of breaking off the battle, Brüning claimed, when Hindenburg overrode him and thereby secured the German triumph. That Brüning was a member of the Catholic Center Party must have particularly galled Ludendorff, consumed as he was at that point by fears of a Catholic conspiracy to control Germany.[37]

Ludendorff waged a years-long battle with Elze over the book, corresponding with the author and threatening legal action. Once again, the archivist Dr. Theobald von Schäfer came to the rescue, writing that while it is true that Prittwitz halted his units before the Weichsel of his own accord, in all other aspects of the battle, Ludendorff and the Eighth Army command were in complete control. Even François's success should be credited to Ludendorff, and "the story of Ludendorff wanting to break off the battle at the decisive moment must be rejected."[38] Eventually Elze partially retracted some of his assertions in a private letter as well as in circulars posted around the Humboldt University in Berlin, where Elze taught.[39] But Ludendorff persisted. Likely he was goaded into further action by the accounts of the battle that circulated following Paul von Hindenburg's death in August 1934, many of which echoed or cited Elze's work.[40]

The conflict simmered until the Reichswehr Ministry intervened in 1935.[41] Rather than have the recently deceased Reichspräsident Paul von Hindenburg's reputation sullied (Elze had relied on Hindenburg's account of August 26 to support his claims), the Reichswehr Ministry attempted to settle the affair out of public view.[42] Their initial response was to reach an understanding with the Propaganda Ministry to ban all further publications on the subject. The military feared that Hindenburg's accomplishments would be overshadowed by Ludendorff's should a debate ensue. Since both the military's identity and its legitimacy in the Third Reich were rooted in the important place occupied by the then-deceased Hindenburg as both Reichspräsident and war hero, the Reichswehr Ministry was loath to see the subject broached.[43]

Ironically, but not surprisingly, this move, undertaken in tacit acknowledgment of Ludendorff's military successes, provoked the general's ire. The ban would impact his own book, *Dirne Kriegschichte*, and so Ludendorff undertook a letter-writing campaign to lift it. Ludwig Beck was sympathetic and hoped to keep the conflict under wraps. It was essential that Ludendorff withdraw his case against Elze lest the proceedings, which seemed likely to cast aspersions on Hindenburg, call the army's legitimacy into question at a time when its relations with the National Socialist state were tense.[44]

As part of an effort to settle outstanding disputes and engage Ludendorff's image for the benefit of the army, Beck visited Ludendorff on January 6, 1935, accompanied by Ludendorff's former colleague, General Georg Wetzell. Wetzell assured Ludendorff that his old comrades from the Eighth Army as well as the OHL knew the truth, that Ludendorff had run the war effort and done the work. Beck presented Ludendorff with a memo drafted by the Reichswehr Ministry. This memo similarly assured Ludendorff that no one in the German military doubted Ludendorff's role at Tannenberg and that everyone endorsed the story of the battle as related not in Elze's book but in Ludendorff's own works.[45]

The memo further promised Ludendorff that now that the Reich's military historical office had moved from the Ministry of the Interior to the Truppenamt, they would have more discretion to intervene against "historical untruths." The decision in December 1934 to ban further publications on Tannenberg was meant, the ministry insisted, only to prevent the controversy from dragging on, thereby leaving Ludendorff's more recently published Tannenberg work as the last word on the subject.[46]

Ludendorff was unmoved. If his comrades were so dedicated, why did he have to fight the many attacks on his "honor" alone for so many years? Being solely responsible for the defense of that honor, he refused to allow any other person or agency to restrict his methods. He then used the occasion to belabor for Beck's benefit the many occasions when he had sought Reichswehr assistance against his various enemies. Though Ludendorff tried to end the discussion on a positive note, praising the Reichswehr for its role in defending Germany, Beck must have quaked when Ludendorff insisted that his anti-Hitler screed, *Weltkrieg droht auf deutschem Boden*, was written with the same purpose in mind.[47] When Ludendorff refused, despite these many entreaties, to withdraw the lawsuit against Elze, it was dismissed by the court in August 1936.[48]

Publications of the Tannenberg League belittled Hindenburg at every opportunity, sometimes quite subtly. In a passage describing Moltke's reliance on Ludendorff in 1914 to halt the Russian advance into East Prussia, one author makes a point of providing the precise dates on which the two commanders received their orders. As soon as he learned of the dangerous situation on the Weichsel River from General von Prittwitz on 21 August, Moltke dispatched a letter to Ludendorff, calling on him to save the situation. "Only on the following afternoon, the twenty-second of August, did the Kaiser name [Hindenburg] as supreme commander. . . . It is clear that Moltke called on Ludendorff first."[49] Nor did Ludendorff shy away from petty attacks. It was Ludendorff who drew attention to the circumstances surrounding the gift of the estate, Neudeck, to Hindenburg in 1927. Ludendorff cried foul and publicized the fact that the estate was in fact deeded to Hindenburg's son, Oskar. Ludendorff saw a scheme to cheat the inheritance tax that would be due upon Hindenburg's death. Hindenburg's supporters saw only a convenience to spare the effort of a transfer, given the field marshal's advanced age.[50]

Ludendorff gleefully reprinted any positive press he received from abroad, particularly as it regarded his wartime performance and the debate over Tannenberg. A quote from a French general, Edmond Buat, crediting Ludendorff with saving Germany repeatedly during the war and absolving him of any blame for defeat, appeared frequently in the pages of *Volkswarte* and other Ludendorff publications.[51] Even more convincing, thought Ludendorff's circle, were the entries in a recently published French dictionary. While Hindenburg's entry had him "commanding the German armies during the World War," Ludendorff's had him "*in reality* commanding the German armies."[52] To one so practiced in reading between the lines as Ludendorff the additional phrase spoke volumes.

No doubt Ludendorff was jealous of the personality cult that grew around Hindenburg among the German right. In a tribute penned in 1922 on the occasion of Hindenburg's seventy-fifth birthday, George von Gravenitz abjured the title field marshal, calling Hindenburg the "Überfeldherr" instead. How Ludendorff could have settled on mere "Feldherr" for his own title remains a mystery.[53]

Certainly Ludendorff was not above using Hindenburg's prestige to advance his own radical political agenda. Already in 1919, observers noted Ludendorff's attempts to use Hindenburg's reputation and events intended to honor the field marshal as opportunities to make political hay.[54] Ludendorff still sought help from the Reichspräsident in February 1932 as a six-week ban was placed on *Volkswarte* at the height of the election season. The fact that Hindenburg referred Ludendorff to General Groener, the minister of the interior whom Ludendorff accused of being a Freemason, only fanned the flames of Ludendorff's suspicions.[55]

Hindenburg, to his credit, seems never to have reciprocated Ludendorff's ire. Several witnesses report that Hindenburg until his death kept a picture of Ludendorff in his study, despite Ludendorff's bitter attacks on him. He once commented to a visitor who expressed surprise that Hindenburg wanted to be reminded of the self-proclaimed Feldherr, that he kept the photo to remind him of wartime camaraderie, the memory of which could not be destroyed.[56] To most Germans, it seemed that the animosity between Hindenburg and Ludendorff was both one-sided (i.e., emanating only from Ludendorff) and unnecessary. "Hindenburg and Ludendorff belong together," wrote one German newspaper in 1932, prompting the usual acrid response from the latter. In his *Volkswarte*, Ludendorff immediately countered with his version of Hindenburg's alleged betrayal upon Ludendorff's dismissal in 1918.[57]

Uncharitable to bitter end, Ludendorff refused to fly the flag at his home in Tutzing at half-mast to honor Hindenburg when the Reichspräsident died in 1934. When someone contacted Ludendorff to see if he had simply misunderstood the Führer's order to fly flags at half-mast, Ludendorff categorically refused to comply.[58]

Relations with Hitler

Between Ludendorff and Hitler there were certainly differences of both ideology and policy, but the feud was largely personal. The two men's fates intertwined in 1923 during the Beer Hall Putsch, but hostility grew quickly thereafter. Hitler's silence during his imprisonment had left Ludendorff free to pursue the leadership of the völkisch movement through the National Socialist Freedom Party (sometimes Movement) (NSFP).

That group enjoyed some modest success in the elections of April 1924, and Ludendorff briefly entered the Reichstag as a delegate. His candidacy for Reich president later that year, however, was a disappointment. He earned only 1 percent of the vote and subsequently blamed Hitler for failing to support his candidacy.

Hitler visited Ludendorff upon his release from prison. While Hitler, according to Ludendorff, refused to enter into any meaningful discussions of strategy or organization, he did reject Ludendorff's plea to have the reborn NSDAP take up the fight against Catholicism with more vigor. As Hitler's silence continued and Ludendorff's frustration mounted, Ludendorff and the leaders of the NSFP looked for ways to ensure that any impending split on the völkisch movement would be pinned on the National Socialists.[59] Instead, Hitler quickly reestablished control of the NSDAP and slowly began rebuilding the group around exclusive loyalty to himself, using the fame he had acquired at their joint trial for treason. The NSFP fizzled, and Ludendorff founded the Tannenberg League, as detailed above. Ludendorff would increasingly describe the split as a "betrayal" akin to the one perpetrated by Hindenburg in 1918.

As early as the summer of 1926, Ludendorff began charging that Hitler was in the thrall of the pope.[60] But Ludendorff began vehemently and publicly to attack Hitler only after the latter's shocking success in the 1930 elections. The opening salvo of the attack came in 1931 with a book titled *Weltkrieg droht auf Deutschem Boden* (World war threatens on German soil).[61] In this book, which the domestic and international press extensively reviewed, Ludendorff details a conspiracy by the usual supranational powers to involve Germany in an even more destructive World War in 1932.[62] Hitler and the NSDAP were to be central to the conspiracy's success. The aim, according to Ludendorff, was to make Germany the battleground for a coming war between France and Italy. By pursuing an illusory alliance with Italy and Britain, the NSDAP would not, as they believed, end Germany's isolation and secure her against French attack. Rather, the alliance would provide the pretext for a French invasion that would devastate Germany. The date for the attack was already set, Ludendorff calculated, for May 1, 1932.[63]

How Ludendorff arrived at this date warrants a brief digression. According to Ludendorff, in certain cabbalistic Jewish traditions, the numbers 10 and 15 (and combinations and multiples thereof) have prophetic

Figure 14. Ad for Erich Ludendorff, *Weltkrieg droht auf Deutschem Boden*, 1931. Institute für Zeitgeschichte, Munich, Library Holdings Ok180.

significance because of their relationship to the Hebrew letters in the name of God, Yahweh.[64] Ludendorff in *Weltkrieg droht* and other works relied on this "insight" both to explain historic events and to predict the future.[65] Ludendorff believed, for example, that Martin Luther had been murdered by fearful Jews.[66] That he died on February 18, 1546, was the "proof" that Ludendorff needed to establish his claim. According to his calculus, $18 + 2 + 15 + 4 + 6 = 45 = 3 \times 15$, making February 18 a "Jehovah Day" in the "Jehovah Year" of 1546 ($15 + 4 + 6 = 25 = 15 + 10$). Even the Nazi "philosopher" Alfred Rosenberg, in a work discussed below, ridiculed Ludendorff on this point while also challenging Ludendorff's math. Rosenberg noted that Ludendorff changed his formula when necessary to achieve the desired result. For example, in order to make 1789 a "Jehovah Year" and thereby make Jews responsible for the French Revolution, Ludendorff separated the digits for the century ($1 + 7 + 8 + 9 = 25$) rather than leave them together as he had for Luther's "murder" above. Even more blatant, in order to make May 1, 1932, auspicious for a planned attack on Germany, Ludendorff merely set the digits for the day and month side by side ($1,5 = 15$, $1 + 9 + 3 + 2 = 15$) rather than adding them, which would yield an invalid result.[67]

According to one insider, in the early 1930s, Haus Ludendorff seethed with hatred of the Nazis.[68] In the same year that *Weltkrieg droht* appeared, Ludendorff published *Hitler's Verrat der Deutschen an den römischen Papst* (Hitler's betrayal of the German people to the Roman pope). This booklet collected essays already published in *Ludendorffs Volkswarte* and packaged them for wider distribution (and greater profits). This publication became the focal point for later discussions of the enmity between the Führer and the Feldherr.

According to Ludendorff, Vatican conspirators had contingency plans that guaranteed their victory. They had succeeded in 1918 in accomplishing their long-term aim of deposing the Protestant house of Hohenzollern. Since 1918, the Catholic Church had been supporting the Center Party as the linchpin of the Weimar system, even under nominal Socialist rule. But with the increasing völkisch awakening in Germany, thanks to Ludendorff, the pope needed a second "trump card"—the NSDAP. Between the Center Party and the NSDAP, the pope was certain to determine Germany's destiny. If one failed, the other would succeed.[69] Hitler was to be the "savior" cynically foisted on the long-suffering German people as they turned away from the failing Socialist system.[70]

Figure 15. Cover, Erich Ludendorff, *Hitler's Verrat der Deutschen an den römischen Papst*, 1931. Institute für Zeitgeschichte, Munich, Library Holdings Ok180.

Several factors led Ludendorff to this "inescapable" conclusion that Hitler and the Nazis were in the pocket of the Catholic Church. Hitler and other Nazi leaders had been born Catholic, and his movement found its home in Catholic Bavaria. Ludendorff noted that even in Protestant areas of Germany, the local party leaders were Catholics.[71] Second, Hitler's party had identified itself as "fascist," which indicated symbolic, if not actual, ties to Mussolini's Italian movement of the same name. For Ludendorff, Italian meant Catholic, despite the occasional evidence of strained relationships between *il Duce* and his papal contemporaries.[72]

The book, compiled in the aftermath of the first stunning electoral victory of the NSDAP in September 1930, suggests that the Catholic Church had not yet anointed Hitler as the leader of papal forces in Germany pending proof that the Nazi's ascendance was more than temporary. National Socialist attacks on "godless Communists" and on Ludendorff himself were supposed to provide evidence of Hitler's loyalty to the pope pending future electoral victories.[73] Further pro-Catholic actions by the Nazis would follow, such as Hitler distancing himself from his own party philosopher, Alfred Rosenberg, whose anti-Catholic views were well known, and the publication of the pro-Catholic *Nationalsozialismus und Katholische Kirche* (National Socialism and the Catholic Church) by Nazi Party member and noted physicist Johannes Stark.[74] That Hitler so quickly withdrew his endorsement of Rosenberg's anti-Catholic book, *Der Mythus des 20. Jahrhunderts* (Myths of the twentieth century), after the Bavarian bishops' protests was proof for Ludendorff not of Hitler's political opportunism but of his loyalty to the Catholic Church and his fear of excommunication.

Ludendorff's attacks prompted an extensive response from the Nazi Party in the *Nationalsozialistiche Monatshefte*, penned by Alfred Rosenberg himself and titled "Der Fall Ludendorff." As always, the Nazis were careful in their handling of war hero and fellow putschist Ludendorff's reputation. Rosenberg's essay begins with a long catalog of Ludendorff's successes and his service to the Fatherland: his work on the General Staff, the victories of Liège and Tannenberg, his ceaseless struggles throughout the World War.[75] After the war, however, condemned to inactivity by the revolution of 1918 and increasingly under the influence of Mathilde, Ludendorff became unhinged, argued Rosenberg. He acknowledged that much of what Ludendorff wrote about Jews, Jesuits, Freemasons, and international finance was correct at the core. But Ludendorff lacked historical sensibility and political judgment. Instead of aiding the struggle against these forces, Ludendorff's fantasies and outlandish claims set the völkisch movement back.

As for the NSDAP being beholden to the Catholic Church, Rosenberg cited the constant attacks of church authorities and their allies. The Center Party, Jesuits, even the pope wished to see the Nazis silenced, so how, asked Rosenberg, could Ludendorff claim that the NSDAP was doing Rome's bidding?[76] Ludendorff's propensity to oversimplify, to see all events as controlled by singular, powerful forces, was too much even for Rosenberg. Rosenberg critiqued Ludendorff's reliance on numerology (see above) and blamed Mathilde for poorly instructing Ludendorff in such mysteries.

It was a perennial theme of Nazi writing on Ludendorff that Mathilde had led him astray. Each time she appears in Goebbels's diaries she is described as "hysterical," "impudent," "arrogant," and an "evil spirit."[77] Goebbels wrote that she had made Ludendorff a laughingstock and lamented that so great a man had fallen under the "spiritual sway of so mediocre a philosopher."[78] In "Der Fall Ludendorff," Rosenberg similarly argued that Ludendorff's "hysterical" claims and "presumptuous" conclusions could only be traced to the influence of a woman.[79]

Never one to let a dispute lapse, Ludendorff immediately commissioned a response to Rosenberg's article by the former Gauleiter, Anton Haselmayer. Haselmayer's retort is noteworthy mainly for making Ludendorff's own literary-fantastic shenanigans seem more reasonable. Haselmayer refuted Rosenberg's work with reference to "imponderables" and the "eternal moral law" that alone prevented France from marching on to Berlin in 1919. Imponderable indeed.[80] Haselmayer required fifty-two pages to rebut Rosenberg's nineteen. He quoted extensively from Rosenberg, Hitler, and Ludendorff in order to bring the argument right back to Ludendorff's: supranational powers control Hitler, France, indeed the world.

Ludendorff reinforced the Hitler-Rome connection graphically in his newspaper at every opportunity (as shown in figure 16). Nor were his alleged links to the Vatican Hitler's only fault, according to Ludendorff. Despite the NSDAP being notoriously antisemitic, Ludendorff insisted that even Hitler's antisemitism was insincere. In their talking points about the relationship between National Socialism and Judaism, the Tannenberg League prominently featured an interview Hitler gave to an American journalist in 1930 in which he insisted that "I am not for curtailing the rights of the Jews in Germany, but I insist that we others who are not Jews shall not have less rights than they."[81] Other clues, such as the occasional reference by Hitler to "respectable Jews" (those with no association with Bolshevism) not being the enemy indicated to Ludendorff and his followers that the Nazis were not serious about the threat Jews posed to Germany. One must reasonably argue that those quotations are suspect taken as they are out of the context of Hitler's many years of vocal and violent public statements against Jews. But to a man practicing the "mosaic work" of detecting insidious conspiracies such tiny fragments are the keys to understanding; they are the slips of the tongue that reveal the real nature of a person or group. Hitler, Ludendorff believed, was "soft" on the Jews.

In his *Volkswarte*, Ludendorff maintained the charge that Hitler was beholden to the Catholic Church for his power. The Nazis were not reviving the spirit of Potsdam, as they claimed, but the "spirit of Charlemagne" wrote one of Ludendorff's followers.[82] In Ludendorff's view, the middle classes, cast into economic misery by the Socialist government

Figure 16. Cartoon from *Ludendorffs Volkswarte*, January 24, 1932. "That thing certainly does have a twist in it . . . but that can be easily straightened out." Institute für Zeitgeschichte, Munich, *Vor'm Volksgericht*, 3, January 24, 1932, 1. ED414/54.

Figure 17. Cartoon from *Ludendorffs Volkswarte*, February 12, 1933. The antisemitic caricature of the Jew shouts "Heil Hitler! We surrender to the facts!" Institute für Zeitgeschichte, Munich, *Vor'm Volksgericht*, February 12, 1933, 1. ED414/150.

and manipulated by the supranational powers, had mistakenly turned to Nazism for salvation.[83] In one of his longer articles against the Nazis, Ludendorff implausibly became a staunch defender of the Weimar constitution. The Enabling Act and other Nazi legislation violated Germans' deep-seated sense of justice and would mean, Ludendorff warned, that the National Socialist "revolution" would never take root.[84] But take root it did, forcing some adjustments to Ludendorff's message while simultaneously fulfilling some of his dreams.

7

LUDENDORFF IN THE THIRD REICH

Now the Lord Siegfried spake: "Me wondereth, since men do give us
such great store from the kitchen, why the butlers bring us not the
wine. Unless men purvey the hunters better, I'll be no more
your hunting-fellow."

—THE NIBELUNGENLIED

Soon after the National Socialists consolidated their power in the summer of 1933, rumors began to circulate that reconciliation between Hitler
and Ludendorff was in the offing.[1] There was some hope that Ludendorff would attend the annual commemoration of the Tannenberg battle,
but he refused. The ceremony proceeded without mention of Ludendorff's
name. At least one völkisch journal lamented his absence, claiming that
"the Germany of Hindenburg and Adolf Hitler needs every great man—
not least General Ludendorff!"[2]

The *New York Times*, for example, reported "with some authority"
that Ludendorff had been won over by Hitler's pleas for national unity
and would attend the anniversary celebration of the Beer Hall Putsch on
November 9.[3] It had been Hitler's "cherished ambition," the paper asserted, to bring the old general back into the Nazi fold and to renew
the friendship between Hindenburg and Ludendorff as well. Negotiations
either stalled or the *New York Times* was misinformed, however. Ludendorff was conspicuously absent from the ceremonies in Munich.

Continued Attacks on NSDAP

In fact, for the first several months of the Third Reich, Ludendorff showed no signs of abandoning his attacks on Hitler, the National Socialists, and their new cabinet allies. He continued to tout his anti-Hitler book *Weltkrieg droht*.[4] Ludendorff took the opportunity to blast his old foe Hindenburg for turning Germany over to the hands of the Nazis. Typical of the cartoons that graced the pages of *Ludendorffs Volkswarte* were those showing corpulent Jewish caricatures waving swastika flags or crasslooking *Sturmabteilung* (SA) men sporting crucifixes on their caps, symbolizing their links (in Ludendorff's eyes) to Rome.[5] The image below reveals a fundamental misunderstanding of Nazi antisemitism, suggesting that a baptized Jew would be welcome in a National Socialist Germany.

For such criticism, Ludendorff's publications endured constant censorship and occasional bans of several weeks.[6] Certain types of criticism

Figure 18. Cartoon from *Ludendorffs Volkswarte*, February 12, 1933. Another antisemitic stereotype, with a baptismal certificate on his chest, proclaims, "Baptized is baptized, Christian is Christian." Institute für Zeitgeschichte, Munich, *Vor'm Volksgericht*, February 12, 1933, 1. ED414/150.

continued, often buried more deeply within some of Ludendorff's longer works or thinly veiled by recourse to sarcasm. What a shame, lamented Ludendorff in *Mein militärischer Werdegang*, that German Protestantism after the Nazi revolution frittered away its newfound strength on attacks on his pagan faith rather than on the real enemy: Roman Catholicism.[7] Lectures also continued, frequently under Gestapo supervision, on the subject of Gotterkenntnis and some subjects to which Nazi officials could hardly object, such as "Ludendorff unmasks the war mongers Rom-Juda."[8]

Despite the many ideological similarities with Nazism, Ludendorff's followers experienced persecution, including their lectures being banned at the last minute or disrupted by SA rowdies. Some Ludendorffers lost their jobs or chances for promotion because of their championing the Feldherr's cause. Some spent time in jail or concentration camps because of their "subversive" belief in Deutsche Gotterkenntnis.[9] Booksellers were required to register with the Reich Publishing Chamber (Reichsschriftumskammer), and Ludendorffers not so registered could count on being reminded of the requirement.[10] Ludendorff's followers who wished to register with the Finanzamt (Finance office) as believers in a nonmainstream religion also faced difficulties with unsympathetic officials. Despite arrangements with Nazi authorities, local offices often refused to register the change to "Deutsche Gotterkenntnis (Ludendorff)" as allowed by a decree of September 14, 1936.[11]

Robert Holtzmann's correspondence consists largely of pleas from these affected individuals, or their relatives, asking him to use his contacts with Himmler, Hess, and the War Ministry to seek redress for their grievances. Not that the police supervision indicated any active subversive behavior on the part of Ludendorffers, as some would claim after 1945.[12] Quite the contrary, instructions from on high urged followers to do all they could to "conquer" the mistrust and to avoid even the appearance of forbidden activities.[13] In a more positive sense, some sought assistance in acquiring a position in the Wehrmacht, once Ludendorff's endorsement in 1935 seemed to raise the prospect for his followers to be welcomed in the new institution.[14] Mathilde Ludendorff's son Hanno von Kemnitz sought Holtzmann's aid in winning government contracts for his industrial firm.[15]

Ludendorff nevertheless sought to capitalize on the new situation and his association with Hitler whenever possible. His publishing company produced a book by Kurt Fügner in 1933 titled *"Wir Marschieren!"*:

General Ludendorff zu Adolf Hitler am 9. November 1923 vor der Marsch durch München ("We march!": General Ludendorff to Adolf Hitler on November 9, 1923, before the march through Munich). In this work Fügner seeks to raise the general's profile by foregrounding his participation in, indeed in Fügner's account his instigation of, the 1923 putsch. According to Fügner, it was Ludendorff, not Hitler, who decided to lead the march through Munich. It was Ludendorff alone who refused to take cover once shots were fired and proceeded straight through the cordon of troops assembled at the Feldherrnhalle. "Is it not our sacred duty," asked Fügner, "in this time of national uprising . . . to show Ludendorff in his true light?"[16] By way of contrast, Hitler, after thanking Ludendorff for guiding the völkisch movement through the period of his (Hitler's) incarceration, broke with Ludendorff over the issue of Catholicism.[17] But despite these misunderstandings and misrepresentations, Ludendorff sought his place as the "freedom-fighter for the German soul" in the new order.[18]

Relations between Hitler and Ludendorff remained icy throughout the first two years of the Third Reich. Ludendorff's enormous public prestige protected him from the fate that befell most vocal critics of the Nazis, but his organizations were subjected to the same process of *Gleichschaltung* (coordination) as other political and voluntary associations. On September 23, 1933, the NSDAP banned the Tannenbergbund and *Ludendorffs Volkswarte*. However, the Ludendorffs still enjoyed what Winfried Martini called "carnival license" (*Narrenfreiheit*).[19] Ludendorff was allowed to restyle his *Volkswarte* as a "purely religious" journal, and it soon reappeared as *Am heiligen Quell Deutscher Kraft*. In this guise, Ludendorff carried on very much as he had before 1933, printing editorials in conflict with the official "party line," to say the least.[20] Frequent critical outbursts resulted in the paper being banned repeatedly in the period 1933–35, but the bans were always temporary and never carried with them the more drastic penalties applied to other Nazi opponents.

Officials of the Tannenberg League in fact continued to operate, disguised as representatives of Ludendorff's publishing company. They tried to keep the Ludendorff message alive by pedaling *Am heiligen Quell* to sympathetic fellow Germans.[21] The publishing company was not able to operate freely, however. Nazis continued to place pressure on Ludendorff and his followers. Ludendorff's associate, Herbert Frank, was convinced his mail was being read.[22] Ludendorff himself feared the newly created

Reich Chamber of Culture and the laws associated with it would mean the end of both his journal and the publishing house.[23] There were reports from company representatives of job discrimination, frequent arrests, interrogations, grave desecration and even bugging of Deutsche Gotterkenntnis lectures. Representatives of the company were advised to avoid anything that might even remotely be construed as forbidden behavior.[24]

While such discrimination rankled, followers of Deutsche Gotterkenntnis were continually at pains to remind officials of exactly how useful their movement could be in promoting Nazi ideals. Complaining of a Prussian ban on public gatherings of the Tannenberg League, Karl von Unruh wrote to Hermann Göring in the latter's capacity as prime minister of Prussia that, far from being a threat to the state, the Tannenberg League supports it "insofar as the League educates Germans to voluntarily integrate themselves into the German national body [*Volksganze*]."[25] Similar letters professing loyalty and common purpose reached Nazi officials at all levels of government in the months following Hitler's assumption of the chancellorship. Karl von Unruh, the editor of *Am heiligen Quell*, urged the Tannenberg leadership to be proactive, to seek out Nazi officials personally to establish relationships in order to forestall difficulties for the group.[26]

Ludendorff bristled at not being included in the festivities commemorating the Battle of Tannenberg in 1933. Instead, Hindenburg alone received the thanks of Göring and the other assembled notables, prompting one Ludendorff associate to charge hypocrisy. The Nazis had acknowledged Ludendorff's role in 1927 when it served their purpose of attacking the Weimar government. But now that they were in power, Ludendorff was to be ignored.[27] In his brief speech, Hindenburg did thank his old comrades, "from the most senior general to the youngest musketeer," which could conceivably have included Ludendorff, but he was certainly not mentioned by name.[28]

In 1934, Ludendorff ostentatiously absented himself from the grandiose funeral of Paul von Hindenburg held at the Tannenberg memorial in East Prussia. Their wartime "happy marriage" had collapsed after 1925 in squabbles over rival presidential candidacies, wartime honors, and myriad perceived slights. Ludendorff refused to offer public or private condolences to the family of the field marshal and hung no flags at his residence as the Hitler regime insisted.[29] "I will not beflag my house in order to honor someone who did so much to deny my military achievements," he wrote to his confidante, Robert Holtzmann.[30]

There were occasional signs of a thaw in relations. In May 1934, Himmler met with one of Ludendorff's associates, Hans Kurth, and granted his permission for the former Tannenbergers to hold public lectures under very strict conditions. The name *Ludendorff* was not to appear on any flyers or announcements of such gatherings, nor were the names of either Erich or Mathilde to be mentioned during the lectures unless strictly necessary and defensible in the context of the subject matter. If these conditions were met, the group could hold lectures on any of their usual subjects: Catholicism, Judaism, Freemasonry, Christianity, Deutsche Gotterkenntnis.[31] Other documents make clear that Ludendorff's people were being closely watched and that attacks against the state would result, not surprisingly, in the immediate dissolution of any gathering.[32]

Ludendorff capitalized on this new arrangement, even preparing a form letter that dropped Himmler's name to be used when applying for police permission for a gathering. The circular including the letter spelled out the procedure to be followed in the case of difficulties, which could (and did frequently) lead to Robert Holtzmann making a personal appeal to Himmler's office in Berlin.[33] Himmler's sympathies were also evident in ads for the SS mouthpiece *Das Schwarze Korps* that appeared alongside those for Ludendorff's *Am heiligen Quell Deutscher Kraft* in pamphlets written by Ludendorff's sympathizers.[34]

Frequently, the line Himmler forced Ludendorff to walk was too fine. Ludendorff was keenly aware of his tenuous situation and took prompt action when potential threats to the precarious concordat arose. In August 1934, for example, Ludendorff circulated a note among his representatives vehemently denying rumors coming out of Königsberg that he was standing as a candidate in an upcoming election.[35] When a campaign gathering signatures to congratulate Ludendorff on the anniversary of the Battle of Tannenberg aroused suspicions of political activity, he asked that it be stopped.[36]

By December, Goebbels had apparently had enough of Ludendorff's provocative screeds (again), and ordered Ludendorff to withdraw both his *Dirne Kriegsgeschichte* and *Tannenberg* books from the shelves.[37] Ludendorff pleaded with Goebbels's staff to lift the ban, and his efforts were crowned with success by the following January, probably thanks to the intervention of Werner von Blomberg and the Reichswehr Ministry.[38] Ironically, the press found that the ban had dramatically increased sales in some areas of both banned books as well as other publications.[39]

Even some outside the circle of the Nazi Party and the Haus Ludendorff attempted to foster better relations between the two. In a series of pamphlets written between 1933 and 1935, G. H. von Teklenburg pleaded for Ludendorff to bury the hatchet with Hitler, Hindenburg, and others in the interests of Germany's revival. He pointed to Hitler's call, in a speech in Munich, for a "harvest of political leadership abilities" to ensure that "no true genius lives among the Volk without being recognized and incorporated" in the party."[40] Teklenburg hoped that Ludendorff would place his own military genius alongside Hitler's political one.

Teklenburg himself was staunchly anticlerical and had positive things to say about both the German Christian movement (Dinter, Reventlow) and Mathilde Ludendorff. While Teklenburg's ideas are repugnant and his hopes misplaced, on certain issues his insights were keen. He rejected Ludendorff's notion that Hitler and the Nazis were tools of the "supranational powers" and focused only on Hitler's refusal, for sensible political reasons, to adopt Ludendorff's uncompromising tactics against the Catholic Church. Teklenburg argued that the masses were simply too hopelessly conservative in such matters to allow for *both* the transformation of the state (which the Nazis accomplished) *and* the transformation of spiritual life. Hitler took the pragmatic course, achieving what he could and leaving the larger battle for later.[41]

The Wehrmacht Intervenes

The German Army was pushing for the rehabilitation of Ludendorff as further proof of the National Socialists' respect for the army. With Hindenburg dead, Ludwig Beck sought energetically over the course of at least a year to use Ludendorff in that role.[42] Beck envisioned Ludendorff as a kind of "Ersatz-Hindenburg" who could take over the latter's role as "protector of the army's independence and sacrosanctity" and secure the military's "quasi-autonomous position in the state."[43]

Officials of the Kriegsakademie certainly linked the two issues in a discussion on January 12, 1935, about the recent Hitler speech concerning tensions between the party and the military. Both sides had concerns, the assembled officers were told, but the army leadership nevertheless had complete confidence in their ability to work together. It was in this context that Blomberg and Fritsch announced their decision to intervene on Ludendorff's behalf. The Feldherr was under attack not only for his political and ideological views (from which they distanced themselves) but also for his leadership and accomplishments during the war. Blomberg and Fritsch explained away Ludendorff's odd behavior and curious beliefs "as the release of pent-up rage, as the thrashings of a wounded lion."[44] The army planned to dispatch General Georg Wetzell to smooth things over with Ludendorff.[45] When Wetzell refused to go alone, General Ludwig Beck joined him, carrying a special, conciliatory message from Hitler himself.[46] The two had a long meeting with Ludendorff, accompanied by his associate Robert Holtzmann on January 6, 1935, at the Ludendorff villa in Tutzing.

Wetzell opened with a few pleasantries about how greatly all officers of the Reichswehr esteemed Ludendorff and his wartime leadership. Ludendorff crankily interrupted that while he was certain of the "inner" respect of his fellow officers, he would have liked more visible signs of support through all the past years and the many indignities suffered. Echoing Siegfried, he declared himself "proud" of his lonely struggle since "the strong [one] is most powerful alone."[47] Beck, as the official representative of the ministry, gave the meeting an official appearance. He read a formal declaration of the Reichswehr minister, clarifying the ministry's stance on the controversy between Ludendorff and Elze discussed above. The Reichswehr Ministry firmly believed that Ludendorff had never wavered in prosecuting the Battle of Tannenberg, particularly on the crucial night of August 26, 1914. It regretted banning Ludendorff's publications on the subject and hoped that the ban's rescission would placate the Feldherr's sense of honor. It did not. Ludendorff cited chapter and verse of the many insults leveled at him in books by Elze, Hindenburg, and many others.

One can only imagine what Beck must have been thinking, sitting dutifully, taking notes concerning seemingly every pinprick ever suffered by a testy sixty-nine-year-old. His notes on the meeting describe Ludendorff as generally supportive of the Reichswehr and welcoming the recognition that the Reichswehr Ministry's recent attentions implied. Ludendorff's bitterness, assumed by and apparent to all, Beck masked with delicate phrases concerning Ludendorff's firm intention to defend his own honor and his desire to postpone a meeting with Hitler until he had had more time to recover from the hardships imposed on himself and his followers.[48]

The public revival of Ludendorff's legend in 1935 also coincided with efforts by the army leadership to restore the names of Kurt von Schleicher and Ferdinand von Bredow after their murder at the hands of the Nazis during the "Night of the Long Knives" in June 1934.[49] The murder of Schleicher, which the Nazis accomplished under the cover of similarly murderous attacks on Ernst Röhm and other SA leaders cast a heavy shadow over the Tannenberg League. Earlier oppression and arrests had created an atmosphere of tension and provoked lengthy, indignant manifestos from those affected.[50] Tannenbergers had their homes searched, were denied passports and weapons permits, faced financial and commercial difficulties such as the denial of pensions or business boycotts. But the brutality of the Night of the Long Knives raised the specter of wholesale liquidation that most members had never imagined possible. Ludendorff's mail ominously stopped at the time of the Röhm Putsch.[51]

Ironically, among the leadership at least, the murder of Röhm and his circle prompted not fear but self-satisfaction. It seems clear that Ludendorff's close associates knew of the impending strike at Röhm in advance and privately rejoiced that Hitler had finally eliminated Röhm. "The events of which you wrote on the twenty-ninth have come to pass," Friedrich Bronsart von Schellendorf wrote to Robert Holtzmann, Ludendorff's eyes and ears in Berlin, "but much more wonderfully than one thought! How long has the Feldherr been warning against that 175er [Röhm]."[52] Some of Ludendorff's followers similarly rejoiced in the murder. Walter Niederstebruch's dubious diary published in 1978 contains material that indicates that it was Röhm's "behavior" and the refusal of Hitler to kick him out of the NSDAP that was the reason for Ludendorff's rejection of Hitler.[53] "I know for a fact that already in 1927 Hitler knew of the unnatural inclination of Röhm and his companion, Herr Heines. . . . Despite that, Hitler called him back into this position. I suspect precisely because of it!"[54]

A second attempt at reconciliation in 1935 allowed the Nazis to capitalize on Ludendorff's fame in conjunction with the several rearmament bombshells of that year. The *London Times* reported that Beck again visited Ludendorff at his home in late February to see if the regime could do something in honor of Ludendorff's upcoming seventieth birthday. Beck carried with him a proposal to grant Ludendorff the title of field marshal at a commemoration of the launching of Operation Michael on March 21, 1918. The army was willing to raise the stakes, obviously, following the flurry of negotiations with Ludendorff in late 1934/early 1935.[55] But the memo remained in Beck's pocket. News of Beck's mission had reached Ludendorff, who dispatched an emissary to forestall Beck's approach.[56] Ludendorff refused the visit while pretending at least not to know Beck's purpose. His representative, Holtzmann, delivered a somewhat cryptic letter to Beck, in which Ludendorff politely but firmly explained that he needed nothing more than his own self-respect to survive. He could serve the Volk knowing that they trusted him, his life experiences, and his historical vision.[57] Two days later, Beck traveled to Tutzing for a brief and pleasant personal visit, returning with an inscribed copy of *Mein militärischer Werdegang*.

Various explanations for his refusal of the field marshal rank have been offered over the years. Some believe Ludendorff insisted that only a sovereign (certainly not a corporal!) could bestow the rank and then only in wartime. Others cited Ludendorff's continued discomfort with being associated with the Nazi regime.[58] One apocryphal story even tells of Hitler arriving at Ludendorff's house, baton in hand, only to be rudely shown the door by the irate general.[59] The latter story is false, of course. Ludendorff commented at his meeting with Beck and Wetzell in January 1935 that birthdays were not the occasions for military honors. The time to have bequeathed such an honor, Ludendorff noted acidly, would have been his fiftieth military anniversary, which passed unnoticed in 1932. His friend, General Friedrich Bronsart von Schellendorf had received a congratulatory telegram at his jubilee, but Ludendorff got nothing.[60]

Actually, Ludendorff simply thought the honor beneath him, having already bestowed on himself the loftier title of Feldherr, putting him in a class with only perhaps Frederick the Great and Napoleon. Field marshals, relatively speaking, are a dime a dozen. "The title field marshal is beneath my dignity," he wrote to Robert Holtzmann.[61] In a letter to Holtzmann from the same period, Ludendorff explained that the mere offer, however well-intentioned, had placed him in a bind. If he had accepted, Freemasons and other enemies would have concluded that only for the sake of such titles had Ludendorff fought in the war. If he declined, he could face retribution from the regime.[62] Fritsch told his fellow officers that Ludendorff refused the offer calmly, and that while Hitler and Ludendorff "do not love each other, they interact politely."[63] Ludendorff is also rumored to have refused the offer of an estate in the Lüneberger Heide on the grounds that only victorious commanders earn such rewards.[64] For his own part, Ludendorff described the meeting as "harmonious" and welcomed the opportunity to lobby for the rights of his followers within the Wehrmacht.[65]

The public announcement of the creation of the Wehrmacht on March 16, 1935, officially abrogating important provisions of the Treaty of Versailles, Ludendorff interpreted, not surprisingly, as a personal victory. "My greatest longing is fulfilled," he said.[66] In an interview granted to the United Press Association, Ludendorff avoided wacky proclamations concerning the supranational powers and instead greeted the introduction of conscription as a "guarantee of peace," returning to the German people their "moral right" to self-defense.[67] On the very next day (March 17, 1935), Defense Minister Werner von Blomberg praised Ludendorff during a speech at the Prussian Opera House celebrating *Heldengedenktag*.[68] Blomberg invoked Hindenburg's memory and then recalled "the man who, from the glorious beginning at Tannenberg, through the whole heroic course of the Great War, stood at Hindenburg's side; who with the strength of Atlas bore a world on his shoulders: we bow before the great *Feldherr* Ludendorff."[69] I am sure Ludendorff appreciated Blomberg's use of the honorific.

In any case, Ludendorff was sufficiently moved to issue a brief statement in a supplement to *Am heiligen Quell*, calling the reinstitution of conscription a "great racial deed," which at least made Germany capable of defending itself from its foreign enemies. He could not resist adding, of course, that Germany also required greater "spiritual unity," which could only be found in an "indigenous apprehension of God"—by which he meant of course his wife's Deutsche Gotterkenntnis. "We want to be free," Ludendorff concluded, "not only from potential enemy neighboring powers, we want also to be free from the supranational powers that secretly destroy our Volk."[70] The statement also included a thinly veiled criticism of the government when it prayed for the German people to be "wisely governed" so as to be able to achieve its great task.[71] Both the *New York Times* and the *London Times* found it significant that Ludendorff ended his statement not with "Heil Hitler" but with his usual "Long

Live Freedom," nor did he mention Hitler or any other National Socialist leader by name.[72]

Some pressure for the rehabilitation of Ludendorff clearly came from Hitler personally. According to Goebbels, Hitler maintained a sincere affection for the old man.[73] Other Nazis lamented the rift between Ludendorff and their movement because they so obviously shared common aims and common enemies.[74] Hitler was determined to ensconce him in the pantheon of Nazi heroes, even if only posthumously.[75]

Seventieth Birthday Celebration

Further extensive negotiations between the Wehrmacht and Ludendorff paved the way for a widely publicized celebration of Ludendorff's seventieth birthday in 1935. Ludendorff still rankled at his treatment at the hands of Hitler since 1924 and agreed to participate in an army- (but not party-) sponsored event, provided that "the two names that begin with 'H' [presumably Hitler and Hindenburg] not be spoken." Blomberg and Fritsch agreed.[76]

Hitler ordered public buildings to hoist flags in Ludendorff's honor and issued a public statement: "The German Volk recalls on this occasion the immortal accomplishments of its greatest commander in the World War."[77] Blomberg and Werner von Fritsch attended a ceremony in Tutzing, as did thousands of additional well-wishers, both military and civilian. In a short speech, Blomberg welcomed the "soldier Ludendorff" back into the army's fold—presumably intending to separate the soldier from the "prophet."[78] The Hohenzollern crown prince attended the ceremony, and the former Kaiser sent greetings from Holland.[79] Military garrisons throughout the country held parades in his honor, and several towns renamed prominent streets "Ludendorffstrasse."[80]

Chief of the Truppenamt, General Ludwig Beck, gave a radio address on the occasion of Ludendorff's birthday that also expressed the desire of the army to claim Ludendorff's legacy as their own. Ludendorff was the "shining symbol of military leadership" for all the young soldiers of the recently minted Wehrmacht. Beck enumerated Ludendorff's accomplishments in a manner befitting Ludendorff's own publications. Ludendorff was the harbinger who even before 1914 saw the need to better exploit technology and to increase the size of the army. He fought his way house to house to capture the citadel at Liège. Tannenberg. Poland. Hindenburg's name appears only in passing. Ludendorff, the Feldherr, belonged in the OHL from the start of the war, Beck believed, not only from 1916 on. When the battle looked hopeless at the end of 1918, Ludendorff, like Frederick the Great, thought only of a glorious defeat.[81]

Müller interprets this speech correctly as an effort by Beck to enlist Ludendorff in his struggle against the "totalitarian" claims of Hitler's leadership. Beck preferred a dualistic model of governance in which military and civilian leadership shared responsibility for policy.[82] By emphasizing Ludendorff's *military* genius and the failure of any corresponding political genius during the Great War, Beck was implicitly arguing against Hitler's claim to total civilian leadership in the Third Reich. Only by combining military genius (in Ludendorff's mold if not Ludendorff himself) with civilian/political genius (Hitler) could the state be strong.[83]

Figure 19. Generals Werner von Blomberg and Werner von Fritsch with Ludendorff on his seventieth birthday, April 9, 1935. Photo by Imagno / Getty Images.

Ludendorff seems to have been less intent on serving Beck's purpose of balancing Nazi power in the state than in using his revived contacts on the "inside" to promote his own interests, such as having Deutsche Gotter-kenntnis literature distributed at military bases or lobbying for the elimination of Freemasons from the ranks of the army.[84] The effort to distribute literature met with only limited success despite an official decree allowing it.[85] Many commanders refused to promote Ludendorff's anti-Christian worldview. Nevertheless, the army officially honored Ludendorff. Beck arranged for Ludendorff's bust to be placed in the Reichswehr Ministry building alongside those of other former chiefs of the General Staff and intervened on Ludendorff's behalf in countless other ways.[86]

Ludendorff personally thanked the Führer for the birthday wishes in a brief telegram, yet otherwise made himself a nuisance.[87] In his own speech on his birthday Ludendorff again lauded the institution of conscription but reminded his listeners that Germany had had a conscript army in 1914 as well. That army, however, had been poisoned by the suprana-tional forces that beset Germany. Only by fighting these forces with the tools provided by his wife's philosophy, could Germany truly be secure.[88] He refused to speak with correspondents from the Nazi press yet made himself easily accessible to foreign correspondents. As Nazi attendees pre-pared to sing the "Horst Wessel Song," Ludendorff's followers burst in with an anti-Catholic tune, with the refrain "save our people from the power of the priests." Other anti-Christian songs angered many attendees and received no coverage in the German press.[89] None of these outbreaks appear in the brief, official Nazi newsreel of the celebration. Instead, one sees marching crowds and Ludendorff, in full uniform, giving an awk-ward "Hitler salute."[90]

The rapprochement was only partial. In an article announcing the launch of the ship *Tannenberg* in September, the *Nationalsozialistiche Korrespondenz* mentioned the significance of the ship being named for the battle and last resting place of the great General-Feldmarschall von Hindenburg—but Ludendorff's name did not appear.[91] Ludendorff still refused publicly to associate with Hitler and failed to attend the lavish twelfth anniversary celebration of the Beer Hall Putsch on the eighth and ninth of November. The "martyrs" of the movement were to be disin-terred and entombed in newly constructed "Temples of Honor" on the Königsplatz in Munich. Hitler nevertheless invoked Ludendorff's memory in a speech on the eighth, recalling Ludendorff's courage in marching at the head of the column despite the danger of armed clashes with the police and army.[92]

While Ludendorff's works such as *Der totale Krieg* received a great deal of public attention, Ludendorff's rapprochement with Hitler was short-lived. By late November 1935, the Prussian Gestapo had again taken action to ban lectures by representatives of Ludendorff's publishing company. The content of the lectures and the behavior of the attendees were creating a public disturbance, the Gestapo argued, and so would be forbidden for the indefinite future. The Ludendorff press tried to canvas its representatives to find out what exactly had prompted the ban but without apparent success. Petitions to Hitler went unanswered.[93]

The pressure continued into 1936 when Hitler cracked down on the various pagan movements in Germany. The leaders of the German Faith Movement, Count Ernst zu Reventlow and Professor Jacob Wilhelm Hauer, both resigned their positions, but the Ludendorffs soldiered on in the face of increasing difficulties.[94] Illustrative of the regime's stance toward Deutsche Gotterkenntnis was the failed effort of Fritz Probst to receive permission to hold a funeral service for one of Ludendorff's followers. The local Kreisleiter objected, saying that any speaker must strictly limit his remarks to narrowly religious ones and not comment on politics in any way. Nor would he be allowed to praise the "Ludendorff movement."[95]

Even after Ludendorff's death and lionization as one of the heroes of the Nazi pantheon, organs of the Nazi Party continued to belittle him and his followers despite the official reconciliation. Julius Streicher's *Der Sturmer* disparaged the Ludendorffers for being "prattlers" who denounced the "supranational powers" but never did anything about them, prompting at least one of Ludendorff's followers to spring to Mathilde's defense in a lengthy letter to the editor.[96]

Throughout this period, Ludendorff's contacts with the military continued. In November 1935, generals von Reichenau and von Bock traveled to Tutzing to visit the Feldherr, ostensibly to discuss purely military matters. Reichenau's reputation as a "political general" make it likely, however, that Beck's messages of the previous spring were reinforced.[97] Ludendorff remained unconvinced and primarily concerned to promote his own movement's interests. Mathilde complained to Holtzmann that the army just wants to hitch its wagon to Ludendorff so that if things went wrong they could blame him again as in 1918, 1920, and 1923.[98] When Army Supreme Command (OKH) Chief Werner von Fritsch followed in February 1936 and asked if Ludendorff wouldn't abandon his ideological struggle for the good of the army, Ludendorff had a fit. He declared the Wehrmacht a bastion of "Christian reactionaries" and later dismissed Holtzmann, his contact to Beck, from his service.[99] Ludendorff refused to allow any public celebrations of his seventy-first birthday in 1936 because of the continuing restrictions placed on his publishing house and his associates.[100]

While Müller describes the meetings over the course of 1935 and 1936 among Beck, Ludendorff, and other representatives of the Wehrmacht Ministry as part of an effort to "rebalance" the arrangement between the Nazis and the Wehrmacht, the public was bound to view the rapprochement between Hitler and Ludendorff quite differently. Unaware of the intrigues inside the Wehrmacht, the German public instead saw a gradual lessening of the hostility between the Führer and the Feldherr that in fact picked up steam where the efforts of Beck, Fritsch, and Blomberg left off. According to Graf von der Schulenburg, Beck's speech on Ludendorff's birthday provoked an "exhalation" in the German people, so pleased were they to hear the Feldherr's name in public again.[101] It was as though a psychological tension had developed around the obvious feuding of the old comrades Hitler and Ludendorff. How could the greatest men of the "old" and the "new" Germany entertain such hostility toward one another? Their fleeting moments of reconciliation raised hopes for resolution of the unspoken inner conflict to the benefit not of the Wehrmacht (at least not in Beck's sense) but to the benefit of Hitler and (to a lesser extent and for a shorter time) Ludendorff.

The chilly atmosphere meant that further efforts were required before Ludendorff's place in the Nazi pantheon was secure. By late 1936, at least, high-ranking National Socialists were engaged in discussions with followers of the general and his wife. One such intermediary was Karl Fischer von Treuenfeld. Treuenfeld later became notorious as a general in the Waffen-SS for his role in the massacres that followed the assassination of Reinhard Heydrich in 1942. As a captain in the Imperial German army, he had worked for Ludendorff in various staff positions from 1915 onward and became a devoted follower after the war.[102] Treuenfeld blamed Freemasons and Jews for the failure of his business enterprise in the 1920 and so found the Ludendorffs' philosophical approach congenial. Throughout the 1930s, Treuenfeld worked to reconcile his old commander with Adolf Hitler, in whom Treuenfeld saw Germany's salvation. Joseph Goebbels in his diaries records a meeting with Treuenfeld on December 12, 1936, in which Treuenfeld reported Ludendorff's displeasure with one of Goebbels's recent speeches before the Reichskulturkammer.[103] A month later, Treuenfeld appeared again, with a proposal for Ludendorff-Hitler meeting.

Goebbels had once been a fervent admirer of Ludendorff, but by 1936 saw little prospect for a reconciliation.[104] In Goebbels's eyes, as in Hitler's, Ludendorff had been poisoned by his association with Mathilde, whom Hitler once referred to as that "hysterical broad."[105] Most high-ranking Nazis attributed Ludendorff's strange behavior to Mathilde's influence. Hitler thought that an unsuccessful surgery performed by Mathilde had imbalanced the old general.[106] Alfred Rosenberg sought deeper psychological explanations for his deep dependence on such a woman.

Ludendorff simply placed too many conditions on the terms of his meeting with Hitler. What was more, Ludendorff persisted in writing embarrassing articles in *Am heiligen Quell.* Just as Treuenfeld appeared to request the meeting, in fact, Goebbels was contemplating banning Ludendorff's paper for three months for several scandalous pieces on the Spanish Civil War.[107] Ludendorff could simply not be allowed to stand outside the law or to enjoy any exceptional license to publish nonsense, thought Goebbels.[108]

Finally, on March 30, 1937, Hitler visited Ludendorff in Munich.[109] No direct account of the meeting exists, but one can surmise the content of their discussions from press releases and other accounts that followed.[110] The official press release acknowledged prior "disagreements and difficulties" but insisted that the "exhaustive conciliatory talks" had overcome them. Ludendorff was said to appreciate the Führer's success in demolishing the Treaty of Versailles and making Germany again "master of the Rhine." For his part, Hitler was pleased that "the Third Reich and its Wehrmacht once again enjoyed the confidence of the great commander of the World War, reminiscent of the ties between the fighters of November 9, 1923, and the old army."[111]

Hitler described the meeting to Joseph Goebbels as "very cordial." Ludendorff was moved to see his old comrade and greeted Hitler with tears in his eyes. Hitler may have broken the ice by playing on Ludendorff's well-known paranoia about Catholic influence. Hitler discussed a recent Italian film, *Condotierri*, which was generating discomfort within National Socialist circles for its starkly Catholic tone. Ludendorff must have been pleased when Hitler revealed his intent to ban the film, despite Italian protests.[112] Surprisingly, for anyone acquainted with Ludendorff's dogmatic character, the general expressed understanding for Hitler's careful tactical approach, especially in church matters.[113] As a result of the meeting, Deutsche Gotterkenntnis was granted equal standing with other religious denominations in German law. Second, Goebbels lifted any extraordinary bans placed on the Ludendorff publishing house, insisting only that it be subject to the "normal" rules governing the media in Nazi Germany.[114] In keeping with the official party stance on "religious neutrality," party members were forbidden to wear uniform while attending Deutsche Gotterkenntnis events but were not otherwise prevented from associating with the Ludendorffs.[115]

Motivations both personal and political drove Hitler to bring Ludendorff back into the fold. According to Goebbels's diaries, Hitler had clear personal feelings for the fellow old fighter. Goebbels admits that there was also a political calculation. When Treuenfeld first broached the subject with Goebbels in December 1936, the Propaganda Minister lamented that Ludendorff wasted his energy on "hopeless extremism," but added, "What we couldn't do with him if he listened to reason!"[116] Once the two parties had come to terms, Goebbels was quick to grasp the possibilities. Ludendorff could be useful in the conflict with the churches since he "could say one thing and another that we [the propaganda ministry] may not say."[117]

Even before the final reconciliation, there are indications that Nazi officials used the Ludendorffs and their publications to further their ideological ends. When it suited the party's purpose, as in 1935 during the drive to "deconfessionalize public life," Ludendorff could be attacked along with other religious groups.[118] When attacks on the Christian churches were welcome, Ludendorff could be let loose. For example, the party authorized the publication in 1936 of Mathilde's book *Der ungesühnte Frevel*, which alleged Jewish involvement in the murder of famous Germans such as Schiller, Mozart, and Luther.[119] After the pope published "Mit brennender Sorge" in 1937, expressing concern at the Nazi's meddling in church affairs, Ludendorff was given free rein.[120]

During the periods of thaw in relations, Ludendorff became effusive in his praise of Hitler in the pages of *Am heiligen Quell*. During his years in the wilderness, Ludendorff had consistently referred to Hitler simply as "Herr Hitler," abjuring the honorific "Führer" that was mandated by Nazi protocol. After March 1937, the "Führer," the "creator of Greater Germany" appeared in the pages of Ludendorff's journal.[121] At the annual gathering of his followers in Tutzing, he reminded those assembled that "we fight for Volk and state with Deutsche Gotterkenntnis," and beseeched them to exercise caution in their demands on the state. Rather than directly addressing matters of policy, speakers should let the teachings of Deutsche Gotterkenntnis speak for themselves. Policy would follow if the movement became more firmly anchored in the people, he assumed. There were also limits to Ludendorff's compliance. He advised against observing such formalities as the Hitler salute. Such formalities were unnecessary and could mask corruption, Ludendorff argued. Inner conviction was more important than superficial ritual.[122]

Benefits of Reconciliation

Ludendorff sought at every opportunity to capitalize on the rekindled relationship with Hitler. He and his associates used the declaration of religious equality to silence criticism of their efforts to convert their fellow citizens to the German faith. To readers of his *Am heiligen Quell Deutscher Kraft*, Ludendorff lauded the removal of restrictions on his followers' activities that the Führer had promised in their March 30 meeting. He and his followers would now be able to "build up the foundations for a completely völkisch state" more effectively.[123] Followers of Ludendorff used public statements such as those made on the occasion of the general's seventieth birthday to deflect criticism of their leader even in private conversations.[124]

Based on his conversations with Hitler in March 1937, Ludendorff believed that he now had the right to insist on Deutsche Gotterkenntnis being included in the curricula of German schools as basic instruction in Christianity was. Frau Ludendorff recognized that the number of teachers qualified to provide such instructions would be small at first, but insisted that progress would be quick. In the summer of 1937, the Ludendorffs sponsored a small conference at which two hundred teachers were (re) acquainted with what such instruction would involve.[125]

Figure 20. Erich and Mathilde outside their villa in Tutzing, April 4, 1935.
Photo by Imagno / Getty Images.

The Ludendorffs believed that only Deutsche Gotterkenntnis could provide the new völkisch state with a sufficiently solid, moral core to survive. Students would be taught about their roots in the Volk and in the state and of their duties to both. They would be acquainted with nature and taught to respect "god's" creation and "god's" will. More importantly, children would be protected from the dangers of atheism (and therefore Bolshevism) that rational people often resorted to after becoming disillusioned with traditional religion.[126] Resistance to this plan, as might be expected, was great. Even in the face of official permission, many school officials refused to provide facilities even for extracurricular instruction in Deutsche Gotterkenntnis, citing lack of interest or fearing the potential controversy among parents and students of mainstream denominations.[127]

Nor apparently, was Ludendorff satisfied with the Nazis' progress in lifting the restrictions on Deutscher Gotterkenntnis. In May 1937, he wrote to Hermann Göring complaining of discrimination against his faith in the new Wehrmacht and questioning the wording of two proposed paragraphs in the criminal code governing religious freedom. He urged Göring to meet with the trusty Major von Treuenfeld, so that Göring might better understand Deutscher Gotterkenntnis and enforce the doctrine of equality established by Hitler at the March meeting. Like Goebbels before him, Göring indulged the old general with a gracious formal reply, but if Goebbels' diary entries are any indication, they resented the petty interference.[128]

The closer relationship sometimes caused problems, as a directive of the party Chancellery makes clear. Books and pamphlets with "problematic content," Ludendorff's included, had been receiving written praise from leading state party officials. These pronouncements would then be misused by the publishers for advertising or to lend the work an air of official approval. Bormann warned his fellow party leaders never to provide such comments unless they had carefully vetted the source and never to write in favor of works of a religious character.[129] Ludendorff is not mentioned by name, but his works certainly fit the description offered by Bormann. Forewords by Göring and other leading representatives of the Nazi regime appeared, and continued to appear in Ludendorff publications after 1937. The Ludendorff press clearly sought to use such commentaries to give a semblance of official imprimatur to their products. The title page of an account of the 1914 Liège battle features words of praise from Franz Halder for Ludendorff, calling him the "exemplar of German soldierdom."[130]

Rumors circulated in November 1937 that Ludendorff had sent a letter critical of National Socialist foreign policy to an acquaintance abroad, but these rumors proved unfounded.[131] On the contrary, Ludendorff became effusive in his praise of Hitler. At the celebration of his fifty-fifth anniversary in military service in April 1937, Ludendorff lauded the Führer in "extraordinarily strong" terms.[132] The two exchanged pleasant telegrams on the anniversary of the Beer Hall Putsch in 1937.[133]

But the arrangement was still not completely satisfactory for the Ludendorffs. At a gathering for Deutsche Gotterkenntnis lecturers in Tutzing on August 4, 1937, Ludendorff explained the group's tenuous relationship to the National Socialist state. While Hitler had promised religious equality at their meeting in March, there existed a danger for those seeking to enlighten their fellow Germans about Deutsche Gotterkenntnis. The party's plank on religion (point 24 of the party program of 1920) contained a paradox, Ludendorff argued, because it both promised "liberty for all religious denominations in the State" but also pledged the party's support for "positive Christianity."[134] Given the Ludendorffers' position on Christianity, positive or otherwise, this was a problem. Would a speaker's attack on Christianity be construed as an attack on the party? Even worse, for those indoctrinated in the Ludendorffs' philosophy, this advocacy of Christianity would necessarily hamper the party's otherwise worthy goal, pledged in the same plank, to "combat the Jewish-materialistic spirit within and around us." Ludendorff had dispatched letters to various agencies seeking clarification of the matter but never apparently received a reply.[135]

In the Ludendorffs' paranoid worldview, "priestly castes" were naturally still sabotaging their work, but as Ludendorff lamented at the speakers' gathering, groups within the National Socialist Party were also working against them. He read from a report authored by an unnamed source that indicated that the party was eyeing *Am heiligen Quell* for a takeover. It was said that the Ludendorffs' journal was needlessly complicated and high-brow. Unseen plotters within the NSDAP reasoned that something simpler, that appeared less frequently, would have a greater impact. Not to worry, Ludendorff assured his listeners. Such a thing could not occur "so long as my wife and I are alive." That condition would not prevail for much longer.[136]

SIEGFRIED'S DEATH

But if you feel at all inclined to do a loyal deed for anyone, noble
King . . . let me commend my dear sweetheart to your mercy. Let her
profit from being your sister. By the virtue of all princes,
stand by her loyally!

—THE MORTALLY WOUNDED SIEGFRIED TO GÜNTHER,
KING OF BURGUNDY, THE NIBELUNGENLIED

So I ask the Germans who listen to me—the dead are better heard
than the living—rally around my wife. Be loyal to her, to the
publishing house, and to *"Am heiligen Quell Deutscher Kraft."*

—LUDENDORFF'S LAST TESTAMENT, 1937

In late November 1937 Ludendorff fell ill with what was reported variously as a bladder infection, kidney, and/or circulation problems.[1] He was treated, ironically, at the Josephinum Clinic in Munich by Catholic nurses whose faith he had scorned and ridiculed for so many years.[2] Concern for the seventy-two-year-old Feldherr was obvious in early press reports of his illness. His family gathered to be at his side. Hitler paid at least one well-publicized visit to the hospital to offer the nation's best wishes for a speedy recovery.[3] That recovery seemed under way in mid-December, as Ludendorff was able briefly to leave his bed and wander the hospital corridors. Goebbels in his diaries wrote frequently of Ludendorff's improvement.[4] On December 19, he was able to sit in a chair and read and even, according to Mathilde's recollection, to use the last of his strength to sign the cards of newly registered members of Deutsche Gotterkenntnis. But later that day, his condition worsened dramatically. Ludendorff did not have a bladder infection, but cancer.[5] Hasty calls went out to family members who had departed in expectation of his gradual improvement.[6]

When Erich Ludendorff died at 8:00 a.m. on December 20, 1937, Hitler issued a formal proclamation that rehearsed the legend that had been built for official purposes during his long rehabilitation. Ludendorff (along with Hindenburg) had tried "to wrench the nation's power of resistance onward to unparalleled achievements" during the First World War. When Germany lost the war thanks to the nation's "lack of character and deplorable weakness," Ludendorff "joined forces with the fighters to reerect the nation both within and without"—an unsubtle reference to the Beer Hall Putsch and others. "From then on," Hitler added more cryptically, "he struggled and fought in his own way."[7]

Press Tributes

German newspapers treated their readers to a recapitulation of the many legends surrounding the former general. There was nearly universal adoption of Ludendorff's self-made title: Feldherr. Much ink had been spilled in the previous two decades over whether Ludendorff deserved the title.[8] But in 1937, in Hitler's Germany, the verdict was in: Ludendorff was the very incarnation of the term.[9] Headline after headline praised the Feldherr of the Great War. Ludendorff was "the great organizer," the master strategist, the brilliant tactician, in short, according to the eulogy delivered by War Minister Werner von Blomberg, he was "one of the greats of Prussian-German soldierdom."[10] To describe Ludendorff, Blomberg twice during his eulogy quoted Clausewitz, which must have caused the long-dead military philosopher to spin in his grave.[11] Clausewitz could have had Ludendorff in mind, Blomberg said, when he wrote of a military leader as "an obelisk towards which the principal streets of a town converge, the strong will of a proud spirit stands prominent and commanding in the middle of the Art of War."[12]

Several papers recounted the stories of Liège and Tannenberg in some detail. After decades of dispute, Ludendorff's view of these events appeared vindicated in these retrospectives. *Der Angriff*, Joseph Goebbels's mouthpiece, even reprinted the relevant section of Ludendorff's memoirs in the December 21 issue. As we have seen in a previous chapter, the battle for the fortress at Liège cemented Ludendorff's reputation as an energetic leader. His assumption of command of the Fourteenth Infantry Brigade from General von Wussow and subsequent capture of the fortress garrison were undisputedly heroic acts. In the days following Ludendorff's death, newspapers recounted colorful moments from the battle, such as when he rallied his stalled forces with the cry: "Fellows! Are you going to allow a general to take on the enemy alone?"[13] General von Blomberg devoted nearly 20 percent of his eulogy to recounting how Ludendorff stormed the Belgian positions and entered the city with his lone brigade. "Accompanied only by his adjutant, he brought about the surrender of the surprised citadel."[14] Ludendorff cultivated an Olympian demeanor and yet relished this image of an officer who led from the front. Numerous accounts of his battles, especially Liège, remarked on his personal bravery during the attack. Even French newspapers lauded his "unusual courage and unusual guts."[15]

Not surprisingly, coverage of his dismissal as first quartermaster general in 1918 reinforced the "stab in the back" legend that Ludendorff had originated. The Deutscher Reichskriegerbund (Kyffhäuser) praised Ludendorff for continuing the fight against Germany's "supranational" enemies even after Germany "fell victim to the cowardly revolt, which broke the power [of Germany's] victoriously led forces."[16] Even General Blomberg's eulogy linked the success of the revolution in 1918 to the insidious forces behind Ludendorff's dismissal.[17] "As Ludendorff was dismissed at the end of October 1918," recalled Blomberg, "the path to the November Revolt lay open."[18]

The uniformity of most accounts testifies to the existence of a "party line" on Ludendorff's historical significance.[19] The most apparent theme in the many treatments of Ludendorff's life was his connection with Hitler and the NSDAP. The red thread that ran through Ludendorff's life and that bound him so closely with Adolf Hitler was his concern for German preparedness (*Wehrhaftigkeit*). Germany could only defend itself if it possessed a large, strong army, if its people were united in spirit, and if it were commanded by an inspiring leader. To those ends, Ludendorff had lobbied for a larger army in 1912, as Blomberg reminded his listeners at the funeral. That he failed to convince the political leadership of the day of the necessity for more divisions to counter Germany's encirclement was only evidence of that leadership's corruption and ineptitude, according to the general.[20]

With the funeral held in Munich, the association with the Beer Hall Putsch of 1923 was unavoidable. Papers described Ludendorff as Hitler's "fellow fighter" for Germany's freedom from Versailles, from international Jewry, and the other supranational forces at work. Ludendorff's work with Hitler and the NSDAP was of a piece with his concern for the spiritual unity of Germany. That Ludendorff had largely retreated from public life in order to devote himself to fostering the spiritual unity of Germany was the common euphemism used to mask his increasing isolation and the hostility of both the Weimar and Nazi regimes from 1925 to 1935.[21]

Germany lost the Great War despite Ludendorff's genius, one newspaper opined, only because Germany lacked a statesman of equal genius. Only after the war would Germany find such a man in Adolf Hitler.[22] In Hitler's Third Reich, many papers pointed out, Ludendorff saw his life's dream fulfilled. He could die a contented man, they argued, because on March 1935, with the renunciation of the disarmament clauses of the Versailles Treaty, Hitler had restored Germany's honor, had restored Germany's sovereignty. Here coverage of the funeral reinforced the linkages made in 1935 as the NSDAP used Ludendorff symbolically to link the Kaiser's army with the new Wehrmacht.[23] Blomberg concluded his eulogy with an expression of the Wehrmacht's pride that Ludendorff had been "one of ours." "His spirit will live on in the German Volk and above all in the German Wehrmacht as an incentive to give our all for Germany."[24]

One of the hallmarks of Nazi propaganda was that it strove to maintain at least some level of verisimilitude. Given Ludendorff's high public profile and notoriously cantankerous behavior, both official and nonofficial retrospectives published in the days following his death often included veiled references to his troubled personality. For the regime that also publicly lionized Field Marshal Paul von Hindenburg after his death in 1934, the well known and public dispute between Ludendorff and Hindenburg over their respective wartime legacies created some awkward moments. "What General Ludendorff accomplished side by side with the field marshal, who preceded him to Valhalla," said General Werner von Blomberg in his eulogy, "belongs for all time to the most beautiful pages of honor in German history."[25] Such phraseology did not account for the acrimonious exchanges between the two generals in the 1920s and 1930s. The two had made a great wartime team, one paper concluded, since Hindenburg's even temperament had softened Ludendorff's "brusqueness," while Ludendorff's initiative and inexhaustible energy had been the driving force behind the Supreme Command.[26] "Brusqueness" was only one of Ludendorff's qualities that were acknowledged in coverage of his funeral. Uncompromising was another. Blomberg called him an "inconvenient prophet" with a "belligerent, uncompromising nature." "Ludendorff followed his own path, upright and unyielding, wrote one German newspaper."[27] "Like all uncompromising fighters of this earth," intoned Ludendorff's former bitter enemy, Adolf Hitler, "the mark of his personality will be more obvious to coming generations than to his contemporaries."[28]

While they could acknowledge the "polarizing" effect he had on people, none of the biographical sketches mentioned Ludendorff's hostility to the Catholic Church—a fact that irked his most dedicated followers.[29] Only in passages quoted from the foreign press could one read more than a passing remark concerning Ludendorff's anti-Christian views. While acknowledging his military abilities, one London newspaper remarked that "by contrast the general's postwar political and literary activities, especially his fight against the Christian church, are judged disparagingly by all sides."[30] Other references were more subtle. Hitler, for example, tacitly acknowledged their strife only by mentioning that Ludendorff strove for "German freedom . . . in his own way."[31]

The main Catholic paper in Germany, *Germania* (Berlin), no doubt on orders from Goebbels, also printed a series of articles on December 20 and the few days following. *Germania*, like most papers, published the speeches and telegrams of Hitler, Goebbels, Blomberg, and other officials. Their own pieces mimic the glorifying tone of the mainstream and völkisch press, even if one can perhaps read some criticism between the lines. The coverage in *Germania* follows the "happy marriage" storyline cultivated in Hindenburg's memoirs and elsewhere, always pairing Ludendorff, the "personification of will," with Hindenburg, calm and with a "deep-seated faith in God." Somewhat strangely, *Germania* acknowledged Ludendorff's postwar fight against the "supranational powers" of Judaism, Freemasonry, and "political Catholicism," and yet maintained a respectful tone, citing Ludendorff's early support for the NSDAP and the cause of national revival.[32]

Despite the published homages, many Catholics rankled at the celebration of a man whose final decades were devoted to often outrageous slanders against Catholicism, the pope, and the priesthood. The Catholic press published the official orders to fly flags at half-mast and to decorate buildings with memorial flags on the day of the burial, but many objected.[33] The bishop of Münster, Clemens Graf von Galen, explained that Catholic churches refused to hang them in honor of the man who had identified Catholicism with the "supranational powers" and with "godless Bolshevism." Galen made sure also to remind his listeners that it was not just Catholicism to which Ludendorff objected. "We cannot decorate Christian churches with flags," he said, "to honor the deluded and dogged enemy of Christianity."[34]

Even the foreign press, for the most part, adopted a reverent tone, and German papers quoted extensively, if selectively, from French, Polish, and British sources. Like the domestic press, foreign papers identified Ludendorff's willpower and energy as his greatest assets. "At all stages of his life Ludendorff carried things to the bitter end. He was always committed to use the most radical means to win quickly, as befitted his fiery spirit, that stood in contrast to his dry demeanor."[35]

German coverage of the foreign press tended to mask critiques of the Feldherr. Germans cited British papers in particular as heaping praise on the "Germany's greatest soldier of the Great War," even suggesting that his abilities surpassed those of their own leadership. Ludendorff innovated as the Allies struggled to learn his lessons.[36] *The Times* argued that alone among the leaders of the belligerent nations, Ludendorff refused to rely on mass to achieve victory and instead developed his own techniques based on surprise.[37] The *Manchester Guardian* called him "the most eminent of the wartime Feldherrn."[38] The British were respectful, but in their actual coverage, *The Times* of London did not ignore Ludendorff's shortcomings: his focus on tactics over strategy, for example, or his apparent blindness to the utility of tanks until it was too late. "Ludendorff is an outstanding lesson in the dangers of the expert," wrote one British journalist. "He proclaimed the doctrine of national war while regarding it as merely a super-size soldier's war."[39]

The American press was likewise guardedly complementary. Several high-ranking officers praised Ludendorff's military genius, and General Robert Bullard, the former commander of the American Second Army, admitted that Ludendorff's tactics were still being studied by the Allies.[40] According to the *New York Times*, Ludendorff was "devastating in onslaught, dogged on defense, ruthless and sly." He almost won the war with his 1918 offensives, and that should be his epitaph, argued the reporter sardonically: "Almost."[41]

Not surprisingly, French coverage was less enthusiastic. The *Paris Journal* rather uncharitably (if not untruthfully) called him "the man who lost the war."[42] French commentators grudgingly noted Ludendorff's energy but not without noting that Ludendorff's exertions had been for an ignoble cause. Several commentators turned the reader's attention back to the incredible sacrifices of the French nation during the war.[43] Not included in the German coverage of the foreign press were the several references to his postwar career in service of Deutsche Gotterkenntnis. The *Petit Parisien*, for example, in its front page story, labeled Ludendorff not only a warrior and a strategist, but also a "prophet."[44]

Coverage in Italian papers was of course profoundly shaped by Fascist Italy's newfound friendship with Nazi Germany. Ludendorff's kind remarks about the Italian Army in one of his postwar writings encouraged reciprocal admiration. Italian papers were effusive in their praise for "Germany's greatest warrior." Some commented on his anti-Catholic stance, but not his overweening hostility to Mussolini, expressed so often in the pages of *Volkswarte*.[45]

All of the major (and several minor!) dignitaries of the Third Reich offered their public condolences to the surviving members of the house of Ludendorff and often rather painfully attempted to weave Ludendorff's life story into their own. Hitler's note to Mathilde Ludendorff was naturally widely publicized, as were the reactions of Göring and Goebbels. Rudolf Hess had private words with Mathilde Ludendorff during the funeral.[46] Even Robert Ley and Walther Darré sent short notes of condolence that found their way into the German press.[47] The National Socialist Economic Service in its journal published a eulogy that praised Ludendorff for seeing the vital link between national defense and the national economy. His efficient administration of the Ober Ost region during the First World War should serve as a model, it wrote.[48] From his exile in Holland, the Kaiser authorized General von Mackensen as his representative to attend the funeral.[49]

Omitted from the discussion so far have been the devotions penned by members of Ludendorff's inner circle and other sympathetic groups. The very qualities that made Ludendorff nearly impossible to work with in real life caused one völkisch newspaper to compare him to Friedrich Nietzsche and describe him as Zarathustra, as a "volcano," an "ocean

Figure 21. Erich Ludendorff in 1935. Photo by Keystone-France / Gamma-Rapho via Getty Images.

of magma . . . controlled by a Nordic Titan's strength, bound by a regal self-mastery, encased in a rugged, jagged, hard, cold field-stone."[50] The Nordic/völkisch newspaper *Sigrune* went to nauseating lengths to lionize Ludendorff and to perpetuate many of the myths surrounding him. Not content with using the title Feldherr, *Sigrune* labeled Ludendorff a "Kriegsgott," whose penetrating blue eyes were the same as those that had caused the ancient Romans to speak of the "terrifying gaze of the Germans." He was a "natural-born, uncrowned king" in whose veins coursed *Wasablut*—the blood of the Swedish dynasty, whose ranks included the illustrious Gustav Adolf, the victor of Breitenfeld.[51]

Funeral

Plans for the funeral were quickly negotiated with the family. Hitler had wanted Ludendorff to be buried at the Neue Soldatenhalle or the Invalidenfriedhof in Berlin or perhaps alongside Hindenburg at the Tannenberg memorial, but Ludendorff himself had refused these offers during prior negotiations.[52] He had made clear to his followers in a 1937 circular that he did not want his funeral to serve as the occasion for official state or military gatherings.[53] Mathilde Ludendorff insisted on carrying out his last wish that he be buried near the family home in Tutzing, but Joseph Goebbels scheduled a complex public ceremony in Munich designed by Georg Buchner (who had also prepared the city for Mussolini's visit in 1937) to honor the fallen hero.[54] Goebbels labored intently over every detail of the ceremony, making changes up to the very last minute.[55]

Upon his death, Ludendorff's body was moved to the nearby headquarters of the Seventh Army Corps. It had been Ludendorff's explicit wish to lie in state surrounded by members of the newly formed armed forces, according to one newspaper account.[56] Staff officers of the army and Luftwaffe solemnly guarded Ludendorff's coffin, surrounded by flags and topped with his *Pickelhaube,* sword, and dozens of decorations. At 5:00 a.m., six noncommissioned officers arrived to carry the coffin (made of oak, naturally) to the waiting gun carriage. Honor guards accompanied the coffin to the main arch of the Siegestor. For several hours, according to reports, thousands of people filed past the coffin to offer their last respects to the war hero Ludendorff. Most touching were those elderly officers of the Kaiser's army who donned their uniforms in order to salute their former commander.[57]

Army bands played for the growing crowd as the time for Hitler's appearance approached. Shortly before 10:00 a.m., the Führer joined Blomberg, Göring, and General Fedor von Bock (standing in for Fritsch) to begin the main procession. Hitler's only formal role during the ceremony was to lay a wreath and offer a short expression of thanks on behalf of the nation. Photos of Hitler's performance show him offering the flag-draped coffin a rigid "German greeting" (as opposed to his more usual bent-elbow salute).[58] Once the parade began, Hitler marched solemnly through the streets of Munich directly behind the coffin, reinforcing his own association with the dead Feldherr.

Buchner plotted the route of the funeral parade to bolster the dominant interpretation proposed by the regime, that Ludendorff had striven all of his life for the same things that Hitler had: German freedom, German power, German racial purity.[59] The parade route passed through the narrow street adjacent to the Feldherrnhalle, "the route through which the dead [of the Beer Hall Putsch] had also passed into the living memory of the nation on the night of 8/9 November."[60] That Ludendorff had marched side by side with the Führer on that fateful evening was central to most coverage of the funeral.

With two more generals thrown in for good measure (Hugo Sperrle and Walther von Reichenau), the group followed the coffin through a cordon of soldiers and party members toward the Feldherrnhalle. According to the *Völkischer Beobachter*, not even the flags dared wave as the solemn procession passed the sacred ground where the martyrs of the party had fallen.[61]

Many nations sent military attachés or other representatives to the funeral. Included in the ceremony (though their participation was complicated by a late arriving train) were representatives of Bulgaria, Finland, Austria, Hungary, Spain (nationalist), Turkey, Great Britain, and the United States.[62] These foreign officials laid one more wreath on the gun carriage before the coffin was loaded into a truck decorated with pine branches for the trip to Tutzing. Despite the cold, gray weather, villagers from Forstenried, Wangen, Starnberg, and Feldafing lined the roads between Munich and Tutzing.

In Tutzing, the family and their associates held a smaller private service before the burial itself, which occurred in the town cemetery with full military honors. Mathilde Ludendorff gave a short speech before a procession numbering several hundred proceeded to the local cemetery.[63] At the cemetery, a band played Ludendorff's favorite song: the appropriately völkisch "Ich hab mich ergeben mit Herz und mit Hand."[64]

Before his death, Ludendorff penned a last testament imploring his followers to remain loyal to his wife. As he departed for Valhalla he must have recalled the words of Siegfried, quoted above, because he wrote, "Schart Euch um meine Frau!"[65]

Hard Times for the House of Ludendorff

Mathilde maintained the outward signs of support for the NSDAP that were required by the Hitler-Ludendorff concordat of 1937. A supplement to *Am heiligen Quell* in April 1938 urging her readers to vote "Yes" in one of Hitler's plebiscites cataloged the many accomplishments of and pledged unshakeable loyalty to Germany's great Führer.[66] But such niceties availed her little in the end. Most former Tannenbergers continued to struggle with the dominance of the National Socialists. Prominent loyalists like Herbert Frank refused to join the party despite increasing pressure at the workplace to do so. He pointedly refused to close his correspondence with "Heil Hitler" and persisted instead with "Long Live Freedom" and other Ludendorff expressions. When his brother Fritz (a member of the Nazi Party) declared, shortly after the invasion of the Soviet Union, that the war must end with the victory of National Socialism, Herbert corrected him: of the German Volk.[67]

While generally unrepentant, most Tannenbergers typically expressed themselves carefully, even in private correspondence. When Nazi officials called the invasion of the Soviet Union a "crusade," alarm bells went off. Was Germany really fighting for the cross, asked Herbert Frank? Jesuits were gaining too much influence in conquered territories, he believed. Was the mere success of a movement proof of its moral value? But gone were the strident denunciations of Nazism of years past. Vague rhetorical questions were the only expressions of dissatisfaction they allowed themselves.[68]

Followers of Ludendorff remained loyal to the Feldherr throughout the war and beyond. One soldier serving on the Eastern Front in August 1943 even saw parallels between the battles raging there and the battle fought twenty-nine years earlier at Tannenberg. On the anniversary of the battle, he reported that German soldiers' accomplishments were worthy of Ludendorff's legacy. "We fought with *the same tactics* [emphasis in original] that the Feldherr Ludendorff used with such success in 1917 on the Western Front." The soldier continued: "Even the antitank tactics Ludendorff introduced in 1917 have once again proven outstanding."[69] The Haus Ludendorff remained concerned for the image of the Feldherr throughout the war. His associate Herbert Frank fired off letters to Goebbels, even to his own uncle when he detected some slight to Ludendorff's honor in the press or in private correspondence.[70]

Other faithful followers saw in the war the fulfillment of Ludendorff's prophesies. While they believed that the war forecast for 1932 (in *Weltkrieg droht*) had only narrowly been averted by Ludendorff's revelations, he was no longer living to avert the second catastrophe. Before his death, he had predicted a war for 1941 (another "Jehovah Year"), and few of his followers were surprised that it came in 1939 instead.[71] No doubt the numerological congruence of the war with the Soviet Union in 1941 (and launched on 6/22 no less!) reassured those whose faith in Ludendorff's numerological predictions had wavered.[72] Once the bombs began to fall on German cities in earnest, Ludendorff's followers certainly saw the consequences of war in terms of Ludendorff's book.[73]

Ludendorff occupied a towering perch in the Weimar Republic and the Third Reich. He represented himself (and many historians have furthered his cause) as the "genius of war"—the Feldherr. He represented Germany's military prowess and its prospects for revenge. He was Siegfried. In this way he also represented, though perhaps less consciously, the paragon of German manhood. But his role as the ultimate man was an ambivalent one. There were the rumors of "loss of nerve" and "breakdown" at Tannenberg and in the Supreme Headquarters in 1918. There was also the curious fact that he fathered no children in his two marriages. Given that he came to the role of ascetic prophet so late in life, and given his commitment to the völkisch principles of race and "blood," this fact is especially noteworthy. While the subjects of infertility and sex in marriage more generally were not topics for public discussion, it is surprising that this issue never surfaces in the documents or the literature, not even among his critics and enemies. There is no evidence or discussion of physical disability. Both of his wives bore children in previous marriages. Perhaps his wives considered their maternal duty done, but it is difficult to believe that a man of Ludendorff's celestial ego would not wish to have his "blood," endowed as it must have been with his enormous gifts, survive. Perhaps, like Hitler, he imagined himself the father of the entire nation. Alfred Rosenberg may not have been far from the truth when he noted that Ludendorff compensated for a profound insecurity by utterly rejecting all male rivals and associations in order to become the noble champion of his wife's cause.[74] The Siegfried of legend, in any case, had no children.

Despite the suspicions of his most loyal followers, Ludendorff's memory was in fact well cared for by the National Socialist regime in the press and elsewhere. Hitler fulfilled the promise made to Rosenberg that Ludendorff would join the heroes of Nazism.[75] For several years, he made regular pilgrimages to Tannenberg, and Ludendorff remained a subject of conversations both private and public. As late as April 1944, the *Rheinische Landeszeitung*, for example, commemorated the Feldherr's birthday with a lengthy article by Dr. Hermann Lange.[76]

But Hitler clamped down on Ludendorff's followers eventually. The war led the National Socialist regime to scale back its attacks on churches and so the anti-Catholic and anti-Christian screeds issuing from the Ludendorff publishing company became less welcome. It was probably a mixture of desire and necessity that led Hitler to cut off paper supplies to *Am heiligen Quell* just prior to start of the war. In his postwar attack on the Ludendorffs, Winfried Martini called the revocation of Mathilde's paper supplies "one of the few kindnesses Hitler ever showed the German people."[77] The publishing house had to inform its subscribers on August 27, 1939, that *Am heiligen Quell* would cease publication.[78] But well into the war, pamphlets praising Ludendorff poured out of his press apparatus, including works on the general's childhood, on Liège, and a more controversial guide to Ludendorff's writings.[79] Older works continued to appear in new editions as well.

Ludwig Beck, who had tried to enlist Ludendorff (or at least to engage his legend) as a counterbalance to Hitler's "totalitarian" claims on the army, lamented that with the Feldherr gone, there was no one whom Hitler respected, no one to act as a restraining force on the Führer's fantasies. Whether anyone could have influenced Hitler along the lines Beck imagined is certainly questionable. Equally questionable is whether Ludendorff's counsel or example would have constituted a restraint or a goad. Nevertheless, Beck made clear that his beloved army was worse off under the Third Reich now that Ludendorff was gone.[80]

"Ludendorff Is Our Siegfried"

Ludwig Beck called Ludendorff "one of the most tragic figures in history."[81] To the nationalist Beck, Ludendorff was the great hero, the genius of the Great War, whose fall in 1918 was also Germany's. That Beck's final encounters with Ludendorff in the mid-1930s found him a prickly recluse obsessed with conspiracy theories probably seemed only a sad denouement. Previous biographers have largely dismissed Ludendorff's postwar activities as the bitter rantings of a broken man.

As this work has shown, Ludendorff did not exit the stage in 1918. Until at least 1925, he was the most influential figure in radical nationalist politics. He authored and sustained the "stab in the back" myth that proved so poisonous to Weimar political culture. He sought the violent overthrow of the democratic system installed in 1919 and repeatedly acted on that desire. Even after his prominence peaked, he remained the embodiment of many Germans' fantasies of revenge.

Though he made many enemies, even Adolf Hitler, his fame remained intact. So famous was Ludendorff, and so intimately associated with the early years of National Socialism, that virtually alone among critics of Hitler, he was untouchable. After 1933, his movement, still numbering in the hundreds of thousands, suffered some persecution, and the Tannenberg League was banned. But his followers persisted, and Ludendorff himself enjoyed a kind of "jester's freedom" to rail against not only Jews and Freemasons, whom the Nazis also targeted, but also against Catholicism, which at times proved convenient for Hitler. Ludendorff's opinion on military affairs remained valued both in public and in military circles, even if few professional soldiers could tolerate his presence. Many old soldiers still revered their wartime commander, the Feldherr Ludendorff.

The red thread that runs through this post–World War I story of Erich Ludendorff is Siegfried. It is perhaps not surprising, given the prominence of the Siegfried story in German national mythology, that wartime operations and positions would receive names like Siegfried, Hagen, and Alberich, drawn from the epic poem. During the war, Ludendorff, the tireless warrior, reminded some of his associates of the mighty hero. But by creating the "stab in the back" myth and ceaselessly calling for revenge against the shadowy enemies who had allegedly brought about Germany's downfall in 1918, Ludendorff took the association to another level in the interwar period. He sometimes consciously, sometimes unconsciously began to use the power of the Nibelungen legend to build his own.

Ludendorff was the "self-made" hero, who rose through the ranks of the military on the basis of his talent alone, without the benefit of a noble birth or courtly connections. Ludendorff was personally courageous at Liège; he was an operational genius and national savior at Tannenberg; in 1917, he brought the Russian colossus to its knees. Only treachery, he and his followers argued, could have brought down so mighty a hero. Revenge became his sole obsession, as it had become Kriemhild's in the poem.

Ludendorff found his own Kriemhild in Mathilde von Kemnitz. After their marriage in 1926, Mathilde provided the pseudo-intellectual trappings to support Erich's already firm conviction that Jews, Catholics, and Freemasons were behind Germany's defeat and virtually everything else in the world besides. By cultivating a philosophy that would bring their followers closer to the pagan Siegfried and their own Germanic roots, the pair promised to open Germany's eyes and steel it against the influence of these pernicious forces. Sometimes subtly, in their iconography, and sometimes more overtly in their publications, the Ludendorffs nurtured the association of Siegfried and the Feldherr, of Ludendorff's betrayal and Germany's revenge.

That Ludendorff's mission, revenge for 1918, was also Adolf Hitler's is neither coincidental nor inconsequential. Ludendorff was both idol of and mentor to the young Hitler. Ludendorff's critical role during the Beer Hall Putsch, while often neglected, helped to bring Hitler to national prominence. Most of the ideas that would guide the Nazis—nationalism, militarism, Greater Germany, autarky—were Ludendorff's long before they were Hitler's. The hostility to Jews might be one exception, with Ludendorff seeming to come to the idea just as he was introduced to Hitler and other virulent antisemites in Bavaria.

When Ludendorff broke with Hitler in 1925–26, he became a critic of the Nazis from an even more radical antisemitic position. In Ludendorff's view, Hitler was "soft" on the Jews and was himself part of a conspiracy to destroy Germany that was being orchestrated by Jews. It is too much, however, to see in Ludendorff's fantasies the origins of the Final Solution.[82] By the time of Ludendorff's death in 1937 even Hitler himself had not yet imagined the Holocaust, however extreme his rhetoric with respect to Jews. That Final Solution required the catalyst of war. Ludendorff's antisemitism was very real but also very dry and almost intellectual. It expressed itself through the revelation of secrets and hidden plots—his "mosaic work" with documents. Ludendorff's movement never seemed to attract the kinds of brutes who would carry out pogroms in the Sturmabteilung (SA) or devise systems of murder in the Schutzstaffel (SS).

Ludendorff was proud and litigious. He was dogmatic and unwilling to play political games of any sort. His attacks on the NSDAP earned him the enmity, though he still held the respect, of Hitler, Goebbels, and other Nazi leaders. His pronounced anti-Christian stance alienated many Germans and practically guaranteed that his would not be a mass movement. But Ludendorff was never irrelevant. To the hundreds of thousands who did join his various associations, read his journals, and buy his books, he was a powerful leader, promising insight into critical problems based on long experience. To those Germans wanting national redemption and revenge for a lost war, he was their Siegfried, slayer of dragons.

Epilogue

Kriemhild's Revenge

Ye full lusty heroes, now go nigher to the stairs and avenge my
wrongs. For this I will ever serve, as I should by right. I'll pay Hagen
well for his overweening pride. Let none at all escape from the house,
and I bid the hall be set on fire at all four ends. Thus all my
wrongs shall be well avenged.

—Kriemhild to Etzel's soldiers, The Nibelungenlied

Making a virtue of necessity, Mathilde pleaded with her followers for renewed dedication in the difficult environment after Erich's death.[1] "The
Feldherr," she claimed, had intentionally resisted the urge for tight organization and strong central authority. "We should revel in the freedom
and volunteerism of a purely cultural struggle for an idea, which slowly
and quietly grows in the Volk and slowly, despite all opposition, strikes its
roots all the more strongly and deeply in the Volk."[2] Only such vague and
desperate language could attempt to mask the increasing marginalization
and irrelevance of Ludendorff's organization just one year after his death.

With the Feldherr gone, sales of *Am heiligen Quell*, the publishing
house's most important source of income, began to fall. The leadership
speculated that many casual readers of the journal had done so only for
the essays by Ludendorff.[3] The organization fostered the memory of Erich's great deeds, dutifully commemorating his birthday as well as the an-
niversaries of his great battles, such as Liège and Tannenberg.[4] They tried
to keep their followers called to military service supplied with materials

and published pamphlets designed especially to fit in a uniform breast pocket.[5]

Some of Ludendorff's followers believed that even the dead Feldherr shaped the course of history. In September 1940 one admirer penned a long essay titled, "On the Unity of the Volk," which claimed that Ludendorff's death inspired Germany's eternal enemies to renew their alliance. It was only the strength of the combined forces of Juda and England in Asia, for example, that had driven Russia to seek Germany's (in 1940 still-standing) friendship.[6]

Bund für Gotterkenntnis (L) after 1945

The collapse of the Third Reich in 1945 allowed Mathilde to begin contacting her followers once again. She circulated letters, hand-copied at first, imploring her readers to remain faithful to the cause. What followed makes for an interesting story in the constitutional history of the Federal Republic. In the course of 1946, her organization reformed as the not-too-cleverly disguised Bund für Gotterkenntnis (L). The "(L)" must have been an attempt to foreground the spiritual character of the group to authorities while signaling to true believers that "Ludendorff" was still at the core. Incredibly, an initial denazification proceeding pronounced Mathilde Ludendorff "politically untainted" and permitted her to resume her activities.

No one was fooled by the (L) apparently, and opponents of her movement quickly got the ear of the authorities. One journalist, a few years later, lamented the Americans' willingness to exonerate her as follows: "Yes, the [occupation forces] are inclined to agree with "Madame" that she truly had been persecuted by Nazism—although a more careful examination would prove that poor Nazism had been persecuted by the Ludendorffs: for being lukewarm!"[7] Chiefly responsible for the renewed official investigations was Winfried Martini, a Munich journalist, author, and radio commentator.[8] His 1949 book, *Die Legende vom Haus Ludendorff*, exposed for any who needed reminding the depth of the Ludendorffs' antisemitism and their consistent espousal of racist and militarist doctrines. Martini had apparently been taken aback when, during the Third Reich, he passed a Ludendorff bookstore and heard two Ludendorff supporters cursing the Nazis for being too soft on the Jews.[9] Martini linked Erich Ludendorff's descent into conspiracy theories to his inability to process the reality of Germany's defeat in 1918. His alleged nervous collapse in that summer was the result of the dissonance between Ludendorff's self-perception as a military genius and his still unacknowledged recognition that the war was going to be lost. The "stab in the back" and the scapegoating of Jews, Catholics, and Freemasons were the result of his vain attempts to reconcile those conflicting forces.

To Martini, Erich and Mathilde worked as a team, with Erich focusing his energies as a publicist against the "anti"—the enemies of Germany, the supranational powers. Mathilde, meanwhile, developed the "pro"—the positive catalyst for Germany's rebirth—Deutsche Gotterkenntnis.[10] Based on the somewhat limited materials available to him, Martini outlined the major tenets of the Ludendorff's beliefs: their hostility to Judaism and Christianity, the similarity of their ideas to those of National Socialists like Himmler, Rosenberg, and Dinter. He subjected the ideas of the Haus Ludendorff to scathing criticism, pointing out, for example, Mathilde's lack of qualifications to analyze the Bible, and the maddening inconsistency of their argumentation even within the skewed universe they inhabited.[11]

Thanks at least in part to Martini, the Spruchkammer in Munich took over the investigation of Mathilde's activities. The judgment of that court, rendered in January 1950, reclassified Mathilde as "Hauptschuldig"—a principal offender in the language of the denazification regulations. An appeal lasting the remainder of 1950 ameliorated that judgment somewhat, classifying her as second-order offender (Belasteten/Aktivisten), which nevertheless carried with it a seven-year ban on practicing a profession or owning a business. In addition, she was forbidden to work as a "teacher, preacher, editor, author or radio-commentator" for the same period.[12] This judgment did not, however, impact the activities of the bund per se, which continued to spread Ludendorff's philosophy as before.[13]

As part of the investigation, the court referred to a psychiatric investigation that had been performed on Frau Ludendorff in 1947. That study had found no evidence of mental illness, notwithstanding the bizarre and irrational nature of Mathilde's work. In the doctor's findings, which clearly reflected on Erich Ludendorff's state of mind as well, the seeming insanity of the worldview the couple produced was a "normal

Figure 22. Mathilde Ludendorff before the Spruchkammer, November 23, 1949.
Photo by ullstein bild / ullstein bild via Getty Images.

system of propaganda, developed with extreme consistency and unscru-
pulousness."[14] One recent study of the Ludendorff's cultlike organization
concluded that the Ludendorffs' "business savvy stands in direct contra-
diction to insanity."[15]

The Ludendorffs were renowned for employing tenacious lawyers, and
Mathilde was able to circumvent the most onerous aspects of the ban
before it even went into effect by transferring ownership and copyright of
her materials in 1949 to her son-in-law, Franz Freiherr Karg von Bebenburg, nicknamed Siegfried.[16] The press was dubbed "Hohe Warte" (High
watchtower) and still publishes.[17] The transfer of ownership allowed even
her previous books and unpublished manuscripts to appear in print despite her being forbidden to work as an author.[18]

Practically, the ban on speaking amounted to little more than an incon-
venience, though the perceived humiliation rankled. Through various sub-
terfuges, Mathilde had relatively little difficulty having her voice and her
opinions heard. She could be interviewed and those interviews could then
appear in publications like *Der Quell* (The source) the group's revived

journal. She could still be published in foreign newspapers and then accounts of those articles could be covered by German journals—such as *Der Quell*. Apparently, even recordings of her voice were not covered by the ban on speaking, so groups of Ludendorffers occasionally resorted to listening to tape recordings of Mathilde, such as those made for gatherings in 1952–53.[19] In July 1954, the Munich court lifted the speaking ban after only four years.[20]

Antisemitism after the War

In an effort to avoid prosecution for their antisemitism, authors for the Ludendorff press inserted occasional caveats in their texts. According to one observer, they "selected very clever formulations, which make prosecution difficult."[21] For example, Walter Leon's *Überstaatliche Mächte und Völkerfreiheit* (Supranational powers and the freedom of the Volk), published in 1953, rails against Bolsheviks, Catholics, and Jews in familiar fashion but adds, "In order for there to be no misunderstanding, I want to very clearly emphasize, that we do not in any way equate this world power, Juda, with the Jewish people. . . . Therefore, when we speak for example of the 'world power Juda,' we mean neither the Jewish people nor individual Jews as members of this people."[22]

Legal troubles and publicity problems continued to dog the bund and the press. In 1959, an article with clear antisemitic overtones appeared in *Der Quell*, leading to investigations in several states. The author was the former leader of the National Socialist Student League, Johann von Leers, in exile in Egypt.[23] The ensuing trial in Weilheim, and a lengthy article in *Spiegel* about Mathilde, raised public awareness of the group's activities and beliefs at the same moment that vandalism at synagogues in Germany was making headlines. When police searched the houses of Ludendorff adherents, they found documents that spoke of the "new creation of the German Volk out of the unity of its racial inheritance," a "Führer-state," and an electoral franchise based on the "achievement principle." Lectures and publications produced by Verlag Hohe Warte described the Federal Republic as a "false democracy" ruled by the "supranational power." On May 25, 1961, the Interior Ministry deemed that sufficient evidence existed to ban the group as hostile to the constitution of the Federal Republic.[24]

The notoriously litigious Ludendorffers appealed, naturally. The appeal dragged on for years. Ludendorff's lawyers based their arguments on jurisdiction (state courts should have no authority over nationwide organizations), freedom of religion, and freedom of speech. At one hearing, they exercised that freedom by reciting antisemitic literature for hours and denouncing the "imperialism of the Jews," who were responsible for the wars and revolutions that ravaged the earth. Such diatribes availed them little, as the court drew parallels to the lenient 1924 verdict against Adolf Hitler. "Stronger measures [in 1924] might have hindered much," the state's lawyer added.[25] In 1966, a court confirmed the ban.

Notwithstanding the publicity associated with the trials, it seems certain that the number of dedicated Ludendorffers dwindled rapidly after the war. Winfried Martini estimated the number of Ludendorff followers in 1949 at around one hundred thousand, though circulation figures for the group's newsletters would suggest a lower number.[26] In 1960, *Der Quell* and *Volkswarte* had print runs of seventy-one hundred and eight thousand copies, respectively.[27] Bettina Amm estimates that as few as four or five hundred followers remained at the time of Mathilde's death in 1966.[28]

The much-reduced association remained active, however. In 1957, the bund published a Festschrift in honor of Mathilde, which summarized her philosophy and even tried to make the Ludendorffs' economic stance relevant to the Cold War environment. In a stance surprising from a group founded by the creator of the Hindenburg Program, the bund declared planned economies "destructive" since they deny individuals the freedom to satisfy their wants.[29] Instead, a free market and a healthy stock market would naturally set prices to the benefit of the Volk, while the only regulation necessary would be the punishment of greed.[30]

Education of the young remained an important goal of the Ludendorff group after 1945. Children must be taught, they insisted, to recognize the "godly" in everything, not simply in a single God, as allegedly preached by Christians.[31] According to the government of the Federal Republic, the Bund für Gotterkenntnis hosted on average thirty gatherings each month all over Germany, many of which were devoted to the subject of youth and education.[32]

The group founded a special school ("Hochschule für Gotterkenntnis") in 1955 and planned lecture tours throughout West Germany.[33] In 1960, a reporter described the leadership of the bund as a "General Staff" at its headquarters marking up maps of the Federal Republic as if they were planning "lecture fronts." The reporter noted wryly that "currently, according to the Tutzinger General Staff map, a Ludendorff-Enlightenment battle is being unleashed in North Rhine Westphalia, along the line Krefeld-Hückeswagen."[34]

Fritz Vater's *Sigfried*

Nor did the death of Erich Ludendorff and the birth of a new, democratic Germany in the West impair the cultivation of the Siegfried legend. In 1953, Fritz Vater published *Sigfried: Die Saga von Germaniens Befreiung* (Sigfried: the saga of Germany's liberation) in the Hohe Warte press, under the editorship of the Ludendorffs' son-in-law Franz Karg von Bebenburg.[35] The work deserves some attention as evidence both of the persistence of the Siegfried-Ludendorff connection and as a work illustrative of the produce of the Ludendorff press after 1945.

On one level, *Sigfried* is an imaginative telling of the story of Arminius/Hermann the Cherusker, legendary victor at the Battle of Teutoburg Forest in 9 CE over the Roman legions of Varus. Vater was by no means the first to point to Hermann as the possible basis for the legend of Siegfried detailed in the Nibelungenlied. The novel takes many liberties, few of them entirely original, in filling in the gaps of Hermann/Siegfried's life in order better to blend the historical and the purely fanciful.[36] In Vater's rendition, the hero of the battle is named Sigfried, or, at times, Armin or Arminius among the Romans. The son of the elected headman of the Cherusker, Sigfried is self-reliant and learns smithing at an early age. The "dragon" in this version is the power of Rome, with whom Sigfried's father struck an uneasy alliance. The dragon is embodied in the person of Quinctilius Varus and the three legions he commands, quartered in Sigfried's territory. The Romans' increasing demands for tribute rankle the freedom-loving German tribes nearby. Sigfried therefore hatches a plot to expel the Romans and unite the tribes. He plans a successful *Handstreich* (note the similarity to Ludendorff's Liège narrative) against the Roman fortress that sends the legions streaming in disarray toward the safety of the nearest Roman town. Sigfried displays not only military prowess but considerable political and strategic savvy as well. One section of the work is even titled: "Feldherr."[37] He has already arranged with his friend Hunwalt der Atli (Attila the Hun) to block the Romans' passage through the mountains with his own forces.[38] Harried by German fighters as they trek through the woods, the legions find themselves surrounded and very poorly led. The slaughter of the Battle of Teutoburg Forest ensues, securing both Sigfried's leadership of the new tribal union and the independence of Germania from Roman rule.

As with Siegfried of the Nibelungenlied, so too does Sigfried in Vater's story arouse jealousy, even within his own family. His cousin Siggast and especially his uncle Ingomar envy Siegfried's success. Ingomar, after several failed attempts to overthrow Sigfried by allying with Rome and other enemies, plots the hero's dastardly murder.

The novel provided the author the opportunity both to glory in the racial and proto-nationalist accomplishments of the Ur-German Hermann and to foreground the legend of Siegfried, with its fantasies of triumphant revenge, for his postwar readers. But it also cunningly enabled Ludendorff's followers, to whom the book was advertised, to cultivate their hatred of the "supranational powers" without drawing the unwelcome attention of censors on the prowl for libel and antisemitism. It is a convenient historical truth that Hermann's enemies were Roman, so that when the novel railed against the power, greed, and urge of "Rome" to dominate, it read a great deal like one of Ludendorff's own anti-Catholic screeds from *Volkswarte* in which the Eternal City stood in for the church. Though overt antisemitism is not in evidence in Vater's book, the Romans do allow certain merchants to ply their wares among the German tribes. It would not have been difficult for the seasoned antisemites among the Ludendorffers to decode the description of these merchants (greedy, unscrupulous, cowardly, obsequious worshippers of Mercury [god of trade]) as traditional antisemitic stereotypes.[39]

In order to accommodate the new regime, Mathilde and her followers made some structural adjustments and offered some variations on their old themes. Members even sought Mathilde's advice on filling out the notorious "Fragebogen," the questionnaires designed by American occupation authorities to root out Nazism and militarism among the Germans. Herbert Frank thanked Frau Dr. Ludendorff (through an intermediary, of course) for her advice on the wording of his answers. He agreed that "we strive for racial unity" was a far better formulation of the group's aims than "we condemn racial mixing" in materials meant for the occupiers.[40]

Postwar Fabrications

The Haus Ludendorff went even further by fabricating two stories about Erich in order to make him *salonfähig* in the new democratic Germany and to augment his status as prophet. Notwithstanding the final judgment in the denazification proceedings, Mathilde and her followers insisted that Erich had in fact tried to prevent Hitler from coming to power and to topple him once he became chancellor.

Mathilde could, of course, point to the many articles and handful of books produced by the Ludendorff press, particularly *Weltkrieg droht* and *Hitlers Verrat*, which pilloried Hitler and the Nazis.[41] That these works did so from an even more radical antisemitic position (i.e., that Hitler was part of the conspiracy directed by the supranational powers to destroy Germany) she obfuscated, of course. Equally telling, the group insisted, was the apocryphal letter that Erich wrote to his former comrade, Paul von Hindenburg, two days after Hitler's appointment as chancellor, warning of the catastrophe Hitler would bring upon Germany. Though historians have now established with a reasonable degree of confidence that Ludendorff wrote no such letter, the story of the letter served the Ludendorffs' purposes well, not least because it was inadvertently given credence by the noted political scientist Hans Buchheim in 1958 when he mentioned the letter (without citation) in a publication of the Institute für Zeitgeschichte in Munich.[42] For the family, the letter helped to establish Ludendorff's prophetic abilities and anti-Nazi credentials.

Even more fanciful is the family's insistence that Ludendorff was the spiritual father of the July 20, 1944, conspiracy to assassinate Hitler. The key to making this story even remotely believable was the fact that Ludwig Beck, one of the most important members of the conspiracy, had visited Ludendorff on several occasions as described in chapter 7 of this book. Those meetings, which the reader will recall were intended to bring about the reconciliation of Hitler and Ludendorff, were now described as the foundations of the military resistance to Hitler. The story first appeared in an affidavit issued by Mathilde in 1949, in which she wrote that Beck, along with Werner von Fritsch and Werner von Blomberg, wished to bring about a change in the Nazi regime by convincing Ludendorff to lead the army against the regime. He refused, according to Mathilde, but encouraged the men to remain firm in their opposition to any war of aggression, thereby, presumably, providing the marching orders for the conspiracy.[43] Ludendorff's one-time associate, Robert Holtzmann, saw in Ludendorff the only hope for resistance to Hitler. Ludendorff's dreamy semi-isolation, his failure to act against the Führer, would haunt his legacy because "he was the only one in a position" to do anything, Holtzmann believed.[44] Mathilde's son-in-law Franz Freiherr Karg von Bebenburg supported the claim in a 1952 issue of *Der Quell*.[45]

Equally outlandishly, Mathilde once claimed to a Swiss reporter that Hitler had notably waited until after Erich had passed away "before daring to move against the Jews"—as if Ludendorff's reputation had somehow protected Jews previously—and from Hitler, whom Ludendorff had portrayed as in the pocket of the supranational powers![46] And as the chapter on Ludendorff's rehabilitation in the Third Reich showed, Ludendorff's followers rankled under the various manifestations of discrimination during the Third Reich partly because they so fervently desired to contribute to the ideological mission of the National Socialists.

In 1971, the Bundesverwaltungsgericht referred the ban on the Bund für Gotterkenntnis (L) back to Bavarian courts, arguing that while the group did violate constitutional prohibitions against "aggressive antisemitic expressions," special care must be taken to protect constitutionally guaranteed freedom of conscience. The lower court was instructed to investigate whether some penalty short of an outright ban might be appropriate.[47] Finally, in 1977, the Bavarian courts lifted the ban. Mathilde did not live long enough to witness this constitutional victory. Mathilde Ludendorff died on May 12, 1966, at the age of eighty-eight after several years of failing health. As pallbearers carried her casket out of the front door of the Tutzing house to a waiting crowd of mourners, a reporter from *Die Zeit* noticed that next to the entry of the house, behind glass, hung a painting of a half-naked Siegfried, challenging the dragon.[48]

NOTES

1. Mythic Life

1. Robert B. Asprey, *The German High Command at War: Hindenburg and Ludendorff Conduct World War I* (New York: W. Morrow, 1991), 467.

2. The Spartacus and Wallenstein references are from G. H. Teklenburg, *Lärm um Ludendorff* (Hamburg: Uhlenhorst, 1935).

3. Walter Görlitz, *History of the German General Staff, 1657–1945* (New York: Praeger, 1959), 184.

4. H. L. Mencken, "Ludendorff," *Atlantic Monthly*, June 1917.

5. The photo appears in a later chapter. Franz von Pfeffer, an intimate associate of both Ludendorff and Hitler, insisted that "until the year 1924, Ludendorff was unquestionably tacitly seen as the leader of all opposition efforts." Institut für Zeitgeschichte (hereafter IfZ) ZS177/21 Bennecke Gespräch mit Pfeffer, October 12, 1959.

6. Andreas Dorpalen, *Hindenburg and the Weimar Republic* (Princeton, NJ: Princeton University Press, 1964), 31.

7. The best work on the life and ideas of Mathilde Ludendorff (née Spieß) is Annika Spilker, *Geschlecht, Religion und Völkischer Nationalismus: Die Ärztin und Antisemitin Mathilde von Kemnitz-Ludendorff (1877–1966)*, Reihe "Geschichte und Geschlechter" (Frankfurt: Campus Verlag, 2013).

8. The best concise study of the sum of Ludendorff's writing is Roger Chickering's contribution to a recent volume on the subject of total war. Roger Chickering, "Sore Loser:

Ludendorff's Total War," in *The Shadows of Total War: Europe, East Asia, and the United States, 1919–1939*, ed. Roger Chickering and Stig Förster (New York: Cambridge University Press, 2003). Chickering accurately summarizes Ludendorff's most important works and captures very well the frustrations of studying his ideas. Chickering goes too far, however, to minimize Ludendorff's significance, describing him, especially after 1925 as an isolated, marginal character. The dismissive title captures the essence of the argument well.

9. D. J. Goodspeed, *Ludendorff; Genius of World War I* (Boston: Houghton Mifflin, 1966), 295.

10. Chickering, "Sore Loser," 166.

11. Richard M. Watt, *The Kings Depart: The Tragedy of Germany—Versailles and the German Revolution* (New York: Simon & Schuster, 1968), 501.

12. Manfred Nebelin, *Ludendorff: Diktator im Ersten Weltkrieg* (Munich: Siedler, 2011), 13–14.

13. John Lee, *The Warlords: Hindenburg and Ludendorff* (London: Weidenfeld & Nicolson, 2005), 177.

14. A letter from the nerve specialist Hochheimer to his wife describes the encounter. Wolfgang Foerster, *Der Feldherr Ludendorff im Unglück; eine Studie über seine Seelische Haltung in der Endphase des Ersten Weltkrieges* (Wiesbaden: Limes Verlag, 1952), 74–76. Georg von Müller, chief of the Kaiser's Naval Cabinet, met with Ludendorff on September 12, 1918, expecting, based on the accounts of friends, to find "a broken man." Müller found nothing strange in Ludendorff's demeanor that day. Georg Alexander von Müller and Walter Görlitz, *The Kaiser and His Court: The Diaries, Note Books, and Letters of Admiral Georg Alexander von Müller, Chief of the Naval Cabinet, 1914–1918* (London: MacDonald, 1961), 388.

15. Paul Frederick Lerner, *Hysterical Men: War, Psychiatry, and the Politics of Trauma in Germany, 1890–1930* (Ithaca, NY: Cornell University Press, 2003), 40–41.

16. Ibid., 50. George L. Mosse, *The Image of Man: The Creation of Modern Masculinity* (New York: Oxford University Press, 1996), 85.

17. Nebelin, *Ludendorff*. Steven Thomas Naftzger covers the postwar period of Ludendorff's life, focused especially on his movement's relationship with Nazism; he also gives a concise overview of Mathilde Ludendorff's philosophy. Naftzger, "'Heil Ludendorff': Erich Ludendorff and Nazism, 1925–1937" (PhD diss., City University of New York, 2002).

18. Alexander Watson, *Ring of Steel: Germany and Austria-Hungary in World War I* (New York: Basic Books, 2014), 369–70. Martin Kitchen, *The Silent Dictatorship: The Politics of the German High Command under Hindenburg and Ludendorff, 1916–1918* (New York: Holmes & Meier, 1976), 84.

19. Müller and Görlitz, *Kaiser and His Court*, 334. Kitchen mentions this episode as well and adds that the Kaiser included the Freemasons in the conspiracy. The reference to Freemasons is not in the English translation of the diaries. Kitchen, *Silent Dictatorship*, 179. "Groß-Orient-Loge" appears in the German original. Georg Alexander von Müller and Walter Görlitz, *Regierte der Kaiser? Kriegstagebücher, Aufzeichnungen und Briefe des Chefs des Marine-Kabinetts Admiral Georg Alexander von Müller, 1914–1918* (Göttingen: Musterschmidt, 1959), 355.

20. Ludendorff refers to these forces in his rationale for his program of Patriotic Instruction in 1917. See "Leitsätze für den vaterländischen Unterricht unter den Truppen," including the appendices of Erich Ludendorff, *Urkunden der Obersten Heeresleitung über ihre Tätigkeit, 1916–1918*, 3rd ed. (Berlin: E. S. Mittler und Sohn, 1922), 271–78. Also cited in Kitchen, *Silent Dictatorship*, 59.

21. Raffael Scheck, *Alfred von Tirpitz and German Right-Wing Politics, 1914–1930* (Atlantic Highlands, NJ: Humanities Press, 1998), 74.

22. Ibid., 214.

23. Nicholas Reynolds, "Dokumentation: Der Fritsch-Brief vom 11. Dezember 1938," *Vierteljahrshefte für Zeitgeschichte* 28, no. 3 (1980): 358–71. Cited in Wilhelm Deist, "Anspruch und Selbstverständnis der Wehrmacht: Einführende Bemerkungen," in *Die Wehrmacht: Mythos und Realität*, ed. Rolf-Dieter Müller, Hans Erich Volkmann, and Militärgeschichtliches Forschungsamt (Munich: Oldenbourg, 1999), 43n19.

24. A 1947 report on Mathilde Ludendorff's state of mind found no evidence of mental illness. The report implies a commentary on Erich Ludendorff's written work as well, calling it a consistent, if unscrupulous system of propaganda, not the product of insanity. Psychiatric report from 1947 by Professor Sterz, cited in Bettina Amm, *Die Ludendorff-Bewegung: Vom Nationalistischen Kampfbund zur Völkischen Weltanschauungssekte*, Reihe Soziologie (Hamburg: Ad Fontes, 2006), 272n20. See epilogue below for more.

25. Herfried Münkler develops this idea in a broader context in his book, *Siegfrieden*, and I acknowledge my debt to that work for providing the language with which to discuss "mythic politics" as imagined by Ludendorff. Herfried Münkler and Wolfgang Storch, *Siegfrieden: Politik mit einem deutschen Mythos* (Berlin: Rotbuch-Verlag, 1988).

26. Ian Kershaw, *The "Hitler Myth": Image and Reality in the Third Reich* (New York: Oxford University Press, 1987).

27. Ibid., 4.

28. Ibid.

29. Wolfram Pyta, *Hindenburg: Herrschaft zwischen Hohenzollern und Hitler* (Munich: Siedler, 2007).

30. Ibid., 287–90. Pyta invokes Weber when describing Hindenburg as "charismatic" but warns against a passive understanding of Hindenburg's "genius" in this regard. Hindenburg's charismatic power involved an active exchange with the public and the self-conscious cultivation of an image by Hindenburg and his allies.

31. Münkler and Storch, *Siegfrieden*, 50. Herfried Münkler, in this work as well as his 2008 *Die Deutschen und ihre Mythen*, has studied how political myths constructed around the *Nibelungenlied* and similar stories operate in a broad sense in German political culture. Both works deal with the *Nibelungenlied* extensively, and my work is indebted to his insights. This work, in contrast, will demonstrate how one man and his followers attempted to operationalize that myth in the service of their cause. Herfried Münkler, *Die Deutschen und ihre Mythen* (Berlin: Rowohlt, 2008).

32. Münkler, *Die Deutschen und ihre Mythen*, 14–15s.

33. Jan Assmann, "Mythen, Politische," in *Handbuch der politischen Philosophie und Sozialphilosophie. Bd. 1 a—M*, ed. Robin Celikates and Stefan Gosepath (Berlin: De Gruyter, 2008), 872.

34. Ibid.

35. Münkler, *Die Deutschen und ihre Mythen*, 11.

36. Pyta, *Hindenburg*, 63.

37. Kershaw, *"Hitler Myth,"* 3.

38. Jesko von Hoegen, *Der Held von Tannenberg: Genese und Funktion des Hindenburg-Mythos*, Stuttgarter Historische Forschungen; 4; Variation: 4 (Cologne: Böhlau, 2007), 8, 17.

39. Anna von der Goltz, *Hindenburg: Power, Myth, and the Rise of the Nazis* (New York: Oxford University Press, 2009), 6.

40. Pyta, *Hindenburg*, 61.

41. In conversation in November 1915 Hindenburg called Cincinnatus "an attractive figure" because he was able to "return to his plow" after the military emergency had passed. Paul Dehn, "Hindenburg als Erzieher," cited in Fritz Endres and Paul von Hindenburg,

Hindenburg; Briefe, Reden, Berichte (Ebenhausen bei München: W. Langewiesche-Brandt, 1934), 41. Jesko von Hoegen, in his work on the Hindenburg-Mythos, points out that personal narratives often rely on preexisting mythic models. Hoegen, *Der Held von Tannenberg*, 17.

42. The "Hitler is Germany" motif appears frequently in Nazi propaganda, perhaps most famously in Leni Riefenstahl's 1934 film, *Triumph of the Will*. In introducing Hitler, his deputy Rudolf Hess says, "You are Germany, when you act, the nation acts, when you judge, the people judge!" Kershaw, *"Hitler Myth,"* 253.

43. Michael Geyer has written a great deal about political violence and describes "mythmaking and storytelling, narrating violence," as a way for both individuals and communities to overcome the effects of trauma. It is clear to me that the myth of Siegfried served this purpose both for Ludendorff personally and for the many nationalist Germans unwilling to accept the lost war after 1918. M. Geyer, "Some Hesitant Observations concerning 'Political Violence,'" *Kritika-Explorations in Russian and Eurasian History* 4, no. 3 (2003): 697.

44. The subhead epigraph comes from Will Vesper and E. R. Vogenauer, *Die Nibelungen-Sage* (Oldenburg, i.O.: G. Stalling, 1921), 22.

45. It is important to note that there are many variations to this story, drawn as it is from numerous medieval epics and tales. For my purposes, I have adopted the 1965 English translation of the *Nibelungenlied* by Arthur Thomas Hatto as the standard. I will mention other sources in the notes as I make use of them. A. T. Hatto, *The Nibelungenlied*, Penguin Classics (London: Penguin, 2004).

46. Westfalen-Treubund, quoted in Niederdeutsche Zeitung. Nationales Tageblatt für Norddeutschland, #279, November 29, 1923. NSDAP Hauptarchiv reel 42, folder 843.

47. Burton Raffel, *Das Nibelungenlied = Song of the Nibelungs* (New Haven, CT: Yale University Press, 2006), xvi.

48. Münkler and Storch, *Siegfrieden*.

49. In her work on theater, Uwe-Karsten Ketelsen argues that "the heroic protagonist ("heroische Held") is not related to victory, but to defeat. Uwe-Karsten Ketelsen, *Heroisches Theater: Untersuchungen zur Dramentheorie des Dritten Reichs*, Literatur und Wirklichkeit, Bd. 2 (Bonn: H. Bouvier, 1968), 138. Cited in Jay W. Baird, *To Die for Germany: Heroes in the Nazi Pantheon* (Bloomington: Indiana University Press, 1990), 249n4.

50. Münkler and Storch, *Siegfrieden*, 130.

51. Hatto, *Nibelungenlied*, 302n1.

52. Werner Hoffmann, "The Reception of the Nibelungenlied in the Twentieth Century," in *A Companion to the Nibelungenlied*, ed. Winder McConnell (Columbia, SC: Camden House, 1998), 133.

53. William O. Cord, *An Introduction to Richard Wagner's Der Ring des Nibelungen: A Handbook*, 2nd ed. (Athens: Ohio University Press, 1995), 58.

54. Hoffmann, "Reception of the Nibelungenlied in the Twentieth Century," 133–34. Friedrich Hebbel was a well-known German playwright of the mid-nineteenth century. His Nibelungen trilogy premiered in 1861 and was performed 1,094 times between 1918 and 1945.

55. Münkler and Storch, *Siegfrieden*, 65.

56. Erich Ludendorff, *Mein militärischer Werdegang. Blätter der Erinnerung an unser stolzes Heer* (Munich: Ludendorff, 1933), 7.

57. Translation by Thomas Dunlap available on the website, German History in Documents and Images, maintained by the German Historical Institute. http://www.germanhistory docs.ghi-dc.org/sub_document.cfm?document_id=755. Accessed November 13, 2007.

58. Hoffmann, "Reception of the Nibelungenlied in the Twentieth Century," 143–44.

59. Liszt's remarks, made in November 1914, are quoted at length in Münkler and Storch, *Siegfrieden: Politik mit einem deutschen Mythos*, 74–75. Herfried Münkler insists that political myths must be flexible to succeed. Münkler, *Die Deutschen und ihre Mythen*, 85.

60. Münkler and Storch, *Siegfrieden*, 53.

61. Ibid., 56.

62. Francis G. Gentry, *The Nibelungen Tradition: An Encyclopedia* (New York: Routledge, 2002), 313–15.

63. Hoffmann, "Reception of the Nibelungenlied in the Twentieth Century," 152.

64. Many of these references can be found in Gentry, *Nibelungen Tradition*, 305–19.

65. Goodspeed, *Ludendorff; Genius of World War I*, 210.

66. On the late war offensives, see David T. Zabecki, *The German 1918 Offensives: A Case Study in the Operational Level of War* (London: Routledge, 2006). Hoffmann, "Reception of the Nibelungenlied in the Twentieth Century," 146. Gentry, *Nibelungen Tradition*, 308, 318. Gentry et al. point out that the Allies called the fortifications the "Hindenburg Line" during World War I and later erroneously referred to the World War II fortifications (known to Germans as the Westwall) as the "Siegfried Line." As mentioned above, the prevalence of the myth, including these incidents, are discussed at length in Münkler and Storch, *Siegfrieden*. See especially pages 83–85. The Hagen offensive's main thrust, into Flanders, was never carried out.

67. Winfried Martini, *Die Legende vom Hause Ludendorff* (Rosenheim: Leonhard Lang, 1949), 66–67.

68. It is inconsequential that Siegfried was killed with a spear and the German Army attacked with a dagger. The iconography is virtually identical. The use of a dagger simply enhances the sense of cowardice and betrayal in a modern mind. For the same reason, American anti-Japanese propaganda often showed the Japanese holding a dagger.

69. Wilhelm Deist spells out the dire situation of the German Army in his article "Der militärische Zusammenbruch des Kaiserreichs: Zur Realität der 'Dolchstoßlegende,'" in *Das Unrechtsregime: Internationale Forschung über den Nationalsozialismus*, ed. Ursula Büttner et al., *Hamburger Beiträge zur Sozial- und Zeitgeschichte; Bd. 21–22* (Hamburg: Christians, 1986). The heavy losses of the spring and summer offensives completely drained the army's capabilities and reserves. After the clear failure of the Michael offensive by March 1918, dispirited German soldiers carried out a tacit military "strike"—refusing to fight, evading service, or outright deserting their units. See also Joachim Petzold, *Die Dolchstosslegende; eine Geschichtsfälschung im Dienst des deutschen Imperialismus und Militarismus*, Deutsche Akademie der Wissenschaften zu Berlin. Schriften des Instituts für Geschichte. Reihe I: Allgemeine und deutsche Geschichte, Bd. 18 (Berlin: Akademie-Verlag, 1963).

70. Gerd Krumeich, "Die Dolchstoss-Legende," in *Deutsche Erinnerungsorte*, ed. Etienne François and Hagen Schulze (Munich: Beck, 2001), 588, "ist uns in den Rucken gefallen." Another good recent essay on the subject is Holger H. Herwig, "Of Men and Myths: The Use and Abuse of History and the Great War," in *The Great War and the Twentieth Century*, ed. J. M. Winter, Geoffrey Parker, and Mary R. Habeck (New Haven, CT: Yale University Press, 2000).

71. Ludwig Beck to Gertrud Beck, November 28, 1918, reproduced in Klaus-Jürgen Müller, *General Ludwig Beck: Studien und Dokumente zur Politisch-Militärischen Vorstellungswelt und Tätigkeit des Generalstabchefs des deutschen Heeres 1933–1938*, Schriften des Bundesarchivs, 30 (Boppard am Rhein: H. Boldt, 1980), 323. Also Wolfgang Foerster, *Ein General Kämpft gegen den Krieg; aus Nachgelassenen Papieren des Generalstabchefs Ludwig Beck* (Munich: Münchener Dom-Velag, 1949), 12.

72. Krumeich, "Die Dolchstoss-Legende," 592, "von hinten erdolcht."

73. Görlitz, *History of the German General Staff, 1657–1945*, 203.

74. Hoffmann, "Reception of the Nibelungenlied in the Twentieth Century," 146–47. Hoffmann cites Annelise Thimme, *Flucht in den Mythos; die Deutschnationale Volkspartei und die Niederlage von 1918* (Göttingen: Vandenhoeck & Ruprecht, 1969), 76.

75. Krumeich, "Die Dolchstoss-Legende," 593. Lee, *Warlords*, 188.

76. Dorpalen, *Hindenburg and the Weimar Republic*, 50. Chickering, "Sore Loser," 158. Johannes Erger, *Der Kapp-Lüttwitz-Putsch. Ein Beitrag zur deutschen Innenpolitik 1919/20* (Düsseldorf: Droste, 1967), 71–72. Walter Schwengler, in his work on Allied demands for the extradition of German war criminals after 1918, seems to doubt Ludendorff's authorship. Walter Schwengler, *Völkerrecht, Versailler Vertrag und Auslieferungsfrage: Die Strafverfolgung wegen Kriegsverbrechen als Problem des Friedensschlusses 1919/20*, Beiträge zur Militär- und Kriegsgeschichte; 24. Bd. (Stuttgart: Deutsche Verlags-Anstalt, 1982), 277. According to Schwengler, the Hindenburg declaration is reprinted in Erich Ludendorff, *Vom Feldherrn zum Weltrevolutionär und Wegbereiter Deutscher Volksschöpfung: Meine Lebenserinnerungen von 1919–1925*, vol. 1 (Munich: Ludendorffs Verlag, 1941). Ludendorff claims authorship in that work on pages 74–75 and discusses the testimony pages 75–79.

77. Quoted in Krumeich, "Die Dolchstoss-Legende," 594. Translation from Paul von Hindenburg and Frederic Appleby Holt, *Out of My Life* (New York: Cassell and Co., 1920), 440.

78. Mencken, "Ludendorff," 826.

79. Margarethe Ludendorff and Walther Ziersch, *Als Ich Ludendorff's Frau War* (Munich: Drei Masken Verlag, 1929), 204. Wilhelm II did not officially abdicate until later in the month.

80. Uwe Lohalm, *Völkischer Radikalismus: Die Geschichte des Deutschvölkischen Schutz- und Trutz-Bundes, 1919–1923*, Hamburger Beiträge zur Zeitgeschichte (Hamburg: Leibniz-Verlag, 1970), 187–88.

81. Tagesbefehl Estorffs, Nachlaß Luetgebrune, Microfilm roll 5, Nr. 1456475, reproduced in Erger, *Der Kapp-Lüttwitz-Putsch. Ein Beitrag zur deutschen Innenpolitik 1919/20*: 304–5.

82. Hatto, *Nibelungenlied*, 20.

83. Diary Notes of Oberst von Thaer, excerpt from October 1, 1918. Albrecht von Thaer, Siegfried A. Kaehler, and Helmuth K. G. Rönnefarth, *Generalstabsdienst an der Front und in der O.H.L. aus Briefen und Tagebuchaufzeichnungen, 1915–1919*, Abhandlungen der Akademie der Wissenschaften in Göttingen. Philologisch-Historische Klasse. 3. Folge; Nr. 40; Variation: Akademie der Wissenschaften in Göttingen; Philologisch-Historische Klasse; Abhandlungen; 3. Folge, Nr. 40 (Göttingen: Vandenhoeck & Ruprecht, 1958), 234. Translation available at the World War I Document Archive, http://net.lib.byu.edu/~rdh7/wwi/1918/thaereng.html. Accessed November 13, 2007. Münkler uses Thaer's remarks as the first appearance of the "stab in the back" to explain the army's collapse, not to draw the Ludendorff-Siegfried connection. Münkler and Storch, *Siegfrieden*, 86.

84. A. Oskar Klausmann and Herbert Lentz, *Die Nibelungen*, 3. Aufl. (Bayreuth: Loewes Verlag, 1978), 8.

85. "Der Tote Feldherr," *Sigrune*, January 10, 1938.

86. There is a very warm letter from Moltke to Ludendorff dated January 1915 reproduced in Moltke's memoirs: Helmuth von Moltke and Eliza von Moltke, *Erinnerungen, Briefe, Dokumente, 1877–1916. Ein Bild vom Kriegsausbruch, Erster Kriegsführung und Persönlichkeit des Ersten Militärischen Führers des Krieges* (Stuttgart: Der Kommende Tag, 1922), 420.

87. Klausmann and Lentz, *Die Nibelungen*, 7.

88. Berliner Lokalanzeiger, September 21, 1917, cited in Nebelin, *Ludendorff*, 8–9.

89. Writing in the aftermath of Ludendorff's trial for treason in 1924, an American journalist noted Ludendorff's role. Leonard Spray, "Ludendorff-Leader of German 'Revenge,'" *Current History* (New York) 20, no. 5 (1924).

90. An instructional guidebook published by the Ludendorff publishing house in 1942 explicitly acknowledges the use of the Siegfried story to support the aims of Ludendorff and his followers. It follows a curriculum designed by Mathilde Ludendorff and dwells on the value of the Siegfried story and other Norse legends. Ferdinand Diepold, *Das Unterrichtswerk der deutschen Lebenskunde* (Munich: Ludendorffs Verlag, 1942). In Myers Collection, 1557. After the war, the publishing house continued to cultivate awareness of the story through its publications. Ulrich von Motz, *Siegfried-Armin; Dichtung und Geschichtliche Wirklichkeit* (Pähl: Verlag Hohe Warte, 1953). The book was widely advertised in other works, such as Walter Leon, *Uberstaatliche Mächte und Völkerfreiheit: Eine Auseinandersetzung Grundsätzicher Art im Geiste Erich Ludendorffs* (Pähl: Verlag Hohe Warte, 1953). Myers 1608.

2. Victor of Liège and Tannenberg

1. The epigraphs are from Daniel Bussier Shumway, *The Nibelungenlied: Translated from the Middle High German with an Introductory Sketch and Notes* (Boston: Houghton Mifflin, 1909), 7; and Klausmann and Lentz, *Die Nibelungen,* 7, respectively. There has been virtually no dispute over the details of Erich Ludendorff's early life despite the dearth of sources. The information comes primarily from his own brief account of his youth as well as the more fulsome tale provided by his maternal aunt Henny von Tempelhof. Ludendorff, *Mein militärischer Werdegang*; Henny von Tempelhoff, *Mein Glück im Hause Ludendorff; ein Familiengeschichte,* 4. und 5. Tausend. ed. (Berlin: A. Scherl, 1918).

2. The mistake appears throughout the scholarly literature, sometimes from ignorance, but more often as a sort of "mental typo." Given his career it just seems that he *should* have been an aristocrat. The American edition of his memoirs, published in 1919, list the author's name as Erich Von Ludendorff. Some other examples include his entry in the index of Larry Eugene Jones and James N. Retallack, eds., *Between Reform, Reaction, and Resistance: Studies in the History of German Conservatism from 1789 to 1945* (Providence: Berg, 1993). General *von* Ludendorff makes an appearance in the English translation of General Max Hoffmann's postwar work, *War of Lost Opportunities,* though the German edition lacks the error. Max Hoffmann and Eric Sutton, *War Diaries and Other Papers,* vol. 2, *War of Lost Opportunities* (London: M. Secker, 1929), 95. The recent spate of literature on the Great War continues to repeat the mistake. See Nick Lloyd, *Hundred Days: The Campaign That Ended World War I* (New York: Basic Books, 2014). A search for "von Ludendorff" on Google books returns 769 hits, including articles from *Time Magazine* and the *American Historical Review.* August Lindner, who maintained a long correspondence with Ludendorff, investigated the question of Ludendorff receiving a patent of nobility intensively after the war. The closest he came to solving the mystery was the intimation that the Kaiser had briefly entertained the idea of bestowing the Schwarzen Adler-Orden on Ludendorff in 1918, which imparted nobility. He found no confirmation, however. See correspondence in Bundesarchiv, Koblenz (hereafter BA) N1245-28 Lindner.

3. Hans Hohlfeld Johannes Scheele, *Ahnentafel des Feldherrn Erich Ludendorff* (De-Mnbsb) 7781349 (Leipzig: Zentralstelle für Deutsche Personen- und Familiengeschichte, 1939), 3. Found in IfZ ED414-83. A shorter version, going back four generations, is in Bundesarchiv-Militärarchiv, Freiburg (hereafter BAMA) N77-7.

4. "Der tote Feldherr," *Sigrune,* January 10, 1938.

5. Scheele, *Ahnentafel des Feldherrn Erich Ludendorff,* 12. Found in IfZ ED414-83.

6. Most Prussian officers came up through regimental ranks as Fahnenjunker rather than enrolling in a cadet academy. John Moncure, *Forging the King's Sword: Military Education between Tradition and Modernization; The Case of the Royal Prussian Cadet Corps, 1871–1918* (New York: P. Lang, 1993), 15.

7. Ludendorff, *Mein militärischer Werdegang*, 6. While Ludendorff certainly had many postwar admirers, at least some recalled him being thoroughly hated by his fellow officers. See the correspondence between Gerold von Gleich and Wilhelm Groener, September 13, 1936, BAMA N46/33/117.

8. Sixteen was relatively young to become a Fähnrich. A more typical career would see the student entering the "Voranstalt" (in Ludendorff's case, Plön) at age ten, passing to the Hauptkadettenanstalt (HKA) at Groß-Lichterfelde at fifteen or sixteen, with the admission to Selekta status only occurring (if at all) at age seventeen or eighteen. See the charts in Moncure, *Forging the King's Sword*, 150–51.

9. See table 1 covering 1860–1972 in Detlef Bald, *Der deutsche Generalstab 1859–1939: Reform und Restauration in Ausbildung und Bildung*, Schriftenreihe Innere Führung. Reihe Ausbildung und Bildung; Heft 28 (s.l.: Bundesministerium der Verteidigung Führungsstab der Streitkräfte I 15, 1977).

10. In 1909, for example, 60 percent of general officers were aristocrats (table 1, ibid.). Dennis Showalter rightly tempers the common association of the officer corps with the aristocracy by highlighting the more modern, bureaucratic features of the German military system. Showalter, "The Political Soldiers of Bismarck's Germany: Myths and Realities," *German Studies Review* 17, no. 1 (1994). Still, Bald's data does not lie, and there is a tangible sense in which men like Ludendorff or Wilhelm Groener, a prominent and bourgeois contemporary of Ludendorff's, were "new men."

11. Görlitz, *History of the German General Staff, 1657–1945*, 96.

12. Ludendorff, *Mein militärischer Werdegang*, 7.

13. A complete resumé of his military career is printed in the papers of August Lindner, BA N1245 folder 26.

14. 8. westfälischen Infanterieregiment Nr. 57, part of the VII Armeekorps.

15. Ludendorff, *Mein militärischer Werdegang*, 14.

16. Ibid., 10.

17. Ibid., 13.

18. On the sporting activities in the military schools, see Moncure, *Forging the King's Sword*, 220–32.

19. Ludendorff, *Mein militärischer Werdegang*, 20.

20. Ibid., 21.

21. Ibid., 22. His term with the navy predated the large expansion undertaken by Wilhelm II in the 1890s.

22. Other military schools predated the nineteenth century, including Frederick the Great's Académie des Nobles (1765). Bronsart von Schellendorf, *The Duties of the General Staff by the Late General Bronsart von Schellendorff*, trans. General Staff War Office, 4th ed. (London: HMSO, 1905), 42.

23. Görlitz, *History of the German General Staff, 1657–1945*, 96.

24. Ludendorff, *Mein militärischer Werdegang*, 29.

25. Ludendorff doesn't mention this promotion, but it is documented in Lindner BA N1245 folder 26.

26. The numbers grew over the course of the century from roughly one hundred to slightly over two hundred. One finds varying numbers for any given date, depending on whether non-Prussian officers were included (Saxon, Württemberger) and whether the large

railroad division is included. Walter Görlitz puts the total number of Prussian officers in 1888 at 197. Görlitz, *History of the German General Staff, 1657–1945*, 96.

27. Walter Görlitz writes that in 1905, of the 102 officers on the General Staff, forty-four were of bourgeois extraction. Half of the officers at that time possessed a classical Gymnasium education while a declining number were products of cadet schools like the one Ludendorff had attended (ibid., 139).

28. Schellendorf, *Duties of the General Staff by the Late General Bronsart von Schellendorff*, 5.

29. Ludendorff, *Mein militärischer Werdegang*, 87. Görlitz, *History of the German General Staff, 1657–1945*, 77, 116. Schellendorf, *Duties of the General Staff by the Late General Bronsart von Schellendorff*, 48.

30. Ludendorff, *Mein militärischer Werdegang*, 32.

31. This report has not survived, to my knowledge.

32. Schellendorf, *Duties of the General Staff by the Late General Bronsart von Schellendorff*, 48.

33. Scheele, *Ahnentafel des Feldherrn Erich Ludendorff*, 3.

34. Hoffmann and Sutton, *War Diaries and Other Papers*, 2; *War of Lost Opportunities*, 34.

35. Karl Hampe, Folker Reichert, and Eike Wolgast, *Kriegstagebuch 1914–1919*, Deutsche Geschichtsquellen des 19. und 20. Jahrhunderts (R. Oldenbourg, 2004), 467–69.

36. Hindenburg and Holt, *Out of My Life*, 84.

37. Resumé in Lindner BA N1245 folder 26.

38. Görlitz, *History of the German General Staff, 1657–1945*, 116.

39. Ludendorff saw in Schlieffen's book on Cannae a powerful expression of his own military philosophy. Ludendorff, *Mein militärischer Werdegang*, 108. Ludendorff would later identify Moltke with a Masonic plot to entangle Germany in the Great War (ibid., 89–90).

40. Ibid., 86. The titles can be confusing at times. The GGS consisted first of "Abteilungen"—usually translated as "section." Each Abteilung was, however, further divided into "Sektionen," which I ranslate here as "division" to avoid confusion. For German readers, Ludendorff was first Sektionschef of the army Sektion, then promoted to Abteilungschef of the "Deutsch-" or "Aufmarschsabteilung."

41. Ibid., 105–9.

42. Ibid., 89. "Broken" or "bound" were code-adjectives used to describe those under the influence of the supranational powers, in contrast to the "free" Germans of Ludendorff's circle.

43. Ibid., 117. Ludendorff recalled seeing a flight demonstration by the "Wrigth" [*sic*] brothers, whose machine he thought pitiful. He was much more impressed with a French craft clearly intended for military use (ibid., 121).

44. Ludendorff, *Urkunden der Obersten Heeresleitung über ihre Tätigkeit, 1916–1918*, 25–26.

45. Ludendorff, *Mein militärischer Werdegang*, 101–2. For a concise discussion of the army increase issue, see Stig Förster, "Dreams and Nightmares: German Military Leadership and the Images of Future Warfare, 1871–1914," in *Anticipating Total War: The German and American Experiences, 1871–1914*, ed. Manfred F. Boemeke, Roger Chickering, and Stig Förster (New York: Cambridge University Press, 1999). Roger Chickering's essay on the Deutsche Wehrverein's role is also useful. Roger Chickering, "Der 'Deutsche Wehrverein' und die Reform der deutschen Armee 1912–1914," *Militärgeschichtliche Mitteilungen* 1 (1979).

46. Ludendorff, *Urkunden der Obersten Heeresleitung über ihre Tätigkeit, 1916–1918*, 58–59. Walter Görlitz somehow puts the numbers much higher, at 540,000 men and five army corps. Watson, *Ring of Steel*, 34.

47. Dennis Showalter in his essay on soldiers of the Bismarck era, cited above, reminds us of August Bebel's lament that the Prussian Guards regiment—"eighty percent Berliners and ninety percent Social Democrats"—would not hesitate to fire on him if ordered. Showalter, "Political Soldiers of Bismarck's Germany," 64.

48. Chickering, "Der 'Deutsche Wehrverein' und die Reform der deutschen Armee 1912–1914," 22. Walter Görlitz has Keim introducing Ludendorff to Class, but later work has questioned or omitted the link. Görlitz, *History of the German General Staff, 1657–1945*, 149. Roger Chickering questions whether any direct contact between Keim and Ludendorff existed but admits they certainly shared the same goal. Roger Chickering, *We Men Who Feel Most German: A Cultural Study of the Pan-German League, 1886–1914* (Boston: Allen & Unwin, 1984), 275. Nebelin seems to agree. Nebelin, *Ludendorff*, 84.

49. Ludendorff, *Mein militärischer Werdegang*, 108–9. Ludendorff studied the Franco-Prussian War in preparation for his duties at the Kriegsakademie.

50. Ibid., 103. Ludendorff cites the French General Edmond Buat for this number, but does not indicate which of Buat's works it came from. Buat authored several books in the early 1920s on Hindenburg, Ludendorff, and the Imperial German Army.

51. Detlef Bald, *Der deutsche Offizier: Sozial- und Bildungsgeschichte des deutschen Offizierkorps im 20. Jahrhundert* (Munich: Bernard & Graefe, 1982), 14, 113.

52. Ludendorff, *Mein militärischer Werdegang. Blätter der Erinnerung an unser stolzes Heer*: 144. Ludendorff also reproduces in his memoir several letters from other officers crediting him with the additions that were made in 1913. Ibid., 164–66. Ludendorff's desire for a larger, more modern force was shared by large portions of the General Staff in particular, but met with opposition from the War Ministry and other sources. These conflicts are explored in Stig Förster, *Der doppelte Militarismus: Die deutsche Heeresrüstungspolitik zwischen Status-Quo-Sicherung und Aggression, 1890–1913* (Stuttgart: F. Steiner Verlag Wiesbaden, 1985).

53. Ludendorff, *Mein militärischer Werdegang*, 131; and chapter 8 below for obituaries.

54. Moltke's letter of congratulation is reprinted in Ludendorff, *Urkunden der Obersten Heeresleitung über ihre Tätigkeit, 1916–1918*, 60. The medal was the Königlicher Kronen-Orden 2. Klass, which was a fairly common decoration.

55. Ludendorff, *Mein militärischer Werdegang*, 169.

56. Ibid. Also Lindner BA N1245 folder 26.

57. Holger Herwig has Ludendorff himself surveying the city from his open-top automobile parked on a promontory overlooking Liège. But it is typical of the way material on Ludendorff is recycled that Herwig cites the mediocre biography by D. J. Goodspeed, which itself provides no evidence for the event. Holger H. Herwig, *The Marne, 1914: The Opening of World War I and the Battle That Changed the World* (New York: Random House, 2009), 105; D. J. Goodspeed, *Ludendorff: Soldier, Dictator, Revolutionary* (London: Hart-Davis, 1966), 1. Robert Foley references the Ludendorff visit, citing Uhle-Wetter's biography published by a right-wing press. Uhle-Wetter claims to possess a copy of a panoramic postcard of the city sent by Ludendorff to his mother in 1908. Robert T. Foley and Alfred Graf von Schlieffen, *Alfred von Schlieffen's Military Writings* (Portland, OR: Frank Cass, 2003), 259. Franz Uhle-Wettler, *Erich Ludendorff in seiner Zeit: Soldat-Stratege-Revolutionär; eine Neubewertung* (Berg: K. Vowinckel, 1996), 93. Manfred Nebelin found a postcard in BAMA N77-17, Nebelin, *Ludendorff*, 115. And Ludendorff mentions visits to the region in Ludendorff, *Mein militärischer Werdegang*, 130.

58. It had been Ludendorff's insistence while on the General Staff to press for the importance of the huge 30.5 cm and 42 cm howitzers that were used to reduce the fortifications in 1914. Ludendorff, *Mein militärischer Werdegang*, 128.

59. Generalquartiermeister v. Stein, reported in the Berliner Lokal-Anzeiger, August 18, 1914, in Eberhard Buchner, *Kriegsdokumente: Der Weltkrieg 1914 in der Darstellung der*

Zeitgenössischen Presse (Munich: Albert Langen, 1914), 231–32. This process is also described in Reichsarchiv (Germany) and Kriegsgeschichtliche Forschungsanstalt, *Der Weltkrieg 1914 bis 1918*, 14 vols. (Berlin: E. S. Mittler, 1925), 118.

60. Moltke comments in Terence Zuber, *German War Planning, 1891–1914: Sources and Interpretations* (Woodbridge, Suffolk, UK: Boydell, 2004), 203–4.

61. Reichsarchiv (Germany) and Kriegsgeschichtliche Forschungsanstalt, *Der Weltkrieg 1914 bis 1918*, vol. 1, *Die Grenzschlachten im Westen* (Berlin: E. S. Mittler, 1925), 109; Asprey, *German High Command at War*, 53.

62. Reichsarchiv (Germany) and Kriegsgeschichtliche Forschungsanstalt, *Der Weltkrieg 1914 bis 1918*, 111.

63. Brialmont lamented the decision not to fortify Visé because of the ease with which an enemy could bypass Liège. Clayton Donnell, *The Forts of the Meuse in World War I* (New York: Osprey, 2007), 9.

64. As in so many other cases, numbers vary widely and are important for any judgment of success or failure. Herwig says only 33,000 in the initial brigades, following Der Weltkrieg. See Reichsarchiv, Kriegsgeschichtliche Forschungsanstalt, *Der Weltkrieg 1914 bis 1918*, 109n1. Sixty thousand more troops were added on August 8 by Bülow and Moltke anxious about the slow pace. These troops were Ninth and Seventh Corps under the command of Karl von Einem-Rothmaler. See Herwig, *Marne, 1914*, 115. Lipkes, a recent and strongly pro-Belgian author, gives the number as 130,000. Jeff Lipkes, *Rehearsals: The German Army in Belgium, August 1914* (Leuven: Leuven University Press, 2007), 58.

65. Léon van der Essen, *The Invasion and the War in Belgium from Liège to the Yser, with a Sketch of the Diplomatic Negotiations Preceding the Conflict* (London: T. F. Unwin, 1917), 39.

66. Donnell, *Forts of the Meuse in World War I*, 8. The fortresses were truly an (ironically) international project. French firms manufactured the cement while the German firm Krupp provided guns and some of the steel turrets. Ibid., 13.

67. Erich von Tschischwitz, *Antwerpen, 1914: Unter Benutzung der amtlichen Quellen des Reichsarchivs*, 2. Aufl., Schlachten des Weltkrieges, 2. Aufl.; Bd. 3 (Oldenburg i.O.: G. Stalling, 1925), 99. Essen, *Invasion and the War in Belgium*, 40.

68. Georges Leman and Georges Hautecler, *Le rapport du Général Leman sur la défense de Liège en août 1914*, Académie Royale des Sciences, des Lettres et des Beaux-Arts de Belgique. Commission Royale d'Histoire. Publications in-Octavo, vol. 69 (Brussels: Palais des académies, 1960), 36.

69. Ibid., 34.

70. Donnell, *Forts of the Meuse in World War I*, 9.

71. The information that follows is derived almost entirely from Leman and Hautecler, *Le rapport du Général Leman sur la défense de Liège en août 1914*, 34–35. Horne corroborates most details. Charles F. Horne, Walter F. Austin, and Leonard Porter Ayres, *The Great Events of the Great War* (New York: National Alumni, 1923), 38.

72. Donnell, *Forts of the Meuse in World War I*, 33.

73. Reichsarchiv and Kriegsgeschichtliche Forschungsanstalt, *Der Weltkrieg 1914 bis 1918*, Die Grenzschlachten im Westen, 1:108.

74. Leman and Hautecler, *Le rapport du Général Leman sur la défense de Liège en août 1914*, 37.

75. Ibid., 38. The prewar population of Liège was 150,000. Thomas Gerhards, "Lüttich," in *Enzyklopädie Erster Weltkrieg*, ed. Gerhard Hirschfeld, Gerd Krumeich, and Irina Renz (Paderborn: Schöningh, 2004), 686.

76. Donnell, *Forts of the Meuse in World War I*, 37.

77. Wyrall details the size of the garrisons in Horne, Austin, and Ayres, *Great Events of the Great War*, 39. Wyrall also provides the 22,000 man estimate for the total Belgian force. Lipkes says 25,000 soldiers plus a 4,500-man garrison. Lipkes, *Rehearsals*, 61.

78. Reichsarchiv and Kriegsgeschichtliche Forschungsanstalt, *Der Weltkrieg 1914 bis 1918*, Die Grenzschlachten im Westen, 1:108; John N. Horne and Alan Kramer, *German Atrocities, 1914: A History of Denial* (New Haven, CT: Yale University Press, 2001), 10–11.

79. Account in Camille Buffin, ed., *Brave Belgians* (New York: G. P. Putnam's Sons, 1918), 1–9.

80. Essen, *Invasion and the War in Belgium*, 54.

81. Leman and Hautecler, *Le rapport du Général Leman sur la défense de Liège en août 1914*, 111.

82. Ludendorff role in Reichsarchiv and Kriegsgeschichtliche Forschungsanstalt, *Der Weltkrieg 1914 bis 1918*, 110.

83. Essen, *Invasion and the War in Belgium*, 62.

84. Ibid. Somville says the Germans suffered 1,800 killed and wounded at Pontisse. Gustave Somville, *Vers Liége, le chemin du crime, août 1914* (Paris: Perrin, 1915), 228, cited in Essen, *Invasion and the War in Belgium*, 63.

85. Essen, *Invasion and the War in Belgium*, 72.

86. Erich Ludendorff, *Meine Kriegserinnerungen, 1914–1918. Mit zahlreichen Skizzen und Plänen* (Berlin: E. S. Mittler und Sohn, 1919), 27.

87. Kurt Fügner, *General Ludendorff im Feuer vor Lüttich und an der Feldherrnhalle in München*, 2nd ed. (Munich: Ludendorffs Verlag, 1935), 2–4.

88. Ibid. Other sources corroborate this account, sometimes with a slight variation in the exhortation. Reichsarchiv and Kriegsgeschichtliche Forschungsanstalt, *Der Weltkrieg 1914 bis 1918*, 115–16.

89. Reichsarchiv and Kriegsgeschichtliche Forschungsanstalt, *Der Weltkrieg 1914 bis 1918*, 115–16.

90. Ludendorff, *Meine Kriegserinnerungen, 1914–1918*, 28.

91. Leman and Hautecler, *Le rapport du Général Leman sur la défense de Liège en août 1914*, 100–104. Leman wanted to preserve the remaining men of the Third Division for the defense of the Gette River.

92. Essen, *Invasion and the War in Belgium*, 70–71.

93. Ludendorff, *Meine Kriegserinnerungen, 1914–1918*, 28.

94. Ibid., 28–29. La Chartreuse was the site of a convent whose grounds had seen the construction of several fortifications since the seventeenth century. In the post-Napoleonic period a more modern fortress, designed to support the citadel in central Liège, was constructed and stands, albeit in disrepair, to this day. In 1914 it did not form a part of the defense network.

95. Gerhards, "Lüttich," 686. This ignores the contingent apparently from the Thirty-Fourth Brigade that had penetrated to central Liège earlier in the day in an effort to kidnap or kill General Leman but was repulsed (see above). It is assumed they were killed or captured.

96. Ludendorff, *Meine Kriegserinnerungen, 1914–1918*, 29.

97. The account in *Der Weltkrieg* mentions that Ludendorff was leading the Twenty-Seventh IR at the time and had driven ahead of them in an automobile. The Belgians surrendered to Ludendorff and "the few men accompanying him"—so there may have been more than just the aide. Reichsarchiv and Kriegsgeschichtliche Forschungsanstalt, *Der Weltkrieg 1914 bis 1918*, 116.

98. Görlitz, *History of the German General Staff, 1657–1945*, 158–59; Herwig, *Marne, 1914*, 113. Many accounts of this incident get the date wrong. By comparing sources on Ludendorff with the general narrative of the battle, however, the course of events become clear and occurred as described above.

99. Horne, Austin, and Ayres, *Great Events of the Great War*, 43.

100. Leman and Hautecler, *Le rapport du Général Leman sur la défense de Liège en août 1914*, 109–10.

101. Lengthy fragments of this report are quoted in Ludendorff, *Mein militärischer Werdegang*, 139–40. For a similar report addressed to the War Ministry, see Ludendorff, *Urkunden der Obersten Heeresleitung über ihre Tätigkeit, 1916–1918*, 5. Nebelin, *Ludendorff*, 80.

102. Leman and Hautecler, *Le rapport du Général Leman sur la défense de Liège en août 1914*, 114–30.

103. Horne, Austin, and Ayres, *Great Events of the Great War*, 169.

104. Leman and Hautecler, *Le rapport du Général Leman sur la défense de Liège en août 1914*, 118.

105. Ibid., 150.

106. "Efforts to Embroil the Porte," *London Times*, September 7, 1914, 6.

107. Exact time indicated by Leman, Leman and Hautecler, *Le rapport du Général Leman sur la défense de Liège en août 1914*, 135.

108. Horne, Austin, and Ayres, *Great Events of the Great War*, 44. Powder figure from Donnell, *Forts of the Meuse in World War I*, 51.

109. H. Depester, *Nos héros et nos martyrs de la Grande Guerre*, 2nd ed. (Tamines: Duculot-Roulin, 1926).

110. Horne, Austin, and Ayres, *Great Events of the Great War*, 44–45.

111. Leman and Hautecler, *Le rapport du Général Leman sur la défense de Liège en août 1914*, 131.

112. Horne and Kramer, *German Atrocities, 1914*, 13. Herwig, *Marne, 1914*, 112.

113. Reichsarchiv and Kriegsgeschichtliche Forschungsanstalt, *Der Weltkrieg 1914 bis 1918*: 113.

114. Herwig, *Marne, 1914*, 117. Herwig cites Émile Galet, *Albert, King of the Belgians, in the Great War; His Military Activities and Experiences Set Down with His Approval*, trans. Joseph Swinton (Boston: Houghton Mifflin, 1931), 126.

115. Ludendorff's successor as quartermaster general in 1918, Wilhelm Groener, credited Ludendorff with the victory. On the twenty-fifth anniversary of the battle, General Franz von Halder wrote to Ludendorff's wife (Ludendorff died in December 1937) that even the simplest German man understood that the "hero of Lüttich" was a "model of true soldierdom." Groener commenting on an anonymous manuscript prepared by the Reichsarchiv on the "operational concept for a two front war," in Zuber, *German War Planning, 1891–1914*, 256. Halder in Werner Kybitz, *Ludendorffs Handstreich auf Lüttich; Erinnerungen und Erkenntnisse eines Alten Lüttichkämpfers zur 25. Wiederkehr des Lüttichtages*, Laufender Schriftenbezug; Reihe 9; Heft 1 (Munich: Ludendorffs Verlag, 1939), 1. See also Kuratorium für das Reichsehrenmal Tannenberg, *Tannenberg: Deutches Schicksal, deutsche Aufgabe* (Oldenburg i.O.: G. Stalling, 1939), 25.

116. The letter from Moltke to Ludendorff, dated August 21, 1914, explaining the decision is in BAMA N77-15.

117. Dennis E. Showalter, *Tannenberg: Clash of Empires, 1914* (Washington, DC: Brassey's, 2004). Asprey, *German High Command at War*, 73. Showalter's book, originally published in 1991, is the standard on the subject. Useful synopses of the battle appear in several general works on the Great War, including Holger H. Herwig, *The First World War: Germany and Austria-Hungary, 1914–1918* (New York: St. Martin's, 1997), 81–86.

118. Showalter, *Tannenberg*, 192–93.

119. Asprey, *German High Command at War*, 70. Asprey cites Hoffmann and Sutton, *War Diaries and Other Papers*, vol. 2, *War of Lost Opportunities*, 33–34.

120. Showalter, *Tannenberg*, 246; Herwig, *First World War*, 84.

121. Showalter, *Tannenberg*, 250–55.

122. Ibid., 323; Herwig, *First World War*, 86.

123. Showalter, *Tannenberg*, 324

124. Herwig, *First World War*, 87.

125. Hans von Seeckt, Friedrich von Rabenau, and Dorothee von Seeckt, *Seeckt: Aus seinem Leben, 1918–1936* (Leipzig: V. Hase & Koehler, 1940), 437.

126. BAMA N46/63 105–25. Groener lecture "Persönlichkeit und Strategie Ludendorffs" delivered to the Mitwochgesellschaft 1936. Quote is on 109.

127. Max Hoffmann and Eric Sutton, *War Diaries and Other Papers*, vol. 1, *War Diaries* (London: M. Secker, 1929), 19. Both Groener and Novak also cited in Asprey, *German High Command at War*, 64.

128. Kuratorium für das Reichsehrenmal Tannenberg, *Tannenberg: Deutches Schicksal, deutsche Aufgabe*, 88.

129. There is a dispute over who suggested the name. Ibid., 105. The work above gives credit to Hoffmann for suggesting the name to Ludendorff, then on p. 168 credits Ludendorff with the insight.

130. Herwig, "Of Men and Myths," 313.

131. Gerd Krumeich, "Langemarck," in *Deutsche Erinnerungsorte*, ed. Etienne François and Hagen Schulze (Munich: Beck, 2001), 294.

132. Frithjof Benjamin Schenk, "Tannenberg/Grunwald," in *Deutsche Erinnerungsorte*, ed. Etienne François and Hagen Schulze (Munich: Beck, 2001), 446.

133. One striking irony never seemed to have dawned on Ludendorff. Until the early nineteenth century, the defeat of Ulrich von Jungingen, the grand master of the *Catholic* Order of Teutonic Knights was generally seen positively by Enlightenment and Protestant commentators. That Ludendorff would link himself in this way with a medieval Catholic order is surprising. See Schenk's discussion of the changing view of Tannenberg over the centuries in ibid., 438–42.

134. Hatto, *Nibelungenlied*, 22.

3. The Feldherr

1. The quote in the epigraph comes from Klausmann and Lentz, *Die Nibelungen*, 40.

2. Kurt Fügner, *"Wir Marschieren!": General Ludendorff zu Adolf Hitler am 9. November 1923 vor der Marsch durch München* (Munich: Ludendorffs Verlag, 1933). One edition of Ludendorff's memoirs makes the connection as well. Erich Ludendorff, *Auf dem Weg zur Feldherrnhalle: Lebenserinnerungen an die Zeit des 9.11.1923, mit Dokumenten in 5 Anlagen* (Munich: Ludendorff, 1937).

3. On those occupied territories, see Vejas G. Liulevicius, *War Land on the Eastern Front: Culture, National Identity and German Occupation in World War I* (New York: Cambridge University Press, 2000), 9.

4. In the recent flood of literature on the Great War, the best history of the war from the German perspective is Watson, *Ring of Steel: Germany and Austria-Hungary in World War I*. This work covers much the same ground as Holger Herwig's 1997 work, but is thoroughly updated and focuses on cultural and moral issues to a greater extent. Herwig, *The First World War: Germany and Austria-Hungary, 1914–1918*. For works that take a more personal focus on Ludendorff in the war, Lee, *The Warlords: Hindenburg and Ludendorff*, is probably the clearest survey in English. German readers will profit from Nebelin, *Ludendorff*, which is a definitive wartime biography and the most comprehensive and up to date work on Ludendorff's wartime activities.

5. Moltke in a letter to Bethmann-Hollweg, January 8, 1915, in Moltke and Moltke, *Erinnerungen, Briefe, Dokumente, 1877–1916*, 395–98.

6. BAMA N46/63 110, Groener lecture "Persönlichkeit und Strategie Ludendorffs" delivered to the Mitwochgesellschaft 1936.

7. Roger Chickering, *Imperial Germany and the Great War, 1914–1918*, 3rd ed. (New York: Cambridge University Press, 2014), 68.

8. The intrigue is detailed in chapter 8, "Ober-Ost versus Oberste Heeresleitung" in Nebelin, *Ludendorff*.

9. Chickering, *Imperial Germany and the Great War, 1914–1918*, 55–57.

10. Vejas Liulevicius, *War Land on the Eastern Front: Culture, National Identity and German Occupation in World War I* (New York: Cambridge University Press, 2000), 54.

11. Ibid., 252.

12. Ibid., 71. The quotation also appears in Hew Strachan, *The First World War* (New York: Viking Penguin, 2004), 149.

13. After the war, Hans von Seeckt would occasionally remark that Falkenhayn and Ludendorff should have led Germany's armies in the reverse order. Whether Seeckt meant that Ludendorff's "eastern focus" would have been better in 1915 or whether Ludendorff's superior organizational abilities and offensive-mindedness would have turned the tide against the Allies is unclear. Seeckt el al., *Seeckt: Aus seinem Leben, 1918–1936*, 268.

14. Nebelin, *Ludendorff*, 219.

15. See chapter 6 of this book for a discussion of Hindenburg's "Mythos."

16. Otto Geßler and Kurt Sendtner, *Reichswehrpolitik in der Weimarer Zeit* (Stuttgart: Deutsche Verlags-Anstalt, 1958), 339.

17. Kitchen, *Silent Dictatorship*, 22.

18. Chickering, *Imperial Germany and the Great War, 1914–1918*, 76–77.

19. Walter Görlitz titles the chapter on the second half of the war "The Silent Dictatorship." Görlitz, *History of the German General Staff, 1657–1945*. Kitchen, *Silent Dictatorship*. Neither scholar makes clear the provenance of the term, however. Neither mentions any wartime source for the expression. If it is an invention of Görlitz's, Kitchen does not acknowledge it. The phrase also appears as the title of chapter 6 in George von Müller's diaries. Müller and Görlitz, *Regierte der Kaiser? Kriegstagebücher, Aufzeichnungen und Briefe des Chefs des Marine-Kabinetts Admiral Georg Alexander von Müller, 1914–1918*, 189. The most recent German biography abjures "silent," simply calling Ludendorff "dictator in the First World War." Nebelin, *Ludendorff*.

20. Mencken, "Ludendorff."

21. The standard work on the subject is still Gerald D. Feldman, *Army, Industry, and Labor in Germany, 1914–1918* (Princeton, NJ: Princeton University Press, 1966). See also Chickering, *Imperial Germany and the Great War, 1914–1918*, 77–83. Chickering provides a lucid summary of the program's major elements in *Imperial Germany and the Great War, 1914–1918*, 76.

22. Chickering, *Imperial Germany and the Great War, 1914–1918*, 78. Nebelin, *Ludendorff*, 246. Michael Geyer, "German Strategy in the Age of Machine Warfare, 1914–1945," in *Makers of Modern Strategy: From Machiavelli to the Nuclear Age*, ed. Peter Paret, Gordon Alexander Craig, and Felix Gilbert (Princeton, NJ: Princeton University Press, 1986), 541.

23. Ludendorff met August and Fritz Thyssen while he was stationed in Dusseldorf before the war. Nebelin, *Ludendorff*, 106. Kitchen, *Silent Dictatorship*, 68.

24. Görlitz, *History of the German General Staff, 1657–1945*, 149. Roger Chickering is careful not to claim any direct connection between Keim and the General Staff. Chickering, *We Men Who Feel Most German*, 274. He explores the issue in somewhat more detail in Chickering, "Der "Deutsche Wehrverein" und die Reform der deutschen Armee 1912–1914." Given Keim's prior service on the General Staff and the similarity of their ideas, it seems unlikely that the two did not know each other, even in the absence of direct documentation.

25. Görlitz, *History of the German General Staff, 1657–1945*, 149.

26. Ludendorff, *Urkunden der Obersten Heeresleitung über ihre Tätigkeit, 1916–1918*, 65–67.

27. Nebelin, *Ludendorff*, 257. Gerhard Hirschfeld, Gerd Krumeich, and Irina Renz, *Deutschland im Ersten Weltkrieg* (Frankfurt am Main: S. Fischer, 2013), 128.

28. Groener Nachlaß BAMA N46-118.

29. Ludendorff, *Urkunden der Obersten Heeresleitung über ihre Tätigkeit, 1916–1918*, 75–76. Nebelin, *Ludendorff*, 257. Chickering, *Imperial Germany and the Great War, 1914–1918*, 81.

30. Ludendorff, *Urkunden der Obersten Heeresleitung über ihre Tätigkeit, 1916–1918*, 68.

31. Nebelin, *Ludendorff*, 259–60.

32. Ludendorff to Kaempf (president of Reichstag), Ludendorff, *Urkunden der Obersten Heeresleitung über ihre Tätigkeit, 1916–1918*, 85–86. Hindenburg expressed a similar view in two memos to Bethmann on November 1–2, 1916. Ibid., 82 and 84–85.

33. Ludendorff, *Meine Kriegserinnerungen, 1914–1918. Mit Zahlreichen Skizzen und Plänen*, 238ff, cited in Jan Philipp Reemtsma, "The Concept of the War of Annihilation: Clausewitz, Ludendorff, Hitler," in *War of Extermination: The German Military in World War II, 1941–1944*, ed. Hannes Heer and Klaus Naumann (New York: Berghahn Books, 1999).

34. The final debate on the bill makes clear the concerns of the majority Social Democrats (who ultimately supported the law) as well as the outright opposition of the increasingly vocal far left wing. See the debates of the 79. Sitzung, December 2, 1916. Verhandlungen des Reichstages, Band 308 1916, 2286+. Available at http://www.reichstagsprotokolle.de/Blatt_k13_bsb00003404_00717.html. Accessed July 10, 2015.

35. The so-called Stinnes-Legien agreement of 1919 was the outcome of this compromise. The revisionist (as opposed to revolutionary) attitude of the majority Social Democratic Party in Germany is well known, so the sacrifice of such a high principle of Marxist ideology in favor of a concrete improvement of conditions was not entirely surprising.

36. From Hindenburg's memo to the chancellor, September 13, 1916, in Ludendorff, *Urkunden der Obersten Heeresleitung über ihre Tätigkeit, 1916–1918*, 66–67.

37. Ibid., 88.

38. The results of the census no longer exist. The authoritative analysis of the furor surrounding the census is Werner T. Angress, "Das deutsche Militär und die Juden im Ersten Weltkrieg," *Militärgeschichtliche Zeitschrift*, no. 1 (1976). In English: Werner T. Angress, "The German Army's 'Judenzählung' of 1916: Genesis—Consequences—Significance," *Leo Baeck Institute: Year Book* 23 (1978).

39. Angress, "German Army's 'Judenzählung' of 1916," 124.

40. Thaer, Kaehler, and Rönnefarth, *Generalstabsdienst an der Front und in der O.H.L. aus Briefen und Tagebuchaufzeichnungen, 1915–1919*, 189. Nebelin, *Ludendorff*, 58.

41. Nebelin, in his recent biography of Ludendorff, blames Ludendorff's confidant Max Bauer, a noted antisemite, for pressuring Wild into conducting the census. But even Nebelin sees almost no involvement on Ludendorff's part. Nebelin, *Ludendorff*, 233–34.

42. Ibid., 263, 68. Kitchen, *Silent Dictatorship*, 84.

43. Strachan, *First World War*, 203.

44. Nebelin, *Ludendorff*, 269.

45. Ibid. Kitchen, *Silent Dictatorship*, 145–46.

46. Watson, *Ring of Steel*, 380.

47. Chickering, *Imperial Germany and the Great War, 1914–1918*, 82.

48. Watson, *Ring of Steel*, 381.

49. Nebelin, *Ludendorff*, 217.

50. Michael Geyer, "Rückzug und Zerstörung 1917," in *Die Deutschen an der Somme 1914–1918: Krieg, Besatzung, Verbrannte Erde*, ed. Gerhard Hirschfeld, Gerd Krumeich, and Irina Renz (Essen: Klartext, 2006).

51. Nachlaß Groener, BAMA N46-63 115, "Persönlichkeit und Strategie Ludendorffs," 1936.

52. Watson, *Ring of Steel*, 416. Nebelin, *Ludendorff*, 300. The order to resume was issued on January 9 to take effect February 1.

53. Theobald von Bethmann-Hollweg, *Betrachtungen zum Weltkriege / 2, Während des Krieges* (Berlin: Reimar Hobbing, 1921), 138. Cited in Nebelin, *Ludendorff*, 304.

54. Watson, *Ring of Steel*, 426. A more typical month in the first half of 1917 would see 400,000–500,000 tons sunk.

55. Ibid., 435.

56. Chickering, *Imperial Germany and the Great War, 1914–1918*, 109.

57. Watson, *Ring of Steel*, 426.

58. Ibid., 428.

59. Nebelin, *Ludendorff*, 298.

60. Bethmann issued a Peace Note in late 1916, calling for peace without spelling out Germany's aims or negotiating position. Henning Hoff, "Friedensinitiativen," in *Enzyklopädie Erster Weltkrieg*, ed. Gerhard Hirschfeld, Gerd Krumeich, and Irina Renz (Paderborn: Schöningh, 2004).

61. Nebelin, *Ludendorff*, 315. Kitchen, *Silent Dictatorship*, 39.

62. Hoffmann and Sutton, *War Diaries and Other Papers*, vol. 1, *War Diaries*, 166. Nebelin, *Ludendorff*, 291.

63. Hoffmann and Sutton, *War Diaries and Other Papers*, vol. 1, *War Diaries*, 166–67.

64. Michael Epkenhans, *Tirpitz: Architect of the German High Seas Fleet* (Lincoln, NE: Potomac Books, 2008), 69–70. Görlitz, *History of the German General Staff, 1657–1945*, 186.

65. Werner Jochmann, "Die Ausbreitung des Antisemitismus," in *Deutsches Judentum in Krieg und Revolution 1916–1923*, ed. Werner Eugen Mosse, Arnold Paucker, and T. W. Moody (Tübingen: J. C. B. Mohr, 1971), 430.

66. Kitchen, *Silent Dictatorship*, 272; Nebelin, *Ludendorff*.

67. Erich Ludendorff, *Ludendorff's Own Story, August 1914–November 1918; the Great War from the Siege of Liège to the Signing of the Armistice as Viewed from the Grand Headquarters of the German Army*, vol. 2 (New York: Harper, 1919), 173. The passage is also cited in Zabecki, *German 1918 Offensives*, 81. Zabecki cites the German edition and provides his own translation.

68. Ludendorff, *Ludendorff's Own Story*, 2:58–59. Kitchen, *Silent Dictatorship*, 129.

69. Nebelin, *Ludendorff*, 339.

70. Müller and Görlitz, *Kaiser and His Court*, 282.

71. Max von Baden, quoted in Nebelin, *Ludendorff*, 339.

72. Max Weber in a November 5, 1917, speech. Cited in Wolfgang J. Mommsen, *Max Weber and German Politics, 1890–1920* (Chicago: University of Chicago Press, 1984), 270.

73. Max Weber in December 1917 at a meeting of the Heidelberg Fortschriftliche Volkspartei. Cited ibid.

74. Hoffmann and Sutton, *War Diaries and Other Papers*, vol. 1, *War Diaries*, 169.

75. Ludendorff, *Mein Militärischer Werdegang*, 11.

76. Hans von Haeften, "Zwei Vorschläge zu einer deutschen politischen Offensive im Jahre 1918," in Ludendorff, *Urkunden der Obersten Heeresleitung über ihre Tätigkeit, 1916–1918*, 477. Cited in Nebelin, *Ludendorff*, 407.

77. Zabecki, *German 1918 Offensives*, 76.

78. Nebelin, *Ludendorff*, 348.

79. Zabecki, *German 1918 Offensives*, 76. Zabecki cites Georg Wetzell, "The Future Concentration and Present Peace Aims," September 30, 1917, in BAMA PH 3/267.

80. Ralph Haswell Lutz, W. L. Campbell, and Reichstag. Untersuchungsausschuss über die Wieltkriegsverantwortlichkeit, *The Causes of the German Collapse in 1918: Sections of the Officially Authorized Report of the Commission of the German Constituent Assembly and of the German Reichstag, 1919–1928*, Hoover War Library Publications No. 4 (Stanford, CA: Stanford University Press, 1934), 13. The reference comes from a draft resolution drawn up for the Reichstag Subcommittee by Deputy Dr. Deermann (BVP).

81. Scheck, *Alfred von Tirpitz and German Right-Wing Politics, 1914–1930*, 65.

82. On Tirpitz as chairman of the Fatherland Party, see ibid., 65–77.

83. Liulevicius, *War Land on the Eastern Front*.

84. I. F. W. Beckett, *The Great War, 1914–1918*, 2nd ed. (Harlow: Pearson/Longman, 2007), 185–86, 92–93.

85. Scheck, *Alfred von Tirpitz and German Right-Wing Politics, 1914–1930*, 67.

86. Ibid.

87. Dieter Fricke and Werner Fritsch, *Lexikon zur Parteiengeschichte: Die bürgerlichen und Kleinbürgerlichen Parteien und Verbände in Deutschland (1789–1945); in vier Bänden* (Leipzig: Bibliogr. Inst., 1984), 391.

88. Or at least Class told his audience so in a speech on October 19, 1918. Lohalm, *Völkischer Radikalismus*, 52–53.

89. Erich Ludendorff, *The General Staff and Its Problems: The History of the Relations between High Command and the German Imperial Government as Revealed by Official Documents*, trans. Frederic Appleby Holt, vol. 2 (London: Hutchinson & Co., 1920), 387–89. Anthony Watson describes Ludendorff's propaganda as moderately effective. Watson, *Ring of Steel*, 495–506.

90. Ludendorff, *Ludendorff's Own Story*, 2:68.

91. Ludendorff, *General Staff and Its Problems*, 2:387–89.

92. Ludendorff, *Ludendorff's Own Story*, 2:69.

93. Ibid.

94. 122. Sitzung, Oktober 6, 1917. Verhandlungen des Reichstages, Band 310 1917, 3714+. Available at http://www.reichstagsprotokolle.de/Blatt_k13_bsb00003406_00623.html. Accessed July 10, 2015.

95. 122. Sitzung, Oktober 6, 1917. Verhandlungen des Reichstages, Band 310 1917, 3724. Available at http://www.reichstagsprotokolle.de/Blatt_k13_bsb00003406_00633.html. Accessed July 10, 2015.

96. Ludendorff, *Ludendorff's Own Story*, 2:165.

97. Quoted in Michael S. Neiberg, *The Second Battle of the Marne* (Bloomington: Indiana University Press, 2008), 7.

98. Ludendorff, *Mein Militärischer Werdegang*, 88.

99. Watson, *Ring of Steel*, 516.

100. Neiberg's description of the opening battles of Operation Michael, the first of the March offensives, almost makes it sound like the Germans have found the key to victory. Certainly the British are reeling. Neiberg, *Second Battle of the Marne*, 70.

101. Ibid., 4. For a lengthy account, focusing on the problem of operational art, the offensives are detailed in Zabecki, *German 1918 Offensives*.

102. Neiberg, *Second Battle of the Marne*, 67.

103. Watson, *Ring of Steel*, 520.

104. Neiberg, *Second Battle of the Marne*, 71.

105. The day one German casualties are from ibid., 72. The remaining figures for the Germans and the Allies come from Zabecki, *German 1918 Offensives*, 226.

106. Neiberg, *Second Battle of the Marne*, 87.

107. Hermann von Kuhl's diary in June clearly reflects the toll Ludendorff took on his colleagues. Zabecki, *German 1918 Offensives*, 288.

108. Ludendorff, *Ludendorff's Own Story*, 2:169–70.

109. Neiberg, *Second Battle of the Marne*, 130. Neiberg writes, "The Hundred Days to Victory should begin with the joint triumph at the Second Marne, not the British triumph at Amiens." Ibid., 188.

110. Erich Ludendorff, *My War Memories, 1914–1918*, vol. 2 (London: Hutchinson & Co., 1919), 326.

111. BAMA N46/63 122 Groener, "Persönlichkeit und Strategie Ludendorffs," 1936.

112. See chapter 1 for more on Ludendorff's mental health.

113. Adolf Vogt, *Oberst Max Bauer: Generalstabsoffizier im Zwielicht: 1869–1929*, Studien zur Militärgeschichte, Militärwissenschaft und Konfliktforschung, Bd. 6 (Osnabrück: Biblio-Verlag, 1974), 148–49. Foerster, *Der Feldherr Ludendorff im Unglück*, 74. Vogt hints that Bauer's diagnosis may have been influenced by the beginnings of a movement to replace Ludendorff in the OHL. Bauer circulated a report critical of Ludendorff in October 1918. Questioning his health, and especially his mental state, would have facilitated Ludendorff's removal. When that proved immediately impossible, the rumors dissipated. Prinz von Baden Max, *Erinnerungen und Dokumente* (Leipzig: Deutsche Verlags-Anstalt, 1927), 380. Cited in Nebelin, *Ludendorff*, 471.

114. Nebelin, *Ludendorff*, 441. Nebelin agrees that there is little evidence to suggest a real "nervous breakdown."

115. Ludendorff, *My War Memories, 1914–1918*, 2:367. Ludendorff described the Bulgarian surrender as a "defection." Ibid., 380.

116. Thaer, Kaehler, and Rönnefarth, *Generalstabsdienst an der Front und in der O.H.L. aus Briefen und Tagebuchaufzeichnungen, 1915–1919*, 246–48. Thaer's account is reproduced at length in Nebelin, *Ludendorff*, 465–66.

117. Ludendorff, *My War Memories, 1914–1918*, 2:418.

118. Michael Geyer describes Ludendorff's postwar stance as disingenuous. It was Walther Rathenau who had made the call for a levee en masse, while the army seemed to have little stomach. Michael Geyer, "Insurrectionary Warfare: The German Debate About a Levee En Masse in October 1918," *Journal of Modern History* 73, no. 3 (2001).

119. Ludendorff, *My War Memories, 1914–1918*, 2:423.

120. Ibid., 426.

121. Wolfram Pyta writes that an admirer of Hindenburg who saw a draft of Ludendorff's memoir convinced Ludendorff to expunge passages critical of Hindenburg. Pyta, *Hindenburg*, 431. See the chapter 6 of this book for more on their dispute.

122. Thaer, Kaehler, and Rönnefarth, *Generalstabsdienst an der Front und in der O.H.L. aus Briefen und Tagebuchaufzeichnungen, 1915–1919*, 246–48. Nebelin, *Ludendorff*, 498–99.

123. The Kaiser himself related the encounter to members of his military cabinet that evening. Müller and Görlitz, *Regierte der Kaiser? Kriegstagebücher, Aufzeichnungen und Briefe des Chefs des Marine-Kabinetts Admiral Georg Alexander von Müller, 1914–1918*, 436–37.

124. Seeckt to his wife, October 27, 1918 (from Seeckt Nachlass v.61), cited in Hans Meier-Welcker, *Seeckt* (Frankfurt am Main: Bernard U. Graefe, 1967), 165.

125. Ibid., 521. Meier-Welcker cites Frau von Seeckt's Tagebuch.

126. Wilhelm Keitel praised Hitler as the "greatest Feldherr of all time" after German victories in the Low Countries and France. Later commanders sardonically abbreviated the

phrase to "GröFaZ" after Hitler's reputation was tarnished by the defeats at Stalingrad and elsewhere. Gordon Alexander Craig, *Germany, 1866–1945* (Oxford: Clarendon, 1978), 714.

127. David R. Stone, *The Russian Army in the Great War: The Eastern Front, 1914–1918* (Lawrence: University Press of Kansas, 2015), 233.

128. Watson, *Ring of Steel*, 492–98.

129. Krumeich, "Die Dolchstoss-Legende," 595, citing *Die Ursachen des deutschen Zusammenbruchs im Jahre 1918*, 2. Aufl., Das Werk des Untersuchungsausschusses der Deutschen Verfassunggebenden Nationalversammlung und des Deutschen Reichstages 1919–1926, Reihe 4 (Berlin: Deutsche Verlagsgesellschaft für Politik und Geschichte, 1928), vol. 6, 71.

130. Meier-Welcker, *Seeckt*, 165.

131. See chapter 7.

4. Putschist

1. The epigraph is taken from Shumway, *Nibelungenlied*, 154.

2. Later letters to his first wife Margarethe reflect these frustrations. Ludendorff and Ziersch, *Als Ich Ludendorff's Frau War*, 212.

3. Ludendorff, *Vom Feldherrn zum Weltrevolutionär und Wegbereiter Deutscher Volksschöpfung*, 1:76.

4. Ibid., 23.

5. Ibid., 29. Wilhelm Breucker, *Die Tragik Ludendorffs; eine Kritische Studie auf Grund persönlicher Erinnerungen an den General und seine Zeit* (Stollhamm [Oldb.]: H. Rauschenbusch, 1953), 77. Margarethe's account differs only slightly.

6. Ludendorff and Ziersch, *Als Ich Ludendorff's Frau War*, 209.

7. Ludendorff, *Vom Feldherrn zum Weltrevolutionär und Wegbereiter Deutscher Volksschöpfung*, 1:33. Manfred Nebeling points out that using the initials "E.L." would have the added benefit of not requiring the alteration of his monogrammed luggage. Nebelin, *Ludendorff*, 507.

8. Breucker, *Die Tragik Ludendorffs*, 78.

9. Ibid., 79.

10. Max Bauer, "Ludendorff: 'Meine Kriegserinnerungen,'" *Der Tag*, August 19, 1919.

11. Ibid.

12. Geyer, "Insurrectionary Warfare: The German Debate about a Levee En Masse in October 1918."

13. Ludendorff, *Vom Feldherrn zum Weltrevolutionär und Wegbereiter Deutscher Volksschöpfung*, 1:38.

14. Ibid., 45.

15. Breucker, *Die Tragik Ludendorffs*, 93.

16. This oft-cited quotation appears in Ludendorff and Ziersch, *Als Ich Ludendorff's Frau War*, 209. The translation in the English edition, most often quoted by biographers (Goodspeed, for example) uses the wrong tense: "would be" instead of "was." Margarethe Ludendorff, *My Married Life with Ludendorff*, trans. Raglan Somerset (London: Hutchinson & Co., 1930), 177. The original reads, "Die größte Dummheit der Revolutionäre war es, daß sie uns alle leben ließen."

17. Ludendorff, *Ludendorff's Own Story, August 1914–November 1918*, 2:428.

18. Ibid., 429.

19. Ibid., 126.

20. Alfred Roth, leader of the Reichshammerbund, saw his antisemitic views confirmed and strengthened while serving on the Eastern Front. Lohalm, *Völkischer Radikalismus*, 63.

21. Ludendorff, *Ludendorff's Own Story, August 1914–November 1918*, 2:409.

22. Ibid. Ludendorff's obsession with Bolshevism runs like a red thread especially through volume 2 of the memoir, covering 1917–18.

23. Ibid., 179.

24. Martini, *Die Legende vom Hause Ludendorff*, 37. Erich Ludendorff, *Kriegsführung und Politik* (Berlin: E. S. Mittler & Sohn, 1922), 51.

25. Ludendorff, *Kriegsführung und Politik*, 141.

26. Ludendorff, *Meine Kriegserinnerungen, 1914–1918. Mit zahlreichen Skizzen und Plänen.* Information on translations gleaned from the WorldCat union catalog.

27. Erich Ludendorff, *The General Staff and Its Problem: The History of the Relations between the High Command and the German Imperial Government as Revealed by Official Documents*, trans. Frederic Appleby Holt, vol. 1 (London: Hutchinson & Co., 1920); ibid., 2.

28. Gustav Noske was an SPD politician and first defense minister of the Weimar Republic. Mathias Erzberger belonged to the Catholic Center Party and served as finance minister during this period. Rolland writing in Avenir international, January 31, 1919, quoted in Gilbert Badia, "Rosa Luxemburg," in *Deutsche Erinnerungsorte*, ed. Etienne François and Hagen Schulze (Munich: Beck, 2001), 108.

29. "Von der Goltz Coup Expected in Baltic," *New York Times*, October 3, 1919.

30. Results of a search performed InfoTrac Digital Archive of the *The Times*. For two examples of advertisements, see "Hutchinson & Co," *The Times*, November 14, 1919; "Land & Water," *The Times*, August 28, 1919.

31. Leonard Spray, "Ludendorff Hailed by Berlin Crowds," *New York Times*, March 26, 1919.

32. Hagen Schulze, ed., *Das Kabinett Scheidemann, 13. Februar bis 20. Juni 1919*, Akten der Reichskanzlei. Weimarer Republik; Variation: Akten der Reichskanzlei. Weimarer Republik (H. Boldt, 1971), 97n4.

33. Ludendorff and Ziersch, *Als Ich Ludendorff's Frau War*, 269. The book does not make clear exactly how long the Ludendorffs stayed at the Adlon.

34. Goodspeed, *Ludendorff; Genius of World War I*, 279–80. Goodspeed cites Sir John Wheeler-Bennett, "Ludendorff: The Soldier and the Politician," *Virginia Quarterly Review* 14, no. 2 (1938): 200.

35. Ludendorff, *Vom Feldherrn zum Weltrevolutionär und Wegbereiter Deutscher Volksschöpfung*, 1:52.

36. Ibid., 102.

37. Ibid., 91. James M. Diehl, *The Thanks of the Fatherland: German Veterans after the Second World War* (Chapel Hill: University of North Carolina Press, 1993), 16.

38. Baird, *To Die for Germany*, 27. "Heldenehrung auf dem Königplatz."

39. Ludendorff and Ziersch, *Als Ich Ludendorff's Frau War*, 270–71. Ludendorff, *Vom Feldherrn zum Weltrevolutionär und Wegbereiter Deutscher Volksschöpfung*, 1:51.

40. Vogt, *Oberst Max Bauer*, 250. Ludendorff, *Vom Feldherrn zum Weltrevolutionär und Wegbereiter Deutscher Volksschöpfung*, 1:54–55. Treuenfeld's mother-in-law was named Newman-Hamburg, so one could perhaps assume "Charles" was a visiting relative. Breucker, *Die Tragik Ludendorffs*, 96. Why this name would so closely correspond to his alias at the Adlon (Karl Neumann) is unclear.

41. Yorck was the hero of the Wars of Liberation against Napoleon, who had, against his king's will, made arrangements with the Russians in December 1812 to switch sides in that conflict and harry Napoleon's forces as they retreated westward out of Russia. Ludendorff, *Vom Feldherrn zum Weltrevolutionär und Wegbereiter Deutscher Volksschöpfung*, 1:56–57.

42. Peter Wulf, ed., *Das Kabinett Fehrenbach, 25. Juni 1920 bis 4. Mai 1921*, Akten der Reichskanzlei. Weimarer Republik; Variation: Akten der Reichskanzlei. Weimarer Republik (Boppard am Rhein: H. Boldt, 1972), 281.

43. The report of the Prussian state commissioner above speculated that Ludendorff believed that it was premature in 1919 for a "strong man" to seize power and that he remained not unsympathetic to the monarchists. Anton Golecki, *Das Kabinett Bauer: 21. Juni 1919 bis 27. März 1920*, Akten der Reichskanzlei. Weimarer Republik; Variation: Akten der Reichskanzlei. Weimarer Republik (Boppard am Rhein: H. Boldt, 1980), 282.

44. Vogt, *Oberst Max Bauer*, 356–57.

45. Ludendorff, *Vom Feldherrn zum Weltrevolutionär und Wegbereiter Deutscher Volksschöpfung*, 1:178.

46. Ibid., 117.

47. Ibid., 70.

48. Wolfram Pyta devotes several pages to Hindenburg's appearance. Pyta, *Hindenburg*, 405–9. Pyta is aware of Ludendorff's claim to have written Hindenburg's declaration but questions it. He presents it as a product of Ludendorff, Karl Helfferich, and Hindenburg. Ibid., 407. See especially 970n88.

49. Ludendorff, *Vom Feldherrn zum Weltrevolutionär und Wegbereiter Deutscher Volksschöpfung*, 1:75.

50. See chapter 1.

51. Marianne Weber, *Max Weber: A Biography* (New York: Wiley, 1975), 648–49. As Weber's wife argues, Max Weber was not antisemitic himself but foresaw the reaction of antisemites (like Ludendorff) in whose eyes the good work of the committee would be discredited by the presence of Jewish politicians.

52. The Deutschvölkische Schutz- und Trutzbund had written to the chair of the committee, Warmuth, asking him to arrange it such that "Hindenburg and Ludendorff, these embodiments of Germanness, do not fall victim to the Jewish Inquisition." Lohalm, *Völkischer Radikalismus*, 187.

53. An assembly of Bavarian Social Democrats on October 12 and 13 called for the prosecution of anyone, "no matter how prominent," responsible for blocking peace efforts and causing the terrible suffering of the war. See also the Spartacus League Proclamation issued in Rote Fahne, #29, December 14, 1918, both cited in Schwengler, *Völkerrecht, Versailler Vertrag und Auslieferungsfrage*, 144.

54. http://www.firstworldwar.com/source/versailles227-230.htm. Accessed October 16, 2008.

55. Harald Wiggenhorn, *Verliererjustiz: Die Leipziger Kriegsverbrecherprozesse nach dem Ersten Weltkrieg*, Studien zur Geschichte des Völkerrechts; Bd. 10 (Baden-Baden: Nomos, 2005).

56. Schwengler, *Völkerrecht, Versailler Vertrag und Auslieferungsfrage*, 303. The names of the most prominent among the accused appear on page 305.

57. *Vossische Zeitung* 138 (75), March 16, 1919, in BA R43 I/703 p. 11. Cited ibid., 157n155.

58. Ibid., 171.

59. Weber, *Max Weber*, 657–58.

60. Ibid., 652.

61. Schwengler describes Weber's letter to Ludendorff in *Völkerrecht, Versailler Vertrag und Auslieferungsfrage*, 207.

62. The exchange between the two men was later recorded by third parties who heard Weber tell of it. Italics in original. Weber, *Max Weber*, 653, cited in Schwengler, *Völkerrecht, Versailler Vertrag und Auslieferungsfrage*, 208.

63. Ludendorff, *Vom Feldherrn zum Weltrevolutionär und Wegbereiter Deutscher Volksschöpfung*, 1:104. Also cited in Schwengler, *Völkerrecht, Versailler Vertrag und Auslieferungsfrage*, 208. In this memoir, published posthumously, Ludendorff credits Weber with inciting him to search for the real "keys of history"—the search that would lead him to his

many conspiratorial fantasies. Ludendorff recalled that Weber's suggestion was so alien to him, and that Weber's eyes shone with the same light that emanated from the eyes of a Lithuanian Jew he had met in Kovno during the war, that the deeper connections among events became more apparent. Ludendorff, *Vom Feldherrn zum Weltrevolutionär und Wegbereiter Deutscher Volksschöpfung,* 1:104–5.

64. Weber, *Max Weber,* 654. Italics in original.

65. Schwengler, *Völkerrecht, Versailler Vertrag und Auslieferungsfrage,* 249–50.

66. Ibid., 286–87. Wiggenhorn, *Verliererjustiz;* Schwengler, *Völkerrecht, Versailler Vertrag und Auslieferungsfrage,* 249.

67. Wiggenhorn, *Verliererjustiz,* 130.

68. Karl Eugen Schmidt, "Schmach- oder Ehrenliste," *Der Tag,* February 14, 1920. Cited in Schwengler, *Völkerrecht, Versailler Vertrag und Auslieferungsfrage,* 309.

69. Wiggenhorn, *Verliererjustiz,* 13.

70. The oft-cited book by Schwengler covers the general issue of extradition while Harald Wiggenhorn's *Verlierjustiz* details the few remaining cases. Ibid.

71. Lerner, *Hysterical Men,* 50.

72. Ludendorff, *Ludendorff's Own Story, August 1914–November 1918,* 2:430.

73. Seeckt, Rabenau, and Seeckt, *Seeckt: Aus seinem Leben, 1918–1936,* 147.

74. Kurt Georg Wilhelm Ludecke, *I Knew Hitler: The Story of a Nazi Who Escaped the Blood Purge* (New York: Charles Scribner's Sons, 1938), 62.

75. Ibid.

76. Ibid., 65.

77. Erger, *Der Kapp-Lüttwitz-Putsch,* 16. See also, Mommsen, *Max Weber and German Politics, 1890–1920,* 270.

78. Ludendorff, *Vom Feldherrn zum Weltrevolutionär und Wegbereiter Deutscher Volksschöpfung,* 1, 96–97.

79. Ibid., 100.

80. Ludendorff mentioned the portrait when describing his visit to Kapp in 1919. Ibid., 98.

81. Kapp to Heye, June 5, 1919, in Erwin Könnemann and G. Schulze, *Der Kapp-Lüttwitz-Ludendorff-Putsch: Dokumente* (Munich: Olzog, 2002), 11–13.

82. Kapp to Heye, June 25, 1919 BA H08-87/35 cited in Hagen Schulze, *Freikorps und Republik, 1918–1920,* Wehrwissenschaftliche Forschungen; Abteilung Militärgeschichtliche Studien, 8 (Boppard am Rhein: H. Boldt, 1969), 122.

83. Ibid., 252.

84. Erger, *Der Kapp-Lüttwitz-Putsch,* 85.

85. Vogt, *Oberst Max Bauer,* 244.

86. Erger, *Der Kapp-Lüttwitz-Putsch,* 86.

87. Vogt, *Oberst Max Bauer,* 249.

88. Ibid., 240–41. Erger, *Der Kapp-Lüttwitz-Putsch,* 86 and 98.

89. Vogt, *Oberst Max Bauer,* 242–43. Curiously, Vogt's bibliography indicates that Solf's booklet appeared in 1921, not 1919. Perhaps Bauer's introduction to Solf's book spells out its history.

90. Ibid., 274.

91. Mentioned in note 1 of Golecki, *Das Kabinett Bauer,* 653.

92. Erger, *Der Kapp-Lüttwitz-Putsch,* 90.

93. Kapp to Heye, July 5, 1919, Nachlaß Luetgebrune, Mikrofilm Rolle 5, Nr. 1456478/81, reproduced ibid., 306–7.

94. "Notiz Dr. Schnitlers über die Bereitschaft General v.d.Goltz und der "Eisernen Division" zur Beteiligung an einem Staatsstreich, February 25, 1920, in Könnemann and Schulze, *Der Kapp-Lüttwitz-Ludendorff-Putsch,* 112.

95. Vogt, *Oberst Max Bauer*, 250.

96. Westarp-Manuskript, Teil II, S. 76 f reproduced in Erger, *Der Kapp-Lüttwitz-Putsch*, 314–15.

97. See Bauer's letter of November 19, 1919, describing a concentration of rightist forces in the Nationale Vereinigung. Reproduced in Könnemann and Schulze, *Der Kapp-Lüttwitz-Ludendorff-Putsch*, 67.

98. Ludendorff, *Vom Feldherrn zum Weltrevolutionär und Wegbereiter Deutscher Volksschöpfung*, 1:99.

99. "Sprachregulungen zwischen Oberst Bauer und General Ludendorff für das Auftreten in einem bevorstehenden Prozess," April 23, 1920, in Könnemann and Schulze, *Der Kapp-Lüttwitz-Ludendorff-Putsch*, 492.

100. "Ludendorffs Zeugenschaft in der Voruntersuchung vor dem Reichsgericht in Leipzig," July 8, 1920, ibid., 505.

101. Unterstaatssekretär Schulz in "Beratung der Unterstaatssekretäre und Minister mit Vizekanzler Shiffer über die Situation," March 16, 1920, ibid., 233. Erger, *Der Kapp-Lüttwitz-Putsch*, 94.

102. Erger, *Der Kapp-Lüttwitz-Putsch*, 97. It is well known that these men and other industrialists supported a number of right-wing causes during the 1920s as a way of combating leftist forces, of influencing Reichstag elections, and of ensuring a certain degree of sympathy among right-wing political parties. Erger thinks it very unlikely that Stinnes or others had any indication that a coup was afoot. Stinnes named two ships built by his Vulkan-Werft after Ludendorff and Hindenburg in 1921. Wulf, *Das Kabinett Fehrenbach, 25. Juni 1920 bis 4. Mai 1921*, 475.

103. Vogt, *Oberst Max Bauer*, 251. On Stinnes, Vogt cites a problematic source: Ignaz Timothy Trebitsch-Lincoln, *Der Grösste Abenteurer des 20. Jahrhunderts!?: Die Wahrheit über Mein Leben* (Leipzig: Amalthea Verlag, 1931). On Strauß, he uses the more reliable Breucker. Breucker, *Die Tragik Ludendorffs*.

104. Görlitz, *History of the German General Staff, 1657–1945*, 220; Erger, *Der Kapp-Lüttwitz-Putsch*, 41. E. L. Woodward, *Documents on British Foreign Policy, 1919–1939* (London: H.M. Stationery Office, 1946), series 1, vol. 6, 26. Bauer was not entirely honest about the Hohenzollern issue. His confidant Trebitsch-Lincoln met shortly thereafter with both Wilhelm II and the Crown Prince to discuss the prospects for a restoration (though not a coup). Neither man responded favorably. Vogt, *Oberst Max Bauer*, 280–81.

105. Schwengler, *Völkerrecht, Versailler Vertrag und Auslieferungsfrage*, 324n80. Schwengler cites Erger and Vogt, *Oberst Max Bauer*, 258–60.

106. Woodward, *Documents on British Foreign Policy, 1919–1939*, series 1, vol. 6, 28n5.

107. Ibid., series 1, vol. 6, 29. There is disagreement on this question in the historiography. Erger and Vogt both rely on the official *Documents on British Foreign Policy* series, but Erger insists that Balfour agreed not to intervene while Vogt contends that Balfour refused to answer one way or the other while remaining personally skeptical. Erger, *Der Kapp-Lüttwitz-Putsch*, 42. Vogt, *Oberst Max Bauer*, 258–60.

108. Woodward, *Documents on British Foreign Policy, 1919–1939*, series 1, vol. 6, 111.

109. Bernard Wasserstein, *The Secret Lives of Trebitsch Lincoln* (New Haven, CT: Yale University Press, 1988).

110. Erger, *Der Kapp-Lüttwitz-Putsch*, 102.

111. Ibid., 225–26.

112. Noske statement before the Reichsgericht, Nachlaß Luetgebrune, Mikrofilm Rolle 12, Nr. 1463120f, reproduced ibid., 318.

113. Ludendorff, *Vom Feldherrn zum Weltrevolutionär und Wegbereiter Deutscher Volksschöpfung*, 1:106–7.

114. Ibid., 110.

115. Könnemann and Schulze, *Der Kapp-Lüttwitz-Ludendorff-Putsch*, 142.

116. Ibid., 142–44.

117. Lohalm, *Völkischer Radikalismus*, 91. Könnemann and Schulze, *Der Kapp-Lüttwitz-Ludendorff-Putsch*, 143.

118. Ludendorff, *Vom Feldherrn zum Weltrevolutionär und Wegbereiter Deutscher Volksschöpfung*, 1:110.

119. Schulze, *Freikorps und Republik, 1918–1920*, 272. Schulze cites Karl Brammer and Traugott von Jagow, *Verfassungsgrundlagen und Hochverrat; Beiträge zur Geschichte des Neuen Deutschlands* (Berlin: Verlag für Politik und Wirtschaft, 1922), 76.

120. Geßler and Sendtner, *Reichswehrpolitik in der Weimarer Zeit*, 123–24.

121. Description for the meeting from the proceedings of the ensuing Jagow trial, reproduced in Erger, *Der Kapp-Lüttwitz-Putsch*, 336–37. Tellingly, the document mentions not once but twice that Ludendorff was there "just to visit."

122. Ludendorff, *Vom Feldherrn zum Weltrevolutionär und Wegbereiter Deutscher Volksschöpfung*, 1:111.

123. Erger, *Der Kapp-Lüttwitz-Putsch*, 165.

124. Könnemann and Schulze, *Der Kapp-Lüttwitz-Ludendorff-Putsch*, 145.

125. Erger, *Der Kapp-Lüttwitz-Putsch*, 297.

126. Schiffer hinted as much to Seeckt in a conversation on the afternoon of March 13. Seeckt refused to cooperate at any level with Ludendorff. Meier-Welcker, *Seeckt*, 264.

127. Ibid., 265.

128. As in the unsuccessful attempt to get department directors in the Reichswehr Ministry to cooperate on the thirteenth and fourteenth, described by Major Fleck, chief of staff to General Walter Reinhardt in Erger, *Der Kapp-Lüttwitz-Putsch*, 331.

129. Major Fleck, chief of staff to Prussian war minister Walter Reinhardt recalled Ludendorff intervening in various disputes at the War Ministry. Geßler and Sendtner, *Reichswehrpolitik in der Weimarer Zeit*, 550.

130. "Beratung der Unterstaatssekretäre und Minister mit Vizekanzler Schiffer über die Situation," March 16, 1920, in Könnemann and Schulze, *Der Kapp-Lüttwitz-Ludendorff-Putsch*, 231. Golecki, *Das Kabinett Bauer*, 777. Golecki says the meeting took place on March 15.

131. Karl Brammer, *Fünf Tage Militärdiktatur; Dokumente zur Gegenrevolution, unter Verwendung amtlichen Materials* (Berlin: Verlag für Politik und Wirtschaft, 1920), 61–62. Erger, *Der Kapp-Lüttwitz-Putsch*, 249–51.

132. Brammer and Jagow, *Verfassungsgrundlagen und Hochverrat; Beiträge zur Geschichte des Neuen Deutschlands*, 291. In fact, on March 13 the USPD issued a call to arms to fight the "military dictatorship" of Lüttwitz. It seems preposterous that the same party would support a Ludendorff dictatorship—even one in which they shared power.

133. Geßler and Sendtner, *Reichswehrpolitik in der Weimarer Zeit*, 122.

134. Erger, *Der Kapp-Lüttwitz-Putsch*, 264–65, and Ludendorff's statement, reproduced ibid., 342.

135. Ludendorff, *Vom Feldherrn zum Weltrevolutionär und Wegbereiter Deutscher Volksschöpfung*, 1:114.

136. From a manuscript by General von Hülsen reproduced in Erger, *Der Kapp-Lüttwitz-Putsch*, 344–45.

137. Ibid., 273 and 277.

138. Vogt, *Oberst Max Bauer*, 271.

139. Scheck, *Alfred von Tirpitz and German Right-Wing Politics, 1914–1930*, 86.

140. Weber, *Max Weber*, 689.

141. Erger, *Der Kapp-Lüttwitz-Putsch*, 298.

142. Ludendorff, *Vom Feldherrn zum Weltrevolutionär und Wegbereiter Deutscher Volksschöpfung*, 1:114.

143. Ludendorff and Ziersch, *Als Ich Ludendorff's Frau War*, 278. Ludendorff, *Vom Feldherrn zum Weltrevolutionär und Wegbereiter Deutscher Volksschöpfung*, 1:123–24.

144. Ludendorff, *Vom Feldherrn zum Weltrevolutionär und Wegbereiter Deutscher Volksschöpfung*, 1:131. Breucker makes it sound like the owner, a manufacturer from Kulmbach, provided the villa for free. Breucker, *Die Tragik Ludendorffs*, 98.

145. Ludendorff, *Vom Feldherrn zum Weltrevolutionär und Wegbereiter Deutscher Volksschöpfung*, 1:155.

146. Erger, *Der Kapp-Lüttwitz-Putsch*, 295.

147. Golecki, *Das Kabinett Bauer*, 740–41.

148. "Antwort des Reichsministers der Justiz im Reichstag auf die Anfrage der Abgeordneten Ledebour und Dr. Rosenfeld über die Beziehungen Ludendorffs zum Kapp-Putsch," January 14, 1922, in Könnemann and Schulze, *Der Kapp-Lüttwitz-Ludendorff-Putsch*, 569–71.

149. During my research, I found a letter at an online auction house, allegedly from Ludendorff to Göring, asking Göring to deliver a secret letter to Kapp. The letter, dated April 16, 1920, does appear to be in Ludendorff's hand, though I cannot vouch for its authenticity, nor its current whereabouts. Digital copy in author's possession. Ludendorff to Göring, April 16, 1920, at Hermann Historica (auction house), http://www.hermann-historica.de/auktion/ hhm59.pl?f=NR_LOT&c=&t=temartic_R_GB&db=kat59_ZEI.txt. Accessed May 31, 2012. It has long been rumored that Göring, who spent part of 1919 and 1920 in Sweden, had contact with Kapp at that time, though James Cavallie searched for concrete evidence of meetings and found none. Cavallie, *Ludendorff und Kapp in Schweden: Aus dem Leben zweier Verlierer* (Frankfurt am Main: Peter Lang, 1995), 190.

150. Staatssekretär Albert an den Reichskanler, August 7, 1920, in Wulf, *Das Kabinett Fehrenbach, 25. Juni 1920 bis 4. Mai 1921*, 110–12. In the notes to the document, the editor writes: "In nationalist circles around General Ludendorff and the industrialist Rechberg there existed plans to wage war on the Soviet Russia; Stresemann moved in these circles as well," 111n4.

151. Vogt, *Oberst Max Bauer*, 293.

152. Ibid., 298–301.

153. Ibid., 313.

154. Lohalm, *Völkischer Radikalismus*, 193.

155. Miklós Horthy, Szinai Miklós, and László Szucs, eds., *Confidential Papers* (Budapest: Corvina, 1965), 26. Cited in Vogt, *Oberst Max Bauer*, 321.

156. Ludendorff, *Vom Feldherrn zum Weltrevolutionär und Wegbereiter Deutscher Volksschöpfung*, 1:138. On his fears of separatism, see Bericht der Preußischen Gesandtschaft München an das Auswärtige Amt. München, August 23, 1920, in Wulf, *Das Kabinett Fehrenbach, 25. Juni 1920 bis 4. Mai 1921*, 135n1.

157. Geßler and Sendtner, *Reichswehrpolitik in der Weimarer Zeit*, 241.

158. Ludendorff quickly became estranged from Ehrhardt, however—a pattern that would repeat itself with most people with whom Ludendorff became associated. When plans for a Putsch originating from Munich became apparent in the fall of 1923, the Reich government hoped to be able to exploit such rifts to their advantage. Ibid., 267.

159. Ludendorff, *Vom Feldherrn zum Weltrevolutionär und Wegbereiter Deutscher Volksschöpfung*, 1:160.

160. Hans von Seeckt noted the occasion in a letter to his wife, April 16, 1921, cited in Meier-Welcker, *Seeckt*.

161. Ludendorff, *Vom Feldherrn zum Weltrevolutionär und Wegbereiter Deutscher Volksschöpfung*, 1:116. Only Jagow was convicted. Kapp later returned from Sweden to face

trial but died before the court reached a verdict. The other conspirators escaped arrest by fleeing abroad and were later amnestied after the election of Hindenburg as president in 1925.

162. Etienne François, "Oberammergau," in *Deutsche Erinnerungsorte*, ed. Etienne François and Hagen Schulze (Munich: Beck, 2001), 284.

163. Ludendorff, *Vom Feldherrn zum Weltrevolutionär und Wegbereiter Deutscher Volksschöpfung*, 1:236.

164. Ludecke, *I Knew Hitler*, 133; Ludendorff, *Vom Feldherrn zum Weltrevolutionär und Wegbereiter Deutscher Volksschöpfung*, 1:238.

165. Ludendorff, *Vom Feldherrn zum Weltrevolutionär und Wegbereiter Deutscher Volksschöpfung*, 1:176.

166. Martin Sabrow, *Der Rathenaumord: Rekonstruktion einer Verschwörung gegen die Republik von Weimar*, Schriftenreihe der Vierteljahrshefte für Zeitgeschichte (Munich: Oldenbourg, 1994).

167. Ludendorff, *Vom Feldherrn zum Weltrevolutionär und Wegbereiter Deutscher Volksschöpfung*, 1:154.

168. Meier-Welcker, *Seeckt*, 310–11. On page 320 Meier-Welcker also cites Lieber, Aktenauszüge vom April 1919 bis Ende 1922, Teil III Blatt 36, Nachl Nr. 278 for information on a plot involving the Seventh Division in Bavaria, behind which Seeckt and others sensed Ludendorff's involvement. Presumably Lieutenant General Hans Lieber.

169. Uwe Lohalm details a few of these connections in Lohalm, *Völkischer Radikalismus*.

170. Ludendorff, *Vom Feldherrn zum Weltrevolutionär und Wegbereiter Deutscher Volksschöpfung*, 1:162–63.

171. Ibid., 161. Albrecht Tyrell puts the date in April–May 1921, relying both on Ludendorff's memoir and on statements by Hitler at his trial. Albrecht Tyrell, *Vom Trommler zum Führer: Der Wandel von Hitlers Selbstverständnis zwischen 1919 U. 1924 U. D. Entwicklung D. NSDAP* (Munich: Fink, 1975), 61n391. Tyrell also discredits the claim of Otto Strasser to have introduced Hitler and Ludendorff in October 1920 and points out D. J. Goodspeed's error in placing the meeting as late as May 1923.

172. Martini, *Die Legende vom Hause Ludendorff*, 59.

173. Two excellent perspectives on the Lüdecke memoir are Roland V. Layton Jr., "Kurt Ludecke and 'I Knew Hitler': An Evaluation," *Central European History* 12, no. 4 (1979); Arthur L. Smith Jr., "Kurt Ludecke: The Man Who Knew Hitler," *German Studies Review* 26, no. 3 (2003). Both authors expose Lüdecke as a consummate con artist, and yet both (but especially Layton) place a great deal of faith in at least the broad outline of Lüdecke's story.

174. Ludecke, *I Knew Hitler*, 60–61.

175. Joseph Goebbels and Elke Fröhlich, *Die Tagebücher von Joseph Goebbels: Sämtliche Fragmente. Teil I, Aufzeichnungen 1924–1941* (Munich: K. G. Saur, 1987). Entry of August 19, 1924.

176. Kurt Lüdecke tells the story differently, arguing that Ludendorff was brought in only at the last minute and without consultation. (Though, as discussed below, Lüdecke does credit Ludendorff with the idea for the ill-fated march through Munich to arouse the population.) Ludecke, *I Knew Hitler*, 175.

177. From trial testimony, reproduced in Fügner, *"Wir Marschieren!,"* 2.

178. Fügner, *General Ludendorff im Feuer vor Lüttich und an der Feldherrnhalle in München*, 15–16. Ludendorff frequently suspected Catholic plots to partition and thereby weaken Germany. An independent Catholic Bavaria would further this aim.

179. Ludendorff, *Vom Feldherrn zum Weltrevolutionär und Wegbereiter Deutscher Volksschöpfung*, 1:248.

180. Ludecke, *I Knew Hitler*, 133.

181. Ibid., 142.

182. Scheck, *Alfred von Tirpitz and German Right-Wing Politics, 1914–1930*, 101.

183. Notizen aus Ausfuhrungen des Herrn Gelberg bei einer inoffiziellen Besprechung der Vaterländischen Verbände in Hagen am 27.8.1923 in IfZ Fa88 Fasz.297.

184. Ludendorff, *Vom Feldherrn zum Weltrevolutionär und Wegbereiter Deutscher Volksschöpfung*, 1:252.

185. Meier-Welcker, *Seeckt*, 245. Meier-Welcker cites Erlaß Nr. 78 Stab P. vom 18.10.1919, Nachl. Nr. 119, reproduced in Hans Meier-Welcker and Manfred Messerschmidt, *Offiziere im Bild von Dokumenten aus drei Jahrhunderten*, Beiträge zur Militär- und Kriegsgeschichte, Bd. 6 (Stuttgart: Deutsche Verlags-Anstalt, 1964), 220.

186. Ludendorff, *Vom Feldherrn zum Weltrevolutionär und Wegbereiter Deutscher Volksschöpfung*, 1:220–21. The meeting was hosted by Friedrich Minoux at the villa later made infamous when the "Wannsee Conference" that signaled the beginning of the Final Solution was held there in 1942. Steven Lehrer confirms the meeting in his book on the villa. Steven Lehrer, *Wannsee House and the Holocaust* (Jefferson, NC: McFarland, 2000). Lehrer relies heavily on Johannes Tuchel, *Am Grossen Wannsee 56–58: Von der Villa Minoux zum Haus der Wannsee-Konferenz*, Publikationen der Gedenkstätte Haus der Wannsee-Konferenz, Bd. 1 (Berlin: Hentrich, 1992), and mentions (but does not cite) memoirs by Geßler and Seeckt.

187. There are at least two different accounts of the meeting. Seeckt himself denied offering Ludendorff any prominent leadership position, but Joachim von Stülpnagel wrote in his diary on the basis of conversations with both Seeckt and Ludendorff, that the two men had discussed making Ludendorff army commander. Seeckt's commentary is probably the more reliable, but surely Ludendorff's name and influence over both the army *and* the paramilitary groups would have been significant for Seeckt. Seeckt, Rabenau, and Seekt, *Seeckt: Aus seinem Leben, 1918–1936*, 330–31; Geßler and Sendtner, *Reichswehrpolitik in der Weimarer Zeit*, 266; Meier-Welcker, *Seeckt*, 358–60.

188. Seeckt and Ludendorff had clashed during the war, and it was widely assumed that Seeckt's tenure with the Turkish Army at the time was a form of banishment imposed by Ludendorff. Geßler and Sendtner, *Reichswehrpolitik in der Weimarer Zeit*, 265–66 and 286.

189. Johann Aigner, "Ein Beitrag zur Geschichte der nationalen Erhebung," in NSDAP Hauptarchiv, reel 5, folder 116. Account of the ride is on page 8 of the nineteen-page manuscript.

190. Ludendorff, *Vom Feldherrn zum Weltrevolutionär und Wegbereiter Deutscher Volksschöpfung*, 1:256.

191. Ludecke, *I Knew Hitler*, 164. Lüdecke also has former Admiral Otto von Hintze lamenting Hitler's choice of wardrobe. "Hitler too—dressed in a morning-coat, that most difficult of all garments to wear, let alone a badly cut morning-coat, and let alone a man with as bad a figure as Hitler, with his short legs and long torso. When I saw him jump on the table in that ridiculous costume, I thought, "the poor little waiter!" Ibid., 185.

192. Ibid., 167.

193. Bericht über den 8. Und 9. November 1923 von Hauptmann a.D. Richard Kolb, in NSDAP Hauptarchiv, reel 5, folder 116.

194. Seeckt, Rabenau, and Seekt, *Seeckt: Aus seinem Leben, 1918–1936*, 378–79.

195. Fügner, *"Wir Marschieren!*, 3.

196. Albrecht von Graefe, "Die Wahrheit über München," *Das Deutsche Tageblatt* 167 (1923). Item available online at the Deutsches Historisches Museum, http://www.dhm.de/datenbank/img.php?img=d2942017&format=1. Accessed June 29, 2016. Quoted in Fügner, *"Wir Marschieren!,"* 5. A draft of the essay is in NSDAP Hauptarchiv, reel 5, folder 116.

197. Ernst Röhm, *Die Geschichte eines Hochverräters*, [Nachdr. d.] 6. Aufl. (Munich: Eher, 1934; reprint Bremen: Faksimile-Verlag, 1982).

198. Röhm quote reproduced in Fügner, *"Wir Marschieren!,"* 4. Fügner also cites the essay by Albrecht von Graefe, *Die Wahrheit über München*, to the same effect.

199. NSDAP Hauptarchiv, reel 5, folder 116, Auszug aus dem Bericht von Pg. Johann Aigner, München, Lämmerstr.1/3 vom 15.12.1937, cited in Baird, *To Die for Germany*, 43. The translation here is Baird's.

200. Ludendorff had no need to embellish his deeds that day. Numerous sources corroborate the account rendered in his memoir. Ludendorff, *Vom Feldherrn zum Weltrevolutionär und Wegbereiter Deutscher Volksschöpfung*, 1:259–61.

201. Baird, *To Die for Germany*, 46. Liulevicius, *War Land on the Eastern Front*, 258–59.

202. Jay W. Baird, *The Mythical World of Nazi War Propaganda, 1939–1945* (Minneapolis: University of Minnesota Press, 1974), 43.

203. A. Rxxmann, "Der neunte November 23 (Aufzeichnungen aus meinem Erlebnissen)," NSDAP Hauptarchiv, reel 5, folder 116. Name unclear.

204. Ludendorff, *Vom Feldherrn zum Weltrevolutionär und Wegbereiter Deutscher Volksschöpfung*, 1:261.

205. Renzo De Felice, *Mussolini e Hitler: I rapporti segreti 1922–1933: Con documenti inediti*, Quaderni Di Storia, 33 (Firenze: Le Monnier, 1975), 67. General Luigi Capello visited Ludendorff on behalf of Mussolini in March 1924. He was told that police guarded the approaches to Ludendorff's house but encountered no one on the dark snowy night he arrived. Capello also mentions Ludendorff's conviction that he was likely to be killed.

206. Fügner, *"Wir Marschieren!,"* 3.

207. Ibid., 5. Lüdecke supports this view as well. Ludecke, *I Knew Hitler*, 170.

208. Ludecke, *I Knew Hitler*, 155.

209. Ibid., 164.

210. Meier-Welcker, *Seeckt*, 410.

211. Geßler and Sendtner, *Reichswehrpolitik in der Weimarer Zeit*, 488–89.

212. Meier-Welcker, *Seeckt*, 405n81.

213. Ludendorff, *Vom Feldherrn zum Weltrevolutionär und Wegbereiter Deutscher Volksschöpfung*, 1:269–70.

214. Ibid., 314.

215. Ibid., 269.

216. Ludendorff and Ziersch, *Als Ich Ludendorff's Frau War*, 304.

217. Scheck, *Alfred von Tirpitz and German Right-Wing Politics, 1914–1930*, 115.

218. Kasche to Ludendorff, 1. Lenzing (March) 1925, and Ludendorff's reply, March 6, 1925, in IfZ Fa88 Fasz. 199.

219. Scheck, *Alfred von Tirpitz and German Right-Wing Politics, 1914–1930*, 123.

220. De Felice, *Mussolini e Hitler*, 67.

221. Ibid., 93.

222. Spray, "Ludendorff-Leader of German 'Revenge.'"

223. Ludendorff, *Vom Feldherrn zum Weltrevolutionär und Wegbereiter Deutscher Volksschöpfung*, 1:327.

224. Ibid., 329.

225. Raffael Scheck, "Politics of Illusion: Tirpitz and Right-Wing Putschism, 1922–1924," *German Studies Review* 18, no. 1 (1995): 39.

226. Scheck, *Alfred von Tirpitz and German Right-Wing Politics, 1914–1930*, 146–47.

227. Ludendorff, *Vom Feldherrn zum Weltrevolutionär und Wegbereiter Deutscher Volksschöpfung*, 1:336.

228. Ibid., 348 and 351, "Die Macht der reinen Idee."

229. Ibid., 351.

230. Ludendorff claimed to have been influenced by his future wife's book: Mathilde von Kemnitz, *Das Weib und seine Bestimmung, ein Beitrag zur Psychologie der Frau und zur Neuorientierung ihrer Pflichten* (Munich: E. Reinhardt, 1917).

231. Especially Mathilde von Kemnitz, *Triumph des Unsterblichkeitwillens* (Munich: E. Reinhardt, 1922).

232. Richard Steigmann-Gall, "Rethinking Nazism and Religion: How Anti-Christian Were the 'Pagans'?," *Central European History* 36, no. 1 (2003): 80–81. Here Steigmann-Gall relies on Breucker, *Die Tragik Ludendorffs.*

233. Ludendorff, *Vom Feldherrn zum Weltrevolutionär und Wegbereiter Deutscher Volksschöpfung*, 1:377. For some reason that Ludendorff does not elaborate, the "Rüstzeug" was printed but never used.

234. Ibid., 395. This is one of the passages that is curiously missing from the 1940 edition.

235. "Aufruf an den ehemaligen Angehörigen der Nationalsozialistischen Deutschen Arbeiterpartei," *Völkischer Beobachter*, February 26, 1925, 1. Also cited in Fügner, "*Wir Marschieren!*," 8.

236. Ludendorff, *Vom Feldherrn zum Weltrevolutionär und Wegbereiter Deutscher Volksschöpfung*, 1:202.

237. Ibid., 405. It is a mystery how or why these passages, amounting to several pages, made their way into the later edition. They are boldly critical of Hitler and blame him for sabotaging Ludendorff's efforts to unify the völkisch movement in 1924. See chapters 6 and 7 for more on the relationship between Ludendorff and Hitler after 1925.

238. Ibid., 405–7.

239. Foreign observers were quick to point out Ludendorff's failings. According to Capello, Mussolini's informal ambassador to the German right, Ludendorff was too "crudely military" to hold high office. De Felice, *Mussolini e Hitler*, 83.

240. Letter from Hermann Fobke to Dr. Adalbert Volk, July 29, 1924, reporting Hitler's response to the Weimar meeting of NSDAP and DFP representatives, in Werner Jochmann, *Nationalsozialismus und Revolution: Ursprung und Geschichte der NSDAP in Hamburg, 1922–1933: Dokumente* (Frankfurt am Main: Europäische Verlag, 1963), 122–23.

5. Prophet

1. The epigraph comes from Fügner, "*Wir Marschieren!*," 29. Translation from Lee M. Hollander, *The Poetic Edda*, 2nd ed. (Austin: University of Texas Press, 1986), 142.

2. More on Ludendorff's income below.

3. An unsurprisingly tendentious autobiography appeared posthumously: Mathilde Spiess Ludendorff, *Statt Heiligenschein und Hexenzeichen mein Leben* (Pähl: von Bebenburg, 1967). For more on Mathilde's life, see Frank Schnoor, *Mathilde Ludendorff und das Christentum: Eine radikale völkische Position in der Zeit der Weimarer Republik und des NS-Staates*, Deutsche Hochschulschriften, 1192 (Egelsbach: Hänsel-Hohenhausen, 2001); and Spilker, *Geschlecht, Religion und Völkischer Nationalismus: Die Ärztin und Antisemitin Mathilde von Kemnitz-Ludendorff (1877–1966).*

4. Spilker, *Geschlecht, Religion und Völkischer Nationalismus*, 12.

5. Ingeborg, born August 20, 1906, and twins Asko and Hanno born April 1, 1909. Ibid., 108, 15. Schnoor, *Mathilde Ludendorff und das Christentum*, 18.

6. Mathilde Spiess, *Triumph des Unsterblichkeitwillens* (Munich: Reinhardt, 1922). Hitler owned a copy of one of Mathilde's works. A copy inscribed by Mathilde to Hitler exists in the Library of Congress's collection from Hitler's personal library. More on the contents of her philosophy below. Philipp Mattern and Daniel S. Gassert, *The Hitler Library: A Bibliography* (Westport, CT: Greenwood, 2001), 166.

7. Ludendorff, *Vom Feldherrn zum Weltrevolutionär und Wegbereiter Deutscher Volksschöpfung*, 1:252.

8. Ibid., 323; ibid., 328.

9. Amm, *Die Ludendorff-Bewegung*, 95–96.

10. The proceedings are well covered, using the divorce documents in the Bayerisches Hauptstaatsarchiv, ibid., 95–97.

11. Ludendorff, *Kriegsführung und Politik*, 40.

12. Ibid., 43–44.

13. Ludecke, *I Knew Hitler*, 63. We must treat Lüdecke's quotation, recorded fifteen years after the fact, with skepticism. Lüdecke was writing from exile in America after having escaped the Oranienburg concentration camp in February 1934. Judging from his memoir, he clearly remained committed to the ideals of National Socialism despite his estrangement from the party. One senses that he looks back at the prospect of Ludendorff's leadership of the German right with a degree of longing. He obviously knew of Ludendorff's later work and may have been putting words into Ludendorff's mouth drawn from those later writings. Yet the quotation is similar enough to Ludendorff's written work circa 1922 to be included.

14. Ibid., 65.

15. Hans Buchheim, "Die organisatorische Entwicklung der Ludendorff-Bewegung und ihr Verhältnis zum Nationalsozialismus," in *Gutachten des Instituts für Zeitgeschichte*, *Veröffentlichungen des Instituts für Zeitgeschichte* (Munich: Institut für Zeitgeschichte, 1958).

16. Erich Ludendorff, *Vom Feldherrn zum Weltrevolutionär und Wegbereiter Deutscher Volksschöpfung: Meine Lebenserinnerungen von 1926–1933* (Stuttgart: Verlag Hohe Warte, 1951), 2:30.

17. Amm, *Die Ludendorff-Bewegung*, 146. Both Hierl and Ahlemann later defect to the NSDAP. Naftzger, "'Heil Ludendorff,'" 82, 84.

18. Note the surely self-conscious inversion of National Socialism. Ludendorff, *Vom Feldherrn zum Weltrevolutionär und Wegbereiter Deutscher Volksschöpfung*, 2:33.

19. Ibid., 32.

20. Hans-Georg von Waldow, "Unsere Idee und unser staatspolitischer Wille," n.d., F-7, 4. From the context it seems clear that Moltke is the Elder, not the Younger.

21. Hans-Georg von Waldow, "Unsere Idee und unser staatspolitischer Wille," n.d., F-7, 2.

22. Stefan Breuer, *Die Völkischen in Deutschland: Kaiserreich und Weimarer Republik* (Darmstadt: Wiss. Buchges., 2008). Annike Spilker, in her study of Mathilde Ludendorff, also links the DVSTB to the Ludendorffs' later antisemitism and yearning for rebirth. The group became largely irrelevant after being banned in 1922 for involvement in the murder of Foreign Minister Walther Rathenau. Spilker, *Geschlecht, Religion und Völkischer Nationalismus*, 61.

23. Lohalm, *Völkischer Radikalismus*, 127.

24. Dieter Fricke and Werner Fritsch, *Lexikon zur Parteiengeschichte: Die bürgerlichen und kleinbürgerlichen Parteien und Verbände in Deutschland (1789–1945); in vier Bänden* (Leipzig: Bibliogr. Inst., 1986), 180.

25. For one example among many that appeared in official publications, see Walter Groß, "Von der politischen zur geistigen Revolution," *Nationalsozialistische Parteikorrespondenz*, no. 238 (1935).

26. Tannenbergbund E.V. Landesleitung Groß-Berlin-Brandenburg, *Die Wahrheit über Ludendorff* (Berlin: Jac. Schmidt & Co., 1928). Reference in an advertisement for Ludendorff's *Deutsche Wochenschau* on the back cover.

27. "Großdeutsche Kundgebung in Hamburg," 20 Lenzings (March) 1926, F-7, 13.

28. "Großdeutsche Tagung in Friedrichsruh-Aumühle, 21 Lenzings (March) 1926), F-7, 15. "Heim ins Reich" (Return home to the Reich) was also the rallying cry of the Nazis bemoaning the loss of territory in Poland, the independent status of the Saar region, and other areas where Germans lived outside the territorial borders of Germany. In this case the subject was Austria.

29. Holtzmann to Ludendorff, April 8, 1929, in Hoover Institution, Robert Holtzmann Papers, box 1, Correspondence with Ludendorff, 1923–32.

30. Holtzmann to Ludendorff, 14 Erntemond (September) 1929, in Hoover, Robert Holtzmann Papers, box 1, Correspondence with Ludendorff, 1923–32.

31. See correspondence letters from Holtzmann to Ludendorff, April 8, 1929, and April 26, 1930, in Hoover, Robert Holtzmann Papers, box 1, Correspondence with Ludendorff, 1923–32. Attendance at lectures was often recorded in the regular Gestapo reports on the group. Albrecht Eckhardt and Katharina Hoffmann, *Gestapo Oldenburg Meldet—: Berichte der Geheimen Staatspolizei und des Innenministers aus dem Freistaat und Land Oldenburg, 1933–1936*, Veröffentlichungen der Historischen Kommission für Niedersachsen und Bremen (Hannover: Hahnsche Buchhandlung, 2002); Gerd Steinwascher, *Gestapo Osnabrück Meldet—: Polizei- und Regierungsberichte aus dem Regierungsbezirk Osnabrück aus den Jahren 1933 bis 1936*, Osnabrücker Geschichtsquellen und Forschungen (Osnabrück: Selbstverlag des Vereins für Geschichte und Landeskunde von Osnabrück, 1995).

32. Claus Heinrich Bill, "Der Tannenbergbund in Schleswig-Holstein," *Informationen zur Schleswig-Holsteinischen Zeitgeschichte* 28 (1995), 17.

33. Tannenbergbund E.V. Landesleitung Groß-Berlin-Brandenburg, *Die Wahrheit über Ludendorff*, 47; Amm, *Die Ludendorff-Bewegung*, 161.

34. Tannenberg League e.V. Landesleitung Ost, "Merkblatt über Organization," Julmonds (July) 1932, in ED414-54.

35. Tannenberg League e.V. Landesleitung Ost, "Merkblatt über Kampf," Julmonds (July) 1932, in ED414-54.

36. Detailed essays on these subjects were produced by the Landesleitung Nord for use in the Kampfschulen, ED414–54.

37. Tannenbergbund E.V. Landesleitung Groß-Berlin-Brandenburg, *Die Wahrheit über Ludendorff*, 15, 18. It had been Chancellor Bethmann, under the influence of Freemasons, who had arranged the passport, according to the booklet.

38. Ibid., 8.

39. Ludendorff, *Urkunden der Obersten Heeresleitung über ihre Tätigkeit, 1916–1918*, 271–78.

40. On the Schutz- und Trutzbund see Lohalm, *Völkischer Radikalismus*, 196.

41. Ludendorff, *Vom Feldherrn zum Weltrevolutionär und Wegbereiter Deutscher Volksschöpfung*, 1:114.

42. Mailing lists for Landesverband Ost were among the records made available to Steven Naftzger by Franz Karg von Bebenburg. Naftzger, " 'Heil Ludendorff,' " 21.

43. Holtzmann to Ludendorff, n.d. (early November 1929), in Hoover, Robert Holtzmann Papers, box 1, Correspondence with Ludendorff, 1923–32. Preceding letter is October 29, following is November 6.

44. Tannenbergbund E.V. Landesleitung Groß-Berlin-Brandenburg, *Die Wahrheit über Ludendorff*, 36.

45. Fobke to Volck July 29, 1924, reporting Hitler's reaction to the Weimar meeting of NSDAP and DFP representatives. Jochmann, *Nationalsozialismus und Revolution*, 123.

46. Tannenbergbund E.V. Landesleitung Groß-Berlin-Brandenburg, *Die Wahrheit über Ludendorff*, 37.

47. Ibid., 39.

48. Herbert Frank, "Aristocratische Führung in der Grossindustrie?," undated manuscript in ED414-52. The document was written under the pseudonym "Heinz Falke" for some reason. Perhaps Frank was too well known as a Ludendorffer.

49. "Tannenbergbund," *Mühlheimer General-Anzeiger*, May 13, 1932, in ED414-51.

50. Tannenbergbund E.V. Landesleitung Groß-Berlin-Brandenburg, *Die Wahrheit über Ludendorff*, 33.

51. Ibid., 34.

52. Naftzger, " 'Heil Ludendorff,' " 21.

53. Ludendorff, *Vom Feldherrn zum Weltrevolutionär und Wegbereiter Deutscher Volksschöpfung*, 1:88.

54. Tutzing-Tagung August 1937, Programme, ED414-83, 88.

55. Mathilde Spiess Ludendorff and Walter Löhde, *Christliche Grausamkeit an deutschen Frauen* (Munich: Ludendorff, 1934); Lena Osswald, *Geschlechterverhältnis und Ehe im völkischen Deutschland* (Munich: Ludendorff, 1935); Lena Wellinghusen, *Die deutsche Frau, Dienerin oder Gefährtin* (Munich: Ludendorff, 1933).

56. L. Oßwald, "Warum in Ludendorff's Tannenberg League?" n.d., 5, ED414-54.

57. On church membership, Steigmann-Gall, "Rethinking Nazism and Religion," 91.

58. Amm, *Die Ludendorff-Bewegung*, 222.

59. As a guide to understanding for new or potential members of the Tannenberg League, Mathilde distilled her ideas into a condensed form in Mathilde Spiess Ludendorff, *Deutscher Gottglaube* (Leipzig: Weicher, 1927). Karla Poewe also nicely summarizes the "basic findings" of Ludendorff's Gotterkenntnis in Karla O. Poewe, *New Religions and the Nazis* (New York: Routledge, 2006), 94–97.

60. Mathilde von Kemnitz, *Das Weib und seine Bestimmung, ein Beitrag zur Psychologie der Frau und zur Neuorientierung ihrer Pflichten* (Munich: E. Reinhardt, 1917); Kemnitz, *Erotische Wiedergeburt* (Munich: Reinhardt, 1919).

61. Kemnitz, *Triumph des Unsterblichkeitwillens*.

62. Mathilde Spiess Ludendorff, *Der Seele Ursprung und Wesen. 1. Schöpfungsgeschichte* (Pasing vor München: W. Simon, 1924); Mathilde Spiess Ludendorff, *Der Seele Wirken und Gestalten 1. Des Kindes Seele und der Eltern Amt* (Munich: Ludendorff, 1930).

63. Karla Poewe has a good, short summary of Mathilde Ludendorff's philosophy. Poewe, *New Religions and the Nazis*, 161–67.

64. Mathilde Spiess Ludendorff, *Höhenwege und Abgründe; Zwei Einführungsvorträge in Deutsche Gotterkenntnis* (Munich: Ludendorff, 1937), 3.

65. Erich Ludendorff, *Hitlers Verrat der Deutschen an den Römischen Papst* (Munich: Ludendorffs Volkswarte Verlag, 1931), 13.

66. Both Mathilde and her first husband, Gustav von Kemnitz, were early members of the Deutsche Monistenbund, founded in Jena in 1906. The Monistenbund found traditional religions unsatisfying and sought to unify science and spirituality. Spilker, *Geschlecht, Religion und Völkischer Nationalismus*, 111.

67. Ludendorff, *Höhenwege und Abgründe; Zwei Einführungsvorträge in Deutsche Gotterkenntnis*: 7.

68. Fügner, *"Wir Marschieren!,"* 25.

69. Tutzing-Tagung August 1937, Programme, ED414-83, 85.

70. Martini, *Die Legende vom Hause Ludendorff*, 24.

71. Wilhelm Prothmann, *Was will Ludendorff? Festrede der Feier des 70. Geburtstages des Generals der Infanterie A. D. Erich Ludendorff* (Berlin: Struppe & Winckler, 1935), 16.

72. Ibid.

73. Tutzing-Tagung August 1937, Programme, ED414-83, 88.

74. "Mathilde Ludendorff: Gotterkenntnis (L)," *Der Spiegel*, February 17, 1960, 30.

75. Mathilde Spiess Ludendorff, *Erlösung von Jesu Christo* (Munich: Ludendorff, 1931).

76. Ludendorff and Löhde, *Christliche Grausamkeit an deutschen Frauen*.

77. Martini, *Die Legende vom Hause Ludendorff*, 22.

78. Other scholars have noted this characteristic of her work. Bettina Amm mentions the recurrence of the "sudden recognition" and the "enlightening of core being [*Aufleuchten des Urwesen*]." Karla Poewe highlights the importance of "uncovering" (*enthüllen*) of hidden truths. Amm, *Die Ludendorff-Bewegung*, 106. Karla Poewe, "Scientific Neo-Paganism and the Extreme Right Then and Today: From Ludenorff's Gotterkenntnis to Sigrid Hunke's Europas Eigene Religion," *Journal of Contemporary Religion* 14, no. 3 (1999): 163.

79. Kemnitz, *Erotische Wiedergeburt*, 3.

80. Prothmann, *Was will Ludendorff?*, 16.

81. Books sometimes appeared with the imprint Ludendorffs Volkswarte Verlag as well.

82. The bibliography of this work will contain many of the important works, but by no means all of the output, of the Haus Ludendorff.

83. Nebelin, *Ludendorff*, 191. Cited in Uhle-Wettler, *Erich Ludendorff in Seiner Zeit*. Using "v. Gayl Nachlaß BA NL31/2 Blatt 138, 141.

84. Ludendorff and Ziersch, *Als Ich Ludendorff's Frau War*, 311.

85. "Eine halbe Stunde bei Ludendorff," NSDAP Hauptarchiv, reel 5, folder 116.

86. Tannenbergbund E.V. Landesleitung Groß-Berlin-Brandenburg, *Die Wahrheit über Ludendorff*, 41.

87. Amm, *Die Ludendorff-Bewegung*, 273.

88. Ludendorff an die Herren Landesführer! February (Hornung) 20, 1930, ED414-31. Also cited in Naftzger, " 'Heil Ludendorff,' " 92.

89. C. Hülsmann claims to have interviewed Ludendorff in 1922 and discussed the idea. Deutsche Aufbauhilfe, Monats-Betrachtung, February 22, 1938, 6. ED414-83. Marginal note reads: "daß Wort "überstaatl. Mächte hat Ludendorff gesagt nicht Hülsmann." Frank frequently used marginalia to express dismay, anger.

90. Lohalm, *Völkischer Radikalismus*, 178.

91. When confronted, Erich and Mathilde would always espouse a uniform anti-Christian stance, but as Richard Steigmann-Gall points out, their vehement anti-Catholicism rarely found an equivalent anti-Protestantism. He speculates that their reticence reflects their common Protestant upbringing. Steigmann-Gall, "Rethinking Nazism and Religion: How Anti-Christian Were the 'Pagans'?," 83. Erich Ludendorff was raised a Protestant in Posen, of course. Though Mathilde's father studied theology and worked briefly as a pastor, Mathilde described him as unconventional. In the 1890s, he had published a German translation of Michael Servet's (also Servetus) sixteenth-century treatise "Christianism restitutio" ("The Restoration of Christianity"), for which Servet had been burned at the stake. Spilker notes some similarity between Servet's ideas and Mathilde's. Spilker, *Geschlecht, Religion und Völkischer Nationalismus*, 91–92.

92. "Zum Christentum," undated, BA Holtzmann N1079 1/27.

93. Lohalm, *Völkischer Radikalismus*, 59.

94. Holtzmann to Ludendorff, December 20, 1929, in Hoover, Robert Holtzmann Papers, box 1, Correspondence with Ludendorff, 1923–32. Langbehn and Woltmann were marginal nineteenth-century authors whose theories about the intersection of race and culture contributed to the milieu from which the racist ideas of the National Socialists and others sprang. See George L. Mosse, *The Crisis of German Ideology: Intellectual Origins of the Third Reich* (New York: Grosset & Dunlap, 1964).

95. Steigmann-Gall, "Rethinking Nazism and Religion: How Anti-Christian Were the 'Pagans'?," 84.

96. Ibid., 85.

97. Ludendorff, *Mein militärischer Werdegang*, 51–52.

98. Ibid., 46.

99. *Ludendorff und wir Bayern: Ein Spiegelbild für die "Völkischen"* (Munich: Verlag "Bayerischer Kurier," 1924), 32.

100. Erich Ludendorff and Mathilde Spiess Ludendorff, *Das grosse Entsetzen; die Bibel nicht Gottes Wort* (Munich: Ludendorff, 1936); Hans Freiherr von Soden, *Hat Ludendorff Recht? Deine Kirche* (Marburg: Volksmissionarisches Amt). Soden was a prominent member and eventual leader of the Confessing Church in the Third Reich and is the namesake for a theological research institute founded in 2003 at the University of Marburg.

101. Soden, *Hat Ludendorff Recht?*, 4–5, 18.

102. Ibid., 18–19.

103. "Abfuhr für den Tannenbergbund," *Fridericus*, c. June 1, 1932, in ED414-51.

104. "Lotte," *Tecklenburger Sonntagsblatt*, July 17, 1932, in ED414-51. The author cites a South Asian expert from the University of Leipzig, Dr. Johannes Hertel, to dispute Mathilde's charge. Ludendorff and Ludendorff, *Das grosse Entsetzen; die Bibel nicht Gottes Wort.*

105. Hansgeorg Schroth, *Ludendorffs Kampf gegen das Christentum*, Stoffsammlung für Schulungsarbeit, 51 (Berlin: Apologetische Centrale, 1936).

106. Ibid., 3.

107. Ibid., 5.

108. Erich Ludendorff, *Kriegshetze und Völkermorden in den letzten 150 Jahren*, 61 bis 70 Tausend ed. (Munich: Ludendorff, 1931), cited in Schroth, *Ludendorffs Kampf gegen das Christentum*, 7.

109. Schroth, *Ludendorffs Kampf gegen das Christentum*, 11.

110. Ludendorff, *Vom Feldherrn zum Weltrevolutionär und Wegbereiter Deutscher Volksschöpfung*, 1:89.

111. Tannenberg League e.V. Landesleitung Ost, "Merkblatt über Kampf," Julmonds (July) 1932 in ED414-54. The significance of Fraktur to nationalist and right-wing groups is obvious to anyone familiar with the press and political advertising of the time. To use the typescript, or its handwritten equivalent, was to establish prima facie one's nationalist credentials.

112. Tannenberg League e.V. Landesleitung Ost, "Merkblatt über Kampf," Julmonds (July) 1932 in ED414-54.

113. See chapter 7.

114. Eitzen to Hanstein, June 26, 1936, in ED401. Eitzen encourages Hanstein to peruse the military articles in *Am heiligen Quell* and to understand that Hanstein's Christianity was incompatible with a truly "German soldierly bearing."

115. Herbert Frank, "An die Handelsvertreter," August 2, 1934, ED414-63.

116. Ludendorff, *Mein militärischer Werdegang*, 14.

117. Ibid., 25; Ludendorff, *Kriegshetze und Völkermorden in den letzten 150 Jahren.*

118. Herbert Frank, Rundschreiben Nr. 14, August 2, 1934, ED414-63. Erich Ludendorff, *Wie der Weltkrieg 1914 "gemacht" Wurde* (Munich: Ludendorffs Verlag, 1934); Ludendorff, *Mein militärischer Werdegang.*

119. Herbert Frank, Rundschreiben Nr. 26, March 25, 1935, ED414-63.

120. Herbert Frank, Rundschreiben Nr. 26, March 25, 1935, ED414-63. Erich Ludendorff, *Des Volkes Schicksal in Christlichen Bildwerken* (Munich: Ludendorffs Verlag, 1934). Erich Ludendorff, *Der totale Krieg* (Munich: Ludendorffs Verlag, 1935). More complete discussion of this last work below.

121. Eitzen to Heinrichs, January 23, 1926, in ED401.

122. Tannenberg League e.V. Landesleitung Ost, "Merkblatt über Kampf," Julmonds (July) 1932, in ED414-54.

123. Heinrich Dauer letter of 7 Scheidings (September) 1935, ED414-63.

124. Lehrbriefe für unsere Mitarbeiter, "Die Bedeutung des Quell-Postbezuges für Kampf und Verlag des Hauses Ludendorff," n.d., in ED401.

125. Once Deutsche Gotterkenntnis was granted official status by the Nazi authorities, new members had to register with Ludendorff.

126. Holtzmann to Ludendorff, n.d. (fall 1929) in Hoover, Robert Holtzmann Papers, box 1, Correspondence with Ludendorff, 1923–32. Letter begins "der Abend in Charlottenburg."

127. Eckhardt, "Reaktionärer oder revolutionärer Nationalismus," August 12, 1926, F-7, 26.

128. Eckhardt, "Unser sozialistisches Schicksal," October 12, 1926, F-7, 30.

129. Ansprache des Feldherrn Ludendorffs bei der 2. Tützinger Tagung, recorded by Herbert Frank, ED414-83.

130. Tutzing-Tagung, August 1937, Programme, ED414-83, 84.

131. Holtzmann, in a letter to Ludendorff, explained that he was consulting a lawyer and trying to clarify the procedures. Holtzmann to Ludendorff, January 21, 1930, in Hoover, Robert Holtzmann Papers, box 1, Correspondence with Ludendorff, 1923–32.

132. Buchheim, "Die organisatorische Entwicklung der Ludendorff-Bewegung und ihr Verhältnis zum Nationalsozialismus," 359–60. Fricke says they were banned in June. Fricke and Fritsch, *Lexikon zur Parteiengeschichte*, 183. More on the Ludendorffs during the Third Reich in chapter 7.

133. Amm, *Die Ludendorff-Bewegung*, 177.

134. Eitzen to local Tannenberg members, January 20, 1934, "Im Auftrage des Feldherrn . . ." in ED401.

135. Buchheim, "Die organisatorische Entwicklung der Ludendorff-Bewegung und ihr Verhältnis zum Nationalsozialismus," 360.

136. Before the ban in 1933, *Ludendorffs Volkswarte* had a circulation of 61,000. *Am heiligen Quell* sold 5,000 copies of its monthly edition in summer of 1935. By April 1935, circulation of its biweekly edition had risen to 50,000, which indicates that there may have been some loss of membership and revenue due to the ban, but not a catastrophic one. Subscription totals continued to rise, to 86,000 before Erich Ludendorff's death in December 1937. Amm, *Die Ludendorff-Bewegung*, 8, 190, 96.

137. Mathilde Spiess Ludendorff, *Angeklagt wegen Religionsvergehens* (Munich: Ludendorffs Volkswarte Verlag, 1930), 44. Cited in Martini, *Die Legende vom Hause Ludendorff*, 67.

138. Erich Ludendorff, "Ludendorff zur Abrüstung," *Ludendorffs Volkswarte*, February 7, 1932. in ED414-104. Wehrhaft can also mean "able-bodied" (as in eligible for the draft) and literally translates as "capable of defense." "Prepared" only partially captures the sentiment.

139. Erich Ludendorff, "Militärische Gleichberechtigung Deutschlands," *Ludendorffs Volkswarte*, April 2, 1933, 1, in ED414-104.

140. Ludendorff, *Mein militärischer Werdegang*, 36.

141. See chapter 2. The story of the army increase is repeated in numerous publications, including Prothmann, *Was will Ludendorff?*, 5.

142. *Am heiligen Quell*, April 1935, quoted ibid., 17.

143. One such armband can be found in ED414-54.

144. Ludendorff, *Der totale Krieg*. This book had an enormous public profile. It went through numerous German editions, and by 1941 it had been translated into English, French, Spanish, Portuguese, Chinese. It was published, apparently in the German original, in Tokyo in 1941. Information from OCLC WorldCat. Reviews appeared in major newspapers throughout Europe and the United States.

145. Herbert Frank, Rundschreiben Nr. 34, ED414-63.

146. Walter Görlitz says the book "strengthened Hitler's convictions" and was "carefully read by the General Staff," though the latter rejected the book's conclusions. Unfortunately, Görlitz provides no evidence for his assertion. Görlitz, *History of the German General Staff, 1657–1945*, 302.

147. Chickering, "Sore Loser."

148. Müller, *General Ludwig Beck*, 55.

149. Ansprache des Oberbefehlshaber des Heeres an die höhere Generalität . . . (n.d.), reproduced ibid., 562–79. Reference to "totalen Krieg" (quotes in original) on page 570. The document authored by Beck was intended to be read by Brauchitsch at a meeting of senior army commanders. Beck hoped to garner the unanimous support of the assembled generals for his stance against war with Czechoslovakia. Brauchitsch did raise concerns about the planned campaign but failed to rally his colleagues for Beck's *démarche*. The context of the document is discussed in Foerster, *Ein General Kämpft gegen den Krieg*, 109–19.

150. "Die Lehre vom totalen Kriege," in Ludwig Beck and Hans Speidel, *Studien* (Stuttgart: K. F. Koehler, 1955), 229–58.

151. Müller, *General Ludwig Beck*, 33. Beck was at many points critical of Ludendorff's wartime dictatorship as well as his postwar teachings concerning the primacy of the "Feldherr," but he certainly did not dismiss the work out of hand.

152. Foerster, *Ein General Kämpft gegen den Krieg*, 137.

153. Erich Ludendorff, "Wehrhaftigkeit," *Ludendorf's Volkswarte*, November 29, 1931.

154. Ibid.

155. Ludendorff, *Der totale Krieg*, 5.

156. Andreas Hauser writes that "both [Hitler and Ludendorff] defined entire populations as enemies, and Hitler and his supporters set out to annihilate or enslave them." Hew Strachan and Andreas Herberg-Rothe, eds., *Clausewitz in the Twenty-First Century* (Oxford: Oxford University Press, 2007), 151–52.

157. G. Ka., "Der totale Krieg: Eine aktuelle Schrift des Generals Ludendorff," *Nationalsozialistische Parteikorrespondenz*, no. 263 (1935), 3.

158. Görlitz, *History of the German General Staff, 1657–1945*, 302; Chickering, "Sore Loser," 175–76.

159. In his 1937 work, *Das Weltkriegsende*, Bernhard Schwertfeger made his case for the consideration of political, not just narrowly military, matters by reference to the consensus surrounding the new "totality of war." Bernhard Heinrich Schwertfeger, *Das Weltkriegsende, Gedanken über die deutsche Kriegführung 1918*, 5. Aufl. (Potsdam: Akademische Verlagsgesellschaft Athenaion, 1937), 7.

160. Görlitz, *History of the German General Staff, 1657–1945*, 302.

161. Chickering, "Sore Loser," 175–76.

162. A sampling: Friedrich Franz Feeser, "Der totale Krieg," *Zeitschrift für Politik* 36, no. 10 (1936); Hans Barth and George Wack, "Reality and Ideology of the Totalitarian State," *Review of Politics* 1, no. 3 (1939); "Editorial: Some Reflections on the War," *Review of Politics* 1, no. 4 (1939); Sigmund Neumann, "The Rule of the Demagogue," *American Sociological Review* 3, no. 4 (1938); "Periodical Literature," *American Sociological Review* 2, no. 1 (1937).

163. Wilhelm Müller-Loebnitz, "Politik und Wehrmacht als Mittler der Kriegführung. Eine Historische Betrachtung—II. Teil," *Militärwissenschaftliche Rundschau*, no. 6 (1936): especially pages 729–32.

164. Konstantin Julius Friedrich von Altrock, "Ludendorff: Mein militärischer Werdegang," review of *Mein militärischer Werdegang. Blätter der Erinnerung an unser stolzes Heer* by Erich Ludendorff (Munich: Ludendorff, 1933), in *Militär-Wochenblatt* 118, no. 9 (1933).

165. There is a telling incident when Robert Holtzmann tells Ludendorff of a planned gathering in Berlin. If Ludendorff would come, it would surely be a huge success. Ludendorff answered that it would depend on when the national gathering (also in Berlin) was scheduled. "To come to Berlin twice in such a short time," he wrote, "is not possible for me." Holtzmann to Ludendorff, date missing, in Hoover, Robert Holtzmann Papers, box 1, Correspondence with Ludendorff, 1923–32. Letter begins "1) Einen geigneten Führer . . ." and Ludendorff's response January 9, 1930.

166. Amm, *Die Ludendorff-Bewegung*, 163.

6. Duelist

1. The epigraph comes from Klausmann and Lentz, *Die Nibelungen*, 15–16.

2. Mosse, *Image of Man*, 100. On willpower and mental health, see Lerner, *Hysterical Men*, discussed in chapter 1.

3. See chapters 4 and 7 for Ludendorff's participation in the Beer Hall Putsch and relations with the National Socialists.

4. Erich Ludendorff and Mathilde Spiess Ludendorff, *Die Judenmacht, ihr Wesen und Ende* (Munich: Ludendorffs Verlag, 1939), 450. Originally published in issue 9 of *Am heiligen Quell Deutscher Kraft* in 1936 [Volksschöpfung].

5. Pyta, *Hindenburg*, 430–31. Dorpalen, *Hindenburg and the Weimar Republic*, 31. Dorpalen says the omitted portion is reprinted in Erich Ludendorff, *Vom Feldherrn zum Weltrevolutionär und Wegbereiter Deutscher Volksschöpfung: Meine Lebenserinnerungen von 1919–1925*, vol. 1 (Munich: Ludendorffs Verlag, 1940), 363 and 50–51.

6. In his memoir, Ludendorff mentions Hindenburg's efforts to dissuade him from resigning but no sense of the betrayal of which he would later complain. Ludendorff, *Ludendorff's Own Story*, 2:425–27.

7. Erich Ludendorff, "Herr Paul von Hindenburg," Sonderdruck aus *Ludendorffs Volkswarte*, Folge 13, 30 Lenzing 1930, in ED414-150.

8. Breucker, *Die Tragik Ludendorffs*, 115. See the chapter 3 for details of Ludendorff's dismissal.

9. Thanks to my research assistant Eric Klinek for noting the trend.

10. Erich Ludendorff, "General von Hindenburg und ich," *Ludendorffs Volkswarte*, November 20, 1932, 1, in ED414-150.

11. Ibid.

12. Ibid.

13. Correspondence reproduced in Fügner, *"Wir Marschieren!,"* 27.

14. Erich Ludendorff, "General von Hindenburg und ich," *Ludendorffs Volkswarte*, November 20, 1932, 1, in ED414-150.

15. In the English edition, Hindenburg and Holt, *Out of My Life*, the offending passage quoted above is on pages 94–95.

16. Hindenburg biographer Wolfram Pyta indicates that Otto Hoetzsch, an instructor at the Kriegsakademie, wrote Hindenburg's memoirs. Pyta, *Hindenburg*, 149. Erich Ludendorff, "General von Hindenburg und ich," *Ludendorffs Volkswarte*, November 20, 1932, 2, in ED414-150.

17. Ibid., 533.

18. The story is from a booklet titled "Das Herz des Hauses Hindenburg" by Ludwig Hoppe. Mentioned in Herbert Frank, "Die 'Gemütstiefe und Seelenruhe' des Generalfeldmarchalls von Hindenburg," manuscript in ED414-52.

19. Fügner, *General Ludendorff im Feuer vor Lüttich und an der Feldherrnhalle in München*, 7. Schäfer was the author of numerous books, including two flattering works that examined Ludendorff and Tannenberg directly: Theobald von Schäfer, *Tannenberg*, ed. Reichsarchiv (Germany), Schlachten des Weltkrieges, in Einzeldarstellungen (Oldenburg i. O.: Stalling, 1927), and Theobald von Schäfer, *Ludendorff, der Feldherr der Deutschen im Weltkriege* (Berlin: K. Siegismund, 1935).

20. Kuratorium für das Reichsehrenmal Tannenberg, *Tannenberg: Deutches Schicksal, deutsche Aufgabe*, 202.

21. Ibid., 203.

22. Ibid., 209.

23. Schenk, "Tannenberg/Grunwald," 449.

24. Ibid., 446, 49.

25. Kuratorium für das Reichsehrenmal Tannenberg, *Tannenberg: Deutches Schicksal, deutsche Aufgabe*, 212.

26. Fügner, *"Wir Marschieren!,"* 19.

27. Schenk, "Tannenberg/Grunwald," 448–49. Thea von Harbou et al., *Die Nibelungen* (New York: Kino on Video, 2002), videorecording, 2 videodiscs (291 min.).

28. Schenk, "Tannenberg/Grunwald," 452.

29. Ludendorff, *Vom Feldherrn zum Weltrevolutionär und Wegbereiter Deutscher Volksschöpfung*, 1:362–63.

30. Seeckt, Rabenau, and Seeckt, *Seeckt: Aus seinem Leben, 1918–1936*, 406.

31. Dorpalen, *Hindenburg and the Weimar Republic*, 132.

32. Alfred Rosenberg and Hans Günther Seraphim, *Das politische Tagebuch Alfred Rosenbergs aus den Jahren 1934/35 und 1939/40: Nach der photographischen Wiedergabe der Handschrift aus den Nürnberger Akten* (Göttingen: Musterschmidt, 1956), 42. The editor of Rosenberg's diary incorrectly lists the date of the memorial's dedication as 1928.

33. Dorpalen, *Hindenburg and the Weimar Republic*, 133.

34. Volker Ackermann, *Nationale Totenfeiern in Deutschland: Von Wilhelm I. bis Franz Josef Strauss: Eine Studie zur politischen Semiotik*, Sprache und Geschichte, Bd. 15 (Stuttgart: Klett-Cotta, 1990), 123; Kuratorium für das Reichsehrenmal Tannenberg, *Tannenberg: Deutches Schicksal, deutsche Aufgabe*. Photo of Hindenburg and Ludendorff busts appears in an appendix. On the reconciliation with Hitler, see chapter 7.

35. Walter Elze, *Tannenberg; das deutsche Heer von 1914, seine Grundzüge und deren Auswirkung im Sieg an der Ostfront* (Breslau: F. Hirt, 1928). Elze was an admirer of Hindenburg according to Pyta's biography; see Pyta, *Hindenburg*, 534.

36. Erich Ludendorff, *"Dirne Kriegsgeschichte" vor dem Gericht des Weltkrieges* (Munich: Ludendorff, 1930); Elze, *Tannenberg: Das deutsche Heer von 1914*. Ludendorff's title defies simple translation, but perhaps turning Dirne into a verb suffices: " 'Prostituting military history': Facing the court of the World War." This book was apparently one of the central problems for Ludendorff and one of the reasons the Wehrmacht decided to intervene on his behalf in 1935. This despite the Reichsarchiv's apparent approval of the book. "Besprechung auf Grund der Bemerkungen des Ministers (von Blomberg) und des Chef HL (Fritsch) am 12.I.1935," ED1, 80.

37. Erich Ludendorff, "Reichspräsident und geschichtliche Wahrheit," *Ludendorffs Volkswarte*, September 25, 1932, 2, in ED414-150.

38. Fügner, *General Ludendorff im Feuer vor Lüttich und an der Feldherrnhalle in München*, 9.

39. Müller, *General Ludwig Beck*, 74.

40. Ludendorff admits as much in his notes on the Wetzell/Beck meeting discussed below. Ibid., 408–9.

41. See chapter 7 on the Reichswehr's interest in rehabilitating Ludendorff.

42. See also Müller, *General Ludwig Beck*, 74ff.

43. Ibid., 76.

44. Ibid., 402.

45. Ludendorff, *"Dirne Kriegsgeschichte" vor dem Gericht des Weltkrieges*; Erich Ludendorff, *Tannenberg: Zum 20. Jahrestag der Schlacht* (Munich: Ludendorffs Verlag, 1934).

46. Erklärung des Reichswehrministers über die Haltung der Reichswehrführung gegenüber Gen. d. Inf. Ludendorff in Müller, *General Ludwig Beck*, 400–403.

47. Aufzeichnung General d. Inf. a.D. Ludendorffs über eine Besprechung mit General Wetzell und General Beck am 06.01.1935 in Tutzing, ibid., 403–11.

48. Ibid., 76.

49. Tannenbergbund E.V. Landesleitung Groß-Berlin-Brandenburg, *Die Wahrheit über Ludendorff*, 9–10. Other pamphlets emphasize the sequence of events. Fügner, *"Wir Marschieren!,"* 15.

50. Dorpalen, *Hindenburg and the Weimar Republic*, 136–37n68.

51. Buat was the chief of the French General Staff in 1920 and wrote the foreword to the French translation of Ludendorff's *Kriegserinnerungen*. Fügner, *"Wir Marschieren!,"* is one such work that prominently features the Buat quote. Fügner, *General Ludendorff im Feuer vor Lüttich und an der Feldherrnhalle in München*. Also Hermann Andress, *Luther! Friedrich der Grosse!! Ludendorff!!!: Priesterschaft oder Deutscher Gottglaube?* (Düsseldorf: Verlag Deutsche Revolution, 1935).

52. "v.Hindenburg-Ludendorff," *Ludendorffs Volkswarte*, January 8, 1933, 1.

53. Paul Lindenberg and Paul von Hindenburg, *Hindenburg-Denkmal für das deutsche Volk eine Ehrengabe für den General-Feldmarschall* (Berlin: Weller, 1922), 392. Cited in Schenk, "Tannenberg/Grunwald," 447.

54. Golecki, *Das Kabinett Bauer*, 431.

55. Transcript of telegraphic exchange between Hindenburg and Ludendorff c. February 26, 1932, in ED414-150.

56. "Der schlagfertige Hindenburg," *Münsterischer-Anzeiger*, February 21, 1932, in ED414-150.

57. Erich Ludendorff, "General von Hindenburg und ich," *Ludendorffs Volkswarte*, November 20, 1932, 1, in ED414-150. This story is repeated by Kurt Fügner in Fügner, *General Ludendorff im Feuer vor Lüttich und an der Feldherrnhalle in München*, 14.

58. Rosenberg and Seraphim, *Das Politische Tagebuch Alfred Rosenbergs aus den Jahren 1934/35 und 1939/40*, 41.

59. Ludendorff, *Vom Feldherrn zum Weltrevolutionär und Wegbereiter Deutscher Volksschöpfung*, 1:396–97.

60. Siegfried Kasche to Ludendorff, June 21, 1926, in IfZ Fa88 Fasz. 199. Kasche asked for clarification from Ludendorff whether he had really suggested that Hitler was "bound to Rome."

61. Erich Ludendorff, *Weltkrieg droht auf Deutschem Boden* (Munich: Ludendorff, 1931).

62. It was even taken seriously in some quarters (presumably those who had not read it!). The Women's International League for Peace and Freedom, based in Washington, DC, used the book to heighten the sense of urgency and anxiety surrounding the prospects for a future war. They treated Ludendorff's prediction of war in 1932 as a serious assessment based on intimate knowledge of military affairs. Document 21, *International Economics versus National Politics* (Washington, DC: Women's International League for Peace and Freedom, 1930). The Records of the Women's International League for Peace and Freedom, U.S. Section, 1919–1959, Swarthmore College Peace Collection (microfilm, reel 33, frames 974–77). Available at http://alexanderstreet6.com/wasm/wasmopen/chemwar/doc21.htm. Accessed April 7, 2008. That the league referred to Ludendorff as a "friend of Adolph [sic] Hitler" only increases one's suspicion that they had not actually read the book.

63. Ludendorff, *Weltkrieg droht auf Deutschem Boden*. Nor was this the first time Ludendorff had prophesied world war. In 1931 he published a long article in *Volkswarte* warning of "preventive war" to be launched against Germany in July 1931. As proof he cited the "fact" that firms in Munich doing business with France had been warned not to enter into long-term contracts because of the impending conflict. Like most doomsday prophets, Ludendorff merely updated his story for the later work. Erich Ludendorff, "Der 'Präventivkrieg' 1931," *Ludendorffs Volkswarte*, n.d. 1931.

64. In Ludendorff's mind, there were other indicators of the significance of those numbers: ten commandments, five books of Moses, and more.

65. Ludendorff, *Kriegshetze und Völkermorden in den letzten 150 Jahren*; Ludendorff, *Weltkrieg droht auf Deutschem Boden.*

66. As Richard Steigmann-Gall points out, Luther was a hero to many pagans with an ambiguous relationship to Christianity, like Ludendorff or his erstwhile antagonist, the Nazi Alfred Rosenberg, as well as Heinrich Himmler. According to them, Luther destroyed the power of the priesthood and developed a "Germanic" Christianity. Steigmann-Gall, "Rethinking Nazism and Religion," 89, 102.

67. Ludendorff, *Kriegshetze und Völkermorden in den letzten 150 Jahren*, 292–93, 306; Alfred Rosenberg, "Der Fall Ludendorff," *Nationalsozialistiche Monatshefte* 2, no. 16 (1931).

68. Hans Kurth to Lindner February 23, 1953, BA N1245-28.

69. Ludendorff, *Hitlers Verrat der Deutschen an den römischen Papst*, 3.

70. Herbert Frank, "Adolf, der Erlöser," May 1, 1932, manuscript in ED414-52.

71. Ludendorff, *Hitlers Verrat der Deutschen an den römischen Papst*, 6. According to the philosophy of Deutsche Gotterkenntnis, traditional religions used the power of suggestion to brainwash people at an early age. Once thus "programmed," one did the bidding of the Catholic Church whether conscious of it or not. The Ludendorffs frequently used the phrase "dogmentreuer Katholik" to describe Hitler almost solely on the basis that he had been subject to Catholic "suggestion" as a child. Mathilde Ludendorff develops the "suggestion" idea in her *Des Kindes Seele und der Eltern Amt*. Mathilde Spiess Ludendorff, *Des Kindes Seele und der Eltern Amt* (Munich: Ludendorffs Volkswarte Verlag, 1930). See Tannenbergbund e.V. Landesleitung Nord, "Nationalsozialistische Deutsche Arbeiterpartei: Wofür kämpft die N.S.D.A.P.?" n.d., in ED414-54.

72. Richard Bosworth details Mussolini's relations with the popes who served during his tenure as dictator of Italy. R. J. B. Bosworth, *Mussolini* (London: Arnold, 2002).

73. Ludendorff, *Hitlers Verrat der Deutschen an den römischen Papst*, 2–3.

74. Johannes Stark, *Nationalsozialismus und Katholische Kirche* (Munich: F. Eher, 1931). It is typical that for all of the similarities between Rosenberg's philosophy and Ludendorff's, as spelled out by Martini in his *Legende vom Haus Ludendorff*, Ludendorff still condemns Rosenberg's work as "thoroughly Christian and full of the gravest errors." Ludendorff, *Hitlers Verrat der Deutschen an den römischen Papst*, 7.

75. Rosenberg, "Der Fall Ludendorff," 290.

76. Ibid., 305.

77. Entries of March 3, 1929; January 23, 1937; and November 11, 1937. Goebbels and Fröhlich, *Die Tagebücher von Joseph Goebbels.*

78. Entries of August 25, 1937 and December 22, 1937. Ibid.

79. Rosenberg, "Der Fall Ludendorff," 295.

80. Anton Haselmayer, *Der Fall Rosenbergs- und fällt Hitler mit? Eine Streitschrift zu "Der Fall Ludendorff" von Rosenberg* (Munich: Ludendorffs Volkswarte Verlag, 1931).

81. Tannenbergbund e.V. Landesleitung Nord, "Nationalsozialistische Deutsche Arbeiterpartei: Wofür kämpft die N.S.D.A.P.?" n.d., in ED414-54. Interview by Karl von Wiegand in *New York American*, January 5, 1930. This is the Hearst paper *Journal-American*, apparently.

82. Unknown, "Die Gleichschaltung und ihre Gefahren für deutsches Geistesgut," n.d., in ED414-82. The Gleichschaltung reference clearly places it after the appointment of Hitler as chancellor.

83. Erich Ludendorff, "Revolution in Deutschland," *Ludendorffs Volkswarte*, March 26, 1933.

84. Ibid., 2.

7. Ludendorff in the Third Reich

1. The epigraph comes from Shumway, *Nibelungenlied*, 130–31.

2. G. H. Teklenburg, *Ludendorff- zu Hitler!* (Hamburg: Curt Brenner, 1935), 13.

3. "Hitler and Ludendorff Likely to Be Reconciled," *New York Times*, November 8, 1933.

4. Advertisements for the book disappeared quickly from Ludendorff publications in 1933, probably due to threats of censorship, but references to it abound in a manner typical of the Ludendorff network. In the conclusion of the 1935 edition of *General Ludendorff im Feuer*, Kurt Fügner reminds his readers that Ludendorff had warned Germany in 1930 that "World War Threatened," setting the phrase off with indentation and quotation marks without directly referencing the book. Fügner, *"Wir Marschieren!,"* 22.

5. See figures 16 and 17 in the previous chapter. It is telling of Ludendorff's misreading of Nazi intentions that at least one Jewish caricature prominently displayed a baptismal certificate as he joined the ranks of the SA.

6. The issue of *Vor'm Volksgericht* mentioned above had black lines blocking words or sentences in nearly every paragraph.

7. Ludendorff, *Mein militärischer Werdegang*, 52.

8. Gestapo Oldenburg, Lagebericht 10. September 1935. Eckhardt and Hoffmann, *Gestapo Oldenburg Meldet—: Berichte der Geheimen Staatspolizei und des Innenministers aus dem Freistaat und Land Oldenburg, 1933–1936*, 249. The now-banned Tannenberg League, the publishing house, and the Ludendorff movement in general were regular topics of Gestapo reports from Oldenburg and Osnabrück, at least for the years available in the Eckhardt book and in Steinwascher, *Gestapo Osnabrück Meldet—, Polizei- und Regierungsberichte aus dem Regierungsbezirk Osnabrück aus den Jahren 1933 bis 1936*.

9. Countless examples exist in N1079 volumes 6–10. A police report sent to the Osnabrück district Gestapo in May 1935 mentioned taking a prominent farmer and Ludendorff-follower from Groß-Drehle into "protective custody" for statements against the regime. According the report, even the brief arrest (one day) had the intended deterrent effect, both on the farmer and the surrounding community. Steinwascher, *Gestapo Osnabrück Meldet—, Polizei- und Regierungsberichte aus dem Regierungsbezirk Osnabrück aus den Jahren 1933 bis 1936*, 156.

10. Bund Reichsdeutscher Buchhandler e.V. to Eitzen, c. November 1936 in ED401. Eitzen adopted the ruse that he did not sell but only recommended and advertised books that he liked in order to avoid registration.

11. *Am heiligen Quell* 14, October 20, 1936; and 23, March 5, 1937, in ED401 Eitzen.

12. See epilogue.

13. IfZ ED414-063 Herbert Frank, "An die Handelsvertreter," Rundschreiben Nr. 6, February 24, 1934.

14. Some officials mocked these requests. General Walter von Reichenau even mocked one applicant for readmission for calling September "Scheiding." Reichenau to Holscher, October 1, 1935, N1079 Holtzmann folder 7 Nr. 97.

15. Hanno v. Kemnitz to Robert Holtzmann, October 4, 1935. N1079 Holtzmann 6/99–105 alt.

16. Fügner, *"Wir Marschieren!,"* 6.

17. Ibid., 8.

18. Ibid., 31.

19. Martini, *Die Legende vom Hause Ludendorff*, 81.

20. Heinrich Himmler recognized the special position Ludendorff's publishing house had been granted. See his note reproduced in Martin Broszat et al., *Gutachten des Instituts für*

Zeitgeschichte (Munich: Institut für Zeitgeschichte, 1958), 361. "Ludendorff's Society Dissolved by Prussia," *New York Times*, September 24, 1933.

21. The publishing house made it clear in numerous circulars that selling the paper was the highest priority and offered small kickbacks to salespeople for each new subscriber. Herbert Frank, Rundschreiben Nr. 1, November 2, 1933, ED414-63.

22. Herbert Frank, Rundschreiben Nr. 9, May 29, 1934, ED414-63.

23. Fügner, "An alle Mitarbeiter," Julmonds (December) 4, 1933, ED414-63

24. Unruh to Reich Interior Minister, March 30, 1933, BAMA 507k Holtzmann, Unruh to Reich Interior Minister; May 2, 1933, BAMA 507k Holtzmann, Herbert Frank, Rundschreiben Nr. 6, February 24, 1934, ED414-63.

25. Unruh to Göring, May 23, 1933, Hoover Institution, Holtzmann collection (507k).

26. Unruh, "An die Herren Landesführer!," May 16, 1933, Hoover Institution, Holtzmann collection (507k).

27. Fügner, *"Wir Marschieren!,"* 17–18. According to Fügner's other work, Ludendorff's name was not even mentioned at the ceremony. Fügner, *General Ludendorff im Feuer vor Lüttich und an der Feldherrnhalle in München*, 7.

28. Kuratorium für das Reichsehrenmal Tannenberg, *Tannenberg: Deutches Schicksal, deutsche Aufgabe*, 220.

29. "Ludendorff to Avoid Hindenburg Funeral; Friends Parted in 1925 over the Presidency," *New York Times*, August 7, 1934. See earlier chapter on personal conflicts. Rosenberg and Seraphim, *Das Politische Tagebuch Alfred Rosenbergs aus den Jahren 1934/35 und 1939/40*, 41–42.

30. Ludendorff to Holtzmann, September 6, 1934, BA N1079 4/227

31. Herbert Frank, Rundschreiben Nr. 9, May 29, 1934, ED414-63.

32. Wurtt. Politisches Landespolizeiamt, Betreff: Vorträge der Vertreter des Ludendorff-Verlages, October 12, 1934, IfZ FA119/1.

33. BA N1079 1/23.

34. Andress, *Luther! Friedrich der Grosse!! Ludendorff!!!*, 32.

35. Herbert Frank, "An die Handelsvertreter," August 15, 1934, ED414-63.

36. Herbert Frank, Rundschreiben Nr. 15, ED414-63

37. Herbert Frank, "An die Handelsvertreter," December 28, 1934, ED414-63. Ludendorff, *Tannenberg*; Erich Ludendorff, *"Dirne Kriegsgeschichte" vor dem Gericht des Weltkrieges: Zum Feldzuge in Süd-Polen Anfang Oktober 1914* (Munich: Ludendorff, 1934).

38. Herbert Frank, Rundschreiben Nr. 20, January 6, 1934 [*sic*—1935], ED414-63. See below on the first effort of the National Socialist state to bring Ludendorff back into the fold. It is likely that the Reichswehr Ministry intervened on Ludendorff's behalf as part of the negotiations leading to that rehabilitation.

39. Herbert Frank, Rundschreiben Nr. 26, March 25, 1935, ED414-63.

40. Hitler speech cited in Teklenburg, *Ludendorff- zu Hitler!*, 14.

41. Teklenburg, *Lärm um Ludendorff*, 14. Teklenburg is also the author of G. H. Teklenburg, *Roms Germanenhass und Judaverehrung*, Hamburg 24 (Berlin: Schliessfach, 1935).

42. Müller, *General Ludwig Beck*, 59. Müller argues that Beck's efforts bordered on the conspiratorial and that Beck hoped to use Ludendorff's prestige to silence National Socialist radicals and allow Beck's dualistic model of governance by military and party to prevail.

43. Ibid., 82.

44. "Besprechung auf Grund der Bemerkungen des Ministers (von Blomberg) und des Chef HL (Fritsch) am 12.I.1935," ED1, 80.

45. The Wetzell/Beck mission was also part of the long-running feud between Ludendorff and Elze, discussed in chapter 6. Ludendorff's proposed legal action against Elze worried the

army leadership because of the possibility that Hindenburg's reputation would be besmirched, thereby complicating army-party relations. For an excellent analysis of these events and their implications for the relationship between the army and the state, see Müller, *General Ludwig Beck*, 74–100.

46. Ibid., 75.

47. Aufzeichnung General d. Inf. a. D. Ludendorffs über eine Besprechung mit General Wetzell und General Beck am 06.01.1935 in Tutzing, reproduced ibid., 403–11.

48. Aufzeichnung Becks über eine Besprechung mit Gen d. Inf. a.D. Ludendorff am 06.01.1935 and Vortragsnotiz Becks über eine Mitteilung des Gen. D. Inf. a.D. Ludendorff an Hitler, both reproduced ibid., 412–13.

49. "Honour of German Generals," *The Times*, March 23, 1935.

50. Dozens of these are held in the papers of Robert Holtzmann, who fielded such complaints within his regional purview as well as more serious complaints from elsewhere in the Reich that Ludendorff wished to bring to the attention of the army or Berlin officials. See especially BA N1079 vol. 4. See Hermann Burr to Ludendorff, August 1934, BA N1079 Holtzmann 4/209–215 (with six enclosures!), Herbert Frank to Regierungspräsident Hildesheim, October 6, 1934, 4/237ff.

51. Bronsart to Holtzmann, July 3, 1934, BA N1079 Holtzmann, 4/155.

52. Ibid. "175er" is an idiomatic term for a homosexual. Paragraph 175 of the German Criminal Code criminalized sexual relations between men as well as bestiality.

53. Walter Niederstebruch, *Erich Ludendorff in Tagebuchnotizen: 1934–1937*, Tutzinger Schriften; Variation: Tutzinger Schriften (Pähl: Verlag Hohe Warte, 1978), 7. Niederstebruch's diary must be approached with extreme caution, of course. It was published after the war by the Ludendorff press that was anxious to distance itself from Nazism. Many of the published passages of the diary could not have been better suited to portray Ludendorff as a champion of justice and the rule of law. While in Niederstebruch's account of the conversation, Ludendorff disparages Röhm's homosexuality as "unnatural" and recalls a similar incident when he had to dismiss a regimental commander lest he lead young soldiers astray, Ludendorff immediately insists that a proper trial should mete out punishment. The diaries also recall Ludendorff very formally denouncing war, Hitler's imperialistic ambitions, and Jewish policy.

54. Ibid., 10.

55. See the discussion of the Elze affair in chapter 6.

56. N1079 Holtzmann 23 #17 contains a transcription of Beck's note on the subject, including the reason the message was never delivered. See also Müller, *General Ludwig Beck*, 82–83.

57. Ibid. Ludwig Beck's note to that effect is penciled at the bottom of the original memo. Ibid., 415 note f.

58. "Gen. Ludendorff, Piqued, to Retire to Mountains," *New York Times*, May 20, 1935; "German Churches Snub Ludendorff," *New York Times*, April 9, 1935. It is important to remember that Ludendorff's reluctance sprang not from the appropriate moral reservations (as some sympathizers would suggest) but from Ludendorff's conviction that the Nazis were tools of the Catholic Church.

59. I am unaware of the source of the rumor. Ackermann suggests the origin is Ferdinand Sauerbruch, *Das war mein Leben* (Bad Wörishofen: Kindler und Schiermeyer, 1951), 561f. Ackermann, *Nationale Totenfeiern in Deutschland*, 123. Ackermann has Ludendorff "brusquely" refusing the honor. Domarus says Hitler sent both Blomberg and Fritsch with the baton. Adolf Hitler and Max Domarus, *Speeches and Proclamations, 1932–1945: The Chronicle of a Dictatorship*, vol. 2, *The Years 1935 to 1938* (Wauconda, IL: Bolchazy-Carducci, 1990), 661.

60. Müller, *General Ludwig Beck*, 407–8.

61. Ludendorff to Holtzmann, undated, N 1079 Holtzmann 11/123. Holtzmann penciled in the date "February/March 1935."

62. Ludendorff to Holtzmann February 25, 1935, N 1079 Holtzmann 11/125.

63. "Ausführung des Chef HL (Fritsch) am 24.4.1935," ED1, 83.

64. "Erich Ludendorff—Erinnerung an einen großen Soldaten," *Deutsche Monatshefte* 38, no. 12 (1987). Both the offer and Ludendorff's grounds for rejection must be treated very warily. The *Deutsche Monatshefte* and its publisher (Türmer-Verlag) were closely associated with right-wing radicals in Germany after the Second World War. The article in question casts Ludendorff in a very favorable light. Mackensen and Hindenburg did receive estates from the Nazis at around the same time. According to Tobias, Hitler in January 1941 improved the estate at Kurszewnia in Posen where Ludendorff was born and bequeathed it to Ludendorff's heirs. Fritz Tobias, "Ludendorff, Hindenburg, Hitler: Das Phantasieprodukt des Ludendorff-Briefes vom 30. January 1933," in *Die Schatten der Vergangenheit: Impulse zur Historisierung des Nationalsozialismus*, ed. Uwe Backes, Eckhard Jesse, and Rainer Zitelmann (Berlin: Propyläen, 1990), note 46.

65. Ludendorff to Holtzmann, March 2, 1935 N1079 Holtzmann 11/135–36.

66. "Gedanken zum 16. im Lenzing [March] 1938!," pamphlet, page 1, in ED401.

67. "Interview der United Press of America mit General Ludendorff," BA N1079 Holtzmann 1/25.

68. "Nazis and General Ludendorff," *The Times*, March 19, 1935.

69. Ibid.

70. Prothmann, *Was will Ludendorff?*, 5.

71. Ibid., 18.

72. "General Ludendorff on Conscription," *The Times*, March 28, 1935; "Remilitarizing of Reich Praised by Ludendorff," *New York Times*, March 28, 1935.

73. Goebbels and Fröhlich, *Die Tagebücher von Joseph Goebbels*, entry dated December 22, 1937.

74. Rosenberg and Seraphim, *Das politische Tagebuch Alfred Rosenbergs aus den Jahren 1934/35 und 1939/40n*, 42.

75. Ibid. Cited in Ackermann, *Nationale Totenfeiern in Deutschland*, 123.

76. Müller, *General Ludwig Beck*, 84. Citing BA Holtzmann Nr. 11

77. Order reprinted in Hitler and Domarus, *Speeches and Proclamations, 1932–1945*, 2:661. "Nazi Homage to Ludendorff," *The Times*, April 10, 1935.

78. The mention of "the soldier Ludendorff" apparently irked the old man, who considered himself to be much more. As late as 1937 he lamented in a letter to Hermann Göring that some officers persisted in making the distinction between "the Feldherr" and "the author" Ludendorff. See Ludendorff's letter to Göring, dated May 3, 1937, reproduced in Martini, *Die Legende vom Hause Ludendorff*, 85.

79. Otto D. Tolischus, "Ludendorff Cool to Nazis' Acclaim," *New York Times*, April 10, 1935. The Kaiser's letter to Ludendorff is in BAMA N77–15 and specifically mentions Ludendorff's service at Liège and Tannenberg.

80. "Nazi Homage to Ludendorff."

81. Rundfunkansprache Becks vom 09.04.1935 anläßlich des 70. Geburtstages des Generals d. Inf. a. D. Ludendorff in Müller, *General Ludwig Beck*, 426–34.

82. Klaus-Jürgen Müller, "Clausewitz, Ludendorff and Beck: Some Remarks on Clausewitz' Influence on German Military Thinking in the 1930s and 1940s," *Journal of Strategic Studies* (Great Britain) 9, no. 2–3 (1986): 245.

83. Oddly, neither Müller nor Beck seems ever to clarify who exactly would fulfill the military leadership role. Surely, Beck didn't imagine Ludendorff, in his seventies, to still be up the job. Perhaps he envisioned himself in that position? The documents do not make this clear.

84. Müller, *General Ludwig Beck*, 89.

85. See Erlaß des Reichskriegsministers betr. religiöse Anschauungen, vom 25 Juni 1937, which seems to counter an earlier decree banning non-Christian practices, like Gotterkenntnis, from the Wehrmacht. Both reproduced in Klaus-Jürgen Müller and Ernst Willi Hansen, *Armee und Drittes Reich, 1933–1939: Darstellung und Dokumentation*, Sammlung Schöningh zur Geschichte und Gegenwart (Paderborn: F. Schöningh, 1987), 237–39.

86. Müller, *General Ludwig Beck*, 89. Ludendorff had of course not been chief—that was Hindenburg's role.

87. "News in Brief," *The Times*, April 11, 1935. Domarus claims that the birthday wishes went unanswered on Ludendorff's part. Hitler and Domarus, *Speeches and Proclamations, 1932–1945*, 2:662.

88. "Nazi Homage to Ludendorff." According to the *New York Times*, the speech nearly led to a fight between Ludendorff supporters and others in the audience. Tolischus, "Ludendorff Cool to Nazis' Acclaim."

89. Tolischus, "Ludendorff Cool to Nazis' Acclaim."

90. March of Time—outtakes—Various Nazi leaders: Story RG-60.0367, tape 164, available at http://resources.ushmm.org/film/display/main.php?search=simple&dquery=keyword%28LUDENDORFF%2C+ERICH%29&cache_file=uia_siZNVa&total_recs=1&page_len=25&page=1&rec=1&file_num=684. Accessed June 16, 2008.

91. Klaus Danzer, "Trägerin eines stolzen Namens," *Nationalsozialistische Parteikorrespondenz* (1935).

92. "Hitler 'Putsch' Commemorated," *The Times*, November 9, 1935. The text of the speech reproduced in the November 9 edition mistakenly reads "I must refer to one who is present tonight, General Ludendorff." It should have read "one who is not present." *The Times* corrected the error in further coverage on November 11.

93. Herbert Frank, Rundschreiben Nr. 35, November 30, 1935, ED414-63.

94. "Pagan Faith Head in Germany Quits," *New York Times*, April 9, 1936.

95. In typical fashion, the Ludendorff group took umbrage even at these restrictions and protested directly to Rudolf Hess. Correspondence of Fritz Probst with Kreisleiter Krannich and Rudolf Hess in January 1937, copied to Herbert Frank in ED414-82.

96. Wilhelm Prothmann to Karl Holz, April 18, 1938, in ED401 Eitzen.

97. Müller, *General Ludwig Beck*, 93.

98. Holtzmann Nachlaß 31 Aufzeichnung Holtzmann über einen Besuch in Tutzing bein Ludendorff im Dezember 1935, cited ibid., 98.

99. Ibid., 95–96.

100. "Ludendorff Forbids Fete on His Birthday," *New York Times*, March 21, 1936.

101. Müller, *General Ludwig Beck*, 87. Presumably citing Holtzmann (31 Holtzmann Brief vom April 17, 1935), but footnote is missing in the text.

102. Ludendorff and Ziersch, *Als Ich Ludendorff's Frau War*, 270. Treuenfeld arranged for the itinerant Ludendorffs to stay at his mother-in-law's house in Berlin during 1919.

103. Goebbels and Fröhlich, *Die Tagebücher von Joseph Goebbels*, entry of December 12, 1936.

104. Goebbels describes an early encounter with Ludendorff as "shattering." Ibid. Entry of August 19, 1924.

105. Martini, *Die Legende vom Hause Ludendorff*, 79

106. Rosenberg and Seraphim, *Das politische Tagebuch Alfred Rosenbergs aus den Jahren 1934/35 und 1939/40*, 42. I have found no other references to such a glandular operation (*Drusenoperation*) being performed, let alone by Mathilde. Ibid.

107. Ludendorff rather predictably asserted that German "volunteers" in Spain were doing the bidding of Jesuits on behalf of the Franco regime. Goebbels and Fröhlich, *Die Tagebücher von Joseph Goebbels*, entries of January 22 and 23, 1937.

108. Ibid. Entries of February 27 and March 10, 1937. It is interesting that Goebbels wants to deny Ludendorff "Schimpffreiheit," the very sort of license Martini insists Ludendorff already enjoyed.

109. There is some confusion over where the meeting took place. Some sources have Hitler visiting Ludendorff at home in Tutzing. *The Times* says only that it was *not* at Tutzing. Goebbels (diary entry of April 6, 1937) says meeting took place at the former Bavarian War Ministry building. An article in *Deutsche Monatshefte* says it was at the Generalkommando in Munich.

110. An article in a right-wing journal published on the fiftieth anniversary of Ludendorff's death (1987) suggests implausibly that the meeting was prompted by Blomberg's suggestion to Hitler that he seek Ludendorff's advice about the Spanish Civil War. According to the article Ludendorff warned Hitler that his aggressive foreign policy would lead Germany into an even greater and more destructive war. The article provides no evidence or sources for its assertions. "Erich Ludendorff—Erinnerung an einen großen Soldaten." The same article praises the keen military vision of Ludendorff's *Weltkrieg droht* and credits its publication with preventing the war predicted for 1932.

111. Hitler and Domarus, *Speeches and Proclamations, 1932–1945*, 2:884–85. Ludendorff's description of the meeting is nearly identical. Erklärung March 31, 1937, in ED401.

112. Goebbels and Fröhlich, *Die Tagebücher von Joseph Goebbels*, entry March 31, 1937.

113. Ibid. Entry April 6, 1937.

114. Martini, *Die Legende vom Hause Ludendorff*, 83

115. Martin Bormann, Rundschreiben Nr.151/37, November 11, 1937, in Db.02 1937

116. Goebbels and Fröhlich, *Die Tagebücher von Joseph Goebbels*, entry December 12, 1936.

117. Ibid. Entry April 6, 1937.

118. Broszat et al., *Gutachten des Instituts für Zeitgeschichte*, 361.

119. Mathilde Spiess Ludendorff, *Der ungesühnte Frevel an Luther, Lessing, Mozart und Schiller* (Munich: Ludendorff, 1936). Mentioned in Martini, *Die Legende vom Hause Ludendorff*, 81. Martini cites a 1947 article in *Die Zeit* as his source for this information.

120. Gert Borst, "Die Ludendorff-Bewegung, 1919–1961, eine Analyse monologer Kommunikationsformen in der sozialen Zeitkommunikation" (diss., Ludwig-Maximilian-Universität, 1969), 242.

121. Martini, *Die Legende vom Hause Ludendorff*, 84

122. Ansprache des Feldherrn Ludendorffs bei der 2. Tutzinger Tagung, recorded by Herbert Frank. ED414-83.

123. Hitler and Domarus, *Speeches and Proclamations, 1932–1945*, 2:885. Ludendorff says not "completely völkisch" but "total, völkisch" in his announcement. Erklärung March 31, 1937 in ED401.

124. Eitzen to Herr von Hanstein, June 8, 1936, in ED401. Eitzen practically orders Hanstein (an officer) to recant his statement that Ludendorff was "staatsfeindlich" based on the statements of his "three highest commanding officers": Hitler, Blomberg, and Fritsch.

125. "Begründing der Notwendigkeit der Aufnahme Deutscher Lebenskunde . . . in den planmäßigen Schulunterricht." February 12, 1938, in ED401.

126. Ibid.

127. Ibid.

128. Goebbels and Fröhlich, *Die Tagebücher von Joseph Goebbels*, entry of January 22, 1936 [*sic*—1937]. See entries of March 12, April 11, and May 1, 1937, for a few examples among many.

129. Martin Bormann, Rundschreiben Nr. 176/37, December 14, 1937. Db.02 1937.

130. One example among many: Kybitz, *Ludendorffs Handstreich auf Lüttich*.

131. Martin Bormann, Rundschreiben Nr. 157/37, November 17, 1937. Db.02 1937.

132. Goebbels and Fröhlich, *Die Tagebücher von Joseph Goebbels*, entry of April 17, 1937.

133. Hitler and Domarus, *Speeches and Proclamations, 1932–1945*, 2:976.

134. Benjamin C. Sax and Dieter Kuntz, *Inside Hitler's Germany: A Documentary History of Life in the Third Reich* (Lexington, MA: D. C. Heath, 1992), 74.

135. Ansprache des Feldherrn Ludendorffs bei der 2. Tutzinger Tagung, recorded by Herbert Frank. ED414-83.

136. Ibid.

8. Siegfried's Death

1. The epigraphs come from Hatto, *Nibelungenlied*, 132, and remarks printed in *Am heiligen Quell*, January 5, 1938, and reprinted periodically, as in "An die Leser des 'Am heiligen Quell!,'" ED401. "Schwere Erkrankung General Ludendorffs," *Rhein und Ruhr Zeitung*, November 30, 1937, 1, in ED414-084. It is surprising how much confusion exists still about the cause of Ludendorff's death. Domarus says he died of a "circulatory debility." Hitler and Domarus, *Speeches and Proclamations, 1932–1945*, 2:987.

2. The irony was not lost on some of Ludendorff's followers, who expressed their dismay that Mathilde had trusted a Catholic hospital to treat the Feldherr. Eitzen to Frau Dr. Ludendorff February 22, 1938, in ED401. Mathilde responded, via a deputy, that it was necessary to use the Josefinum Clinic so that Erich could be treated by the noted urologist, Dr. Kielleuthner. Bornemann to Eitzen, February 26, 1938, in ED401.

3. "Der Führer besuchte General Ludendorff," *Völkischer Beobachter*, December 8, 1937; also Hitler and Domarus, *Speeches and Proclamations, 1932–1945*, 2:985.

4. Goebbels and Fröhlich, *Die Tagebücher von Joseph Goebbels*. Ludendorff's improving health is mentioned in the entries for December 1, 3, and 7, 1937.

5. Nebelin, *Ludendorff*, 9.

6. "Wie Ludendorff starb," newspaper clipping without masthead, dated December 21, 1937, in ED414-84.

7. Hitler and Domarus, *Speeches and Proclamations, 1932–1945*, 2:987.

8. See chapters 3 and 6.

9. Photo caption reads "Ludendorff—das war die Inkarnation des Begriffs Feldherr." "'Kerls, wollt ihr einen General allein gegen den Feind gehen lassen?,'" *12 Uhr*, December 21, 1937, 3.

10. "Stratege und Taktiker Ludendorff," *Munchner Neueste Nachrichten* (*MNN*), December 22, 1937, 3. Blomberg's speech was cited extensively in newspaper coverage, including *Westdeutscher Beobachter*, December 23, 1937. According to Walter Görlitz, it was at Ludendorff's funeral that Blomberg first mentioned to Hitler his intent to remarry. It was the checkered past of Blomberg's betrothed that formed the pretext for his dismissal the following year. Görlitz, *History of the German General Staff, 1657–1945*, 312.

11. See chapter 5 on "Total War" and Ludendorff's dismissive critique of Clausewitz.

12. *Westdeutscher Beobachter*, December 23, 1937. Translation from Carl Clausewitz from Anatol Rapoport, *On War* (New York: Penguin Books, 1982), 164.

13. Cited without attribution in the article of the same title, "Kerls, wollt Ihr einen General allein gegen den Feind gehen lassen?," *12 Uhr*, December 21, 1937, 3.

14. *Westdeutscher Beobachter*, December 23, 1937.

15. "Wie Frankreich den Feldherrn sieht," *12 Uhr*, December 21, 1937, 2.

16. "Stratege und Taktiker Ludendorff," *MNN*, December 22, 1937, 3.

17. Several newspapers reprinted Blomberg's eulogy, including *Völkischer Beobachter*, December 23, 1937.

18. Blomberg eulogy, cited in Ackermann, *Nationale Totenfeiern in Deutschland*, 126. Ackermann makes clear that the "As" in Blomberg's statement should be read as "Because," thereby establishing the causal link.

19. Press guidelines were in fact issued. Bundesarchiv Koblenz, ZSg. 110/6, p. 305ff, cited ibid., 124.

20. *Westdeutscher Beobachter*, December 23, 1937.

21. Blomberg used the phrase in his eulogy.

22. *Linzer Tagespost* coverage from *MNN*, December 22, 1937, ED414-84.

23. Ackermann, *Nationale Totenfeiern in Deutschland*, 126.

24. *Völkischer Beobachter*, December 23, 1937.

25. Ibid., ED414-84.

26. "Feldherr des Weltkrieges—Mitkämpfer des Führers," *Der Angriff*, December 21, 1937, 2, in ED414-84.

27. *Westdeutscher Beobachter*. The language of Blomberg's eulogy and many of the newspaper retrospectives loudly echoed the brief positive assessment of Ludendorff's past written by Alfred Rosenberg in "Der Fall Ludendorff," *Nationalsozialistische Monatshefte* 2, no. 16 (July 1931): 289–307. Rosenberg, like Blomberg, called Ludendorff an "unbequemer Mahner." Ibid., 290.

28. "Aufruf des Führers zum Tode Ludendorffs," *12 Uhr*, December 21, 1937, 1.

29. One newspaper described Ludendorff retreating into private life after his failed presidential candidacy in 1925 to dedicate himself to the fight against Jewry and Freemasonry. Ludendorff's longtime associate Herbert Frank angrily penciled the comment "and Rome!" into the margin. "Ludendorff Privat," *Rheinische Landeszeitung*, December 21, 1937, in ED 414-84.

30. "Die Kriegsgegner ehren Ludendorff," *Rheinisch-Westfälische Zeitung*, December 21, 1937, 1.

31. "Der Führer zum Tode Ludendorffs," *Rheinisch-Westfälische Zeitung*, December 21, 1937.

32. "Der Heerführer," *Germania*, December 20, 1937, 67/352, 1–2.

33. "Halbmast am Beisetzungstage," *Germania*, December 21, 1937, 67/353, 1.

34. Galen cited in Ackermann, *Nationale Totenfeiern in Deutschland*, 256–57.

35. *Gazeta Polska*, cited in "Stratege und Taktiker Ludendorff," *MNN*, December 22, 1937, 3, in ED414-84.

36. *Daily Telegraph*, cited in "Stratege und Taktiker Ludendorff," *MNN*, December 22, 1937, 3.

37. "Stratege und Taktiker Ludendorff," *MNN*, December 22, 1937, 3.

38. "General Ludendorff Dead," *Manchester Guardian*, December 21, 1937.

39. "The Lessons of Ludendorff," *The Times*, December 21, 1937. This article is most likely the one cited in the German coverage. It mentions Ludendorff's tactical innovations to create surprise.

40. "Stratege und Taktiker Ludendorff," *MNN*, December 22, 1937, 3.

41. "Ludendorff," *New York Times*, December 21, 1937, 22.

42. "Ludendorff est mort," *Le Journal* (Paris), December 21, 1937, 1.

43. "Wie Frankreich den Feldherrn sieht," *12 Uhr*, December 21, 1937, 2.

44. "Ludendorff est mort," *Le Petit Parisien*, December 21, 1937, 1.

45. "Rom: Ein großer Soldat, aber auch ein großer Staatsbürger," *12 Uhr*, December 21, 1937, 2. Typical of the Italian coverage is "La morte di Ludendorff," *La Stampa*, December 21, 1937, 5.

46. *Völkischer Beobachter*, December 23, 1937, 1.

47. "Weitere Beileidskundgebungen," *MNN*, December 22, 1937, in ED414-84.

48. Abschrift aus: "Die Deutsche Volkswirtschaft," Nationalsozialistischer Wirtschaftsdienst, 6. Jahrgang, 3. Dezemberheft 1937, in ED414-82.

49. It appears that Mackensen was unable to attend and sent a representative instead. "Des Feldherrn letzter Weg," *National-Zeitung*, December 23, 1937. Goebbels acidly remarked that the Kaiser had to send a representative because he wouldn't dare show his face after his "cowardly treason" against Ludendorff in 1918. Goebbels and Fröhlich, *Die Tagebücher von Joseph Goebbels*, entry of December 22, 1937.

50. "Der tote Feldherr," *Sigrune*, January 10, 1938, 3–4.

51. Ibid.

52. Adolf Hitler, Henry Picker, and Gerhard Ritter, *Tischgespräche im Führerhauptquartier, 1941–42* (Bonn: Athenäum-Verlag, 1951), 233. Hitler and Domarus, *Speeches and Proclamations, 1932–1945*, 2:1333n276.

53. Mitteilungen Ludendorffs, August 20, 1937, in ED401 Eitzen.

54. Buchner prepared Munich for Mussolini's visit earlier in 1937—the same visit documented in the film *Mussolini Visits Hitler* (though the film concentrates more on the Berlin segment of the journey).

55. Goebbels and Fröhlich, *Die Tagebücher von Joseph Goebbels*. See diary entries of December 21–23, 1937.

56. "Der Staatsakt für Ludendorff," *Westfälische Landeszeitung*, December 22, 1937.

57. The best coverage of the funeral proceedings was in the *Völkischer Beobachter* on December 23, 1937. The description above is drawn primarily from this source. Where details vary among accounts, I have indicated in the footnotes. There are curious discrepancies among the various accounts, however. The *National-Zeitung* mentions Goebbels attending, yet none of the other papers do. Also, the *National-Zeitung* has the foreign military attachés appearing at a different point in the proceedings.

58. *Völkischer Beobachter*, December 23, 1937. Photo captioned "Der letzte Gruß des Führers an der Feldherrnhalle."

59. Ackermann highlights the coincidence that Franz Josef Strauß's funeral ceremony in 1988 shared many elements of the Ludendorff parade. Ackermann, *Nationale Totenfeiern in Deutschland*, 293n43.

60. *Völkischer Beobachter*, December 23, 1937.

61. "Führer und Volk nahmen Abschied von dem toten Feldherrn," *Völkischer Beobachter*, December 23, 1937, 1.

62. "Führer und Volk nahmen Abschied von dem toten Feldherrn," *Völkischer Beobachter*, December 23, 1937, 2.

63. "The Last Salute to Ludendorff," *The Times*, December 23, 1937.

64. "Führer und Volk nahmen Abschied von dem toten Feldherrn," *Völkischer Beobachter*, December 23, 1937, 2. This song was a favorite of the German fraternities (Burschenschaften). Written in 1820 by Hans F. Maßmann, it speaks of working and dying for the sacred Fatherland. The song also refers to Germany as "Hermann's land," with reference to Arminius/Hermann the Cherusker, usually taken to be the historical basis for the character Siegfried. It had been played at Tannenberg events for over a decade, at least. See "Großdeutsche Kundgebung in Hamburg," 20 Lenzings (March) 1926, F-7, 13.

65. Printed in *Am heiligen Quell*, January 5, 1938, and reprinted periodically, as in "An die Leser des 'Am heiligen Quell!,'" ED401. Also BA N1245/32, "Das Vermächtnis des Feldherrn." Goebbels and Fröhlich, *Die Tagebücher von Joseph Goebbels*, entry dated January 11, 1938.

66. Beilage *Am heiligen Quell*, April 5, 1938, ED414-83.

67. Herbert Frank to Fritz Frank, August 22, 1941, in ED414-75.

68. Ibid.

69. Unsigned letter (copy), "die militärische Lage," August 29, 1943, ED414-82.

70. See Herbert Frank to Goebbels, January 17, 1941, and Herbert Frank to Karl Frank, June 14, 1942, both in ED414-75. The letter to Goebbels even elicited an apology of sorts. A representative of the Propaganda Ministry assured that the problematic article in the *National-Zeitung*, which had downplayed Ludendorff's contribution to World War I, was mistaken and that "appropriate steps were being taken."

71. Herbert Frank to Fritz Frank, August 22, 1941, in ED414-75.

72. In a letter late 1941, Fritz Frank's wife Anna refers to Ludendorff's prophecy of 1941 obliquely. Fritz Frank to Herbert Frank, December 21, 1941, in ED414-75. 6 + 2 + 2 = 10 for those keeping score.

73. Herbert Frank to Karl Frank, June 14, 1942, ED414-75.

74. Rosenberg and Seraphim, *Das politische Tagebuch Alfred Rosenbergs aus den Jahren 1934/35 und 1939/40*, 42.

75. Ibid.; see chapter 7.

76. The essay was so positive that it pleased even Herbert Frank, who wrote to the editor of the paper to thank the author. Frank's only complaint was that Ludendorff's struggle against the Catholic Church had been neglected by Dr. Lange, "who no doubt had his reasons for not mentioning it." Herbert Frank to *Rheinische Landeszeitung*, April 12, 1944, ED414-75.

77. Martini, *Die Legende vom Hause Ludendorff*, 88.

78. Rundschreiben des Verlags, September 27, 1939, in ED401.

79. Kybitz, *Ludendorffs Handstreich auf Lüttich*; Erich Ludendorff and Mathilde Spiess Ludendorff, *Weihnachten im Lichte der Rasseerkenntnis* (Munich: Ludendorffs Verlag, 1933); Walter Löhde, *Erich Ludendorffs Kindheit und Elternhaus* (Munich: Ludendorff, 1938); Walter Löhde, *Ludendorffs gerader Weg, ein Gang durch die Werke und Schriften des Feldherrn* (Munich: Ludendorffs Verlag, 1940).

80. Aufzeichnung Holtzmanns über einen Besuch bei Beck am 16.11.1938, reproduced in Müller, *General Ludwig Beck*, 579–82.

81. The quote used as a subhead here is from Westfalen-Treubund, quoted in *Niederdeutsche Zeitung. Nationales Tageblatt für Norddeutschland* 279, November 29, 1923. NSDAP Hauptarchiv, reel 42, folder 843. Ludwig Beck to Gertrud Beck, November 28, 1918, reproduced in Müller, *General Ludwig Beck*, 325.

82. A sensationalistic and poorly researched biography of Ludendorff implies the connection in a chapter titled "Ludendorff Moves to Murder the Jews and Fight a New War." Will Brownell, Denise Drace-Brownell, and Alexander Rovt, *The First Nazi: Erich Ludendorff, the Man Who Made Hitler Possible* (Berkeley, CA: Counterpoint, 2016).

Epilogue

1. The epigraph comes from Shumway, *Nibelungenlied*, 284.

2. "Lehrbriefe" Mathilde Ludendorff, September 1, 1938.

3. Lehrbriefe für unsere Mitarbeiter, "Die Bedeutung des Quell-Postbezuges für Kampf und Verlag des Hauses Ludendorff," n.d., in ED401.

4. See for example, Holscher on Ludendorff's birthday 1938, and *Am heiligen Quell* 9, July 28, 1939, both in IfZ ED414-80.

5. Mathilde Ludendorff Rundschreiben 6, February 15, 1940, and "Wichtige Mitteilung über Schriften, die sich auch besonders gut für unsere Soldaten eignen," attached Lehrbrief 11, September 15, 1940, both in IfZ ED414-80.

6. Dr. Fritz Michael, "Von der Geschlossenheit des Volkes," dated September 1940 in IfZ ED414-80. Passage on Russia is on page 9.

7. Hans Eberhard Friedrich, "'Feldherr' und 'Philosophin' zwischen Machtgier und Wahn," *Neue Zeitung*, May 29, 1949.

8. Martini's biography is interesting as well. He enjoyed some success as a foreign correspondent and newspaper representative during the Third Reich but was banned after 1943 from practicing his profession. After the war, he became a vocal anti-Communist and critic of the Bundesrepublik. In addition to his booklet on the Ludendorff movement, two books published in the postwar period achieved significant notoriety: Winfried Martini, *Das Ende aller Sicherheit; eine Kritik des Westens* (Stuttgart: Deutsche Verlags-Anstalt, 1954); Winfried Martini, *Freiheit auf Abruf: Die Lebenserwartung der Bundesrepublik* (Cologne: Kiepenheuer & Witsch, 1960). On his activities, see "Personalien: Winfried Martini," *Der Spiegel*, July 25, 1956; Rudolf [Moritz Pfeil pseud.] Augstein, "Martini am Letzten," *Der Spiegel*, August 24, 1960.

9. "Deutschland: Am heiligen Quell Deutscher Kraft," review of *Die Legende vom Hause Ludendorff* by Winfried Martini, *Der Spiegel*, June 23, 1949, 6.

10. Martini, *Die Legende vom Hause Ludendorff*, 37.

11. Ibid., 16, 42. According to an article in *Der Spiegel* in 1949, Martini spoke to his dog in Hebrew and liked to joke that his miniature pinscher, Nelly, knew more of the language than Mathilde did. "Deutschland: Am heiligen Quell Deutscher Kraft," 6.

12. Schnoor, *Mathilde Ludendorff und das Christentum*, 36.

13. Borst, "Die Ludendorff-Bewegung, 1919–1961," 274.

14. 1947 Psychiatric Report by Professor Sterz, cited in Amm, *Die Ludendorff-Bewegung*, 272n20.

15. Ibid., 273.

16. Dietrich Strothmann, "Tod in Tutzing," *Die Zeit*, 1966.

17. http://www.hohewarte.de. Two recent additions to their catalog are Adelheid Duppel, *Grundgedanken zum Sinn des Lebens: Eine Einführung in die Philosophie Mathilde Ludendorffs* (Pähl: Verlag Hohe Warte, 2010); and Adelheid Duppel, *Kinderseele und Erziehung: Eine Einführung in die Philosophie Mathilde Ludendorffs* (Pähl: Verlag Hohe Warte, 2011). English translations of a few of Mathilde's works are also still in print. Verlag Hohe Warte, "Preisliste," http://www.hohewarte.de/Preise.pdf. Accessed January 25, 2013.

18. Borst, *Die Ludendorff-Bewegung, 1919–1961, eine Analyse monologer Kommunikationsformen in der sozialen Zeitkommunikation*, 279.

19. Various tricks are detailed ibid., 280–82.

20. Ibid., 283.

21. Dr. Hans Lamm to Dr. van Dam (Zentralrat), October 31, 1958, in Zentralarchiv, B1/7/58.

22. Leon, *Uberstaatliche Mächte und Völkerfreiheit*, 7, in Zentralarchiv, B/1/7/58.

23. "Mathilde Ludendorff: Gotterkenntnis (L)," 24.

24. "Verbot der Ludendorff-Bewegung," Bulletin des Presse- und Informationsamtes der Bundesregierung, May 26, 1961, 918. In Zentralarchiv, B1/7/58.

25. "Ludendorffs Verein zieht vor den Richter," *Süddeutsche Zeitung*, June 4, 1964, in Zentralarchiv, B1/7/58.

26. Martini, *Die Legende vom Hause Ludendorff*, 8.

27. Amm, *Die Ludendorff-Bewegung*, 276.

28. Ibid., 279.

29. Bund für Gotterkenntnis, *Festschrift zum achtzigsten Geburtstage Mathilde Ludendorffs: Aus dem Kreise ihrer Mitarbeiter* (Pähl: Verlag Hohe Warte, 1957), 170.

30. Ibid., 181.

31. Ibid., 154.

32. "Verbot der Ludendorff-Bewegung," Bulletin des Presse- und Informationsamtes der Bundesregierung, May 26, 1961, 918. In Zentralarchiv, B1/7/58.

33. "Mathilde Ludendorff: Gotterkenntnis (L)," 32.

34. Ibid.

35. Fritz Vater, *Sigfried: Die Saga von Germaniens Befreiung* (Pähl [Oberbayern]: Verlag Hohe Warte, 1953). The book is still for sale. Verlag Hohe Warte, "Preisliste," http://www.hohewarte.de/Preise.pdf. Accessed January 25, 2013.

36. As one might imagine, documentation on the life of Hermann is sparse. Most scholars rely heavily on the material provided by the ancient historians Paterculus, Tacitus, Suetonius, and Dio.

37. Vater, *Sigfried*, 179.

38. Numerous sources link the name "Atli" to fictionalized renditions of Attila the Hun present in Norse and Germanic sagas. Vater uses Atli as an honorific or title for Sigfried's friend Hunwalt, of the Marser. The similarity of Hunwalt der Atli to Attila the Hun makes the connection unmistakable.

39. I searched for but could not find any evidence of the other "supranational power," the Freemasons.

40. Frank to Unruh, April 14, 1946, cited in Borst, *Die Ludendorff-Bewegung, 1919–1961, eine Analyse monologer Kommunikationsformen in der sozialen Zeitkommunikation*, 271.

41. Ludendorff, *Weltkrieg droht auf Deutschem Boden*; Ludendorff, *Hitlers Verrat der Deutschen an den römischen Papst*.

42. Buchheim, "Die organisatorische Entwicklung der Ludendorff-Bewegung und ihr Verhältnis zum Nationalsozialismus."

43. Mathilde Ludendorff, "Eidesstaatliche Erklärung," in Nachlass Lindner, BA N1245-33. Also cited in Amm, *Die Ludendorff-Bewegung*, 210.

44. "Aufzeichnung Holtzmanns über einen Besuch bei Beck am 16.11.1938," reproduced in Müller, *General Ludwig Beck*, 579–82. Quote from page 582. Ludendorff's "resistance" in Holtzmann's sense should not be equated with Beck's later heroic resistance to Hitler in 1944. Holtzmann, like Beck at this stage, was concerned about excesses of the regime but seemed most interested in protecting the place of the army in the state.

45. The article in *Der Quell* is refuted in detail by E. v. Selle (presumably the pilot Erich von Selle) in E. v. Selle, "Wollte er Hitlers Sturz?," *Welt am Sonntag*, May 18, 1952.

46. "Deutschland: Am heiligen Quell Deutscher Kraft," 6.

47. "Antisemitismus verstößt gegen das Grundgesetz," *Juristischer Pressedienst* 7 (1971), in Zentralarchiv, B.1/7/58.

48. Strothmann, "Tod in Tutzing."

BIBLIOGRAPHY

Archives

Bayerische Staatsbibliothek
  Verhandlungen des Reichstages
Bundesarchiv, Koblenz (BA)
  N1022 Nachlaß Bauer
  N1079 Nachlaß Holtzmann
  N1245 Nachlaß Lindner
  506k and 507k Holtzmann (copies of material available at the Hoover Institution)
Bundesarchiv-Militärarchiv, Freiburg (BAMA)
  Db 15.02 Anordnungen des Stellvertreters des Führers (Bormann)
  Militärbiografische Sammlung (MSg1)
    2039 Bronsart von Schellendorff
    2842 Lossow
    2292 Wintzer
  Militärgeschichtliche Sammlung (MSg2)
  N5 Nachlaß Stülpnagel
  N28 Nachlaß Beck
  N37 Nachlaß Hoffmann
  N46 Nachlaß Groener

N77 Nachlaß Ludendorff
N241 Nachlaß Meier-Welcker
N247 Nachlaß Seeckt
N250 Nachlaß Wachenfeld
N429 Nachlaß Hindenburg
N559 Nachlaß Deimling
N738 Nachlaß Adam
RH16 Kriegsakademie der Reichswehr und der Wehrmacht
RW13 Wehrmachtakademie
Deutsche Nationalbibliothek
Publications of the Ludendorffs Verlag
Herbert D. Katz Center for Advanced Judaic Studies, Philadelphia, PA
Publications of the Ludendorffs Verlag
Institut für Zeitgeschichte (IfZ)
ED1 Liebmann
ED401 Georg Eitzen
F7 Alfred Conn
Fa119 Bayerische Politische Polizei
Fa88 NSDAP Hauptarchiv
ED414 Herbert Frank
National Archives and Records Administration, Washington, DC
T-253 Luetgebrune papers
NSDAP Hauptarchiv (microfilm), University of Pennsylvania, Philadelphia
United States Army Heritage and Education Center, Carlisle, PA
Germany Military Journals
Deutsche Wehr
Militärwissenschaftliche Rundschau
Militär-Wochenblatt
Wissen und Wehr
University of Michigan Special Collections, Ann Arbor
Myers collection, books and pamphlets from the Weimar and Nazi periods
Zentralarchiv zur Erforschung der Geschichte der Juden in Deutschland
B1/7 Zentralrat der Juden in Deutschland

Primary Sources

Andress, Hermann. *Luther! Friedrich der Grosse!! Ludendorff!!!: Priesterschaft oder Deutscher Gottglaube?* Düsseldorf: Verlag Deutsche Revolution, 1935.
Bethmann-Hollweg, Theobald von. *Betrachtungen zum Weltkriege / 2, Während des Krieges.* Berlin: Reimar Hobbing, 1921.
Brammer, Karl. *Fünf Tage Militärdiktatur: Dokumente zur Gegenrevolution, unter Verwendung amtlichen Materials.* Berlin: Verlag für Politik und Wirtschaft, 1920.
Breucker, Wilhelm. *Die Tragik Ludendorffs; eine kritische Studie auf Grund persönlicher Erinnerungen an den General und seine Zeit.* Stollhamm (Oldb.): H. Rauschenbusch, 1953.

Buchner, Eberhard. *Kriegsdokumente: Der Weltkrieg 1914 in der Darstellung der Zeitgenössischen Presse.* Munich: Albert Langen, 1914.

Buffin, Camille, ed. *Brave Belgians.* New York: G. P. Putnam's Sons, 1918.

Bund für Gotterkenntnis. *Festschrift zum achtzigsten Geburtstage Mathilde Ludendorffs: Aus dem Kreise ihrer Mitarbeiter.* Pähl: Verlag Hohe Warte, 1957.

Depester, H. *Nos héros et nos martyrs de la Grande Guerre.* 2nd ed. Tamines: Duculot-Roulin, 1926.

Diepold, Ferdinand. *Das Unterrichtswerk der deutschen Lebenskunde.* Munich: Ludendorffs Verlag, 1942.

Die Ursachen des deutschen Zusammenbruchs im Jahre 1918. Das Werk des Untersuchungsausschusses der Deutschen Verfassunggebenden Nationalversammlung und des Deutschen Reichstages 1919–1926; Reihe 4. 2. Aufl. Berlin: Deutsche Verlagsgesellschaft für Politik und Geschichte, 1928.

Duppel, Adelheid. *Grundgedanken zum Sinn des Lebens: Eine Einführung in die Philosophie Mathilde Ludendorffs.* Pähl: Verlag Hohe Warte, 2010.

———. *Kinderseele und Erziehung: Eine Einführung in die Philosophie Mathilde Ludendorffs.* Pähl: Verlag Hohe Warte, 2011.

Eckhardt, Albrecht, and Katharina Hoffmann. *Gestapo Oldenburg Meldet—: Berichte der Geheimen Staatspolizei und des Innenministers aus dem Freistaat und Land Oldenburg, 1933–1936.* Veröffentlichungen der Historischen Kommission für Niedersachsen und Bremen. Hannover: Hahnsche Buchhandlung, 2002.

Elze, Walter. *Tannenberg; das deutsche Heer von 1914, seine Grundzüge und deren Auswirkung im Sieg an der Ostfront.* Breslau: F. Hirt, 1928.

Endres, Fritz, and Paul von Hindenburg. *Hindenburg; Briefe, Reden, Berichte.* Ebenhausen bei München: W. Langewiesche-Brandt, 1934.

Essen, Léon van der. *The Invasion and the War in Belgium from Liège to the Yser, with a Sketch of the Diplomatic Negotiations Preceding the Conflict.* London: T. F. Unwin, 1917.

Foerster, Wolfgang. *Der Feldherr Ludendorff im Unglück; eine Studie über seine seelische Haltung in der Endphase des Ersten Weltkrieges.* Wiesbaden: Limes Verlag, 1952.

———. *Ein General Kämpft gegen den Krieg; aus nachgelassenen Papieren des Generalstabchefs Ludwig Beck.* Munich: Münchener Dom-Velag, 1949.

Foley, Robert T., and Alfred Graf von Schlieffen. *Alfred von Schlieffen's Military Writings.* Cass Series—Military History and Policy, no. 2. Portland, OR: Frank Cass, 2003.

Fügner, Kurt. *General Ludendorff im Feuer vor Lüttich und an der Feldherrnhalle in München.* 2nd ed. Munich: Ludendorffs Verlag, 1935.

———. *"Wir Marschieren!": General Ludendorff zu Adolf Hitler am 9. November 1923 vor der Marsch durch München.* Munich: Ludendorffs Verlag, 1933.

Galet, Émile. *Albert, King of the Belgians, in the Great War; His Military Activities and Experiences Set Down with His Approval.* Translated by Joseph Swinton. Boston: Houghton Mifflin, 1931.

Goebbels, Joseph, and Elke Fröhlich. *Die Tagebücher von Joseph Goebbels: Sämtliche Fragmente. Teil I, Aufzeichnungen 1924–1941.* Munich: K. G. Saur, 1987.

Golecki, Anton. *Das Kabinett Bauer: 21. Juni 1919 bis 27. März 1920*. Akten der Reichskanzlei. Weimarer Republik; Variation: Akten der Reichskanzlei; Weimarer Republik. Boppard am Rhein: H. Boldt, 1980.

Hampe, Karl, Folker Reichert, and Eike Wolgast. *Kriegstagebuch 1914–1919*. Deutsche Geschichtsquellen des 19. und 20. Jahrhunderts. R. Oldenbourg, 2004.

Haselmayer, Anton. *Der Fall Rosenbergs- und fällt Hitler mit? Eine Streitschrift zu "Der Fall Ludendorff" von Rosenberg*. Munich: Ludendorffs Volkswarte Verlag, 1931.

Hatto, A. T., ed. and trans. *The Nibelungenlied*. Penguin Classics. London: Penguin, 2004.

Hindenburg, Paul von, and Frederic Appleby Holt. *Out of My Life*. New York: Cassell and Co., 1920.

Hitler, Adolf, and Max Domarus. *Speeches and Proclamations, 1932–1945: The Chronicle of a Dictatorship*. Vol. 2, *The Years 1935 to 1938*. Wauconda, IL: Bolchazy-Carducci, 1990.

Hitler, Adolf, Henry Picker, and Gerhard Ritter. *Tischgespräche im Führerhauptquartier, 1941–42*. Bonn: Athenäum-Verlag, 1951.

Hoffmann, Max, and Eric Sutton. *War Diaries and Other Papers*. Vol. 1, *War Diaries*. London: M. Secker, 1929.

———. *War Diaries and Other Papers*. Vol. 2, *War of Lost Opportunities*. London: M. Secker, 1929.

Hollander, Lee M. *The Poetic Edda*. 2nd ed. Austin: University of Texas Press, 1986.

Horne, Charles F., Walter F. Austin, and Leonard Porter Ayres. *The Great Events of the Great War*. New York: National Alumni, 1923.

Horthy, Miklós, Szinai Miklós, and László Szucs, eds. *Confidential Papers*. Budapest: Corvina, 1965.

Kemnitz, Mathilde von. *Das Weib und seine Bestimmung, ein Beitrag zur Psychologie der Frau und zur Neuorientierung ihrer Pflichten*. Munich: E. Reinhardt, 1917.

———. *Triumph des Unsterblichkeitwillens*. Munich: E. Reinhardt, 1922.

Klausmann, A. Oskar, and Herbert Lentz. *Die Nibelungen*. 3. Aufl. Bayreuth: Loewes Verlag, 1978.

Kuratorium für das Reichsehrenmal Tannenberg. *Tannenberg: Deutches Schicksal, deutsche Aufgabe*. Oldenburg i.O.: G. Stalling, 1939.

Kybitz, Werner. *Ludendorffs Handstreich auf Lüttich; Erinnerungen und Erkenntnisse eines alten Lüttichkämpfers zur 25. Wiederkehr des Lüttichtages*. Laufender Schriftenbezug; Reihe 9; Heft 1; Munich: Ludendorffs Verlag, 1939.

Leman, Georges, and Georges Hautecler. *Le rapport du Général Leman sur la défense de Liège en août 1914*. Académie Royale des Sciences, des Lettres et des Beaux-Arts de Belgique. Commission Royale d'Histoire. Publications in-Octavo. Vol. 69. Brussels: Palais des académies, 1960.

Leon, Walter. *Überstaatliche Mächte und Völkerfreiheit: Eine Auseinandersetzung grundsätzlicher Art im Geiste Erich Ludendorffs*. Pähl: Verlag Hohe Warte, 1953.

Lindenberg, Paul, and Paul von Hindenburg. *Hindenburg-Denkmal für das deutsche Volk eine Ehrengabe für den General-Feldmarschall*. Berlin: Weller, 1922.

Löhde, Walter. *Erich Ludendorffs Kindheit und Elternhaus*. Munich: Ludendorff, 1938.

———. *Ludendorffs gerader Weg, ein Gang durch die Werke und Schriften des Feldherrn*. Munich: Ludendorffs Verlag, 1940.

Ludecke, Kurt Georg Wilhelm. *I Knew Hitler: The Story of a Nazi Who Escaped the Blood Purge.* New York: Charles Scribner's Sons, 1938.

Ludendorff, Erich. *Auf dem Weg zur Feldherrnhalle: Lebenserinnerungen an die Zeit des 9.11.1923, mit Dokumenten in 5 Anlagen.* Munich: Ludendorff, 1937.

———. "Der 'Präventivkrieg' 1931." *Ludendorffs Volkswarte* [n.d.], 1.

———. *Der totale Krieg.* Munich: Ludendorffs Verlag, 1935.

———. *Des Volkes Schicksal in christlichen Bildwerken.* Munich: Ludendorffs Verlag, 1934.

———. *"Dirne Kriegsgeschichte" vor dem Gericht des Weltkrieges.* Munich: Ludendorff, 1930.

———. *The General Staff and Its Problems: The History of the Relations between the High Command and the German Imperial Government as Revealed by Official Documents.* Translated by Frederic Appleby Holt. 2 vols. London: Hutchinson & Co., 1920.

———. *Hitlers Verrat der Deutschen an den römischen Papst.* Munich: Ludendorffs Volkswarte Verlag, 1931.

———. *Kriegsführung und Politik.* Berlin: E. S. Mittler & Sohn, 1922.

———. *Kriegshetze und Völkermorden in den letzten 150 Jahren.* Munich: Ludendorff, 1931.

———. *Ludendorff's Own Story, August 1914–November 1918: The Great War from the Siege of Liège to the Signing of the Armistice as Viewed from the Grand Headquarters of the German Army.* Vol. 2. New York: Harper, 1919.

———. *Meine Kriegserinnerungen, 1914–1918: Mit zahlreichen Skizzen und Plänen.* Berlin: E. S. Mittler und Sohn, 1919.

———. *Mein militärischer Werdegang. Blätter der Erinnerung an unser stolzes Heer.* Munich: Ludendorff, 1933.

———. *My War Memories, 1914–1918.* Vol. 2. London: Hutchinson & Co., 1919.

———. "Revolution in Deutschland." *Ludendorffs Volkswarte,* March 26, 1933, 1.

———. *Tannenberg: Zum 20. Jahrestag der Schlacht.* Munich: Ludendorffs Verlag, 1934.

———. *Urkunden der Obersten Heeresleitung über ihre Tätigkeit, 1916–1918.* 3rd ed. Berlin: E. S. Mittler und Sohn, 1922.

———. *Vom Feldherrn zum Weltrevolutionär und Wegbereiter Deutscher Volksschöpfung: Meine Lebenserinnerungen von 1919–1925.* Vol. 1 Munich: Ludendorffs Verlag, 1940.

———. *Vom Feldherrn zum Weltrevolutionär und Wegbereiter Deutscher Volksschöpfung: Meine Lebenserinnerungen von 1919–1925.* Vol. 1. Munich: Ludendorffs Verlag, 1941.

———. *Vom Feldherrn zum Weltrevolutionär und Wegbereiter Deutscher Volksschöpfung: Meine Lebenserinnerungen von 1926–1933.* Vol. 2. Stuttgart: Verlag Hohe Warte, 1951.

———. "Wehrhaftigkeit." *Ludendorffs Volkswarte,* November 29, 1931, 1.

———. *Weltkrieg droht auf Deutschem Boden.* Munich: Ludendorff, 1931.

———. *Wie der Weltkrieg 1914 "gemacht" wurde.* Munich: Ludendorffs Verlag, 1934.

Ludendorff, Erich, and Mathilde Spiess Ludendorff. *Das grosse Entsetzen: Die Bibel nicht Gottes Wort.* Munich: Ludendorff, 1936.

———. *Die Judenmacht, ihr Wesen und Ende.* Munich: Ludendorffs Verlag, 1939.

———. *Weihnachten im Lichte der Rasseerkenntnis.* Munich: Ludendorffs Verlag, 1933.

Ludendorff, Margarethe. *My Married Life with Ludendorff.* Translated by Raglan Somerset. London: Hutchinson & Co., 1930.

Ludendorff, Margarethe, and Walther Ziersch. *Als Ich Ludendorff's Frau War.* Munich: Drei Masken Verlag, 1929.

Ludendorff, Mathilde Spiess. *Angeklagt wegen Religionsvergehens.* Munich: Ludendorffs Volkswarte Verlag, 1930.

———. *Der Seele Ursprung und Wesen. 1. Schöpfungsgeschichte.* Pasing vor München: W. Simon, 1924.

———. *Der Seele Wirken und Gestalten 1. Des Kindes Seele und der Eltern Amt.* Munich: Ludendorff, 1930.

———. *Der Ungesühnte Frevel an Luther, Lessing, Mozart und Schiller.* Munich: Ludendorff, 1936.

———. *Des Kindes Seele und der Eltern Amt.* Munich: Ludendorffs Volkswarte Verlag, 1930.

———. *Deutscher Gottglaube.* Leipzig: Weicher, 1927.

———. *Erlösung von Jesu Christo.* Munich: Ludendorff, 1931.

———. *Höhenwege und Abgründe; Zwei Einführungsvorträge in Deutsche Gotterkenntnis.* Munich: Ludendorff, 1937.

———. *Statt Heiligenschein und Hexenzeichen mein Leben.* Pähl: Von Bebenburg, 1967.

Ludendorff, Mathilde Spiess, and Walter Löhde. *Christliche Grausamkeit an deutschen Frauen.* Munich: Ludendorff, 1934.

Ludendorff und wir Bayern: Ein Spiegelbild für die "Völkischen." Munich: Verlag "Bayerischer Kurier," 1924.

Lutz, Ralph Haswell, W. L. Campbell, German Reichstag, eds. Untersuchungsausschuss über die Wieltkriegsverantwortlichkeit. *The Causes of the German Collapse in 1918: Sections of the Officially Authorized Report of the Commission of the German Constituent Assembly and of the German Reichstag, 1919–1928.* Hoover War Library Publications No. 4. Stanford, CA: Stanford University Press, 1934.

Max, Prinz von Baden. *Erinnerungen und Dokumente.* Berlin: Deutsche Verlags-Anstallt, 1927.

Michaelis, Herbert, and Ernst Schraepler. *Ursachen und Folgen. Vom deutschen Zusammenbruch 1918 und 1945 bis zur staatlichen Neuordnung Deutschlands in der Gegenwart; eine Urkunden- und Dokumentensammlung zur Zeitgeschichte.* Berlin: H. Wendler, 1958.

Moltke, Helmuth von, and Eliza von Moltke. *Erinnerungen, Briefe, Dokumente, 1877–1916. Ein Bild vom Kriegsausbruch, Erster Kriegsführung und Persönlichkeit des ersten militärischen Führers des Krieges.* Stuttgart: Der Kommende Tag, 1922.

Motz, Ulrich von. *Siegfried-Armin: Dichtung und geschichtliche Wirklichkeit.* Pähl: Verlag Hohe Warte, 1953.

Müller, Georg Alexander von, and Walter Görlitz. *The Kaiser and His Court: The Diaries, Note Books, and Letters of Admiral Georg Alexander von Müller, Chief of the Naval Cabinet, 1914–1918.* London: MacDonald, 1961.

———. *Regierte der Kaiser? Kriegstagebücher, Aufzeichnungen und Briefe des Chefs des Marine-Kabinetts Admiral Georg Alexander von Müller, 1914–1918.* Göttingen: Musterschmidt, 1959.

Müller, Klaus-Jürgen. *General Ludwig Beck: Studien und Dokumente zur politisch-militärischen Vorstellungswelt und Tätigkeit des Generalstabschefs des deutschen Heeres 1933–1938*. Schriften des Bundesarchivs, 30. Boppard am Rhein: H. Boldt, 1980.

Niederstebruch, Walter. *Erich Ludendorff in Tagebuchnotizen: 1934–1937*. Tutzinger Schriften. Pähl: Verlag Hohe Warte, 1978.

Osswald, Lena. *Geschlechterverhältnis und Ehe im völkischen Deutschland*. Munich: Ludendorff, 1935.

Prothmann, Wilhelm. *Was will Ludendorff? Festrede der Feier des 70. Geburtstages des Generals der Infanterie A. D. Erich Ludendorff*. Berlin: Struppe & Winckler, 1935.

Raffel, Burton, ed. and trans. *Das Nibelungenlied = Song of the Nibelungs*. New Haven, CT: Yale University Press, 2006.

Reichsarchiv (Germany). Heer. Kriegsgeschichtliche Forschungsanstalt. *Der Weltkrieg 1914 bis 1918*. 14 vols. Berlin: E. S. Mittler, 1925.

——. Heer. Kriegsgeschichtliche Forschungsanstalt. *Der Weltkrieg 1914 bis 1918*. Vol. 1. *Die Grenzschlachten im Westen*. Berlin: E. S. Mittler, 1925.

Röhm, Ernst. *Die Geschichte eines Hochverräters*. [Nachdr. d.] 6. Aufl. Munich: Eher, 1934. Bremen: Faksimile-Verlag, 1982.

Rosenberg, Alfred. "Der Fall Ludendorff." *Nationalsozialistische Monatshefte* 2, no. 16 (July 1931): 289–307.

Rosenberg, Alfred, and Hans Günther Seraphim. *Das politische Tagebuch Alfred Rosenbergs aus den Jahren 1934/35 und 1939/40: Nach der photographischen Wiedergabe der Handschrift aus den Nürnberger Akten*. Göttingen: Musterschmidt, 1956.

Sauerbruch, Ferdinand. *Das war mein Leben*. Bad Wörishofen: Kindler und Schiermeyer, 1951.

Schäfer, Theobald von. *Ludendorff, der Feldherr der Deutschen im Weltkriege*. Berlin: K. Siegismund, 1935.

——. *Tannenberg*. Schlachten des Weltkrieges: In Einzeldarstellungen. Edited by Reichsarchiv (Germany). Oldenburg, i.O.: Stalling, 1927.

Scheele, Hans Hohlfeld Johannes. *Ahnentafel des Feldherrn Erich Ludendorff* (De-Mnbsb) 7781349. Leipzig: Zentralstelle für Deutsche Personen- und Familiengeschichte, 1939.

Schellendorf, Bronsart von. *The Duties of the General Staff by the Late General Bronsart von Schellendorff*. Translated by General Staff War Office. 4th ed. London: HMSO, 1905.

Schroth, Hansgeorg. *Ludendorffs Kampf gegen das Christentum*. Stoffsammlung für Schulungsarbeit, 51. Berlin: Apologetische Centrale, 1936.

Schulze, Hagen, ed. *Das Kabinett Scheidemann, 13. Februar bis 20. Juni 1919*, Akten der Reichskanzlei. Weimarer Republik; Variation: Akten der Reichskanzlei. Weimarer Republik: H. Boldt, 1971.

Schwertfeger, Bernhard Heinrich. *Das Weltkriegsende, Gedanken über die deutsche Kriegführung 1918*. 5. Aufl. Potsdam: Akademische Verlagsgesellschaft Athenaion, 1937.

Seeckt, Hans von, Friedrich von Rabenau, and Dorothee von Seeckt. *Seeckt: Aus seinem Leben, 1918–1936*. Leipzig: V. Hase & Koehler, 1940.

Shumway, Daniel Bussier, ed. and trans. *The Nibelungenlied: Translated from the Middle High German with an Introductory Sketch and Notes*. Boston: Houghton Mifflin, 1909.

Soden, Hans Freiherr von. *Hat Ludendorff Recht?* Deine Kirche. Marburg: Volksmissionarisches Amt, 1936.

Somville, Gustave. *Vers Liége, le chemin du crime, août 1914.* Paris: Perrin, 1915.

Spiess, Mathilde. *Triumph des Unsterblichkeitwillens.* Munich: Reinhardt, 1922.

Stark, Johannes. *Nationalsozialismus und Katholische Kirche.* Munich: F. Eher, 1931.

Steinwascher, Gerd. *Gestapo Osnabrück Meldet—: Polizei- und Regierungsberichte aus dem Regierungsbezirk Osnabrück aus den Jahren 1933 bis 1936.* Osnabrücker Geschichtsquellen und Forschungen. Osnabrück: Selbstverlag des Vereins für Geschichte und Landeskunde von Osnabrück, 1995.

Tannenbergbund E.V. Landesleitung Groß-Berlin-Brandenburg. *Die Wahrheit über Ludendorff.* Berlin: Jac. Schmidt & Co., 1928.

Teklenburg, G. H. *Lärm um Ludendorff.* Hamburg: Uhlenhorst, c. 1935.

———. *Ludendorff- zu Hitler!* Hamburg: Curt Brenner, 1935.

———. *Roms Germanenhass und Judaverehrung.* Hamburg 24, Schliessfach: Berlin, 1935.

Tempelhoff, Henny von. *Mein Glück im Hause Ludendorff; ein Familiengeschichte.* 4. und 5. Tausend. ed. Berlin: A. Scherl, 1918.

Thaer, Albrecht von, Siegfried A. Kaehler, and Helmuth K. G. Rönnefarth. *Generalstabsdienst an der Front und in der O.H.L. aus Briefen und Tagebuchaufzeichnungen, 1915–1919.* Abhandlungen der Akademie der Wissenschaften in Göttingen. Philologisch-Historische Klasse. 3. Folge; Nr. 40. Göttingen: Vandenhoeck & Ruprecht, 1958.

Trebitsch-Lincoln, Ignaz Timothy. *Der grösste Abenteurer des 20. Jahrhunderts!?: Die Wahrheit über mein Leben.* Leipzig: Almathea Verlag, 1931.

Tschischwitz, Erich von. *Antwerpen, 1914: Unter Benutzung der amtlichen Quellen des Reichsarchivs.* Schlachten des Weltkrieges, 2. Aufl.; Bd. 3. 2. Aufl. Oldenburg i.O.: G. Stalling, 1925.

Vater, Fritz. *Sigfried: Die Saga von Germaniens Befreiung.* Pähl (Oberbayern): Verlag Hohe Warte, 1953.

Vesper, Will, and E. R. Vogenauer. *Die Nibelungen-Sage.* Oldenburg, i.O.: G. Stalling, 1921.

Wellinghusen, Lena. *Die deutsche Frau, Dienerin oder Gefährtin.* Munich: Ludendorff, 1933.

Woodward, E. L. *Documents on British Foreign Policy, 1919–1939.* London: H.M. Stationery Office, 1946.

Wulf, Peter, ed. *Das Kabinett Fehrenbach, 25. Juni 1920 bis 4. Mai 1921,* Akten der Reichskanzlei. Weimarer Republik; Variation: Akten der Reichskanzlei. Weimarer Republik. Boppard am Rhein: H. Boldt, 1972.

Secondary Sources

Ackermann, Volker. *Nationale Totenfeiern in Deutschland: Von Wilhelm I. bis Franz Josef Strauss: Eine Studie zur politischen Semiotik.* Stuttgart: Klett-Cotta, 1990.

Amm, Bettina. *Die Ludendorff-Bewegung: Vom nationalistischen Kampfbund zur völkischen Weltanschauungssekte.* Reihe Soziologie. Hamburg: Ad Fontes, 2006.

Angress, Werner T. "Das deutsche Militär und die Juden im Ersten Weltkrieg." *Militärgeschichtliche Zeitschrift* 1 (1976): 77–146.

——. "The German Army's 'Judenzählung' of 1916: Genesis—Consequences—Significance." *Leo Baeck Institute Year Book* 23 (1978): 117–37.

Anonymous. "Erich Ludendorff—Erinnerung an einen großen Soldaten." *Deutsche Monatshefte* 38, no. 12 (December 1987): 27–31.

Asprey, Robert B. *The German High Command at War: Hindenburg and Ludendorff Conduct World War I.* New York: Morrow, 1991.

Assmann, Jan. "Mythen, Politische." In *Handbuch der politischen Philosophie und Sozialphilosophie. Bd. 1 a—M*, edited by Robin Celikates and Stefan Gosepath, 869–73. Berlin: De Gruyter, 2008.

Badia, Gilbert. "Rosa Luxemburg." In *Deutsche Erinnerungsorte*, edited by Etienne François and Hagen Schulz, 105–21. Munich: Beck, 2001.

Baird, Jay W. *The Mythical World of Nazi War Propaganda, 1939–1945.* Minneapolis: University of Minnesota Press, 1974.

——. *To Die for Germany: Heroes in the Nazi Pantheon.* Bloomington: Indiana University Press, 1990.

Bald, Detlef. *Der deutsche Generalstab 1859–1939: Reform und Restauration in Ausbildung und Bildung.* Schriftenreihe Innere Führung. Reihe Ausbildung und Bildung; Heft 28. s.l.: Bundesministerium der Verteidigung Führungsstab der Streitkräfte I 15, 1977.

——. *Der deutsche Offizier: Sozial- und Bildungsgeschichte des deutschen Offizierkorps im 20. Jahrhundert.* Munich: Bernard & Graefe, 1982.

Beck, Ludwig, and Hans Speidel. *Studien.* Stuttgart: K. F. Koehler, 1955.

Beckett, I. F. W. *The Great War, 1914–1918.* 2nd ed. Harlow: Pearson/Longman, 2007.

Bill, Claus Heinrich. "Der Tannenbergbund in Schleswig-Holstein." *Informationen zur Schleswig-Holsteinischen Zeitgeschichte* 28 (December 1995): 8–36.

Borst, Gert. "Die Ludendorff-Bewegung, 1919–1961, eine Analyse monologer Kommunikationsformen in der sozialen Zeitkommunikation." Diss., Ludwig-Maximilian-Universität, Berlin, 1969.

Bosworth, R. J. B. *Mussolini.* New York: Arnold, 2002.

Breuer, Stefan. *Die Völkischen in Deutschland: Kaiserreich und Weimarer Republik.* Darmstadt: Wiss. Buchges., 2008.

Broszat, Martin, Hans Buchheim, H. Heiber, and P. Kluke. *Gutachten des Instituts für Zeitgeschichte.* Munich: Institut für Zeitgeschichte, 1958.

Brownell, Will, Denise Drace-Brownell, and Alexander Rovt. *The First Nazi: Erich Ludendorff, the Man Who Made Hitler Possible.* Berkeley, CA: Counterpoint, 2016.

Buchheim, Hans. "Die organisatorische Entwicklung der Ludendorff-Bewegung und ihr Verhältnis zum Nationalsozialismus." In *Gutachten des Instituts für Zeitgeschichte.* Veröffentlichungen des Instituts für Zeitgeschichte, 356–80. Munich: Institut für Zeitgeschichte, 1958.

Cavallie, James. *Ludendorff und Kapp in Schweden: Aus dem Leben zweier Verlierer.* Frankfurt am Main: Peter Lang, 1995.

Chickering, Roger. "Der 'Deutsche Wehrverein' und die Reform der deutschen Armee 1912–1914." *Militärgeschichtliche Mitteilungen*, no. 1 (1979): 7–33.

——. *Imperial Germany and the Great War, 1914–1918.* New York: Cambridge University Press, 1998.

———. *Imperial Germany and the Great War, 1914–1918.* 3rd ed. New York: Cambridge University Press, 2014.

———. "Sore Loser: Ludendorff's Total War." In *The Shadows of Total War: Europe, East Asia, and the United States, 1919–1939,* edited by Roger Chickering and Stig Förster, 151–78. New York: German Historical Institute, 2003.

———. *We Men Who Feel Most German: A Cultural Study of the Pan-German League, 1886–1914.* Boston: Allen & Unwin, 1984.

Cord, William O. *An Introduction to Richard Wagner's Der Ring des Nibelungen: A Handbook.* 2nd ed. Athens: Ohio University Press, 1995.

Craig, Gordon Alexander. *Germany, 1866–1945.* Oxford: Clarendon, 1978.

De Felice, Renzo. *Mussolini e Hitler: I rapporti segreti 1922–1933: Con documenti inediti.* Firenze: Le Monnier, 1975.

Deist, Wilhelm. "Anspruch und Selbstverständnis der Wehrmacht: Einführende Bemerkungen." In *Die Wehrmacht: Mythos und Realität,* edited by Rolf-Dieter Müller, Hans Erich Volkmann, and Militärgeschichtliches Forschungsamt, 39–46. Munich: Oldenbourg, 1999.

———. "Der militärische Zusammenbruch des Kaiserreichs: Zur Realität der 'Dolchstoßlegend.'" In *Das Unrechtsregime: Internationale Forschung über den Nationalsozialismus,* edited by Ursula Büttner, Werner Johe, Angelika Voss-Louis, and Werner Jochmann, 21–22. Hamburger Beiträge zur Sozial- und Zeitgeschichte. Hamburg: Christians, 1986.

Diehl, James M. *The Thanks of the Fatherland: German Veterans after the Second World War.* Chapel Hill: University of North Carolina Press, 1993.

Donnell, Clayton. *The Forts of the Meuse in World War I.* New York: Osprey, 2007.

Dorpalen, Andreas. *Hindenburg and the Weimar Republic.* Princeton, NJ: Princeton University Press, 1964.

Epkenhans, Michael. *Tirpitz: Architect of the German High Seas Fleet.* Lincoln, NE: Potomac Books, 2008.

Erger, Johannes. *Der Kapp-Lüttwitz-Putsch. Ein Beitrag zur deutschen Innenpolitik 1919/20.* Düsseldorf: Droste, 1967.

Feldman, Gerald D. *Army, Industry, and Labor in Germany, 1914–1918.* Princeton, NJ: Princeton University Press, 1966.

Förster, Stig. *Der doppelte Militarismus: Die deutsche Heeresrüstungspolitik zwischen Status-Quo-Sicherung und Aggression, 1890–1913.* Stuttgart: F. Steiner Verlag Wiesbaden, 1985.

———. "Dreams and Nightmares: German Military Leadership and the Images of Future Warfare, 1871–1914." In *Anticipating Total War: The German and American Experiences, 1871–1914,* edited by Manfred F. Boemeke, Roger Chickering, and Stig Förste, 343–76. New York: Cambridge University Press and Publications of the German Historical Institute, 1999.

François, Etienne. "Oberammergau." In *Deutsche Erinnerungsorte,* edited by Etienne François and Hagen Schulze, 274–91. Munich: Beck, 2001.

Fricke, Dieter, and Werner Fritsch. *Lexikon zur Parteiengeschichte: Die bürgerlichen und kleinbürgerlichen Parteien und Verbände in Deutschland (1789–1945); in vier Bänden.* Leipzig: Bibliogr. Inst., 1986.

Gassert, Philipp, and Daniel S. Mattern. *The Hitler Library: A Bibliography*. Westport, CT: Greenwood, 2001.

Gentry, Francis G. *The Nibelungen Tradition: An Encyclopedia*. London: Routledge, 2002.

Gerhards, Thomas. "Lüttich." In *Enzyklopädie Erster Weltkrieg*, edited by Gerhard Hirschfeld, Gerd Krumeich, and Irina Renz, 686–87. Paderborn: Schöningh, 2004.

Geßler, Otto, and Kurt Sendtner. *Reichswehrpolitik in der Weimarer Zeit*. Stuttgart: Deutsche Verlags-Anstalt, 1958.

Geyer, Michael. "German Strategy in the Age of Machine Warfare, 1914–1945." In *Makers of Modern Strategy: From Machiavelli to the Nuclear Age*, edited by Peter Paret, Gordon Alexander Craig, and Felix Gilbert. Princeton, NJ: Princeton University Press, 1986.

———. "Insurrectionary Warfare: The German Debate about a Levee en Masse in October 1918." *Journal of Modern History* 73, no. 3 (2001): 459–527.

———. "Rückzug und Zerstörung 1917." In *Die Deutschen an der Somme 1914–1918: Krieg, Besatzung, verbrannte Erde*, edited by Gerhard Hirschfeld, Gerd Krumeich, and Irina Renz, 163–79. Essen: Klartext, 2006.

———. "Some Hesitant Observations concerning 'Political Violence.'" *Kritika-Explorations in Russian and Eurasian History* 4, no. 3 (Summer 2003): 695–708.

Goltz, Anna von der. *Hindenburg: Power, Myth, and the Rise of the Nazis*. New York: Oxford University Press, 2009.

Goodspeed, D. J. *Ludendorff: Genius of World War I*. Boston: Houghton Mifflin, 1966.

———. *Ludendorff: Soldier, Dictator, Revolutionary*. London: Hart-Davis, 1966.

Görlitz, Walter. *History of the German General Staff, 1657–1945*. New York: Praeger, 1959.

Harbou, Thea von, Fritz Lang, Paul Richter, Margarete Schoen, Theodor Loos, Hanna Ralph, Hans von Schlettow, et al. *Die Nibelungen*. Video recording, 2 video discs. Kino on Video, 2002.

Herwig, Holger H. *The First World War: Germany and Austria-Hungary, 1914–1918*. New York: St. Martin's, 1997.

———. *The Marne, 1914: The Opening of World War I and the Battle That Changed the World*. New York: Random House, 2009.

———. "Of Men and Myths: The Use and Abuse of History and the Great War." In *The Great War and the Twentieth Century*, edited by J. M. Winter, Geoffrey Parker, and Mary R. Habeck, 299–330. New Haven, CT: Yale University Press, 2000.

Hirschfeld, Gerhard, Gerd Krumeich, and Irina Renz. *Deutschland im Ersten Weltkrieg*. Frankfurt am Main: S. Fischer, 2013.

Hoegen, Jesko von. *Der Held von Tannenberg: Genese und Funktion des Hindenburg-Mythos*. Cologne: Böhlau, 2007.

Hoff, Henning. "Friedensinitiativen." In *Enzyklopädie Erster Weltkrieg*, edited by Gerhard Hirschfeld, Gerd Krumeich, and Irina Renz, 510–12. Paderborn: Schöningh, 2004.

Hoffmann, Werner. "The Reception of the Nibelungenlied in the Twentieth Century." In *A Companion to the Nibelungenlied*, edited by Winder McConnell, 127–52. Columbia, SC: Camden House, 1998.

Horne, John N., and Alan Kramer. *German Atrocities, 1914: A History of Denial.* New Haven, CT: Yale University Press, 2001.

Jochmann, Werner. "Die Ausbreitung des Antisemitismus." In *Deutsches Judentum in Krieg und Revolution 1916–1923*, edited by Werner Eugen Mosse, Arnold Paucker, and T. W. Moody, 409–510. Tübingen: J. C. B. Mohr, 1971.

——. *Nationalsozialismus und Revolution: Ursprung und Geschichte der NSDAP in Hamburg, 1922–1933: Dokumente.* Frankfurt am Main: Europäische Verlag, 1963.

Jones, Larry Eugene, and James N. Retallack, eds. *Between Reform, Reaction, and Resistance: Studies in the History of German Conservatism from 1789 to 1945.* Providence: Berg, 1993.

Kershaw, Ian. *The "Hitler Myth": Image and Reality in the Third Reich.* New York: Oxford University Press, 1987.

Ketelsen, Uwe-Karsten. *Heroisches Theater; Untersuchungen zur Dramentheorie des Dritten Reichs.* Bonn: H. Bouvier, 1968.

Kitchen, Martin. *The Silent Dictatorship: The Politics of the German High Command under Hindenburg and Ludendorff, 1916–1918.* New York: Holmes & Meier, 1976.

Klausmann, A. Oskar, and Herbert Lentz. *Die Nibelungen.* Bayreuth: Loewes Verlag, 1978.

Könnemann, Erwin, and G. Schulze. *Der Kapp-Lüttwitz-Ludendorff-Putsch: Dokumente.* Munich: Olzog, 2002.

Krumeich, Gerd. "Die Dolchstoss-Legende." In *Deutsche Erinnerungsorte*, edited by Etienne François and Hagen Schulze, 585–99. Munich: Beck, 2001.

——. "Langemarck." In *Deutsche Erinnerungsorte*, edited by Etienne François and Hagen Schulze, 292–309. Munich: Beck, 2001.

Layton, Roland V. Jr. "Kurt Ludecke and 'I Knew Hitler': An Evaluation." *Central European History* 12, no. 4 (1979): 372.

Lee, John. *The Warlords: Hindenburg and Ludendorff.* London: Weidenfeld & Nicolson, 2005.

Lehrer, Steven. *Wannsee House and the Holocaust.* Jefferson, NC: McFarland, 2000.

Lerner, Paul Frederick. *Hysterical Men: War, Psychiatry, and the Politics of Trauma in Germany, 1890–1930.* Ithaca, NY: Cornell University Press, 2003.

Lipkes, Jeff. *Rehearsals: The German Army in Belgium, August 1914.* Leuven: Leuven University Press, 2007.

Liulevicius, Vejas G. *Land War on the Eastern Front: Culture, National Identity, and German Occupation in World War I.* New York: Cambridge University Press, 2000.

Lloyd, Nick. *Hundred Days: The Campaign That Ended World War I.* New York: Basic Books, 2014.

Lohalm, Uwe. *Völkischer Radikalismus: Die Geschichte des Deutschvölkischen Schutz- und Trutz-Bundes, 1919–1923.* Hamburg: Leibniz-Verlag, 1970.

Martini, Winfried. *Das Ende aller Sicherheit; eine Kritik des Westens.* Stuttgart: Deutsche Verlags-Anstalt, 1954.

——. *Die Legende vom Hause Ludendorff.* Rosenheim: Leonhard Lang, 1949.

——. *Freiheit auf Abruf: Die Lebenserwartung der Bundesrepublik.* Cologne: Kiepenheuer & Witsch, 1960.

Meier-Welcker, Hans. *Seeckt.* Frankfurt am Main: Bernard U. Graefe, 1967.

Meier-Welcker, Hans, and Manfred Messerschmidt. *Offiziere im Bild von Dokumenten aus drei Jahrhunderten.* Stuttgart: Deutsche Verlags-Anstalt, 1964.

Mommsen, Wolfgang J. *Max Weber and German Politics, 1890–1920.* Chicago: University of Chicago Press, 1984.

Moncure, John. *Forging the King's Sword: Military Education between Tradition and Modernization; The Case of the Royal Prussian Cadet Corps, 1871–1918.* New York: P. Lang, 1993.

Mosse, George L. *The Crisis of German Ideology; Intellectual Origins of the Third Reich.* New York: Grosset & Dunlap, 1964.

———. *The Image of Man: The Creation of Modern Masculinity.* New York: Oxford University Press, 1996.

Müller, Klaus-Jürgen. "Clausewitz, Ludendorff and Beck: Some Remarks on Clausewitz' Influence on German Military Thinking in the 1930s and 1940s." *Journal of Strategic Studies* (Great Britain) 9, nos. 2–3 (1986): 240–66.

Müller, Klaus-Jürgen, and Ernst Willi Hansen. *Armee und Drittes Reich, 1933–1939: Darstellung und Dokumentation.* Paderborn: F. Schöningh, 1987.

Münkler, Herfried. *Die Deutschen und ihre Mythen.* Berlin: Rowohlt, 2008.

Münkler, Herfried, and Wolfgang Storch. *Siegfrieden: Politik mit einem deutschen Mythos.* Berlin: Rotbuch-Verlag, 1988.

Naftzger, Steven Thomas. "'Heil Ludendorff': Erich Ludendorff and Nazism, 1925–1937." PhD diss., New York: City University of New York, 2002.

Nebelin, Manfred. *Ludendorff: Diktator im Ersten Weltkrieg.* Munich: W. J. Siedler, 2011.

Neiberg, Michael S. *The Second Battle of the Marne.* Bloomington: Indiana University Press, 2008.

Petzold, Joachim. *Die Dolchstosslegende; eine Geschichtsfälschung im Dienst des deutschen Imperialismus und Militarismus.* Berlin: Akademie-Verlag, 1963.

Poewe, Karla. *New Religions and the Nazis.* New York: Routledge, 2006.

———. "Scientific Neo-Paganism and the Extreme Right Then and Today: From Ludenorff's Gotterkenntnis to Sigrid Hunke's Europas Eigene Religion." *Journal of Contemporary Religion* 14, no. 3 (October 1999): 387–400.

Pyta, Wolfram. *Hindenburg: Herrschaft zwischen Hohenzollern und Hitler.* Munich: Siedler, 2007.

Reemtsma, Jan Philipp. "The Concept of the War of Annihilation: Clausewitz, Ludendorff, Hitler." In *War of Extermination: The German Military in World War II, 1941–1944,* edited by Hannes Heer and Klaus Naumann, 13–35. New York: Berghahn Books, 1999.

Reynolds, Nicholas. "Dokumentation: Der Fritsch-Brief vom 11. Dezember 1938." *Vierteljahrshefte für Zeitgeschichte* 28, no. 3 (1980): 358–71.

Sabrow, Martin. *Der Rathenaumord: Rekonstruktion einer Verschwörung gegen die Republik von Weimar.* Munich: Oldenbourg, 1994.

Sax, Benjamin C., and Dieter Kuntz. *Inside Hitler's Germany: A Documentary History of Life in the Third Reich.* Lexington, MA: D. C. Heath, 1992.

Scheck, Raffael. *Alfred von Tirpitz and German Right-Wing Politics, 1914–1930.* Atlantic Highlands, NJ: Humanities Press, 1998.

——. "Politics of Illusion: Tirpitz and Right-Wing Putschism, 1922–1924." *German Studies Review* 18, no. 1 (1995): 29–49.

Schenk, Frithjof Benjamin. "Tannenberg/Grunwald." In *Deutsche Erinnerungsorte*, edited by Etienne François and Hagen Schulze, 438–54. Munich: Beck, 2001.

Schnoor, Frank. *Mathilde Ludendorff und das Christentum: Eine radikale völkische Position in der Zeit der Weimarer Republik und des NS-Staates*. Egelsbach: Hänsel-Hohenhausen, 2001.

Schulze, Hagen. *Freikorps und Republik, 1918–1920*. Boppard am Rhein: H. Boldt, 1969.

Schwengler, Walter. *Völkerrecht, Versailler Vertrag und Auslieferungsfrage: Die Strafverfolgung wegen Kriegsverbrechen als Problem des Friedensschlusses 1919/20*. Stuttgart: Deutsche Verlags-Anstalt, 1982.

Showalter, Dennis E. "The Political Soldiers of Bismarck's Germany: Myths and Realities." *German Studies Review* 17, no. 1 (February 1994): 59–77.

——. *Tannenberg: Clash of Empires, 1914*. Washington, DC: Brassey's, 2004.

Smith, Arthur L. Jr. "Kurt Ludecke: The Man Who Knew Hitler." *German Studies Review* 26, no. 3 (2003): 597–606.

Spilker, Annika. *Geschlecht, Religion und völkischer Nationalismus: Die Ärztin und Antisemitin Mathilde von Kemnitz-Ludendorff (1877–1966)*. Frankfurt: Campus Verlag, 2013.

Steigmann-Gall, Richard. "Rethinking Nazism and Religion: How Anti-Christian Were the 'Pagans'?" *Central European History* 36, no. 1 (2003): 75–105.

Stone, David R. *The Russian Army in the Great War: The Eastern Front, 1914–1918*. Lawrence: University Press of Kansas, 2015.

Strachan, Hew. *The First World War*. New York: Viking Penguin, 2004.

Strachan, Hew, and Andreas Herberg-Rothe, eds. *Clausewitz in the Twenty-First Century*. Oxford: Oxford University Press, 2007.

Thimme, Annelise. *Flucht in den Mythos; die Deutschnationale Volkspartei und die Niederlage von 1918*. Göttingen: Vandenhoeck & Ruprecht, 1969.

Tobias, Fritz. "Ludendorff, Hindenburg, Hitler: Das Phantasieprodukt des Ludendorff-Briefes vom 30. January 1933." In *Die Schatten der Vergangenheit: Impulse zur Historisierung des Nationalsozialismus*, edited by Uwe Backes, Eckhard Jesse, and Rainer Zitelmann, 319–42. Berlin: Propyläen, 1990.

Tuchel, Johannes. *Am Grossen Wannsee 56–58: Von der Villa Minoux zum Haus der Wannsee-Konferenz*. Berlin: Hentrich, 1992.

Tyrell, Albrecht. *Vom Trommler zum Führer: Der Wandel von Hitlers Selbstverständnis zwischen 1919 und 1924 und die Entwicklung der NSDAP*. Munich: Fink, 1975.

Uhle-Wettler, Franz. *Erich Ludendorff in seiner Zeit: Soldat-Stratege-Revolutionär; eine Neubewertung*. 2. Aufl. Berg: K. Vowinckel, 1996.

Vogt, Adolf. *Oberst Max Bauer: Generalstabsoffizier im Zwielicht: 1869–1929*. Osnabrück: Biblio-Verlag, 1974.

Wasserstein, Bernard. *The Secret Lives of Trebitsch Lincoln*. New Haven, CT: Yale University Press, 1988.

Watson, Alexander. *Ring of Steel: Germany and Austria-Hungary in World War I*. New York: Basic Books, 2014.

Watt, Richard M. *The Kings Depart: The Tragedy of Germany—Versailles and the German Revolution.* New York: Simon & Schuster, 1968.

Weber, Marianne. *Max Weber: A Biography.* New York: Wiley, 1975.

Wheeler-Bennett, Sir John. "Ludendorff: The Soldier and the Politician." *Virginia Quarterly Review* 14, no. 2 (Spring 1938): 187–202.

Wiggenhorn, Harald. *Verliererjustiz: Die Leipziger Kriegsverbrecherprozesse nach dem Ersten Weltkrieg.* Baden-Baden: Nomos, 2005.

Zabecki, David T. *The German 1918 Offensives: A Case Study in the Operational Level of War.* New York: Routledge, 2006.

Zuber, Terence. *German War Planning, 1891–1914: Sources and Interpretations.* Rochester, NY: Boydell, 2004.

INDEX

Page numbers in italics indicate figures